PYTHAGORAS AND RENAISSANCE EUROPE: FINDING HEAVEN

In *Pythagoras and Renaissance Europe: Finding Heaven*, Christiane L. Joost-Gaugier offers the first systematic study of Pythagoras, the ancient Greek sage, and his influence on mathematics, astronomy, philosophy, religion, medicine, music, the occult, and social life – as well as on architecture and art – in the late medieval and early modern eras. Spanning the period between Dante and Petrarch in the fourteenth century and Kepler and Galileo in the seventeenth, this book demonstrates that Pythagoras's influence in intellectual circles – Christian, Jewish, and Arab – was more widespread than has previously been acknowledged. Joost-Gaugier shows that during this period admiration for Pythagoras was great throughout Europe. She also shows how this admiration was translated into ideas that were applied to the visual arts by numerous well-known architects and artists who sought, through the use of a visual language inspired by the memory of Pythagoras, to obtain perfect harmony in their creations. Among these were Alberti, Bramante, Leonardo da Vinci, Michelangelo, and Raphael. Thus, she suggests, some of the greatest artworks in the Western world owe their modernity to an inspirational force that, paradoxically, was conceived in the distant past.

Christiane L. Joost-Gaugier is an internationally known and distinguished scholar. A three-time graduate of Harvard, she has published extensively in research journals, conference proceedings, and international catalogues on subjects ranging from classical literature to medieval architecture to Renaissance art and intellectual history. A recipient of grants from the American Council of Learned Societies, the American Philosophical Society, the Delmas Foundation, the Fulbright Association, and the National Endowment for the Humanities among others, she is the author of *Jacopo Bellini: Selected Drawings, Raphael's Stanza della Segnarch: Meaning and Invention,* and *Measuring Heaven: Pythagoras and His Influence on Thought and Art in Antiquity and the Middle Ages.* In 2005 she was awarded an Honorary Phi Beta Kappa from Harvard University for lifetime achievement.

Frontispiece: Montepulciano, San Biagio (Antonio da Sangallo the Elder) Photo: Allan Foy

PYTHAGORAS AND RENAISSANCE EUROPE

Finding Heaven

CHRISTIANE L. JOOST-GAUGIER

CAMBRIDGE
UNIVERSITY PRESS

CAMBRIDGE UNIVERSITY PRESS
Cambridge, New York, Melbourne, Madrid, Cape Town, Singapore,
São Paulo, Delhi, Dubai, Tokyo

Cambridge University Press
32 Avenue of the Americas, New York, NY 10013–2473, USA

www.cambridge.org
Information on this title: www.cambridge.org/9780521517959

First published 2009

Printed in the United States of America

A catalog record for this publication is available from the British Library.

Library of Congress Cataloging in Publication data
Joost-Gaugier, Christiane L.
Pythagoras and Renaissance Europe : finding heaven / Christiane L. Joost-Gaugier.
p.   cm
Includes bibliographical references and index.
ISBN 978-0-521-51795-9 (hardback)
1. Pythagoras.   2. Pythagoras – Influence.   3. Philosophy, Modern.
4. Philosophy, Renaissance.   I. Title
B243.J66 2009
182′.2–dc22   2008040586

ISBN 978-0-521-51795-9 Hardback

First of all, I never get down to writing except at dead of night when it's absolutely quiet and deep silence reigns over all … in short, when there's such complete peace that if Pythagoras were alive he would be able to hear the music of the spheres quite clearly. At such a time gods and goddesses delight to hold converse with pure minds.

Erasmus, Dialogus Ciceronianus *(trans. Betty I. Knott)*

CONTENTS

List of Illustrations   *page* x
Acknowledgments   xiii

INTRODUCTION   1

PART ONE: PYTHAGORAS, MAN FOR THE RENAISSANCE

ONE: PROLOGUE: THE DIFFUSION OF KNOWLEDGE
ABOUT PYTHAGORAS IN THE RENAISSANCE   15

TWO: THE EMERGENCE OF "SAINT" PYTHAGORAS IN
THE EARLY RENAISSANCE   19
   Early Fifteenth-Century Writers View Pythagoras   19
   Pletho, Bessarion, Cusanus, and Alberti: An International Generation
      Applauds Pythagoras   24
   Ficino's Pythagoras and His Significance as the Jewish "Grandfather"
      of Christianity   27
   Pico's Venerable Pythagoras: Fountainhead of Wisdom   30
   The Dissemination of Information about Pythagoras in
      the Late Fifteenth Century   31

THREE: THE APOTHEOSIS OF PYTHAGORAS IN
THE SIXTEENTH CENTURY   37
   The Authority of Pythagoras in the Early Sixteenth Century   38
   Reuchlin Describes Pythagoras's "Luggage": The Hebrew
      Patrimony of Christianity   42
   Occultism, Virtue, and the "Jewish" Side of Pythagoras: The Heavenly
      Teacher of Wisdom   45
   Mathematics, Exorcisms, and the Inspiration of Painters   51
   Pythagoras: The "Prince of Italian Philosophy"   55

PART TWO: THE MANY FACES OF RENAISSANCE
PYTHAGOREANISM

FOUR: THE PYTHAGOREAN TRADITION IN THE
EARLY FIFTEENTH CENTURY   63
The Resurgence of Pythagoreanism in Florence   65
The Greek Factor: Pletho and Bessarion   66
Intertwined Threads of Balance, Perfection, and Frugality:
   Germany, Florence, and Rome   72

FIVE: THE STRENGTHENING AND DEEPENING OF
PYTHAGOREANISM IN THE LATER FIFTEENTH CENTURY   80
Ficino's Pythagoreanism and His Proselytizing   80
Pico's Version of Pythagoreanism   87
Other Late-Century Pythagoreans in Tuscany   92
Urbino and the Mathematical Angle   93
Other Mathematical Considerations   98
Gaffurio and the Harmonia *of Music*   102
The Roman Connection   103

SIX: THE MATURATION AND VICISSITUDES OF
PYTHAGOREANISM IN THE SIXTEENTH CENTURY   108
Pacioli, Leonardo da Vinci, and Their Friends   109
Roman Perspectives   120
Venice: The Harmonia mundi *of Francesco Zorzi and*
   Pythagorean Musical Traditions   122
Esoteric Pythagoreanism: Reuchlin and His Contemporaries
   in Germany, Italy, England, and the Netherlands   123
International Pythagoreanism and Magic: France,
   Germany, England, and Italy   127
Finding Heaven: On the Brink of a New Science – From
   Copernicus to Kepler and Beyond   133

PART THREE: PYTHAGOREANISM IN ARCHITECTURE AND ART

SEVEN: RENAISSANCE IMAGES OF PYTHAGORAS   145

EIGHT: THE SEARCH FOR HARMONY IN
ARCHITECTURE AND ART IN THE FIFTEENTH CENTURY   162
Early Beginnings in the Florence of Brunelleschi and Michelozzo   162
Pythagorean Concepts Develop: Alberti in Florence and His
   Contemporaries in Pienza and Urbino   176

CONTENTS

Contemplating Harmony at Cortona, Prato, Milan,
  and Rome   192

NINE: FINDING HARMONY: FORM AND MEANING IN
ARCHITECTURE AND ART OF THE SIXTEENTH CENTURY   202
  Prelude: The Pythagorean Experiments of Leonardo,
    Early Michelangelo, and Young Raphael   202
  Bramante and the Perfect Church   211
  Harmonious Unities in the Maturation of Leonardo,
    Michelangelo, Raphael, and Fra Bartolomeo   218
  Venice and the Divinity of Proportion   230
  The Theology of Arithmetic in Spain   233

TEN: CONCLUSIONS: THE PRINCE OF
PHILOSOPHERS AND THE BIRTH OF HARMONY
AS AN AESTHETIC NOTION   240

Appendix A: Pythagorean Works in Six Renaissance Libraries   245
Appendix B: English Translation of Filippo Beroaldo's
       Symbola Pythagorica (1503)   248
Notes   267
Select Bibliography   301
Index   315

ILLUSTRATIONS

Montepulciano, San Biagio (Antonio da Sangallo the Elder)   *page* ii

1   Luca della Robbia, *Pythagoras Teaching Arithmetic to Plato*   146

2   Luca della Robbia, *Pythagoras Discovering Music*   148

3   *Pythagoras Spitting out Mathematical Formulas*   149

4   Jörg Syrlin the Elder, *Pythagoras Singing*   151

5   *Pythagoras in His Study*   152

6   *Jubal Inventing Music, Pythagoras Inventing Harmony, Pythagoras Testing His Theory on a Monochord,* and *Pythagoras Testing His Theory on Flutes*   154

7   *Boethius and Pythagoras*   155

8   Raphael, *Pythagoras* from *School of Athens*   156

9   Pellegrino Tibaldi, *Jubal and Pythagoras as Inventors of Music and Arithmetic*   158

10   Pellegrino Tibaldi, det. from *Jubal and Pythagoras as Inventors of Music and Arithmetic*   159

11   Annibale Carracci, *Hercules Bearing the Globe*   160

12   Florence, Pazzi Chapel, int. (Brunelleschi)   163

13   Florence, San Lorenzo, Sacristy, int. (Brunelleschi)   165

14   Plan of San Lorenzo (Brunelleschi)   166

15   Plan of Santo Spirito (Brunelleschi)   167

16   Florence, Pazzi Chapel, façade (Brunelleschi)   168

17   Plan of Santa Maria degli Angeli (Brunelleschi)   169

18   Florence, Santa Maria degli Angeli (Brunelleschi)   169

19   Plan of Cathedral of Florence Lantern (Brunelleschi)   170

20   Lorenzo Ghiberti, east doors of the Florentine Baptistery   172

21   Masaccio, *Tribute Money*   173

22   Florence, Palazzo Medici, int. courtyard (Michelozzo)   174

23   Florence, Palazzo Medici, ext. (Michelozzo)   175

24   Florence, Palazzo Rucellai (Alberti)   177

25   Matteo dei Pasti, medal for Tempio Malatestiano   178

26	Rimini, Tempio Malatestiano (Alberti)	179
27	Florence, Santa Maria Novella (Alberti)	180
28	Pienza, Cathedral (Bernardo Rossellino)	182
29	Pienza, Palazzo Piccolomini, courtyard (Bernardo Rossellino)	183
30	Pienza, Palazzo Piccolomini, east façade (Bernardo Rossellino)	184
31	Urbino, Palazzo Ducale, Grand Courtyard (Luciano Laurana)	185
32	Urbino, Palazzo Ducale, Cappella del Perdono (Bramante?)	186
33	Urbino, Palazzo Ducale, Tempietto delle Muse (Bramante?)	187
34	Piero della Francesca, *Flagellation*	189
35	Luciano Laurana (?), *Ideal City*	191
36	Cortona, Santa Maria del Calcinaio, int. (Francesco di Giorgio)	192
37	Cortona, Santa Maria del Calcinaio (Francesco di Giorgio)	193
38	Prato, Santa Maria delle Carceri (Giuliano da Sangallo)	194
39	Milan, Santa Maria presso San Satiro, int. (Bramante)	195
40	Milan, Santa Maria delle Grazie, int. (Bramante)	196
41	Milan, Santa Maria delle Grazie (Bramante)	197
42	Rome, Sistine Chapel, original int.	198
43	*Pythagorean Sphere*	199
44	Leonardo, *Benois Madonna*	203
45	Leonardo, *Adoration of the Magi*	205
46	Leonardo, *Madonna of the Rocks*	206
47	Michelangelo, *Madonna of the Steps*	208
48	Michelangelo, *Pietà*	209
49	Raphael, *Three Graces*	210
50	Raphael, *Marriage of the Virgin*	211
51	Rome, Tempietto at San Pietro in Montorio (Bramante)	212
52	Fabio Calvo, view of ancient Rome	213
53	Fabio Calvo, view of ancient Rome	214
54	Cristoforo Caradosso, medal commemorating foundation of St. Peter's (Bramante)	215
55	Montepulciano, San Biagio (Antonio da Sangallo the Elder)	216
56	Todi, Santa Maria delle Consolazione	217
57	Todi, Santa Maria delle Consolazione, int.	218
58	Leonardo, *Burlington House Cartoon*	219
59	Leonardo, *Madonna and Child with St. Anne*	220
60	Raphael, *Canigiani Holy Family*	221
61	Michelangelo, *Pitti tondo*	222
62	Michelangelo, Sistine Ceiling	223
63	Raphael, Ceiling of Stanza della Segnatura	226
64	Raphael, *School of Athens*	227
65	Raphael, *Disputà*	228
66	Raphael, *Parnassus*	229

67	Fra Bartolomeo, *Marriage of St. Catherine*	231
68	Giorgione and Titian, *Fête Champêtre* (*Memorial to Giorgione*)	232
69	Vicenza, Villa Rotonda (Andrea Palladio)	234
70	Granada, Palace of Charles V, courtyard (Pedro Machuca)	235
71	Madrid, El Escorial, plan (Juan de Toledo and Juan de Herrera)	236
72	Luca Cambiaso, *Trinity*, det. of *Gloria* at El Escorial	237

ACKNOWLEDGMENTS

The present volume, following from one that aimed to set the stage for Pythagoras and his influence in Antiquity and the Middle Ages, is devoted to recapturing his influence for the Renaissance and to speculating on its effect on the visual arts and architecture. The subject of Pythagoras's influence on the Renaissance, and specifically on the visual arts, has been obscured by our modern tendency to view different disciplines as separated from each other. The broadly interdisciplinary nature of this problem is challenging because it requires the wider perspective that was understood in the Renaissance. The substructure of thinkers and ideas that lies deeply embedded in the culture of the Renaissance is fertile ground. The testimony of its sources is so suggestive it cannot be overlooked. Our knowledge respecting the contributions of these thinkers to each other is much fuller than is frequently realized. While my understanding may be imperfect, I have here attempted to indulge my curiosity in how Pythagoras served as a conduit enabling those who sought to imitate the past to achieve an original and stunning modernity. I hope my readers will understand that this volume does not purport to give a complete synthesis of Pythagoras and his importance for the Renaissance, but only to offer some suggestions for future exploration and for evaluating his importance for the history of art and architecture. It is this interest that has encouraged me to enlarge my own studies and to seek understanding of the past by listening to its own language. For this gratification I am indebted to many institutions and many people.

First and foremost, those who inspired me in the beginning with the thrill to understand the past left an indelible example for me. These were, especially, Millard Meiss and Federico Zeri, my mentors at Harvard, and Giuseppe Billanovich, who kindly opened his house at Padua to me on many occasions. Among the many libraries that opened their doors to me, I am grateful to the Harvard University libraries, especially the Houghton and Dumbarton Oaks research libraries, as well as to the Biblioteca Apostolica Vaticana, the Library of the Kunsthistorisches Institut in Florence, the Bibliothèque Nationale at Paris, the Library of Congress, the Library of the Folger Institute, and the National Library of Medicine. During the time of my work on this volume, my most beloved home, however, was in the Library of the National Gallery at Washington, where the entire staff was always patient, kind, knowledgeable, and helpful.

I owe a special debt to those of my friends and colleagues whose superior knowledge in many important areas helped me to overcome problems or discover new tools of enlightenment. George Hersey, who sadly is no longer with us, first inspired and encouraged me to see this project through. Throughout its writing he was a confidant and a correspondent. Its realization owes a special debt of gratitude to two scholars whose knowledge, wisdom, grace, and common sense were never in short supply, Arielle Saiber and Mary Garrard. Francisco LaRubia Prado was helpful in innumerable imaginative ways, as was Carolyn Tuttle, whose first English translation of an important Renaissance work on Pythagoras is included as an appendix to this book. Among the many others who have helped me in one way or another to see this work through are Colin Eisler, Lamia Doumato, Yuri Long, Alexander Blachly, Allan Foy, David Alan Brown, Caroline Karpinski, Norberto Gramaccini, Helga DeLisle, Joscelyn Godwin, George Tatge, Shannon Pritchard, Dominique Surh, François Souchal, Carolyn Valone, Antonio Paolucci, Luba Freedman, Mary L. Robertson, Kent Killelea, Elaine Economides Joost, Charlotte DeMonte Phelps, Andrea Zezza, Inge Dupont, John Monfasani, Greg Murr, Gérard Bonneaud, Andrew Oliver, Ariel Cardoso, Elizabeth Welles, and Jorge Sobredo. I would also like to express my gratitude to the Kress Foundation for its support of this work in the form of a subvention. A very special word of thanks is due to Paolo Sfriso, who very kindly allowed the use of his photograph for the front cover.

To all these institutions and people I acknowledge my most vivid gratitude. I am especially honored to have worked, once again, with Cambridge University Press and its ever-wise and ever-gracious editor, Beatrice Rehl. Cambridge's production editor, Camilla Knapp, and copy editor, Susan Greenberg, both helped immeasurably in the process of publication.

INTRODUCTION

Today the name of Pythagoras conjures up, at best, only the theorem attributed to him. Yet his impact on the history of civilization was significant. This book tells the story of how this ancient sage, who left no surviving writings, was revered and even imitated some two thousand years after his death. Similarly to the case of Christ, who also left no writings, a steady stream of thinkers wrote about Pythagoras after his own time and came, increasingly, to be influenced by him. Paradoxically, it would appear that the further away in time scholars lived from when Pythagoras was born (ca. 570 B.C.), the more intense their esteem for him became. By Renaissance times he had come to be identified as an ideal ancestor of scientific investigation, a prophet of Christianity, and an authority on morality and the social good. It was perhaps *because* Pythagoras left no writings that he could be appreciated by many different people in many different ways.

To those of us who have followed, in a previous volume,[1] the reputation of Pythagoras and the various ways in which the admiration of his followers was expressed throughout Antiquity and the Middle Ages, the high regard in which he was held by the end of the medieval centuries is clear. Yet at no time in history were scholars more fascinated by Pythagoras than in the Renaissance. Surprisingly, the remarkable acceleration of interest in him and in the ideas believed to have originated with him that took place at that time has not yet been the subject of a comprehensive study focussed on the visual arts.

This volume will examine the critical fortune of Pythagoras and the ideas attributed to him by those who admired him in the Renaissance. This surge of interest was not so much for discovering the facts of his life as it was for finding his unique fame as a divine polymath useful in expounding a new cultural language. In an age when artists and scientists were not separated as they are today, this new language could be and was, as this book will show, disseminated in the visual world. From about 1394, when the first teacher of Greek arrived on Italian soil from Constantinople and the first Italian humanists (that is, men of learning) journeyed to the East in the hunt for precious Greek manuscripts, its pages will carry us to the early 1600s when, in giving birth to a new appreciation for observational evidence, the "Scientific Revolution" of the seventeenth century overtook the lure of classicism and relegated Pythagoras to the more distant realm of romantic imagination.[2]

The great fondness for Pythagoras in the Renaissance (essentially the fifteenth and sixteenth centuries) was largely due to the introduction of the study of Greek in Italian cities. It was also due to the long history of his previous approval by Christian authorities. Among those early Christians who had admired him were Clement of Alexandria, Saints Jerome and Augustine, the influential monk Cassiodorus, and the erudite bishop of Seville, Isidore. Pythagoras was revered by these scholars, who were perceived from early medieval times as disseminators of classical and Christian truth, as well as by later scholars in the Middle Ages as the first to have recognized the immortality of the soul. All saw him as an authority on morality. Because of the history of their consistent approval, Pythagoras continued to be admired in the Renaissance world as he had been in the Middle Ages.

For the Renaissance Pythagoras and what he stood for were very much alive. Ideas evoked by his influence were not separated, as they are today, into specialized disciplines. Rather, inspired by his memory, they formed part of a general background of thought based on the fundamental importance of the four elements (earth, fire, water, and air) to all living matter. According to this scheme, in which mathematics was the handmaid of the "science of the divine," the ancient significance of Pythagoras was rediscovered, raising his status among the thinkers of the ancient world because his inspiration had ignited the thought of the others.

The ancient threads that make up the thought of Pythagoras's followers were remarkably important for by the end of the Middle Ages they had survived sixteen centuries virtually intact, especially in the Greek world. This complex skein of thoughts came to be known by the general term Pythagoreanism. As we shall see, it shaped the ideas, and often also the lifestyles, of Renaissance thinkers. They conceived of "true" wisdom as a composite of intellectual knowledge, piety, and moral discipline – an ideal similar to that of ancient Pythagoreans for whom the concept of wisdom meant both factual knowledge and divine insight. Some were intellectuals who pondered number and mathematics; others thought it suitable to practice vegetarianism and frugality; yet others were intrigued by both. Old as were the origins of the beliefs they recalled, these provided an avenue for welcoming many interests still regarded as "modern" today – including peace, harmony, concord, ethical conduct, astrology, frugality, meditation, altruism, alternative medicine, the acceptance of women into the

Academy, and vegetarianism along with other dietary taboos. The written evidence from those who lived in the centuries of the Renaissance and the visual evidence left by contemporary architects and artists are compelling. Together they suggest an important story.

Renaissance thinkers were fascinated by the ancient literary and mathematical works that came, along with works of natural philosophy, into their hands. But they did not read them to construct verifiable positivistic theories about the past. Rather they used these works for their inspirational value. Those in the Renaissance who responded to the voice of Pythagoras through his representatives from the past liked what they heard. They used those ancient messages to articulate and create a unified world of their own design, to broaden Christian concerns, and to create a new idealism based on the concept of Pythagorean harmony. Thus was the muffled voice of Pythagoras greatly amplified in the Renaissance, when he became immensely influential.

The aim of this book is to describe how this happened. Studying the various ways in which ancient ideas connected with him were disseminated and transposed into new formulations will help us understand the role Pythagoras and his followers played in the development of Renaissance culture. As they passed from generation to generation, these ideas evoked an essential unity in patterns of belief similar to those Pythagoras was believed to have preached. The translation of this highly appreciated inheritance into a search for a novel language, one that would invest even the most Christian of themes with classical authority, was more intense in the Renaissance, when the two frequently merged, than in the Middle Ages when ancient themes were often relinquished in favor of Christian ones. The many varied aspects of Pythagorean thought – especially in arithmetic, geometry, and music – suggest a common goal: finding harmony. These ideas are particularly evident in the visual arts, where this ancient system of meanings could be, and was by some, especially architects and painters, transposed into fundamentally new concepts of perfection.

The path for my study of this exceptional evolution of thought has been paved by the seminal research of scholars who have provided us with a framework within which to view the significance of Pythagoras and the doctrines attributed to him.[3] François Lenormant was, in the mid-nineteenth century, the first to see the essential unity in the presumed teachings of Pythagoras. In an impressive number of works, Franz Cumont demonstrated, in the first half of the twentieth century, how a knowledge of Pythagorean thought could enhance our understanding of the iconography (subject matter) of ancient Greek and Roman art. Classical art was, of course, important for the Renaissance, when its Pythagorean connections appear to have been better understood than they are now. A philosopher herself, Cornelia de Vogel displayed great wisdom in arguing, in the 1960s, that Pythagoras could not be properly understood exclusively in terms of philosophy but must be studied in terms of his larger social influence.

In the later twentieth century, S. K. Heninger explicated the significance of Pythagorean thought for poetic literature of the Renaissance. Michael J. B. Allen demonstrated the richly interwoven influences of Platonism and its multifaceted impact on Renaissance philosophical thought. Valuable research on the influence of Pythagoras in Florence has been accomplished by Christopher Celenza. In his masterpiece on architectural principles in the Renaissance, Rudolf Wittkower speculated that aesthetic theories in Renaissance building practice were connected with other manifestations of the mind, such as music, science, and mathematics. Though he perceived that number was important for understanding Renaissance architecture, he was handicapped by his conceptualization of numbers in the modern way, as cold integers, rather than in the Pythagorean way, as warm symbols that had character and mysterious meaning. André Chastel pioneered the modern study of the rapport between Florentine late fifteenth-century art and contemporary intellectual currents. George Hersey was the first to propose that Pythagorean ideas were influential on Renaissance architecture by showing their fundamental importance for the new architectural creation known as the Renaissance palace. To date, this work remains unique in its impact on interpretations of Pythagoras in the Renaissance. The work of J. V. Field, though not formally associated with Pythagoreanism, should be acknowledged because it studies, in an insightful and learned way, the relation between mathematics and art in the Renaissance. Though her work concerns times later than the Renaissance, Eileen Reeves wrote an exemplary analysis that was the first to seriously probe the association between astronomy and painting. Other scholars in our times have made important contributions to our knowledge of Renaissance philosophical and scientific thought. These include, to name but a few, Brian Copenhaver, Allen Debus, James Hankins, John Monfasani, Pier Daniele Napolitani, Paul Lawrence Rose, Wayne Shumaker, and Pierre Souffrin.[4]

Indeed, it is now time to enlarge the format of these discussions and to look at the big picture of Renaissance Pythagoreanism. This will, I believe, reveal that consciously or not the legacy of Pythagoras opened up entirely new vistas for mind and eye (in writings as well as in architecture and art). These were intertwined, forming the last – and perhaps the grandest – chapter in the relevance of Pythagoras to the history of civilization and, especially, to Western culture.

Before beginning our journey, which follows the fortune of Pythagoras and the dissemination of his ideas in the Renaissance, it will be useful to describe, in brief, the very ancient roots of the multifaceted "worldview" that his memory evoked and its persistence – indeed, its expansion and development – from Antiquity through the Middle Ages to the dawn of the Renaissance.

Owing to the absence of documents from his own time, a true biography of Pythagoras cannot be written. However, the history of his importance can be evoked based on surviving fragments of works written by those who knew him or had direct knowledge of him. These help us to begin to reconstruct a lost "history," largely that of his reputation.

The surviving words of those who knew and followed Pythagoras in those first generations of his influence speak forcibly of the earliest evidence we have about him – his compassion for animals, his belief that all living beings have souls, his wisdom, and his highly original attempts to introduce the idea of order in the universe. This order enunciated a "law" of contrariety, that of the existence of interacting opposites. In the face of their intrinsic conflict, this interaction found refuge in a middle ground. This was based on the idea that, in making continuous reparation to each other, the four elements established the perfect balance on which the lives of humankind should be modeled. Among the most famous early admirers of Pythagoras were Empedocles of Agrigento, Philolaus of Croton, and Democritus of Abdera. Ancient testimony from these and even from those who, like Heraclitus of Ephesus, may have been his rivals, is unanimous in suggesting that one side of Pythagoras was dedicated to scholarship while another side was occupied with the supernatural – that is, with the mysterious forces of the universe, which some associated with magic. Whether Pythagoras specifically taught metempsychosis – transmigration of the soul – as a doctrine is not clear. However, that he believed that the soul was immortal and could expect to live eternally is clear.

Inevitably, the historical portrait of Pythagoras in Antiquity fades with the passage of time. Correspondingly, a legendary Pythagoras takes over in the writings of those who aimed to reconstruct his life and teachings. These reconstructions, too, are history, for they established the reputation of Pythagoras as it was to be heard by Renaissance ears and, thus, passed down to us.

Though increasingly mythologized in the later centuries of Antiquity, the reputation of Pythagoras does not change his essential historical image. He was, and continued to be, above all, a humble sage. An important new element was, however, introduced during this time. Pythagoras came to be regarded for mathematical discoveries. This was based on a suggestion originally made by Philolaus, one of his earliest followers, that Pythagoras was the first to identify the geometrical solids, or polyhedra (the hexahedron or cube, the tetrahedron or four-sided pyramid, the octahedron, the dodecahedron, and the icosahedron – so named according to the number of plane faces they possess). Because Plato discussed these in his *Timaeus*, a later work, they came to be known as "Platonic solids." Pythagoras's favorite plane geometrical form, it was deduced in late Antiquity, was the circle. Because the circle has no perceivable beginning or end, it stood for the purest divine and eternal continuity. His favorite solid geometrical form was its three-dimensional counterpart, the sphere. Because the sphere displays equality at all points of its surface to and from its center, it was even more favored by him, for it could contain any of the five geometrical solids.

One of these solids, thought to have been of particular importance to Pythagoras, was the cube. It could be described in two ways. As a regular geometrical solid, it had six faces or equal square sides. It could also be described numerically, based on its equal dimensions, as the third power – or cube – of any number (e.g., 4 x 4 x 4 = 64). Awe for this concept was so great that at least one Roman, the architect Vitruvius, wrote that Pythagoras and his followers had composed "books" about the cube, celebrating its primacy.[5]

Another geometric solid particularly admired by Pythagoras and his followers (especially Anatolius, Nicomachus of Gerasa, and Philo of Alexandria) was the pyramid. Having four sides at its base, it symbolized the basic perfection of the number 4, the number commemorating the importance of the four elements. The significance of this number was memorialized in an equilateral triangular display of the first four numbers. This array brought the total of its component integers to 10 and was represented by the famous symbol attributed to Pythagoras, the *tetraktys*:

$$
\begin{array}{cccc}
 & \bullet & & \\
 & \bullet & \bullet & \\
\bullet & & \bullet & \bullet \\
\bullet & \bullet & \bullet & \bullet \\
\end{array}
$$

Aëtius, in the first century A.D., described Pythagoras's *tetraktys* as the source of all nature because it was based on the quaternity, or "fourness," of the elements; a century later, Theon of Smyrna called it "the holy *tetraktys*," for it represented the cosmos, now symbolized by the number 10. In short, the *tetraktys* and the decad together came to be a compendium of Pythagorean mysticism believed to contain the ratios of cosmic harmony.[6] Thus was Pythagoras understood to have pondered geometry.

More important the mathematics attributed to Pythagoras in the centuries following his death introduced the idea that number could explain all features of order in the universe. Thus he came to be universally admired as an arithmetician. But arithmetic was not a stand-alone science (as we now think of it) in Antiquity; rather it and theology were bound together into a form of knowledge that might more properly be called "arithmology" – a knowledge that was both scientific and mystical. Because the seven strings of the lyre reflected the number of the celestial bodies (the five planets known at the time plus the sun and the moon), this instrument was considered ideal for audibly confirming the music of the spheres that Plato had first alluded to and Cicero and Macrobius had later described. It was during Roman times that the geometrical theorem now known as the "Pythagorean theorem" (the square of the hypotenuse of a right triangle is equal to the sum of the squares of the other two sides, or $c^2 = a^2 + b^2$) was first, to our knowledge, attributed to Pythagoras, by Vitruvius.[7]

Other new elements make up the legendary accretions to the life of Pythagoras developed during late Antiquity. These include his associations with moral teachings, dietary restrictions, self-discipline, the practice of silence, the abhorrence of luxury, the pursuit of simplicity, the exercise of piety, the use of secrecy and enigma, and the practice of healing. None of these conflicted with the original aim of Pythagoreans to find and define order in the universe. That concept had simply been enlarged to include the Pythagorean commitment to teaching human beings how to put order in their lives. In essence, Pythagoras's ancient reputation had not changed; these accretions only enriched it.

This enrichment included other elements that are clearly legendary though in some cases (starting as far back as Aristotle in the fourth century B.C.) they had been reported by exacting, scientific scholars. Pythagoras worshipped primarily one god (Apollo), who, as his divine father, had entrusted him, at birth, with the mission to teach morality, purity, and piety to all humankind. Pythagoras had a golden thigh, which he displayed on selected occasions, "proving" his special status as the son of a god. He cured emotional sickness through music therapy induced by playing his lyre with a slower rhythm and longer, stressed (or "spondaic"), beat. This enabled him, ancient sources tell us, to calm frenzied behavior. Numerous other legends, repeatedly reported by many writers in late Antiquity, served as symbols of his divinity.

Such marvelous stories were accepted over time as true, leading some to deduce that because Pythagoras was the son of a god (Apollo) he was a god himself. In late Antiquity, it was thought by such writers as Neanthes Satyrus and Hermippus that this divine man and his followers had been persecuted and died tragic deaths. This idea gave the impression that they had become martyrs. The accumulation of miraculous events attributed to Pythagoras and his followers reached their height in the years of early Christianity. While these accounts served as inspiring symbols to initiates, outsiders such as Lucian of Samosata found them puzzling or even ludicrous.[8] However, it was thought by some that as a divine being who had died a martyr's death, Pythagoras was reborn after having visited Hades and resurrected from the dead. It was this Pythagoras that came to be known to the Roman world. Following Pythagoras's influence in Italy, his divine father, Apollo, the inventor of music and the arts and the master of Parnassus and the Muses, moved from the Greek to the Roman world, keeping his name intact. There Apollo attained a unique popularity as a god of healing. His son, Pythagoras, late-Antique writers explained, was devoted to the nine Muses, who were in charge of unison, harmony, and rhythm, the ingredients that make up concord.[9]

Those who wrote about Pythagoras in late Antiquity came from such disparate areas as Syria (e.g., Nicomachus, Porphyry of Tyre, and Iamblichus of Chalcis),

Alexandria (e.g., Theon of Smyrna, Aristobulus and Philo of Alexandria), Athens (e.g., Proclus), and Rome (Cicero and Varro, among others). Whereas the Syrians tended to emphasize the mystical traits of Pythagoras (divinity and the mysticism of number), Alexandrians stressed his interest in arithmetic and were interested in Pythagoras's connection with Judaism. The *Book of Wisdom*, an apocryphal work believed to have been written by Solomon himself (though it is now connected with Philo), proclaimed that God had created all things according to number, weight, and measure. Romans, particularly Cicero, saw Pythagoras as a great unifier and a builder of community and harmony.[10]

Pythagoras was also noted, especially in late Antiquity, for his ability to practice magic. Interest in this tradition was especially vivid among the Druids. Perhaps remembering their Greek origins, this learned priestly class of Gauls were thought, in Gallo-Roman times, to have taught Pythagorean doctrines. Playing their lyres, they practiced the well-known Pythagorean arts of divination, prognostication, and medicine as they melded into French medieval culture.[11]

Most astonishing, perhaps, is the consistency of medieval traditions about Pythagoras. Though in the Middle Ages there was a tradition of suspicion regarding mathematics (and other forms of esoteric knowledge) as an occult, dark, art, Pythagoras was valued by many who believed his arithmetic had played a pivotal role in understanding the universe. This resulted in the rising importance of the study of geometry and proportion and of the idea that opposing or different concepts instinctually seek mediation, or union, with their counterparts. Among the many routes by which classical learning about Pythagoras was transmitted to the Middle Ages, the most crucial manifested themselves early on. Authoritative writers such as Macrobius, Boethius, and Isidore of Seville sought to explain the cosmological harmony for which Pythagoreans had come to be famous. The tradition of learning established by their works was extremely influential throughout the remaining medieval centuries. Its inspiration led to mathematical interpretations of the universe and the assignment of numerical symbolism to religious concepts by Christians and Jews. Pythagoras was especially revered in the early Middle Ages as the founder of the quadrivium, the four disciplines (arithmetic, geometry, music, and astronomy) that formed the foundation of the Seven Liberal Arts (to which the trivium – grammar, rhetoric, and dialectic – were added). These were celebrated in a bold and florid drama about them concocted by Martianus Capella, which would become required reading for every medieval schoolboy. Now the number 7, revered by Pythagoreans, and memorialized in the Seven Liberal Arts, was put under the protection of none other than the Blessed Virgin.[12] Numbers and geometry were of the greatest importance to medieval writers, not only because scholars such as Boethius had said as much, but because Plato's *Timaeus*, the only complete work of Plato's known in medieval times, was a work they respected.

Here Plato had explained the unity of God and the creation of the world by this divine master craftsman in a way that Christians could follow because the Church Fathers had accepted it. Plato stipulated triangles to be the essential ingredient of the five basic geometrical solids that compose the universe. All geometric plane figures can, he suggested, be analyzed as triangles. Thus did the triangle come to be regarded as basic to the construction of the universe. The *Timaeus* proved that all parts of nature were interconnected through geometry and number in the great sphere of the universe. Behind Plato's god, who laid out the order of the universe from the primeval chaos previously described by Hesiod into a functioning harmony of celestial bodies moving in fixed proportions to one another, was Plato's teacher and inspirator, Pythagoras.[13] Plato's masterpiece thrilled not only Western scholars, who read it in Latin translation, but also Eastern scholars in the Byzantine world, who read it in the original Greek. It would also thrill Renaissance humanists anxious to replace the medieval scholastic obsession with Aristotle with the more unified worldview advocated by Plato in the *Timaeus*, a work known since Antiquity and through the Middle Ages as his most Pythagorean work. The power of Plato's resurgence in the Renaissance was so great that modern concepts such as "Platonism" and "Neoplatonism," which have so concentrated our attention on Plato's methods, ideas, and influence, tend to overlook what Renaissance thinkers knew – that behind Plato was Pythagoras.

Meanwhile, an alchemical tradition, one originating in Antiquity but ever more pronounced during the Middle Ages, connected the transmutation of base metals into gold with the subterranean world that had, supposedly, been inhabited by Pythagoras. This tradition regarded Pythagoras, who had discovered the immortality of the soul, as an authority in a world where even stones were believed to have souls.[14] In the world of medieval divination, inspired in great part by the Druids in France, a considerable literature developed around the authority of Pythagoras as a master prognosticator.[15] Those who knew the secrets of interpreting number – especially medical doctors and priests – could make the necessary predictions involving life and death. Thus everyday people were also acquainted with Pythagoras. Clearly, his high standing in medieval times prevailed in the occult as well as the intellectual world.

It was this expanded world that the Renaissance would inherit when it found its ideal ancestor in the pure soul of Pythagoras. Dante very much admired Pythagoras, just as Renaissance thinkers would admire Dante. Petrarch too thought highly of Pythagoras. During the Renaissance many people could even visualize Pythagoras, because a steady stream of portraits of him survived from Antiquity and the Middle Ages. Pythagorean influence had helped Gothic architects develop the mystical numerical symbolism of their cathedrals, which, as did the oldest surviving Pythagorean temple now known as the Subterranean Basilica at Porta Maggiore in Rome, faced eastward.[16]

This rich inheritance consisted of many pieces that had to be fitted together. The initial steps toward the process of re-presenting Pythagoras in the Renaissance would be inspired by the burgeoning interest in all things Greek. Indeed, the classical tradition had not died out, as is often assumed; on the contrary, it was continued into the Early Renaissance and enriched and accelerated when Greek scholars met their Latin counterparts on the soil of Italy.

This book is, in accordance with the nature of the topic I am studying, divided into thirds. The first, comprising Chapters 1–3, studies the reputation of Pythagoras, the man, as developed in the Renaissance. The second, consisting of Chapters 4–6, examines the testimony and ideas of those authors active in the fifteenth and sixteenth centuries who were interested in Pythagoras's ideas or that suggest that these writers were following what were thought to be his teachings. Because some of them may have actually written about Pythagoras the man, there will, inevitably, be some who reappear in these pages. On the other hand, there are many more who appear to have subscribed to some (but not necessarily all) of the concepts attributed to him by tradition. Both extremes, and others in between, will be considered here. The final part, made up of Chapters 7–9, selects some of those creations in the visual arts of the Renaissance that appear to suggest the impact or inspiration of Pythagoras and what were thought to be his ideas. This part first describes the portrait tradition of Pythagoras in the Renaissance, providing evidence that he was well known in the artistic world. In the pages that follow, evidence suggesting the impact of his ideas on visualizing form, space, and design in Renaissance art and architecture will be offered for consideration. The association of ideas presented in these chapters suggests visual corroboration that the tentacles of Pythagoreanism, as first rediscovered in Italy, spread in the Western world – an extensive area that included Germany, Spain, France, and England. A final chapter summarizes the significance of Pythagoras and the widespread influence of doctrines associated with him from late medieval to early modern times.

The first of two appendixes will, it is hoped, give the reader an idea of the quantity and variety of ancient literature referring to Pythagoras that was collected in Renaissance libraries. The second will provide the reader an opportunity to understand the importance of the "moral" side of Pythagoreanism in the Renaissance with the first translation into English of an Italian Renaissance publication of the *Symbola*. This was an accretion of moral precepts thought, in the public memory, to have been written by Pythagoras himself. These precepts explained to contemporaries how they might put order in their lives reflecting the order he had seen in the universe. Pythagoras's moral authority had had a long and consistent history in Antiquity and the Middle Ages and was to be particularly important in the Renaissance. This fact has been neglected by recent scholarship, which stresses his mathematical or philosophical aspect. In order to understand the complex and multifaceted weight of the influence of Pythagoras, it is essential to acknowledge the respect the Renaissance paid to all aspects of his reputation, including his moral teachings.

Though of course not all thinkers in the Renaissance were Pythagoreans, a surprising number were. There were also many who did not call themselves "Pythagoreans" but who contributed, through their teachings and ideas, in valuable ways to the movement and its development. The testimony of the literary sources is clear. So also is that of architects and artists, though in many cases the latter speak without words. In this volume, their testimony will be reported in a language as free as possible of the jargon of specialists. Art and science were not separate disciplines in the Renaissance, as they are today. Nor were philosophy, religion, mathematics, alchemy, astronomy, and astrology. Nor, for that matter, were cosmology and architecture. So fascinating was Pythagoras's influence that it may be seen as leading Renaissance thinkers to new areas of intellectual exploration where elements that had previously been considered minimally or not at all came to be unified under the challenging mantle of "perfect" harmony. Perfect harmony was also a goal in the world of music. While Pythagorean thinking, which had permeated all aspects of medieval music, especially the makeup of the musical scale, continued to provide the foundation for music theory throughout the fifteenth and sixteenth centuries, in the course of this time the notion of a numerically derived musical scale came to be increasingly important. Relying on ideas of cosmological harmony, numerical arrangements were devised to make music more harmonious and pleasing to the ears.[17] This is revealed in major musical treatises of the Renaissance that, no doubt, followed the lead of musical practice. At the root of all was number, but not exactly in the sense of the modern label "numerology" (which implies a systematic study of the mysterious significance of number).

For Pythagoreans, number was a living language that, in addition to its practical mathematical applications, was believed to have theological and cosmological attributes, and therefore universal inspirational power. Diverse as they seem to modern people, such concerns were not necessarily separated in Antiquity, when numbers denoted the universal divine thought that defined all things. Each number, especially those within the decad, had personality, sex, warmth, and special meanings that could be enhanced when squared (the product of a number multiplied by itself, as $9 = 3 \times 3$ or $16 = 4 \times 4$) or cubed (the product of a number multiplied by itself three times, as $8 = 2 \times 2 \times 2$ or $27 = 3 \times 3 \times 3$) by mathematical processes. Another way of enhancing a number was to view it as a figurate number. A figurate number is one for which that number of equally spaced points can be represented as a geometric figure (for e.g., the numbers 3, 6, or 10 can be arranged to form triangles — such figurate numbers could also be called "triangular" numbers). Other numbers were considered "perfect." A mathematically perfect number is one that is equal to the sum of its divisors ($6 = 1 + 2 + 3$, or $28 = 1 + 2 + 4 + 7 + 14$).[18] Some numbers were called "perfect" simply because reverence for them was so great, as in the case of 3, 4, 10, and 16. For Pythagoreans, both forms of numerical "perfection" – mathematical and symbolic – were valid, and sometimes they were intertwined. In these pages, it will not be necessary to distinguish between mathematically perfect and symbolically perfect numbers, but only to understand that for Pythagoreans many numbers could be "perfect."

This book is an introduction to a new way of thinking about the Renaissance; it invites the reader to understand how and where Pythagoreanism found a home in Renaissance thought and to see visual objects in a new light, different from the conventional stylistic and iconographical limitations of art history, which concentrates on the manner of making art and on what its resulting images represent. My purpose is to follow threads that have not been pursued before and, by doing so, to bring out new evidence concerning the history, authority, stimulus, and influence of one man – who, long dead, left no writings – during this remarkable time in the history of civilization.

Part One:
Pythagoras, Man for the Renaissance

ONE:

PROLOGUE: THE DIFFUSION OF KNOWLEDGE ABOUT PYTHAGORAS IN THE RENAISSANCE

Much is to be learned about Pythagoras by starting from the Renaissance. The rediscovery of Plato's lost works in the Latin West marks, probably above all else, the indeterminate beginnings of this brilliant period in the history of civilization. While the Byzantine world knew most if not all Plato's dialogues, and the Arab world knew a number of his texts through translations, the Latin West knew of his works mainly only through the summaries of his successors.[1] It was the first third of the *Timaeus*, as translated in late Antiquity by Chalcidius, that provided the medieval West with its firsthand knowledge of Plato until, in later medieval times, the *Phaedo* and parts of the *Parmenides* would come to be known. Essentially, then, the only work of his known during the Middle Ages, the *Timaeus* was widely regarded. However, it was so well known throughout that time as a Pythagorean work that it might be said that Pythagoras (as its presumed inspirator) was transported into the Renaissance on Plato's coattails. But Pythagoras had also been popular on his own throughout the Middle Ages. His influence had permeated many aspects of medieval life from cosmology to geometry, mathematics, and proportion, to magic. Not only did the Renaissance inherit what was known about Pythagoras in the Middle Ages, it also enthusiastically sought for, and found, an impressive storehouse of information about his reputation and his doctrines in the literature of Antiquity.

By the beginning of the fifteenth century, the dream of Petrarch (d. 1374) to comprehend the whole of the classical heritage, Greek as well as Latin, seemed possible. Inspired by him, his successors, the early humanists (the literary intelligentsia who read classical Latin if not Greek) of fifteenth-century Italy, began to actively search for ancient works that had been lost to the Latin world during the Middle Ages. Their devotion was motivated not only by intellectual zeal but also by an eagerness to apply the ideas of ancient authors to problems of their time.[2]

Their stimulation, fed by the presence in Italy of Greek émigré scholars, would last for nearly a century and a half. Beginning as early as 1397, when the Byzantine Manuel Chrysoloras delivered his opening lecture at the *studium* of Florence (the future University of Florence), it continued until 1534, when the last major Greek scholar-exile, Janus Lascaris, died in Rome.[3]

The presence of Greek scholars first made itself dramatically felt in Western culture as a result of the Great Council that, in the hopes of uniting the Western and Eastern churches, was convened in Ferrara in 1438 and moved to Florence in 1439.[4] These scholars brought with them from Constantinople, the last great outpost of Greek culture, works of ancient writers that had either languished in the West or been only legendary there. When Constantinople fell to the Turks in 1453, the exodus of Greek scholars was drawn to the West. Bearing texts and inspirited by their vast knowledge of ancient Greek works, they were highly valued as teachers in the flourishing humanist centers of Italy, including Florence, Milan, Bergamo, Padua, Venice, Naples, Verona, Bologna, Ferrara, Rome, and Mantua.[5] Italians were encouraged by these Greek scholars to pay homage to Pythagoras. In the words of one émigré, "Would you not make obeisance before the Easterners who have discovered the beauty of letters and of philosophy itself? Who among the Europeans is wiser than Socrates, Timaeus and Pythagoras?"[6] Thus was the medieval store of knowledge about Pythagoras tremendously augmented, fertilizing a soil previously cultivated. The resulting familiarity with the literary production of numerous ancient writers provided new information about Pythagoras. First known through manuscripts, these writers became ever more familiar after the invention of printing in the 1460s.[7] Thus did Greek influence in Italian scholarly life set the stage for an enduring renewal of respect for Pythagoras.

Interest in Pythagoras was keen from the Early Renaissance. Not only was he widely accepted by humanists, he was also interesting for conservative Christians. The latter had never derogated him as a subverter of Christianity, as they had Plato, for Pythagoras had the stamp of approval of numerous revered ecclesiastics. This approval was based in part on the belief of the Church Fathers that Pythagoras had discovered the immortality of the soul. It was also based on the established tradition that Pythagoras had invented the idea that numbers might serve as symbols to elucidate complex discussions of the divine creation of the universe. This science of number, which had endless theological applications, had been much discussed at the intellectual level in influential mathematical treatises from late Antiquity and Early Christian times that were now introduced to eager readers.

The resurgent interest in Pythagoras extended beyond Plato's devotees to include those familiar with Ovid. Ovid's striking portrait of Pythagoras as a vegetarian in the *Metamorphoses* — a work that enjoyed enormous popularity throughout the Middle Ages and Renaissance — appears to have touched more people during the Renaissance than it had during medieval times. Epic in its scope, entertaining in its ingenuity, and powerful in its intensity, Ovid's work was more popular than ever in the Early Renaissance. It was imitated, quoted, and translated – into English, French, German, Italian, and Spanish – in the fifteenth century and, after the invention of printing later in the century, it was widely distributed.[8] As all schoolboys (for whom the *Metamorphoses* was required reading) knew, Ovid's Pythagoras was a hero for all. In a dazzling display of conviction, he had protested against the killing and eating of animals, which he saw as "life eating life," and expressed piety before his god, Apollo, the sun of the universe and the healer of humankind.

Schoolboys also knew Pythagoras as one of the great Greek sages who had attended a magnificent heavenly wedding in Martianus Capella's grandiloquent fifth century A.D. work, which they also read, *De nuptiis Mercurii et Philologiae* (*The Marriage of Mercury and Philology*). Celebrating harmony and bearing the fabulous Lady Arithmetic on his arm, Pythagoras miraculously and dramatically appears in the wedding march in this work, like the father of the bride, as the inspirator of the magic and mysticism to which it was believed his arithmetic was devoted. As all his disciples, including Plato, assemble to revere the awesome lady with the ten lustrous rays protruding from her forehead, Pythagoras holds a torch aloft over her head. Thus, representing the mystical qualities of Arithmetic, this glorious and majestic figure manifests the importance of the number 10, which, it was believed, Pythagoras had taught was sacred for it embraces everything in the universe. This number confirmed the basic importance of the number 4, whose components when added together produced 10 ($1 + 2 + 3 + 4 = 10$) and form the *tetraktys*.

Attention to Pythagoras expanded as antique authors not familiar to most medieval commentators came to be known to Italian scholars. Among these newly discovered authors were Philo of Alexandria, a famous Pythagorean philosopher of Antiquity; Domninos of Larissa, a Syrian mathematician and follower of the already famous mathematician of late Antiquity, Nicomachus; and Hermes Trismegistus (Hermes "Thrice-Great"), a mysterious author of late Antiquity whose occult works, known as "Hermetic" texts (texts that regarded Pythagoras as an authority on magic), were mistakenly believed in the Renaissance to be much older than they were. Another such text, purported to be by Iamblichus, was known as the *Mysteries of Egypt*.[9] These texts and their influence will be taken into account in the chapters that follow.

As precious works by ancient authors were rediscovered, many of the great libraries of Italy were formed – for example, those in Florence, Naples, Pavia, Milan, Urbino, Novara, and Rome.[10] Humanist texts made their way outside Italy as well, to collections such as those of Cardinal Zelada in Spain and King Mathias Corvinus of Hungary. With their impressive collections of manuscripts and, after the 1460s, printed books, the new Renaissance libraries reveal which authors were copied and collected, and thereby they serve as a gauge to the esteem in which historical personalities and ideas were held. The Pythagorean holdings of six such libraries, selected on the basis of their geographical and sociological diversity, are summarized in Appendix A. These include those of the dukes of Lombardy, a cardinal who regarded Venice as his home, a pope in the Vatican at Rome, an independent intellectual in Florence, a Hebraic scholar in Germany, and a king of Spain.

The contents of these libraries show that the desire to salvage and capture the intellectual heritage of the Greek world was especially instrumental in providing a steady and dependable stream of information about Pythagoras. The information about him that came to be known in the fifteenth century was more complete than that known in medieval times. Students of the "humanitas," devotees of classical Greek and Latin authors, became acquainted with works that had formerly been neglected and incorporated them into the intellectual pedigree of Pythagoras that had survived through the Middle Ages. As great libraries were assembled and new educational methods focusing on Greek studies became a reality, especially in Italy, the humanistic world of the Early Renaissance discovered new perspectives on Pythagoras. These were paralleled by the surging new interest in Plato who had always been, and continued to be, believed to be a follower of Pythagoras.

At the same time, a continuous tradition of the *Golden Verses* and the *Symbola* of Pythagoras – long lists of moral maxims first assembled in late Antiquity and believed throughout medieval times to be authentic works by Pythagoras – were well known to early Renaissance readers, first in manuscript form and later in a succession of printed editions.[11] Purportedly composed by the great sage himself, these maxims guaranteed that the fame of Pythagoras as a teacher and arbiter of morality would flourish throughout the Renaissance – for the common people as well as for the intellectuals.

Thus did Pythagoras come to be well known through the classical heritage of the Renaissance not only as the mathematical intellect behind Plato but also as a social reformer, mystic, and popular hero. All these aspects of Pythagoras were to be reflected in the fabric of developing Renaissance views.

TWO:
THE EMERGENCE OF "SAINT" PYTHAGORAS IN THE EARLY RENAISSANCE

The fusion of Greek and Latin traditions that occurred during the Early Renaissance produced an efflorescence of interest in classical ideas that allowed Pythagoras and his doctrines to become more familiar to scholars and better known to a wider spectrum of people than ever before. With "new" classical sources now before them, not to mention the birth of the printing press that occurred during this century, the appreciation of contemporary thinkers for Pythagoras extended far beyond what had been known in medieval times. Inspired by Antiquity, they demonstrated in a crescendo of writings that his reputation was well known to them. Indeed, Pythagoras was so consistently and increasingly important in the fifteenth century that his reputation came to be enhanced – and enriched – by new literary interpretations (discussed here and in Part II) that in turn inspired artistic productions (discussed in Part III). It was no doubt this great interest that stimulated the appearance, in the closing years of the fifteenth century and the opening decade of the sixteenth, of several new biographies of him.

EARLY FIFTEENTH-CENTURY WRITERS VIEW PYTHAGORAS

In the earliest years of the Renaissance, Coluccio Salutati (1331–1406), an influential chancellor of Florence as well as a great scholar devoted to the search for ancient manuscripts, held up Pythagoras as a moral and intellectual example. Persuading his contemporaries to see Pythagoras as a guide to the virtuous life, this younger contemporary of Petrarch enthusiastically expresses his approbation of the authority of Pythagoras in *De laboribus Herculis* (*The Labors of Hercules*, 1390), a work exploring the relation of the labors of Hercules to the search for divine truth. In several passages, Salutati stresses the significance of what he considers to have been a very important invention of Pythagoras, the letter "Y," in which two branches diverge from a stem. According to the teachings of Pythagoras, he tells us, the choice of virtue or vice was signified by this letter. Pythagoras had taught, he admiringly continues, that one must decide between what is lofty and what is base. He discusses the significance of this letter as that of the choice set before each human to follow virtue or vice – a choice that, as described in both pagan and early Christian literature, affects the eternal life of the soul.[1]

Salutati also expresses deep admiration for Pythagoras in the intellectual realm. In a discussion of musical sequences he demonstrates his familiarity with the doctrines of Pythagoras concerning harmony. He describes "Philolaus the Pythagorean," Plato, Archytas, Macrobius, and Virgil as examples of famous thinkers of Antiquity who disseminated the teachings of Pythagoras respecting celestial harmony. That harmony was born, he exults, in the revolutions of the heavenly spheres, as first discovered and described by Pythagoras. In discussing the interrelation between musical tones, intervals, and number Salutati reminds his readers that Pythagoras's understanding of celestial harmony, symbolized by the singing of the Muses, was later explained by Plato.[2] Celestial harmony bestows enlightenment on those who understand it, enabling them to be virtuous human beings. Thus does Salutati attach the ancient concept of noble virtue (or *virtus*) to the Christian concept of moral virtue. For the pursuit of virtue, he concludes, the teachings of Pythagoras are fundamental.

Continuing to draw from ancient sources, Salutati discusses the extraordinary abilities of Pythagoras in numbers and measurement. He adds that the rule of silence that Pythagoras taught enjoined his listeners never to question what they heard.[3] An entirely new contribution to the teachings of Pythagoras appears in his assertion that Pythagoras taught that the sun was the father and the earth the mother of all.[4]

The humanist tradition established by Salutati was shared by his successor as chancellor of Florence, Leonardo Bruni (ca. 1370–1444). So also was his admiration for Pythagoras. Though Bruni worked as Apostolic Secretary to four popes in Rome, it was for his political and literary contributions to the city of Florence that, in the words of one of his contemporaries, "this greatest ornament of our age and of all learned men" is most well remembered.[5] As one of the first humanists to acquire a command of Greek, he was familiar with numerous Greek texts, many of which – including a number of Plato's newfound dialogues, such as the *Phaedo*, the *Apology*, the *Crito*, and the *Gorgias* – he translated himself.[6] The breadth of his knowledge about Pythagoras, extending over moral as well as intellectual matters, was owed to his careful reading of ancient sources. Bruni's original writings express his deep respect for Pythagoras, "the most eminent of philosophers." Referring to the doctrine of silence reputedly imposed by Pythagoras on his followers, Bruni spiritedly theorizes that the reason Pythagoras instituted the rule of silence was that he thought it inappropriate for people to discuss things about which they knew little or nothing.[7] In praising the wisdom of Pythagoras, he asserts that Pythagoras's advice was always the "best" and the "holiest."[8] As the founder of philosophy, Bruni muses, Pythagoras was a lover of wisdom whose light burned ever brightly. Pairing him with Plato, Bruni says that together they invented the mathematical sciences and investigated them, leaving "almost nothing unknown in heaven and on earth." Pythagoras and Plato were models for him not only of intelligence but also of the contemplative life that had so appealed to Petrarch and that was so exemplary to Christians.[9]

Bruni's respect for Pythagoras was echoed by his younger contemporary, also a distinguished Apostolic Secretary and Chancellor of Florence, Poggio Bracciolini (1380–1459). Through the many letters this cultured international traveler, book collector, and writer wrote detailing his enthusiasm for searching out lost texts of valued Greek and Latin works, we know that he was well acquainted with antique admirers of Pythagoras, including Plato, Vitruvius, Cicero, Quintilian, and Macrobius.[10] This is confirmed in his literary works, in which his great regard for the reputation of "the noble and wise" Pythagoras as the arbiter of social responsibility is revealed.[11] Paraphrasing Cicero, Poggio claims that Pythagoras surpassed all others in wisdom, and, paying tribute to the great renown of Pythagoras in Greece and Italy he adds that in fact all countries were influenced by him. Yet, he reflects, Pythagoras was humble. Poggio compares the humility of Pythagoras with the vanity of philosophers who know little but seek glory, renown, and notoriety.

Other contemporaries of Bruni in the mainstream of early Italian humanism were similarly drawn to Pythagoras. Pier Paolo Vergerio of Padua (ca. 1369–1444), a frequent visitor to Rome and Florence, exalted the example of Pythagoras as a moral guide – an example he may have learned from his studies of Saint Jerome. Perhaps not unlike Jerome, who was drawn to the ascetic life, Vergerio speaks of being forbidden "by God's command" to depart from the example of Pythagoras.[12] A Florentine contemporary and scholar of rhetoric, Lorenzo Valla (1407–1457), who was of a strongly independent mind and widely read in Latin literature, attempted to identify personally with Pythagoras: "It pleases me to believe what Pythagoras thought, that souls 'migrate' into one and another's bodies; and as he himself was Euphorbus … [a reference to ancient accounts of Pythagoras's claim to have been a Trojan hero, Euphorbus, in a previous life] perhaps was I another person who wrote refined works of grace for many generations."[13] Valla wrote admiringly of the example of Pythagoras as a philosopher, arbiter of virtue, and inspirator of Plato. He describes Pythagoras as "morally strong and incontrovertibly exceeding all others who excelled in the zeal for wisdom."[14]

The range of intellectual interests envisioned by the first humanists of the century blossomed in the work of a prominent scholar of Greek in the next generation, Francesco Filelfo (1398–1481). After spending seven years in Constantinople and returning to Italy with a Greek wife and a substantial library of Greek books, Filelfo became, in 1429, the first professor of Greek at the University of Florence prior to his departure for Siena, Milan, Pavia, Bologna, and a variety of princely courts. Evidence of the substantial interest Filelfo cultivated in Pythagoras can be found in a number of his writings. A letter of 1464 describes Pythagoras as having had such "divine" talent that those who did not respect it were left not only lacking in vigor and strength but indeed empty. Pythagoras was the most noble and ancient of philosophers, Filelfo rhapsodizes. Quoting from a biography of Timaeus of Locri (the principal character in Plato's *Timaeus*), whose works though lost to us must have been known to him in fragmentary form, Filelfo singles out Pythagoras as the greatest authority of Antiquity on mathematics and physics. He says Pythagoras "surpassed all other men of his time for his divine grace. He was marvelously preeminent. He was believed to be Apollo incarnate and superior to all mortals because of his divine qualities and his zeal for learning."[15] As this letter develops, it becomes a quasi-biography of Pythagoras. It describes the education of Pythagoras as beginning in Europe and continuing in Egypt and subsequently in Chaldea, where he met Zoroaster himself. Pythagoras returned to Europe to teach, and his learning passed directly to Plato, who became his representative. Filelfo claims that Plato followed Pythagoras in all matters that pertain to intelligence and divine subjects. His references to Pythagoras as the founder of Italic philosophy and to the absolute authority of his word, which no one dared to contradict ("Ipse dixit" [so he said]), show his familiarity with ancient works such as Diogenes Laertius's biography of Pythagoras and Cicero's *De natura deorum*.[16]

Pythagoras is the historic centerpiece in a famous treatise by Filelfo, *De morali disciplina* (*On Moral Philosophy*). Closely following Diogenes Laertius, Filelfo affirms the influence of Pythagoras and his authority on Western philosophy, especially in the area of virtue. He suggests that virtuous people have superior powers of understanding; these powers lead them, following the example of Pythagoras, to study the meaning of numbers. Pythagoras, he says, was the inventor of the idea that the soul is the seat of virtue. Pythagoras viewed the soul as divided into two parts, one higher and the other more tangible, one rational and the other more irrational. It was, Filelfo explains, Pythagoras's discoveries about the soul that, in addition to his physics and mathematics, most influenced Plato, making Plato an "imitator" and "disciple" of Pythagoras.[17]

Another member of this generation, the enterprising merchant-antiquarian Cyriaco of Ancona (1391–1452), sought physical evidence of Pythagoras. Discussing his travels to Greece during the 1440s in search of antiquities, Cyriaco's notebooks describe two ancient letters he "discovered," one from the tyrant of

Agrigento to Pythagoras and the other one personally written by Pythagoras to the king of Syracuse.[18] Thus was the first report that Pythagoras had received and written letters embraced with great enthusiasm in the Early Renaissance, no doubt sparking a hunt to find more. The triumphal language of one of Cyriaco's own letters records his joy when he arrived at Samos (the birthplace of Pythagoras), the "Pythagorean port itself."[19]

Still another facet of the Pythagorean saga was demonstrated by the pioneering archaeologist Flavio Biondo (1392–1463). He refers to an ancient controversy respecting the connection between the early beloved Roman king, Numa Pompilius, and Pythagoras. Overlooking the fact, noted by the later Roman historian Livy, that Pythagoras could not have been the teacher of Numa or even have known him since they were not contemporaries, Biondo explains that this beloved king of ancient Rome "followed the doctrines of Pythagoras" in making sacrifices. Not only did Numa adhere to Pythagoras's tenets in not soiling his altars with blood, he also imitated the "purity" of Pythagoras, Biondo writes, in forbidding the representation of God in Roman temples.[20] This new interpretation of an old story suggesting that Pythagorean religious structures were clean and pure and without representative sculpture cannot but remind us of the fact that the interior of the Subterranean Pythagorean Basilica at Porta Maggiore (a building of the first century A.D. that was not known to Biondo for it had not yet been discovered), the only Pythagorean temple known to us today, is in fact entirely white and is not adorned with any representational sculpture, save for a symbolic image over the altar.[21]

The midcentury saw an expansion of the educated imagination concerning Pythagoras and his example. Visiting the Duke of Milan during these years, the Florentine sculptor, architect, and amateur antiquarian Filarete (Antonio Averlino, ca. 1400–1469) reminded the Duke that it was Pythagoras who, as an astronomer with his eye on the heavens, had discovered the planet Venus. This he knew from the ancient writer Pliny the Elder.[22] Filarete also lists Pythagoras in an ideal assortment of famous men suitable for representation as exemplary heroes in a series of projected paintings.[23] His more sophisticated humanist contemporary Aeneas Sylvius Piccolomini (1405–1464), better known as Pope Pius II, also admired Pythagoras. In a treatise on the education of boys, he proposes that Pythagoras be held up as an example of the ideal educator. Pius informs his readers that boys would do well to curb their wanton behavior by following the methods taught by Pythagoras for restraining their reckless appetites. He also cites the authority of Pythagoras in music, referring to his abilities to use music to quell disorderly behavior as first described by the ancient writer Quintilian.[24] Pius regards Pythagoras, as did his contemporaries, as the inventor of wisdom; it was Pythagoras's great wisdom, he declares, that led to the development of the Seven Liberal Arts.[25]

Pletho, Bessarion, Cusanus, and Alberti: An International Generation Applauds Pythagoras

In the second half of the fifteenth century interest and respect for Pythagoras grew into fascination and near adoration as a consequence of the visit to Florence in 1439 of a Greek scholar, Pletho (ca. 1355–1452).[26] A philosopher who had been trained in the Ottoman city of Adrianople, Pletho, whose real name was George Gemistus, had come to Florence as a member of the Greek delegation to the Council of Florence.[27] There he gave lectures. There also his writings came to be well known. The learning Pletho had acquired in Adrianople, where Eastern, Greek, and Byzantine ingredients were fused, most likely explains his mystical views on ancient philosophy. His greatest heroes were, he stipulates in his most important work, a *Treatise on Law*, first, Pythagoras, and second, Plato, whom he believed was dependent on Pythagoras. Together they carried on the wisdom of the ancient Chaldean prophet Zoroaster (with whom some in Antiquity thought Pythagoras had studied astrology and astronomy).[28] All the most distinguished philosophers were formed in their "school," Pletho maintains. Because it provided outstanding guidance to humankind, we are "bound to follow" its teachings, he declared. In collaboration, he explains, Pythagoras and Plato established a tradition of divinity according to which there can be no real atheists but only those who, in separating themselves from the doctrine of these most distinguished sages, are doomed to failure and unhappiness. The influence of Pythagoras, Pletho continues, inspired great legislators to form the principles of the Western legal tradition.[29]

In other writings, Pletho stresses the oriental education of Pythagoras, who passed on Zoroaster's erudition and knowledge of magic directly to Plato. This made Plato, Pletho assures his readers, an incontrovertible source of truth. Because, like Pythagoras, Plato did not write down all his doctrines, the basic principles of his philosophy reflected the same mystical dimension.[30] Thus was Plato, the great propagator of Pythagoras's doctrines, reintroduced to the West more closely connected to Pythagoras than ever before. From this time, the growing Platonic philosophical tradition in Florence kept the image of Pythagoras very much alive. This tradition, however, had its downside, for it initiated an acrimonious controversy that was to last for decades in the West. Spurred by Pletho's *De differentis* (*On the Difference between Aristotle and Plato*), which esteemed Plato far more than Aristotle, the latter appeared belittled, a fact that inflamed his followers. In describing Aristotle's "fallacies," Pletho justifies the superiority of Plato by demonstrating Plato's closeness to the first students of Pythagoras.[31] Pletho's great esteem for Pythagoras is underlined in the fact that he wrote a commentary on an ancient text of the *Golden Verses* of Pythagoras.[32] (A number of such texts, traditionally believed to have been written by the sage himself, were known since late Antiquity. These contained moral commandments that were believed to embody Pythagoras's teachings on the practice of virtue.) This suggests that for Pletho, Pythagoras was important as a moral example.

Though his visit to Italy lasted only three years, Pletho's influence among Florentine humanists would be felt more later in the century than during the actual time of his presence. The popularity of his lectures in Florence is difficult to measure, since it is not sure who attended them, but even his detractors were constrained to admit that at times he inspired people to throng around him and dance in the streets.[33] Prominent among those who were linked with him was the scholarly Cardinal Bessarion, who had been his pupil. The philosopher-scientist and future cardinal Nicholas Cusanus traveled with him, and the architect Leon Battista Alberti was a probable attendee of his lectures in Florence. The philosopher Marsilio Ficino, who was but a small child at this time, was to inherit Pletho's interests in Plato – and therefore in Pythagoras.[34]

In defending Plato against his detractors, the Greek cardinal Giovanni Basilio Bessarion (1403–1472), one of the most enlightened humanists in fifteenth-century Italy, continued the work of his teacher Pletho after settling in Italy in the 1440s. The first section of his major work, *In calumniatorem Platonis* (*Against the Critic of Plato*), introduces Plato through his teacher and inspirator, Pythagoras.[35] In this work, one of the first books to be printed in Rome (1468), Bessarion offers a bouquet of the various ways in which Pythagoras was important for Plato. Relying on the authority of the ancient works contained in his vast library, Bessarion affirms that it was Pythagoras who taught Plato the art of secrecy and mystery, as well as the importance of virtue and the zeal for learning. According to his information, Pythagoras had left "writings" that he had entrusted to his daughter, Damo, in the form of secret commentaries. Asserting that Damo diligently guarded the secret documents of her father's learning after his death, he quotes from a letter reportedly written by Lysis of Tarentum reprimanding Hipparchus for having publicly divulged the divine precepts of Pythagoras to those who did not understand his teachings on the purification of the soul.[36] Pythagoras taught, he says, that the exercise of memory and discipline protected his most supreme doctrines from being propagated to the masses. Thus, he argued, was Plato protecting ancient learning from the uninitiated as Pythagoras had taught him to do when he used enigma and myth to describe divine truths through mathematical means. This systematic method was inherited by Christians and absorbed into Christian doctrine, Bessarion – a uniquely qualified scholar who represented both the Greek and Latin churches – maintains. Bessarion proposed a new role for Pythagoras, as a conduit from ancient philosophy to Christianity: Not only was Pythagoras a precursor of Christianity, he was one of its inspirators. This learned cardinal and voracious reader also knew that the Druids were followers of Pythagoras, for he expresses his admiration of the Druids and their doctrines of education, secrecy, and conduct, which were, he explains, inspired by those of Pythagoras.

Lauding Pythagoras as "a very famous man of undeniable authority" and "the first philosopher of all and the glory of Italy and of Greece," another learned cardinal, the German Nicholas Cusanus (1401–1464), Bessarion's colleague and friend, also had Pythagoras on his mind.[37] When this philosopher, mathematician, and theologian discussed in his writings the fundamental importance of number for all things earthly and celestial, he was always sure to cite Pythagoras as the ultimate authority on number. According to him, it was the power of Pythagoras's influence that lay behind the doctrine of the "ever adorable Trinity in oneness and Oneness in trinity."[38] Not only did Cusanus the mathematician regard Pythagoras as a fundamental authority on mathematics, but Cusanus the theologian agreed with Bessarion that Pythagoras's influence had helped to shape the doctrines of Christianity.

Pythagoras's mastery of number was also on the mind of the great Florentine architect and contemporary of these two cardinals, Leon Battista Alberti (1404–1472). In his famous treatise on the art of building, *De re aedificatoria* (*On the Art of Building*), composed in about 1450 and inspired by Vitruvius's *De architectura*, Alberti holds aloft the example of Pythagoras. He cites Pythagoras's supposed aversion to statues or effigies in temples in order to reinforce his own argument for architectural "purity" in design. Perhaps more important, in a pointed discussion of the significance of number and the architect's responsibility to rely on the skillful management of number to obtain harmony and proportion, Alberti turns to Pythagoras as his authority. Pythagoras is, he explains, the ultimate source of the idea that dimension and line together define proportion, a harmony equivalent to that of music. He concludes, "I affirm again with Pythagoras: it is absolutely certain that Nature is wholly consistent. That is how things stand."[39] In a less serious vein, while describing the antics of an unscrupulous antihero in a satire on the folly of the gods (*Momus*, ca. 1450), Alberti's main character refers to the "overabundance" of authority that had been invested in Pythagoras through time, as a result of which everyone believed all sorts of things about Pythagoras without questioning his words. Apollo, another character in the satire, responds by insisting that the vast recondite knowledge about Pythagoras and his magical abilities is well founded.[40]

Alberti's interest in Pythagoras was shared by several eminent contemporaries. Cristoforo Landino (1424–1498), a poet and humanist devoted to studying the quest of the soul for virtue, advises the "best young men" of his time to seek virtue despite all difficulties, just as had Pythagoras. As the most important predecessor of Plato and one of the four greatest philosophers of ancient Greece, it was Pythagoras, he says, who first described the celestial paradise in which men's souls were born. These souls knew wisdom and harmony, and enjoyed ambrosia and nectar and the vision of God, a concept that Pythagoras had passed to Plato. Thus was the "divine" Plato, he maintains, the beneficiary of Pythagoras.[41]

FICINO'S PYTHAGORAS AND HIS SIGNIFICANCE AS THE JEWISH "GRANDFATHER" OF CHRISTIANITY

Pythagoras continued to inspire intellectuals even more vigorously during the later decades of the fifteenth century. One of these was Marsilio Ficino (1433–1499). Perhaps the most influential philosopher and Greek scholar of the entire Italian Renaissance, Ficino held Pythagoras in very high regard. In an early work, he describes Pythagoras as the key figure who transmitted "ancient theology" – as it passed from the Egyptians to the Greeks to the Arabs to Dionysius the Areopagite (a Pythagorean of late Antiquity, also known as Pseudo-Dionysius, who had attempted to fuse Platonism with Christianity), and culminating in Saint Augustine.[42] Pythagoras's central position as the link between pagan philosophy and Christian wisdom, already described by Bessarion and Cusanus, was thereby underlined. Indeed, according to Ficino, Pythagoras was to be honored equally with the prophets of the Old Testament.

In the preface to his translation of a medieval manuscript of the *Pimander* (or *Book on the Power and Wisdom of God*), thought at the time of its discovery (1462) to have been written by the legendary ancient Hermes Trismegistus, Ficino establishes a wondrous line of venerable ancient theologians.[43] Starting with Moses, he passes to Hermes Trismegistus, to Orpheus (probably also legendary), to Pythagoras. It was, he says, their contemplation of God's divinity through the study of mathematics that was bequeathed to the "divine" Plato, the greatest teacher of all.[44] Though this work, printed again in 1471, 1472, 1481, 1491, 1492, and 1494, remained influential until the nineteenth century, it was especially stimulating to the next two generations of European scholars, when it was published in at least twenty-four editions and five languages.

Though his ideas changed somewhat as he matured, Ficino always held Pythagoras to be in the first rank, if not at the top, of the world's preeminent theologian-philosophers. By 1469 his list of all-time theological greats was headed by Zoroaster. Pythagoras, however, remained in place as the direct inspirator of Plato.[45]

In the 1470s, Ficino began his major philosophical masterpiece, the *Theologia Platonica* (*Platonic Theology*). The immortality of the soul, a concept that he holds originated in the speculations of Pythagoras, is a central theme in this long, visionary work. In it, he defines the soul's movement as a circle that, having no beginning and no end, infinitely replicates itself, becoming a sphere – as, he says, Pythagoras had demonstrated. Pythagoras also taught, says Ficino, that the soul is indivisible, incorporeal, and divine.[46]

In this work, Ficino struggles to define the soul according to its characteristics. One of these is its divine temperance, or restraint. This was exemplified by Salmoxis, he explains. The slave and disciple of Pythagoras first described by Herodotus, Salmoxis exercised patience in living underground for three years until he was thought to be dead and then emerged to prove his immortality. In describing another characteristic of the soul, its wisdom, he cites the *Golden Verses* of Pythagoras for they define the wisdom of the soul as a search for knowledge directed by light.[47] Pythagoras experienced the "true light," Ficino tells us, when he made his famous discovery concerning the triangle. Pythagoras thanked God, Ficino says, whom he worshipped every day, for allowing him to do this.[48]

Pythagoras's own soul, Ficino tells us, was highly developed because it was nurtured by his having lived underground for ten years, an idea surely derived from Diogenes Laertius, who had cited an ancient report of Pythagoras's living in a subterranean dwelling and then emerging to be considered divine.[49] Depending on the ancient writer Porphyry's description, Ficino says that the calmness of Pythagoras's soul made it inaccessible to outside influences. Ficino's interpretation of the many miracles performed by Pythagoras as a proof of his divinity appears to reflect comments made in late Antiquity by Iamblichus who had explained these miracles by saying that everything is easy for God, for whom nothing is impossible. The concept of God as the Absolute One derives from Pythagoras's view of Apollo, whose very name meant oneness, purity, and the absence of multiplicity.[50] Ficino repeats Iamblichus's assertion that Pythagoras advised his followers to follow God in respecting others. Extrapolating from Macrobius, he says that Pythagoras understood that the forces of nature could be described by points, which are indivisible, drawn on lines that in turn could produce geometric forms such as cubes.[51]

Ficino also offers interpretations of his own. Nature's inability to corrupt the soul because it was created by God was, according to him, a discovery first made by Pythagoras and later established by Plato. In noting Pythagoras's association, in Antiquity, with the idea of the transmigration of the soul, Ficino avoids reproving him. Pythagoras could not easily be criticized, since he had been widely accepted in the Christian world. Ficino's mention of this delicate subject was likely meant to assure that Plato, whose reputation was being established in this celebrated work, would not be held responsible for a view that might prevent his full acceptance by Christians. The *Platonic Theology* closes with an emotionally loaded quote from Pythagoras's *Golden Verses* describing the immortality of the soul as leading it irresistibly and directly, after abandoning the body, to the eternal heavenly ether of God.[52] Though at the time it generated some controversy,[53] Ficino's belief that Pythagoras's greatest discovery was the immortality of the soul was extremely influential. It would result in the acceptance of this idea as sacred dogma at the Lateran Council of 1512.

An abiding interest in Pythagoras is evident also in Ficino's letters, which are so numerous and addressed to such an array of distinguished friends – including statesmen, churchmen, architects, doctors, and humanists – that they constitute a significant collection of historical documents.[54] They provide ample testimony to his view that the immortality of the soul and its eternal life in heaven was the discovery of Pythagoras. They also demonstrate Ficino's eagerness to urge his correspondents to imitate Pythagoras. He exhorts them to study philosophy, as Pythagoras did, in the light of the sun in order to obtain the best wisdom, rather than by lamplight (which suggests weaker knowledge). One letter, to a bishop, addresses the issue of lax morality at banquets and cites as exemplary the prohibitions of Pythagoras against blasphemy and indecency. Another praises Pythagoras's command that things should be held in common. A letter on medicine cites Apollo as the founder of medicine and his followers Pythagoras, Empedocles, and Apollonius of Tyana as healers who cured disease with chants. Ficino praises Pythagoras's teaching of silence and his reluctance to publish, saying that Pythagoras did not need to put things in writing since he was a "living book."[55] His exhortation to "do according to Pythagoras" is directed at the education of the young, who must be shielded from wantonness and iniquity.[56] It was the "divine Pythagoras," Ficino says in several letters, who taught humankind honor.

In a stunning revelation, Ficino, who was a clergyman, tells Lorenzo de'Medici, the ruler of Florence, that he owed his learning to Christ, Pythagoras, and Plato equally. In another letter he says, "I am imitating Jesus … and I am also following Pythagoras."[57] Many letters speak of his admiration for the various teachings of Pythagoras. Such phrases as "Pythagoras commands," "Pythagoras teaches," "according to Pythagoras," are frequently used as Ficino recommends his readers follow the example of Pythagoras. The teachings of the *Golden Verses*, which he repeatedly cites, are transformed into tenets of Christian behavior. Pythagoras's mathematical discoveries led his predecessors, he says, to study the heavenly spheres (astronomy). Indeed, Pythagoras's view of God as the founder and designer of the universe inspired Ficino to sing daily to the accompaniment of his lyre because it imitated the music of the heavenly spheres.[58]

In a work on Christian doctrine, Ficino ponders Pythagoras's thoughts on God. He points out that, like Moses, Pythagoras believed in one eternal god. Thus, returning to an idea of his youth, Ficino connects Pythagoras with Moses – as Aristobulus, Numenius, and Philo had proposed in Antiquity. But he goes further in asserting that Pherecydes, Pythagoras's teacher, was a follower of Moses. He offers another new claim in maintaining that Pythagoras was born of a Jewish father. Thus it is not surprising to read, farther along in these pages, that, for Ficino, Pythagoras was a Jew.[59]

Contemporary Jewish scholars, it would seem, liked this idea. Johanan ben Isaac Alemanno (ca. 1435–1504) insists, in his *Commentary on the Song of Songs*, that Pythagoras studied with the Hebrews. He also claims that Pythagoras was involved with geomancy.[60] This suggests that, contrary to the protestations of Ficino, a strain of the old medieval belief that Pythagoras was a magician persisted in the Renaissance. In the next century, a number of scholars would return to the subject of Pythagoras and Judaism.

PICO'S VENERABLE PYTHAGORAS: FOUNTAINHEAD
OF WISDOM

The concept that the path to eternal salvation had been initiated by Pythagoras did not elude Ficino's younger contemporary, the count from Mirandola in the northerly Italian province of Emilia-Romagna. In an aborted oration known as the *De hominis dignitate* (*Oration on the Dignity of Man*), which Pico della Mirandola (1463–1494) planned for delivery in Rome in 1486 as part of a grand scheme praising philosophical concord, he exalts Pythagoras.[61] Advising his hearers (who became his readers when the oration was published in 1496) to consult "the very wise Pythagoras," this brilliant young philosopher-genius, then only twenty-four, assures them that they would learn to judge wisely, examine carefully, and lead diligent lives. They would also learn basic rules of moral behavior and how to express their piety. As Pythagoras advised, Pico explains, the contemplation of the sun as the symbol of God would enable them to nourish their souls with the "knowledge of divine things." Thus could they be in harmony with the universe.[62]

Not only was Pythagoras a great prophet, Pico explains, he was also a highly original thinker. It was he who discovered the science of numbers. For Pico, there is a big difference between "mercantile" arithmetic and "divine" arithmetic; he makes it clear that it was the latter that Pythagoras explored. Pythagoras taught his followers how to exercise their wisdom. Speaking of magic, Pico reports that Pythagoras had nothing to do with the magic of demons. Rather, he makes plain, Pythagoras explored the heavenly magic of God, proving that God's gift of the "knowledge of divine things" is medicine for the soul. Embodied in the harmony of the universe, this "knowledge of divine things" is a profound and deep mystery that can be experienced only by the contemplation of nature that leads from earth to heaven and from humankind to God.[63] Connecting Pythagoras with the doctrine of the Trinity, he suggests that the mystery of threesomeness, which was to show Christians the path to God, was inspired by Pythagoras and Plato ("whose doctrines are so akin to Christian faith that our Augustine gives great thanks to God that the books of the Platonists came into his hands") and appreciated by the Jews. Pico notes that the ancients regarded the words of Pythagoras as "holy" because they exemplify ancient wisdom.[64]

This oration was intended to introduce Pico's *Conclusiones nongentae*, or *900 Theses*, a manifesto that, with youthful enthusiasm, he hoped would bring together pagan, Jewish, Arabic, medieval, and contemporary beliefs into an overarching Christian synthesis.[65] The vast array of theses he put forward, for which he was denounced by the Pope in 1487 and exonerated in 1493, includes a special section devoted to Pythagoras. Cast in obscure language intended to pass as secret wisdom, these "propositions" purport to illustrate Pythagoras's basic mathematical doctrines. Here Pico "proves" that the number 1 (the monad) is unity and all other numbers are generated from its successors. He discusses the various types of numbers, following Speusippus, Nicomachus, Theon of Smyrna, and other ancient Pythagoreans, whose works he knew well for they were in his library. He lays special emphasis upon triplicity, which, according to him, inspires the triangle, true proportion, and, ultimately, the Trinity. He declares that the three kinds of proportion – arithmetic, geometric, and harmonic – are reflected in symbols of judgment, justice, and peace. The science of perspective is, he holds, based on the triple function of rays that, being direct, reflective, and refractive, recall the triplicity of nature – intellectual, animal, and human. In closing the section, he connects mathematics with music and the soul and adds a reference to the importance of the numbers 4 and 10 (or 4 x 10 = 40), undoubtedly a reference to Pythagoras's *tetraktys*, for which he expresses his admiration not only here but elsewhere.[66]

In grouping the section on Pythagoras with those on Chaldean theologians, the magic of Hermes Trismegistus, and Kabbalist wise men, Pico suggests that these ancient sources of knowledge were largely in agreement. His conclusions to the work as a whole reaffirm his high regard for Pythagoras by reminding his readers that, as Wisdom personified, Pythagoras considered number the principle of all things.[67] Though Pico continued throughout his short life to be an advocate for philosophical unity, it should be noted that he later toned down some of these ideas to be more in line with Christian doctrine.

The *Heptaplus*, a work written and published in 1489, makes it clear that in Pico's view Pythagoras, who was to inspire Christianity, received his inspiration from Moses, who deeply influenced him. Pico illustrates this by showing that, following Moses, Pythagoras repudiated astrology. Pico would later reaffirm this position in a major work on astrology.[68] His letters add his strong admiration for Pythagoras's refusal to kill animals. Had Pythagoras been able to live without food, Pico speculates in one letter, he would have been opposed, as well, to injuring vegetables. In another Pico offers oblique praise for Pythagoras's rule of silence by describing it as being like a medicine that "penetrates to the marrow and blood," as opposed to words that are more comparable to the "surface of the skin."[69]

THE DISSEMINATION OF INFORMATION ABOUT PYTHAGORAS IN THE LATE FIFTEENTH CENTURY

Pythagoras was well known to other members of Pico's generation. The erudite poet Angelo Poliziano (1454–1494) was fascinated by the strength of Pythagoras's belief in the soul's immortality, while he dismissed the idea of its transmigration as legendary. He was unambiguous, however, in honoring Pythagoras, whom he calls the "leader of the silent sect," for his discovery of the importance of number. The number 10 and the cube were especially pleasing to Pythagoras, he reports, for they suggest the universe. Not only was Pythagoras revered in the world of mathematics, Poliziano says, he was also honored for his important discoveries in music.[70] He claims that the relation between Pythagoras's fascination with geometry and proportion and his concept of harmony demonstrate the unity of his learning. Drawing largely on Pliny, Poliziano discusses the accomplishments of Pythagoras in astronomy.[71]

It was during this time that the Greek scholar Constantinus Lascaris (ca. 1434–1501), an émigré from Byzantium and an influential teacher of Greek in Italy, published what appears to be the first Renaissance biography of Pythagoras.[72] Its importance lies less in the amount of new information it contains than in the fact that this little known work is the first to consolidate the ancient information known about Pythagoras from Greek sources. Pythagoras was, Constantinus tells his readers, born in Samos; he was the son of a gem engraver and a pupil of Pherecydes. He studied science and philosophy, first in Egypt and then in Babylonia, with the Magi (a priestly class of astrologers). Eventually, he traveled to Croton (in southern Italy), where he settled with a large number of disciples and friends. There he taught erudite doctrines to more than five hundred citizens who also learned from him life skills, such as peace, concord, morals, and good government through the rule of law. Thus were his disciples able to live together in harmony as a community of friends. He later went to Metapontum (also in southern Italy), where he died, but not before bequeathing three of the books he had composed to his daughter. These were later given to Philolaus. Constantinus lists and provides valuable biographies for a host of early followers of Pythagoras including Empedocles, Timaeus of Locri, Glaucus, Hippasus of Metapontum, Archytas, Lysides, Aristoxenus of Tarentum, and Parmenides of Eleata. Though he settled in Messina, Constantinus became well known throughout Italy, where his works experienced a wide diffusion.[73]

A younger member of this generation, Polydore Vergil (1470–1555), a scholar and priest-diplomat from Urbino, showed that he had accumulated a substantial knowledge about Pythagoras from his extensive readings of classical authors. In 1499, he complimented Pythagoras for his discovery that God was both a circle (as the beginning and end of all things) and the monad (as the single creator of the universe). According to Polydore's compendium of important discoveries, Pythagoras also showed that God regulates universal harmony according to musical order. As the first philosopher, he points out, Pythagoras laid the foundations for philosophy in Italy; he also developed geometry and the science of measuring, and, at the same time, his study of the heavens made astronomy and astrology comprehensible to humankind. Although Polydore is uncertain if Pythagoras was the inventor of numbers, he assigns him an important role in the development of justice and recognizes him as a protector of animals. A chapter on adultery reaffirms the traditional role of Pythagoras as a teacher of moral behavior:

> Asked when one ought to lie with a woman, Pythagoras answered:
> "When you wish to become weaker than you are. ... Though we know

this well enough, women's wiles still draw us into lust, as a dog returns to its vomit, so the saying goes."[74]

The late years of the fifteenth century also saw Pythagoras remembered and admired in a variety of other literary forms. His image as the founder of arithmetic appears in textbooks devoted to this subject.[75] He is also noted in poetry. A Milanese poem published in 1492 cites Pythagoras's ability to restrain drunkenness by using music as medicine, earning him the title "the priest of music."[76]

Professionals involved in music were well aware of the Pythagorean musical proportions that had inspired Alberti. The Franco-Flemish world produced at least two musicians notable for their interest in Pythagoras. A lover of enigma, Johannes Ockeghem (ca. 1420–1497) composed a canon for thirty-six (a perfect numerical square) voices. His regard for Pythagoras is confirmed by a musical eulogy to him composed by a French priest, poet, and musician at the Burgundian court, Antoine Busnoys (d. 1492). The score of this work demonstrates the Pythagorean harmonic proportions (6:4:3), while its words explain that Ockeghem's harmonies were based on the inventions of Pythagoras.[77] At the same time, in Italy, the eminent Milanese composer and theorist Franchino Gaffurio (1451–1522) confirmed the importance of the role Pythagoras had played in the study of music. Discussing the theory of music in 1492, Gaffurio pictures Pythagoras as the first musical therapist (because he was the first to recognize the calming effects of music). This philosopher was so devoted to the study of mathematics and astronomy, Gaffurio says, that he could understand as no one else music and its cosmological applications. Gaffurio honors Pythagoras as the discoverer of consonances and proportion in music. It was Pythagoras's devotion to music, he explains, that enabled him to discover the art of measuring the heavens.[78]

In a work written in 1500, *De harmonia musicorum instrumentorum opus* (*The Musical Harmony of Instruments*), Gaffurio names Pythagoras as the first to conduct serious research in tuning and harmonics as well as the first "to recognize in a rational way the art of music."[79] Pythagoras's study of musical intervals, we are told, led him to discover melody as the product of harmonious mixture. In borrowing the numbers of arithmetic and the quantities of geometry, Pythagoras discovered that music could "create harmonious concord with sonorous strings which produce proportional intervals when struck."[80] Thus was geometric proportion, Gaffurio tells us, related to harmonic division. He explains that when Pythagoras first observed a disdiapason, or lack of harmony, in the extremes of the human voice, he developed a harmonic rule, or mathematical tuning fork, that produced a concord based on diapason.[81] Gaffurio reports that as a result of examining hammers of differing weights in a blacksmith's shop, Pythagoras was able to make the dazzling discovery that the weight of the hammers, correlated with the amount of tension on the strings of an instrument, produced various tones that "proved" the numerical basis of musical pitch and created rational harmony or concord. (This was a repetition of a legend first reported by Nicomachus in the first century A.D. and frequently cited by medieval writers.) In this way was Pythagoras inspired, Gaffurio explains, to understand the proportional laws underlying musical intervals.[82] So great was his authority that no one dared to deviate from the standard Pythagoras established, we are told, nor did anyone dare to add anything to it.

Pythagoras's importance for music is also acknowledged in a pair of encyclopedias written at the end of the fifteenth century in Siena. Not only does their author, the humanist Bishop Francesco Patrizi (1413–1494), praise Pythagoras as an authority on music, he claims that Pythagoras was its inventor. It was this great knowledge that enabled Pythagoras to discover the harmony of the spheres while he was studying the universe. He also notes that Pythagoras was famous for his "sermons," that he abstained from meat, and that he was imitated by Plato in "everything."[83]

Meanwhile, Pythagoras's reputation for cunning (as a practitioner of trickery, magic, and prognostication), first suggested in Antiquity by his contemporary Heraclitus, underlined by Pliny the Elder in Roman times, and developed further in the Middle Ages, was unabated. The widespread regard for Pythagoras in medicine, alchemy, and the literature of magic was, if anything, expanded in the Early Renaissance. Among the texts written by Giovanni Garzoni, a professor of medicine at the University of Bologna from 1466 to 1505, is an oration in praise of the medical sciences that names Pythagoras as one of the founders of Greek medicine.[84] Works on divination, some of which, like the *Experimentarius* (*The Experimenter*), were Arabic in origin, also praised Pythagoras's medical expertise. Use of the "Pythagorean Sphere," which was probably Druidic if not Egyptian in origin, is well documented in fifteenth-century manuscripts. These are drawings that, based on an esteem for the magic of number, invoke the name of Pythagoras in tables of numbers designed for determining lucky and unlucky days and deducing answers to questions about such subjects as life and death, medical practices, marriage, war, economic gain, relief from imprisonment, and the planting of vegetables (fig. 43).[85] Versions of the medieval *Turba philosophorum* (*Assembly of Philosophers*), in which Pythagoras was a grand master of alchemy, provided detailed recipes for performing alchemical transmutations useful to pharmacists, metallurgists, ceramists, chemists, and other tradesmen.[86] These constituted a literary industry that professed to rely on the magical abilities of Pythagoras.

The descendants of such works on magic and compendia on alchemy provided recipes, diagrams, and a vocabulary of symbols in a continuous tradition throughout the fifteenth century.[87] In most of these works Pythagoras lurked in the background as a venerable wise man. These texts on "magical sciences" paralleled those of more intellectual writers like Pico who, disapproving of black magic (magic associated with demons) and astrology, cultivated enigmatic Kabbalistic exegeses that, combining pagan wisdom and Christian theology, attempted to unlock the mysteries of the cosmos.

In Italy, the popularity of Hermetic texts, which relied on the reputation of Hermes as an alchemist and as a fountain of wisdom, celebrated Pythagoras as the first to have revealed the wisdom of Hermes.[88] Their popularity was accelerated by the translation from Greek into Latin of several of these texts, including the *Pimander* and the *Mysteries of Egypt*, by Ficino. The latter text claims that in order to develop their philosophy Pythagoras and Plato studied ancient Egyptian inscriptions written by Hermes himself.[89] This fascination led to other "discoveries," and an efflorescence of texts on magic, fumigation, exorcism, and astrology. Some of these were written by humanists. One such example is the *Tractato iustissimo de la vera e de la falsa alchimia* (*Treatise on True and False alchemy*) by Antonio Cornazzano (ca. 1430–1483), a Lombard humanist who worked for Francesco Sforza, Duke of Milan, and Bartolomeo Colleoni, a mercenary captain of Venice. In this work, Antonio cites Pythagoras as the ultimate authority on alchemy.[90] In Germany, a fifteenth-century alchemical manuscript admonishes its readers to follow the example of Pythagoras, who directed his disciples not to reveal the secrets of this "high art" to "ordinary people."[91] Meanwhile, in Spain, Pythagoras was remembered – despite Ficino's and Pico's views to the contrary – as a great astrologer.[92]

The Early Renaissance was an important time for Pythagoras. It was then that supposed letters written to and from Pythagoras were first "discovered." In addition to having been the direct inspirator of Plato, he was also, as an ancient theologian, a central link between pagan, Hebraic, and Christian religious wisdom. In rediscovering Pythagoras's ancient connection with Moses, fifteenth-century intellectuals invited Pythagoras to the status of a prophet of Christianity. His revelations about the immortality of the soul conferred on him the status of a pre-Christian Christian and helped to secure the same status for Plato, despite the fact that some detractors ridiculed Pythagoras's belief in transmigration of souls.[93]

During the Early Renaissance Pythagoras was enthusiastically regarded as an arithmetician as well as a geometer. Pythagoras and his pupil Plato had, Leonardo Bruni asserted in the 1440s, investigated mathematics with such "incredible" depth that almost nothing remained to be discovered.[94] God had made the universe comprehensible to human beings through the symbolism of number, the fountain and mother of everything, and Pythagoras knew God's secrets. Pythagoras's discovery of the regular solids was well established, as was his theorem of the right triangle (known through Vitruvius). The triangle and the triplicate were precious to him, as were the circle and the sphere. His presumed love of these mathematical forms invited theological speculation: God, the great monad, was also the enduring center of the Trinity. It also invited cosmological speculation: The universe was spherical and made up of circles. The old medieval idea connecting Pythagoras with astrology was modified by avant-garde intellectuals who separated astrology from astronomy and exonerated Pythagoras from any connection with the former.

The fifteenth century also rediscovered Pythagoras's high regard for the law and social good. The ancient Greek idea that the moral teachings of Pythagoras on personal virtue and communal life were important resurfaced in these years, largely because scholars were able to read original works by early witnesses who claimed to have knowledge of his life. His leadership as an arbiter of a moral system that led to that of Christianity was commended by numerous writers. The *Golden Verses*, believed to have been written by him, had a life of their own. In a continuous flow of manuscript and printed editions, they established rules of morality with words that were considered "holy." It was undoubtedly the newly aroused interest in Aristoxenus, an ancient writer who had written on harmony as well as a (now lost) biography of Pythagoras, that inspired interest, toward the end of the century in Milan, in the inventions of Pythagoras in music. His discoveries in music were, it was believed, connected to his interest in the structure and movement of the heavens. Pythagoras knew the road to heaven because he knew, in essence, how to measure heaven.[95]

Pythagoras's significance for this century also touched nonintellectuals, namely, those who relied on popular esoteric cultish knowledge that would help them to unlock the mysteries of the universe and the events that related to their daily lives. For them the symbolism of numbers was important because numbers elucidated medical issues and life decisions as well as playing important roles in magic, alchemy, and astrology, all of which had deep roots extending through the medieval past to Antiquity. Thus was Pythagoras as significant at the popular level as he was at the intellectual level. As a natural magician, or someone who comprehended the "science of the heavenly," he understood occult knowledge as well as scientific knowledge because he had shown the way to both and because both were unified under the rubric of "wisdom," the seat of all knowledge in which he reigned supreme.

All in all, the Early Renaissance rapturously embraced Pythagoras as a great harmonizer for his discoveries of number and form and for his teachings on moral order, which together composed the great unity of the universe symbolized by the concord of its musical tones. Life could indeed be enhanced by the living presence of Pythagoras's discoveries, example, and holiness. Indeed, by century's end, his divine light was burning brightly.

THREE:

THE APOTHEOSIS OF PYTHAGORAS

IN THE SIXTEENTH CENTURY

The light of Pythagoras burned even more brightly during the sixteenth century. Because the previous century had promoted Plato to be the final authority on the mathematical organization of the universe and established his dependence on Pythagoras, for the sixteenth century these were basic facts. As the heir of Pythagoras from whom he had inherited the divine wisdom that he had divulged to humankind Plato, whose works were now widely known through the translations and commentaries of Marsilio Ficino, was well established in the intellectual world.

Plato was more than a teacher of mathematics and the organization of the universe. For Florentines, as for the enormous number of exegetes outside the republic who were in touch with Florentine Platonists, he was, in addition, an authority in the areas of mystical philosophy, harmonics, and theology.[1] After the death of Lorenzo de'Medici in 1492, the chief patron of Ficino and a friend to Platonic studies in Florence (sometimes erroneously called "the Platonic Academy"),[2] the humanist movement came, increasingly, to be centered in Rome. There, at the papal court, humanists found a different preoccupation, as the modern scholar John D'Amico has demonstrated, devoting themselves to theological questions rather than metaphysical speculations.[3] Nonetheless, the fact that most of the humanists of papal Rome came from places other than Rome, and many of them from Tuscany and Umbria (places where Ficino's influence had been strongest), meant that Plato continued to be appreciated for his many-sided learning in Rome as elsewhere in Italy.

As the Plato-Aristotle controversy born in the early fifteenth century (in reaction to the influence of Pletho and other Greek émigrés) began to ease at the turn of the century, the classical heritage came increasingly to be regarded as a unified framework of thought.[4] This unity was characterized by an increased attention to the Church Fathers – Saints Augustine, Jerome, Gregory, and Ambrose. These learned Christians of late Antiquity were regarded by humanists in this "new" Rome of the Renaissance as having been, like themselves, Romans and Christians. Also like them, the Church Fathers had enjoyed a classical education. This made them humanist compatriots, for they had had to adjust the legacy of classical learning to their Christian zeal.[5] In the new Roman humanist world Pythagoras fitted well, for the Church Fathers – especially Saints Augustine and Jerome – had endorsed him. By the opening years of the sixteenth century, not only Rome, but Italy in general, was home to scores of humanists who, under the aegis of the Church Fathers, were well acquainted with Pythagoras and his successor Plato.

THE AUTHORITY OF PYTHAGORAS IN THE EARLY SIXTEENTH CENTURY

In 1494, Luca Pacioli (ca. 1445–1517), a Franciscan friar and esteemed mathematician from the central Italian province of Umbria, published his *Summa de arithmetica geometria proportioni et proportionalita*, known as the *Summa arithmetica* (*The Authority of Arithmetic*), one of the earliest printed books on mathematics and the first general compendium in the field.[6] This enormously influential work, elaborately dedicated to the Duke of Urbino, aimed to make the applied and theoretical traditions of mathematics universally comprehensible. Though Pacioli does not mention Pythagoras directly in this work on the practicalities of mathematics, he does express admiration for Pythagorean mathematicians, as will be discussed in Chapter 6. However, in his vastly influential *De divina proportione* (*On Divine Proportion*), a work that first appeared in 1499 and was published in an expanded version in 1509, Pacioli pays direct tribute to Pythagoras. Twice in this work, which, illustrated by Leonardo da Vinci, focused on the value of mathematics for achieving perfect (or "divine") proportion – mainly in architecture – Pacioli reveals his devotion to Pythagoras.[7] First, he declares that Pythagoras's discovery of the construction of the right triangle merits the highest commendation. Later, returning to the subject, he claims that Pythagoras was so elated upon discovering the proportion of the lines that compose this triangle that he joyfully celebrated this event. "So perfect," is the triangle of Pythagoras, Pacioli exults, that geometers call it "the angle of justice."[8] Pacioli makes it clear that whoever does not know Pythagoras cannot be a practitioner of architecture. His interest in Pythagoras is far greater than these references indicate for, as will be seen in Chapter 6, throughout his works he expresses his debt to Pythagoras and his mathematical doctrines without bothering to mention his name. This suggests that the mathematical doctrines attributed to Pythagoras were too well known to his audience at this time to require identification.

Writing at about the same time, Giovanni Nanni (also known as Annius da Viterbo, ca. 1432–1502) informs his readers that Pythagoras was a teacher of "divine" and "human" law. This surely reflects Nanni's acquaintance with ancient works such as those of Porphyry and Iamblichus in which Pythagoras was respected not only as a religious thinker but also as a political theorist who taught his followers about the many benefits of good government that bring peace and concord.[9] Such works as Nanni's suggest that in the early years of the sixteenth century, those interested in moral, legal, and social integrity, as well as those interested in mathematics, looked to Pythagoras for guidance. Thus could they hope, in addition to pursuing an intellectual life, to live a virtuous life and achieve social good.

The same years saw a cascading interest in the biography of Pythagoras. A quasi-biography of him that appeared in Bologna in 1503 was, effectively, a demonstration of his importance as an arbiter of morals (see Appendix B). Its author, Filippo Beroaldo Senior (1453–1505), a prominent and prolific humanist and erudite philologist of that city, opens and closes his *Symbola Pythagorae* (*Symbols of Pythagoras*), a selection of the moral teachings similar to those contained in the *Golden Verses* attributed since Antiquity to Pythagoras, with an introduction and conclusion that, taken together, describe his esteem for his hero. Pythagoras, he summarizes, taught humankind how to live ethically.[10]

The nature of this claim is described through Beroaldo's early sixteenth-century eyes. His introduction presents what he considers essential facts about Pythagoras: Pythagoras studied cosmology, astronomy, and geometry and he discovered that music could be used therapeutically to calm the emotions and smooth disturbances. After establishing that as the founder of philosophy Pythagoras was the most renowned of ancient philosophers, Beroaldo asserts that Plato imitated the philosophy of Pythagoras. All those following Plato are bound to imitate Pythagoras, becoming, according to Beroaldo, the beneficiaries of his "outstanding influence." This influence was so powerful that disputes could be resolved simply by referring to the infallibility of Pythagoras with the mantra, or formulaic answer, "Ipse dixit" (So he said).

For Beroaldo the "succulent centerpiece" of the ethical teachings of Pythagoras was the well-organized and divine code of living that he taught. The primary doctrines of Pythagoras listed by Beroaldo are respect for justice and the law (a subject on which Beroaldo offers long, passionate discourses); condemnation of tyrants who hold themselves above the law; wise use of time, talent, speech, resources, and emotion; frugality and restraint; avoidance of corrupting or enslaving influences; and the cultivation of silence, achieved by locking the tongue within the "wall" of the teeth. Referring to Pythagoras's practice of enigma and silence in his teaching, he asserts that this "great and wonderful philosopher," invented a "secret realm of divine philosophy." Though it may be meager in words, his philosophy was magnificently abundant in meaning, "like a fruit whose exterior is tough but whose interior is juicy and rich."[11] The enigmatic "symbols" devised by "the divine philosopher" have a sacred and mystical character, Beroaldo explains, pointing out the path that enables humankind to conduct its affairs with honor and providing it with the necessary tools to lead a wholesome life. Thus do Pythagoras's tenets form the basis for the achievement of happiness and the establishment of harmony in the world.

In concluding, Beroaldo offers his assessment of the significance of Pythagoras:

> What high priest, after all, would God be able to find more worthy than Pythagoras, through whom to write down precepts for the human race? He is so renowned for truth-telling that his very name, Pythagoras the Greek, is consigned to posterity as a symbol for truth just as surely as Apollo is referred to as the Pythian. His majesty was so great that he could be worshiped as a god. Let us therefore keep most deeply rooted in our hands, mouths, and hearts these … teachings restored from the sanctuary of his sacred and godlike doctrine.[12]

This religious adulation of Pythagoras as a moral leader may seem odd coming from the pen of one who worked for the Bentivoglio family, one of the most notoriously immoral and cruel ruling families of Renaissance Italy. Beroaldo evidently had discovered the importance of Pythagoras elsewhere – most likely in the course of his work as a scholar, which required numerous absences from the court at Bologna.[13] Other works by Beroaldo discuss, similarly, the good (moral) fortune of all those who benefit from the influence of Pythagoras. As a "god" and divine philosopher, it was he who taught humankind to understand virtue and to place the highest value on leading a happy, honorable, and fruitful life.[14]

Beroaldo's work on Pythagoras, as well as his Latin translation of Philostratus's *Life of Apollonius of Tyana* (a work of late Antiquity that described the religious mystic Apollonius as a disciple of Pythagoras), was surely known to other humanists outside Bologna. This is suggested, for example, by the works of Pietro del Monte, a scholar from Brescia, which, collected in French libraries of the later sixteenth century, cite those of Beroaldo.[15]

A second early sixteenth-century work that may be considered a biography of Pythagoras was published three years after Beroaldo's, in 1506. The *Commentaria Urbana* by Raffaele Maffei (1451–1522), a prominent intellectual from a famous family of Volterran humanists who served the papal court in Rome, is one of the first encyclopedic surveys of the history of classical Antiquity. In this compendium, which was internationally known and internationally influential, Raffaele summarizes, in his entry on Pythagoras, what was known to him from Antiquity concerning Pythagoras's birth, childhood, and education. He includes information on Pythagoras's early voyages to Egypt, where he studied arithmetic, and to Babylon, where he studied the courses of the stars. Raffaele's account contains new information from an unknown source: Pythagoras also went to Crete and

Sparta before settling in southern Italy. The rest of his text is devoted to recounting information derived from well-known classical sources such as those by Cicero, Pompeius Trogus, Livy, Dionysius of Halicarnassus, Philostratus, Diogenes Laertius, Porphyry, and Iamblichus, some of which he names. He describes Pythagoras's activities in Croton (the place where Pythagoras settled in southern Italy) and Metapontum (the nearby place to which he moved and where he later died). Most significant, in his view, was Pythagoras's influence on others in the areas of morality and virtue. Pythagoras taught those accustomed to profligacy to lead virtuous lives. Among the doctrines he taught were the injunction to abstain from meat and the belief in transmigration of the soul. His moral purity had a powerful effect on women as well as on men. Under his influence women forsook their luxurious golden clothes and jewels, while men dedicated themselves to sobriety. He was also important, we are told, as the inventor of the science of numbers.

Speaking of the late years of Pythagoras, Raffaele says that the reason Pythagoras moved from Croton to Metapontum was that he and his followers had been persecuted in Croton. After his death, Raffaele relates, Pythagoras was cherished as a god and his house in Metapontum became a temple. His account closes with a report that a first-century (A.D.) poet named Persius, inspired by Pythagoras's claim to have been a peacock in a previous incarnation, named his peacock "Pythagoras."[16] Raffaele's source for this anecdote is unknown.

The fame of Pythagoras spread as far as early sixteenth-century France, though perhaps not as rapidly as it had in Italy. There one of that country's most acclaimed academics, Jacques Lefèvre d'Étaples (Faber Stapulensis, ca. 1455–1536), expressed his high regard for Pythagoras, which would inspire renewed respect for Pythagoras in France. Indulging his wish to meet Pico della Mirandola and Ficino, Lefèvre was drawn to Italy, where he traveled three times during his youth. Lefèvre's early works on arithmetic and music are largely based on the works of the most important Pythagorean writer on these subjects from late Antiquity, Boethius. The letters prefacing Lefèvre's works reflect his great admiration for Pythagoras and his ancient followers.

One of these letters lists the most important ancient writers on arithmetic and music. Lefèvre names Pythagoras himself, as well as Nicomachus, Plato, the "divine" Boethius, and other Pythagoreans of note. Another letter suggests that Lefèvre acquired much of his information from Martianus Capella, to whose work he frequently refers. It is important to note that Lefèvre, who was known as a religious reformer, greatly admired the moral teachings of Pythagoras. Pythagoras was divine in his eyes, as was Dionyius the Areopagite. Like Ficino, he suggests that Pythagoras and his successor Plato were precursors of Christ.[17] Lefèvre's pupil and collaborator at the University of Paris, Josse Clichtove (d. 1543), an intensely spiritual monk and celebrated humanist, wrote that he looked up to Pythagoras as "the most prestigious and important authority" on the role of mathematics in music, astronomy, and "all subjects of divine contemplation."[18] Thus was the authority of Pythagoras in moral as well as in divine matters acknowledged and sanctioned by eminent defenders of the church in France as well as in Italy.

REUCHLIN DESCRIBES PYTHAGORAS'S "LUGGAGE": THE HEBREW PATRIMONY OF CHRISTIANITY

The authority of Pythagoras in the Renaissance became ever more important in the work of Johannes Reuchlin (1455–1522), a noted German Hebraic scholar and erudite classicist (whose library is discussed in Appendix A).[19] Following his studies in Latin, Greek, and the law, Reuchlin traveled to Italy in the last decade of the fifteenth century. There he came into contact with Pico della Mirandola, the most prominent Christian scholar at that time to have a scholarly interest in Hebrew and the one who opened the study of Kabbalah (or Jewish mystical tradition) to Christians, and Ficino, who had expressed his belief that Pythagoras was a Jew. Both these scholars influenced Reuchlin but particularly Pico, under whose sway he began to study Hebrew in 1492.

Upon Reuchlin's return to Germany, his legal advice was sought by Emperor Maximilian I, who wished to determine whether a decree ordering the burning of Jewish books (which had been demanded by its chief advocate, Johannes Pfefferkorn, a butcher and converted Jew) should be revoked. In his recommendation for revocation, issued in 1510, the erudite Christian Reuchlin found occasion – perhaps designed to assuage the blunt language of the bigoted Pfefferkorn – to praise Pythagoras's linguistic restraint. Referring to Pythagoras as the "first" philosopher, he describes him as the inventor of enigma, an exemplary language that came, Reuchlin says, to be widely imitated not only by philosophers such as Plato, Porphyry, and the Druids in France but also by writers on alchemy and medicine.[20]

Published a few years later, in 1517, Reuchlin's *De arte Cabalistica* (*On the Kabbalah*) was the first scholarly work to claim that the Kabbalah was a source of Christianity. It also was the first work of a Christian thinker to present the doctrines of Pythagoras as a distinct philosophy, different from all those of other ancient philosophers (except his disciple Plato). Pythagoras is one of the main subjects of this work, written in the form of a dialogue with three discussants. The information on Pythagoras expounded here is so extensive and unique that, in essence, it forms a new biography. Not only does it reflect Reuchlin's personal ardor for Pythagoras; in proposing Pythagoras's apotheosis, this work also provides a measure of the strength of his reputation among early sixteenth-century humanists.

In his letter dedicating *De arte Cabalistica* to Pope Leo X, Reuchlin tenders an elaborate explanation as to how the Christian religion was derived from Kabbalistic texts that had long been ignored.[21] He offers to prove to the Pope that it was Pythagoras who, in rescuing these Hebraic texts that had lain dormant since Greek Antiquity and by incorporating them into his doctrines, had laid the groundwork for the Christian religion, thus "parenting" Christianity. Because they were derived from the Kabbalah, Reuchlin argues, the uniqueness of Pythagoras's doctrines makes them worthy of being revived for the benefit of the contemporary sixteenth-century world.[22] Advising the Pope that these doctrines would ensure Pythagoras's "rebirth" as the single greatest intellect of Antiquity, Reuchlin proposes that his scholarly text should become a reference work explaining how Christianity developed from its Hebraic roots under the guidance of Pythagoras.[23]

According to Reuchlin, the tradition of God's secret information (the Kabbalah was primarily an oral tradition that consisted of esoteric revelations couched in the form of enigmatic concepts, symbols, and numbers), first given to Moses, had been understood and revealed to humanity by Pythagoras: "What Moses, the servant of God, received by divine inspiration was handed down to posterity in an interpretation by [Pythagoras] of the nature of the universe."[24] Thus was Jewish mysticism, or Kabbalah, which Reuchlin believed was ancient, incorporated into Christian theology through the teachings of Pythagoras, who had had the wisdom to rescue it from oblivion:

> [O]ur master Pythagoras, that great stream of all learning … drew his stream of learning from the boundless sea of the Kabbalah … and that Pythagoras has led his stream into Greek pastures from which we, last in the line, can irrigate our studies.[25]

Highlighting the special status of Pythagoras, Reuchlin speaks of the "limitations" of the other ancient Greeks. They, he holds, were incapable of understanding such mysteries: "I must make an exception for my mentor Pythagoras … his pre-eminence was derived not from the Greeks, but again from the Jews."[26] Placing Pythagoras's education with the Jews in context, Reuchlin situates it outside Greece, among the Egyptians, the Chaldeans, the Druids in Gaul, the Celts, the Magi in Persia, and lastly (he says) the Jews in India.

Because he was imbued with sacred learning, Reuchlin argues, Pythagoras was uniquely able to understand the secrets of Moses, that is, the eternal truths of Kabbalah. In making them available to the Greek world Pythagoras opened the path for their entrance into the mainstream of Christianity. In this way Christianity was ennobled, through his genius, by the inheritance of its Hebrew patrimony. This view, repeatedly stated in Reuchlin's text, represented a revision of the older notion, expressed by Ficino and Pico, that Pythagoras was merely one of several famous ancient theologian-philosophers of Greek Antiquity. In Reuchlin's text, Pythagoras was the most important one because he had access to the divine revelation of the Kabbalah. Reuchlin's elevation of Pythagoras to this exclusive status was made possible, he assures us, through his careful reading of the works of Aristobulus, Numenius, Hermippus, Philo, Eusebius, and Clement of Alexandria – all ancient writers who had discussed Pythagoras's connections to Judaism. Though these had linked Pythagoras (and his disciple Plato) to Moses, none of them had gone so far as to suggest the thesis proposed by Reuchlin, that it was Pythagoras, the "prince of philosophers," who personally conveyed the wisdom of Kabbalah to Christianity.[27]

Pythagoras taught his disciples the value of silence (which is majestic as compared with idle talk and chatter), the harmonic organization of the cosmos (which is composed of three worlds bound together by their harmonious motion), the importance of friendship (which creates an indissoluble bond of love), and the governing principal of number (on which all things are based). The latter was especially important in Reuchlin's view. Pythagoras taught that the infinite God was symbolized by the monad, or number 1. He also valued the Tetragrammaton, the four letters that in Hebrew spell the name of God, for it was based on the significance of the number 4 for the *tetraktys*, his own "divine" invention. Pythagoras's emphasis on the numbers 3 and 4 was reflected in his celebration of the triangle and the pyramid, each of which fits into the dodecahedron, the symbol of the universe. Added together, Pythagoras taught, these numbers make 7, the number of strings in the lyre.[28]

According to Reuchlin, Pythagoras's influence on the Christian religion was especially profound in the area of the soul's immortality and salvation. His passionate argument on behalf of Pythagoras's influence on Christianity ("Pythagoras has come so close to the beliefs in our own day; Christian teaching is … very similar")[29] is not sidetracked by Pythagoras's alleged belief in metempsychoses, or transmigration. Indeed, Reuchlin asserts, Pythagoras never held such a ridiculous belief. Rather, later writers misinterpreted his belief in the immortality of the soul. The proof is, Reuchlin asserts, that nowhere in his writings (following Diogenes Laertius, Reuchlin believed that Pythagoras was a prolific writer) does Pythagoras mention the subject.[30] "This outstanding man of supreme intelligence," Reuchlin summarizes, deserves special credit because he was alone in his extraordinary pursuits. "This wisdom … he brought home to Italy … in his luggage as it were."[31]

Commenting on the authority of Pythagoras, Reuchlin notes: "I hate his detractors. They are not men but monsters." As though to prove the persuasiveness of his argument, Reuchlin has the most skeptical of the three discussants in his dialogue-text declare to the other two, at the end, his conversion: "See what a receptive pupil you have, and what a good Pythagorean I am!"[32]

Reuchlin paid dearly for his notions about the significance of Jewish thought transmitted by Pythagoras to Christianity. His old adversary, Pfefferkorn, continued agitating against him with a stream of defamatory pamphlets. Although others of inferior education in Germany scoffed as well, Reuchlin won the admiration of the humanists and the literati of Europe, including Erasmus of Rotterdam (Desiderius Erasmus, ca. 1466–1536), who asserted that the detractors of Reuchlin were "ignorant" and "demented enemies of the humanities."[33] Indeed, Erasmus was so inspired by Reuchlin that he wrote a dialogue-play proposing the beatification of Reuchlin. In this work, Reuchlin enters heaven accompanied by his guardian angel. Ranking him with Saint Paul and the Virgin Mary, Erasmus proposes making Reuchlin a saint, for, he says, Reuchlin suffered during his life in defense of the truth.[34] A letter from one of Reuchlin's German humanist colleagues describes him as a "learned and excellent man" who has performed "a great and wonderful service" to the world:

> [F]or a long time we have never had his like in Germany, and he deserves to be handed down to Posterity. ... the greatest general would not match him ... [who] is now engaged on perhaps the most noble enterprise of all. May God Almighty prosper my hero's plans![35]

The exudation of admiration for Reuchlin by humanists not only in the Netherlands and Germany but also in Italy and France testifies to the enthusiasm that was felt at the international level for the originality and significance of his views on the unique importance of Pythagoras. Thus in the early sixteenth century was Pythagoras more fervently admired than he had ever been, not only for his wisdom and virtue but also as the greatest predecessor of Christianity in the pagan world. Because his authority was inspirational, his views on cosmic harmony, no longer "pagan," now belonged to Christianity.

A German contemporary of Reuchlin and a practitioner of medicine, alchemy, and the magic arts, Cornelius Agrippa of Nettesheim (1487–1535), saw Pythagoras from a different perspective. In a remarkably modern text he composed on the superiority of women, Agrippa refers to Pythagoras's innovation of the concept that women should be educated in an equal way with men. He cites the examples of Pythagoras's wife, Theano, and their daughter, Damo, who were reputed in ancient literature to have carried on his teachings after his death, as examples of celebrated intellectual women.[36]

OCCULTISM, VIRTUE, AND THE "JEWISH" SIDE OF PYTHAGORAS: THE HEAVENLY TEACHER OF WISDOM

A different aspect of Agrippa's appreciation for Pythagoras lies in his suggestion that Pythagoras was one of the first to use supernatural powers over natural forces. The connection of Pythagoras with magic had first been discussed in a variety of contexts by the ancient writer Pliny the Elder and reaffirmed by early Christian ecclesiastics.[37] In a work on occult philosophy written in 1510 (though published only in 1530) Agrippa named the great "sages" who were his predecessors in the practice of the occult arts. Pythagoras figures prominently in this list, followed by his slave Salmoxis, and others who came after them – including Hermippus, Porphyry, Iamblichus, Plotinus, and Apollonius of Tyana.[38] Agrippa showed, in another work, that medieval forms of divination such as the Pythagorean Sphere, a method of divination widely known in medieval manuscripts (as described in Chapter 2), was still well known and in active use in the Germany of his time.[39]

Another German contemporary, the brilliant and eccentric physician Philippus Aureolus Bombastus von Hohenheim, more commonly known by his adopted name Theophrastus Paracelsus (ca. 1493–1541), was also interested in Pythagoras's connection with magic. He focused on Pythagoras's mystical doctrines, which, according to him, described wisdom as comprehensible only to initiates. Writing during the 1520s and 1530s, Paracelsus employs a good deal of enigmatic language of his own, speaking, for example, of "magical" and "Kabbalistic" "contemplations." Such concepts, he assures his readers, have the stamp of Pythagoras's authority in addition to the pedigree of Plato, Porphyry, Plotinus, Iamblichus, and others who had been influenced by Pythagoras's doctrines. Pythagoras had borrowed this language of secrecy in which he shrouded his doctrines from Moses, Paracelsus explains, mixing in his writings many things from the law of Moses and the Old Testament.[40] This of course implies that Paracelsus believed Pythagoras had left writings, though perhaps he was referring merely to the *Golden Verses,* which were familiar fare in Renaissance libraries. Paracelsus portrays Pythagoras as one of the most learned men in history because he was an "authentic philosopher" who understood the hidden knowledge and mysteries ("supercelestial operations") of the Magi and could point the way to obtain the precious philosopher's stone. This surely refers to the fact that late medieval alchemical texts such as the *Turba philosophorum* continued to be well known in the Renaissance. Paracelsus, who was himself very interested in magic, minerals, and alchemy, viewed Pythagoras as one of the lofty heroes of "The Art" (alchemy), a fact that shows that the old medieval popular views of Pythagoras's involvement with magic invoked by Paracelsus's own contemporary Agrippa, were still very much alive in mid-sixteenth-century Germany.[41]

Skepticism regarding Pythagoras's purported reputation in the occult arts emerged in the writings of Giovanni Francesco Pico (ca. 1470–1533), biographer of his uncle (Pico della Mirandola) and a savant in his own right. Among his philosophical studies is a work that examines the history of Christian doctrine. Here the name of Pythagoras is omnipresent.[42] Giovanni Francesco is not as persuaded as was his uncle respecting the importance of Pythagoras for Christianity; in addition, he finds Pythagoras's reputation in the occult world worrisome. He cites various matters of contention relating to the life of Pythagoras: the secret doctrines and rites of Pythagoras that were described in the famous letter from

Lysis to Hipparchus that had so fascinated Cardinal Bessarion; Iamblichus's report that Pythagoras and Abaris, a mysterious deity, had understood each other because both were divine beings; and the relation of Pythagoras to magic and the occult. He even questions whether Pythagoras was the son of Apollo. He points to disagreements over whether Pythagoras ate beans or meat.[43] The issues he raises do not mean that Giovanni Francesco was deprecating Pythagoras but rather that, seeing the dangers of adulating the authority of a great philosopher of the past, he was devoting himself to separating what he believed to be fact from fiction. His observations testify to the fact that Pythagoras was well known to him and that his legacy was continuing to enjoy the spotlight as the sixteenth century developed.

Contemporary literati, too, paid attention to Pythagoras. In his masterpiece *Il Cortegiano* (*The Courtier*), a famous treatise on the concept of the educated and graceful gentleman that came to be regarded as one of the most important prose works of sixteenth-century Europe, Baldassare Castiglione of Urbino (1478–1529) casts Pythagoras in two very positive roles. Both are derived from his knowledge of ancient literature. In one (inferred from his reading of Cicero) Pythagoras demonstrated his extraordinary understanding of music in deeming it divine. In the other (inferred from his reading of Plutarch) Pythagoras "ingeniously and admirably" demonstrated his prowess as a mathematician by ascertaining the size of Hercules's body through considering the proportion of his foot to that of the dimensions of a stadium.[44] Thus the elegant and restrained language of Castiglione refers to what must have been well-established topics of social concourse about Pythagoras, his discovery of harmony and the qualities of correct proportions. Equally positive is the interpretation of Pythagoras suggested by Castiglione's contemporary, the poet Ludovico Ariosto (1474–1533), who spent much of his adult life in Ferrara, an important center of humanistic studies. In his famous poem *Orlando Furioso*, Ariosto characterizes as virtuous sages Pythagoras and his early disciple Archytas of Tarentum (the probable actual transmitter of Pythagoras's outlook on the cosmos to Plato).[45]

A contemporary of Castiglione and Ariosto, the Venetian patrician and Franciscan friar Francesco Zorzi (1460–1540, also known as Francesco Giorgio), paid particular tribute to Pythagoras for his discovery that numbers had a divine significance. In his widely read philosophical poetic treatise *De harmonia mundi* (*The Harmony of the World*), already known in 1520 though it was not published until 1525,[46] Zorzi explains that because of Pythagoras's discovery, numbers should be celebrated and even venerated as divine. Surely this is why Zorzi's work is divided into eight books (not only is 8 the first cube as 2 x 2 x 2 = 8, but also it was venerated by Pythagoreans of Antiquity as the number of perfect equilibrium and the "embracer of all harmonies").[47] Plato and his followers were, the ardent follower of Ficino and Pico and enthusiast of Hermetic and Kabbalistic texts declares, devotees of this important discovery of Pythagoras's. They believed and affirmed the numerical system of Pythagoras, which described the concinnity of all parts of the universe. Thus could the universe function harmoniously, a fact reflected in the music that emanates from it (a reference to the "harmony of the spheres" described by Cicero). This function of music is not, he holds, unrelated to Pythagoras's discovery of its soothing function in the treatment of frenzy.[48] Zorzi believed that Pythagoras had left writings, for he suggests he had read them: "According to the writings of Pythagoras, not only the fabric of the soul but also the entire world were arranged and perfected by number and proportion."[49] In a later text, which suggests he was familiar with Reuchlin's recent work, Zorzi goes back beyond even Moses to connect Pythagoras with Jewish history. He declares that Pythagoras was privy to a precious book on the divine light of the intellect that had been given by God to Adam and had been passed down through generations of Jews.[50] Zorzi's Pythagoreanism will be discussed in Chapter 6.

Pythagoras's dependence on Judaism was a popular subject among other Renaissance exegetes in the 1520s, surely due to the influence of Pico and Reuchlin. While the intellectual preacher and reformer Egidio da Viterbo (ca. 1469–1532), Vicar General of the Augustinian order in Rome and humanist defender of Reuchlin, may not have known Zorzi's views on Pythagoras's connection to Adam, he was convinced that it was from Moses that Pythagoras had received his ideas before passing them on to Plato, who published them in his *Timaeus*.[51] Egidio also reminds us of the connection of the letter "Y" with Pythagoras.[52] Invented by Pythagoras, this letter could, he advises, be expressed by painters as a tree, he said, with two diverging branches sharing one trunk, a tradition with which he was no doubt familiar because of its long history in medieval art.[53] Egidio's interest in Pythagoras may well have been prompted by his ardor for Saint Augustine, the founder of his religious order, who was an admirer of Pythagoras in late Antiquity. Perhaps coincidentally, during the lifetimes of Egidio and Francesco Zorzi (both of whom published in Venice), a great diffusion of Jewish Kabbalistic literature took place from the printing presses of Italy, particularly those of Venice.[54]

The distinguished Dutch scholar and humanist Erasmus was a particularly avid admirer of Pythagoras. In many of his works, he used examples about Pythagoras drawn from his extensive readings in classical literature. "Was there ever anyone of more penetration or more learning than Pythagoras?" Erasmus asks in *Antibarbarorum* (*The Antibarbarians*). He "surpassed earlier philosophers in modesty as he conquered them in learning," Erasmus continues.[55] Well known to him, he tells us, were the comments of Saint Jerome on the education of Pythagoras.[56] Erasmus's most famous work, *Moriae encomium* (*Praise of Folly*), memorializes, not without wit, the reputation of Pythagoras for admitting to the transmigration of his own soul:

> And so I could never have enough praise for the famous cock who was
> really Pythagoras. When he had been everything in turn, philosopher,

man, woman, king, commoner, fish, horse, frog, even a sponge, I believe, he decided that man was the most unfortunate of animals, simply because all the others were content with their natural limitations.[57]

This passage suggests that stories about the transmigration of Pythagoras's soul were so well known that they had become legion during the Renaissance. Erasmus makes similar comments in other works. For example, in *Lingua* (*The Tongue*), he says:

> In Lucian, Pythagoras, whose soul is supposed to have changed its abode repeatedly and to have entered into the bodies of creatures of every kind, men and women, bipeds and quadrupeds, admits that he had lived a much happier life as a frog than as a king. All this may sound absurd, but it would not be far from the truth if that heavenly teacher of wisdom had not convinced us that everlasting happiness is laid up for those who have placed all their hopes of bliss … .[58]

In a discussion of the value of sleep, Erasmus pays a clear compliment to Pythagoras by comparing his own toils to his:

> I never get down to writing except at dead of night when it's absolutely quiet and deep silence reigns over all … in short, when there's such complete peace that if Pythagoras were alive he would be able to hear the music of the spheres quite clearly. At such time gods and goddesses delight to hold converse with pure minds.[59]

In other works, he speaks of Pythagoras's reputation for having been handsome – of his noble appearance and pleasing body. Such comments reflect his readings of late-Antique authors such as Porphyry and Iamblichus. Pythagoras's good looks aside, Erasmus has high praise for Pythagoras's virtue and morality, his contributions to medicine, his exceptional wisdom, and his empathy for nature ("Pythagoras says that trees are alive and possess the spirit of life … thus the walnut laments that when it sees a blow coming it cannot dodge by moving its body.")[60] He also admires Pythagoras's reputed chastity and his vegetarianism, which he compares to the virtues of asceticism appropriate to the Christian soldier.[61]

In their own words, Erasmus and his correspondents express their high regard for Pythagoras about whom, it is clear, they knew a lot. His own high regard for the idea of commonality between friends, Erasmus says, was born in his admiration for this principle in the doctrines of Pythagoras. In discussing the moral maxims of Pythagoras, Erasmus asserts, "[They] well deserve their name, the Golden Verses." He expresses particular admiration for the learning

Pythagoras acquired during his travels. In speaking of the few ancient writers whose admiration of Pythagoras was less than ardent – for example, Lucian (some of whose works took aim at Pythagoras as being a charlatan) – he advises caution in reading their works.[62] Certainly, Erasmus must have convinced his friend Ambrogio Leoni to become an admirer of Pythagoras, for in 1518, admitting that "[l]ong ago I used to laugh at Pythagoras," Ambrogio admiringly suggests that Erasmus is a second Pythagoras. He writes:

> Hitherto, dearest Erasmus, I have regarded as fabulous the ancient accounts of Pythagoras … changing himself into various shapes whenever he pleased; … But I no longer smile at such tales as trumpery or fables; I believe them to be history, for I know that we are blest with … [him] in your sole person. In such a short space of time you have often died and returned to life. … First I heard … that you had died in France and a few years later come to life again in Germany, and soon afterwards you reappeared in Italy. … So I thought I must be seeing a second Pythagoras."[63]

In 1522, Erasmus wrote to Pope Adrian VI (a fellow countryman from the Netherlands) in praise of Pythagoras's discovery of the wonders that music can perform in calming youthful agitation. That the moral teachings of Pythagoras must have been widely appreciated is suggested by the text of a letter written to Erasmus by a friend. It proposes that Erasmus remind all youths of the symbolism of Pythagoras's letter (the "Y") so that, as they grow up, they can be persuaded through the example of Pythagoras to choose the path of virtue.[64]

In a letter to King Henry VIII, Erasmus compares Pythagoras and his disciple Apollonius of Tyana to Christ. In another, to a Polish humanist, he refers to Pythagoras as "that heavenly teacher of wisdom," asserting that the various peregrinations of Pythagoras's soul do not appear to be absurd when one takes into account that it was he who convinced us that everlasting happiness awaits the blessed. This happiness Erasmus defines as the most powerful doctrine of Pythagoras: It is this principle, he explains, that identifies the eternal happiness in which the immortal soul places all its hope.[65] Many of Erasmus's humanist friends shared his admiration of Pythagoras. These include not only those mentioned earlier but also Spanish humanists. Though he lived much of his life outside his home country, Juan Luis Vives (1492–1540), for example, appears to have had a deep interest in Pythagoras. As one who was particularly concerned about social issues and Christian charity, his comments betray his special regard for Pythagoras as a model of morality, particularly in the areas of friendship, sharing, and the law, which for him exemplified the correct way to live.[66]

The depth of Erasmus's lifelong admiration for Pythagoras, which was underlined by his avid support of Reuchlin as noted earlier, strongly suggests that he was an active Pythagorean. The subject of Erasmus's Pythagoreanism will be discussed in Chapter 6.

MATHEMATICS, EXORCISMS, AND THE INSPIRATION OF PAINTERS

In a volume on natural history published in 1544, the Ferrarese mathematician and astronomer Celio Calcagnini (1479–1541), Erasmus's younger contemporary and friend, awarded high praise to Pythagoras for having been a great teacher. As Calcagnini exudes, Pythagoras, one of the wisest men of Antiquity, elevated numbers to the status of divinity. He was the first mathematician to discover that harmony was a "computation" that, based on calculation, produced concord. He was also, Calcagnini tells us, the first musician to recognize the wondrous power of music as a medical cure for frenzy. To demonstrate Pythagoras's discovery of concord he repeats the old story first told in the first century A.D. by Nicomachus about Pythagoras and the harmonious blacksmith.[67] Calcagnini is the first person ever to provide a reason as to why, as Aristotle and his successors had claimed in Antiquity, Pythagoras had a golden thigh: "For Pythagoras it was the price and outstanding value of the secret matters he studied that made his thigh golden."[68] This reference to the weightiness of the "secret matters" Pythagoras studied suggests that in the sixteenth century he was still considered to have, beyond his mathematical skills, knowledge of divine things. Calcagnini makes it clear that by his time it was generally assumed that Pythagoras had obtained his secret knowledge (which he calls "theological deductions") from Moses and passed it on to Plato.[69]

In an oral recital in praise of geometry Calcagnini's younger colleague, the renowned mathematician and professor of medicine Girolamo Cardano (1501–1576), noted that Pythagoras had made important contributions to the field of geometry, "increasing knowledge about this art and making it celebrated."[70] Cardano was in his middle age when, after many delays, the magnum opus of the Polish-born, Italian-educated astronomer Nicholaus Copernicus (1473–1543) finally appeared in print.[71] Though Copernicus does not discuss Pythagoras himself, he pays ample tribute to the distant predecessor with whom he shared a passion to measure the beautiful heaven he so loved in the form of his debt to Pythagorean thought, which will be discussed in Chapter 6.

To this generation belongs the eccentric French philologist Guillaume Postel (1510–1581). In a work entitled *Petit Traité de la Signification ultime des Cinq Corps Réguliers* (*Small Treatise on the Ultimate Significance of the Five Regular Bodies*), Postel speaks an obscure language, possibly inspired by Pythagoras (widely described in Antiquity as having presented his doctrines in the form of enigmas to protect them from the uninitiated). His views are, however, clear. He traces the doctrines of Pythagoras back not only to Moses, but, as Zorzi had first suggested, also to Adam. These doctrines eventually reached the ancestors of the French, the Druids, he continues, whose Pythagoreanism was exemplary, as was widely noted in Antiquity. Postel explains that the Druids knew Pythagoras's [not Plato's] five regular solids. Connecting the "wondrous" significance of these five polyhedra with Christianity, he says that though they were elaborated by Plato they were surely derived from Pythagoras and possibly even from Pythagoras's teacher Pherecydes. Postel also expresses his own personal preference – inspired by Pythagoras – for the equilateral triangle and the cube.[72] He wrote with passionate intensity about the symbolism of number. Not only did this self-taught and well-traveled scholar put the imprimatur of Pythagoras on his bizarre ideas, he also connected him with Christian goals. Postel's reveries concerning the harmonious unification of humankind, including the Muslims, under a Christian kingdom were surely not unrelated to his interest in Pythagoras. Such signs of his Pythagoreanism will be discussed in Chapter 6.

Much more conventional was Daniele Barbaro (1513–1570), the Patriarch of Aquilea and a specialist in Vitruvius. In his commentary on Vitruvius's *De architectura*, this Christian dignitary writes glowingly of Vitruvius, who, he says, dedicated his life to understanding the perfect precepts of architecture; accordingly, Barbaro finds several occasions on which to discuss Pythagoras. The lessons of Pythagoras and his accomplices Plato and Democritus were of fundamental importance, he declares, for they were basic to Vitruvius's thought. This included, Barbaro continues, the theory concerning the square of the hypotenuse established by Pythagoras, which was of great significance for architects. He cites the authority of Pythagoras in arithmetic and measurement. The latter was demonstrated when Pythagoras accurately calculated the stature of Hercules. Pythagoras, this Christian patriarch rhapsodizes, was a divine man ("huomo divino") who merits the greatest honor ("grandissima commendatione").[73]

Not everyone was as historically polite as Erasmus, as focused as Cardano and Copernicus, or as imaginative as Postel. In a distinctly crude and coarse commentary on the peregrinations of the soul of Pythagoras, Giovanni Paolo Lomazzo (1538–1600), a painter and writer on art, invited his readers' laughter at the image of Pythagoras as a sleek charlatan whose soul could pick and choose which bodies it entered. His *Libro de sogni* (*Book of Dreams*), a youthful work published in 1563, contains a discussion, composed in the form of an entertaining dialogue-play, between Pythagoras and a military engineer.[74]

Puffed up with pride, a cynical Pythagoras boasts that he had recently left the body of the famous Italian author Pietro Aretino (1492–1556), who had recently died. "Do you know what?" Pythagoras taunts his interlocutor. Then he continues in the form of a long story. In order to establish its background, he explains that while he was in the body of Aretino, an Arab wanted Aretino's spirit. Wearing a strange costume and a crown decorated with Chaldean and

Hebrew letters, the Arab performed an exorcism after closing all the doors and windows and laying out colored lamps that emitted perfumes. This scene inspires Lomazzo's Pythagoras to boast further. And he does. He tells the Arab that he had not only been in the bodies of men but also in those of females and animals. He remembers "inhabiting" the bodies of Helen of Troy and of other women, taking obvious pleasure in comparing their sexual aptitudes. He also inhabited, he brags, the body of an ant in India, from where he had traveled to Greece. It was there that he entered the body of Euphorbus, about whom Homer was later to write. Homer, he adds, did not know anything about this, because he was only six years old at the time. But, Pythagoras vaunts, he enjoyed the body of Aretino more than that of any other. The piece concludes with a bizarre sonnet whose words, accompanied by a lyre, offer a potpourri of famous names, including the poetess Sappho, Adam and his son Cain, the master of magic Pietro d'Abano, and the monk-scholar Cassiodorus. It is not clear, though the words are suggestive, whether or not he inhabited the bodies of these famous historical characters. Though this play includes vulgar passages, it demonstrates Lomazzo's erudition. It suggests that though he regards Pythagoras as a great man worthy to be his subject, he considers the reputation of Pythagoras respecting transmigration of the soul to be flawed. His predecessors Ficino and Erasmus, he implies, had in all sincerity sought to overlook this flaw because Pythagoras was such a significant figure.

In other early works that do not involve the subject of transmigration, Lomazzo is much more respectful of Pythagoras. Linking him with Apollo and the seven-stringed lyre, for example, Lomazzo describes in admiring detail Pythagoras's discovery of the seven planets and the harmonious tones they emit as they move in perfect concord. He is not hesitant to credit Pythagoras with "marvelous investigations" in astronomy and music.[75] Pythagoras also, he says, discovered the microcosm (which is man) while studying the megacosm of the universe.[76] Lomazzo links Pythagoras with Sappho in suggesting that his followers employed a special herb to induce love between a man and a woman. Accordingly, it was because Faon had ingested this very herb that he fell in love with Sappho, and it was this love that occasioned her suicidal leap. Dedicating her leap to Apollo, whose temple crowned the site of this event, Sappho had dramatically demonstrated the power of Apollo to guarantee immortality (a subject regarded in Antiquity as Pythagorean and a subject suitable for an altarpiece in a Pythagorean temple).[77] Lomazzo discusses other herbs with medicinal properties employed by Pythagoras in his role as a healer.[78]

Serious too is Lomazzo's treatment of Pythagoras in a product of his maturity, the *Trattato dell'arte* (*Treatise on Art*), a major sixteenth-century work written after the artist-writer became blind. Here – perhaps longingly – he describes the qualities of color. He notes that Pythagoras disapproved of black, a color suggesting evil, while he required that his priests dress in white linen to symbolize the purity of the sacrifices they attended. Originally Jewish, Lomazzo says, this practice of wearing white was brought to Egypt by Pythagoras.

According to Lomazzo, Pythagoras delighted in the study of perspective because it was he who had discovered the art of measurement. Pythagoras's remarkable skill in that art was, we are told, one of his most admired attributes in the Renaissance. Lomazzo's praise for Pythagoras's mathematical abilities extends to Pythagoras's discoveries of the right triangle and the proportional relationship of musical tones. The ancients, Lomazzo summarizes, most admired Pythagoras for his brilliant mind and his insights. In a passage concerning the portrayal of famous people, Lomazzo reminds us that Pythagoras had a beautiful body and a handsome face.[79]

In the *Idea del tempio della pittura* (*Scheme for a Temple of Painting*) of 1591, Lomazzo respectfully refers to Pythagoras as the first philosopher. Here he explicitly states as fact what Postel had recently suggested: that Pythagoras had discovered the five regular polyhedra, or geometrical solids – the four-sided pyramid or tetrahedron, the cube or hexahedron, the octahedron, the icosahedron, and the dodecahedron, all forms that could be circumscribed in a sphere, his favorite geometrical shape. The pedigree of these solids passed, Lomazzo explains, from Pythagoras to Plato to Chalcidius (whose fourth-century A.D. translation and commentary on Plato's *Timaeus* was printed in the sixteenth century) to Macrobius. Lomazzo goes on to discuss Pythagoras's discoveries of musical, pictorial, and compositional harmony that, he affirms, were disseminated by Empedocles and Plato. He is the first to state unequivocally that Pythagoras and his disciples inspired painters. Under their influence painters, he says, learned to paint with harmony and grace.[80] Lomazzo reserves his greatest praise for Pythagoras in his last work, *Della forma delle muse* (*On the Conformation of the Muses*), written in the early 1590s. Closely connected with Pythagoras, the Muses sing in unison in Apollo's imperium: "[T]his Apollo is none other than the supreme God, as the universally great Pythagoras said."[81] Lomazzo was not alone in claiming that artists paid attention to Pythagoras's discovery of harmony. So also did his contemporary Gregorio Comanini. In a treatise on painting, Comanini emphasizes the importance of the harmonic proportions (the invention, he says, of Pythagoras) for sixteenth-century artists.[82]

Admiration for Pythagoras did not diminish in the later sixteenth century. Many less overtly enthusiastic about him appear to have accepted the doctrines and discoveries historically attributed to him. It appears that these had become so commonplace that it was not necessary to mention him by name in connection with them. Perhaps events such as the Council of Trent (1545–1563), which faced the perils of Protestantism by restoring, reinforcing, and reinvigorating the Catholic Church, and the "scientific revolution," which stimulated discoveries that made of astronomy – once the commonly accepted partner of astrology – a highly abstract science exclusively devoted to the study of the physical universe, were the primary causes of a redirection of interests into religious and scientific paths that came to be separated and well defined. No longer would religion and science be interlocked.

Meanwhile, the memory and inspiration of Pythagoras did not die. In 1580, the great mathematical philosopher and prolific writer Giordano Bruno (1548–1600) remarked on the enduring importance of the "divine" and "wise" Pythagoras and his philosophy of numbers, while reprimanding newer scientists who, because they did not listen to Pythagoras, were "strangers to the truth."[83] His modern cosmology recognized the numerical relationships of Pythagoras. In a moment of ingenious eccentricity prompted by his interest in magic and the Kabbalah, Bruno claimed that because Pythagoras would not want us to despise anything in nature, the ass and the ape might become members of an academy.[84] Pythagoras and Solomon, the wisest of men as Bruno hints in an enigmatic poem, were able to discover wisdom because they understood unity:

> Solomon and Pythagoras
> What is that which is?
> Itself – what it has been.
> What is what it has been?
> Itself – what it is.
> Nothing is new under the sun.
> Cheers!

In pairing the two with the epithet "nothing is new under the sun" he suggests that Pythagoras and Solomon are basic to civilization, that is, that the Pythagorean worldview is as ancient and fundamental as any truth or wisdom to be learned from Solomon.[85]

PYTHAGORAS: THE "PRINCE OF ITALIAN PHILOSOPHY"

Notwithstanding Bruno's equation of Pythagoras and Solomon as the most revered pair of heroes from the past, it would appear that Pythagoras eclipsed Solomon in the variety and number of areas in which his authority reigned supreme. These all fell into place in the late sixteenth century in what is perhaps the least known but certainly the most comprehensive and elaborate biography of Pythagoras ever written. Composed in 1588 by Bernardino Baldi (1553–1617), the most erudite of the many famous mathematicians of Urbino, this biography introduces Pythagoras, in its opening paragraph, as the "prince of Italian philosophy." Thus was Reuchlin's epithet (Pythagoras was the "prince of philosophers") made more precise.

Baldi's biography provides a perfect example of how the Renaissance derived its vigor by looking backward. In describing his search for what he terms the gold of the past, Baldi outlines a scholarly approach that convinces his readers that his aim was to discover the historical "truth" about Pythagoras. Not only did Baldi know the world of mathematics well, he also knew, and was able to read for himself, an enormous number of ancient and medieval works that pertained to Pythagoras, some of which have not come down to us. In so doing, he avoided the pitfall of basing his reporting on vague sources. Realizing that the "true" history of Pythagoras's life will never be known, because he lived so long ago and because so much of the information about him comes from later times and is characterized by conflicting views, Baldi develops a highly original and dazzlingly modern approach. He constructs his *Vita di Pitagora* (*Life of Pythagoras*) by studying and analyzing the various, often conflicting, points of view of his many sources.[86] His concentration on the issues they raise allows him to focus on ideas rather than on chronology.

The first of these issues is the matter of where Pythagoras was born. Though Baldi considers the possibilities of Etruria, Tuscany, and Syria, he concludes that Samos is the most likely. Baldi explains that he reached this conclusion through the discovery of new information that enabled him to trace the genealogy of Pythagoras's family to Phlious, an ancient Neolithic site near Corinth, in Greece. Evidence suggests, he says, that Pythagoras's grandparents emigrated from there to Samos. Also new to the biography of Pythagoras are the names of his mother, maternal grandfather, paternal grandfather, and brother, as well as that of his first teacher, a certain Hermodamante, who taught him poetry and whom Baldi connects with Homer. It was the fact that Pythagoras would later settle in Croton, Baldi ingeniously suggests, that probably had led some, confusing Croton with Cortona (an Etruscan city of Tuscany), to associate Pythagoras with Etruria or Tuscany.[87]

Baldi attempts to explain why and how Pythagoras went to Egypt – perhaps, he suggests, he went as a prisoner. He holds that it was in Egypt that Pythagoras studied geometry and later, in Babylonia, arithmetic and music. Though he lists all the various ancient authors who speculated that Pythagoras had studied with the Hebrews, Baldi discounts their "legends" about Pythagoras having been a student of Moses. On the other hand, he suggests that it was because Pythagoras attended the Olympic Games when he returned to Greece that he developed his great regard for physical health. It was this interest, he proposes, that led Pythagoras to turn his attention to medicine and to deduce that good health was linked to harmony.

Important sections on Pythagoras's love of virtue, disdain for luxury, and love of family follow. Here we learn that his wife (Theano) was a professional philosopher and that together they may have had four children (rather than two, as was commonly believed). After considering the views of numerous antique sources regarding Pythagoras's doctrines, Baldi asserts that the teachings of

Pythagoras centered on arithmetic, geometry, cosmology, and the law, and that he regarded secrecy, enigma, silence, and discipline to be important teaching and learning techniques. Baldi avoids the subject of the many miracles that had been attributed to Pythagoras since the time of Aristotle, including his alleged golden thigh. But he seriously considers, and at great length, the historical debate over whether Pythagoras ate beans, meat, or fish. He concludes that Pythagoras probably did abstain from meat because of his great respect for animals. Baldi lays particular stress on the importance of peace, concord, proportion, and harmony for Pythagoras, and characterizes discord as Pythagoras's greatest enemy.

One of the highlights of Baldi's biography lies in his discussion of the importance of number for Pythagoras. He devotes special attention to Pythagoras's interest in the cube and the various forms of the triangle. Baldi insists that the five regular solids were invented by Pythagoras, though they were later "illustrated" by Plato. It was Pythagoras, he affirms, who perfected geometry. The length and depth of Baldi's discussion of the meanings and symbolisms of number indicate that these were still vital matters in his own time. He pays special tribute to the numbers 1 through 10. Of particular importance are the number 3, which, multiplied by itself twice, produces 27, a "cubical" number, and the number 4, which, multiplied by itself, produces 16, a perfect number.

While Baldi discounts the beliefs of some that Pythagoras was the inventor of music (musicians existed before his time, he assures his readers), he concedes that Pythagoras was, in the sixteenth century, believed to have been connected with the Muses. He explains that Pythagoras attempted to measure the heavens by investigating the distances between each of the planets and the earth and that these distances suggested to him the harmonic proportions that are reflected in the music of the spheres.

Baldi takes a personal interest in Pythagoras. He describes him as serious, melancholy, severe, and austere – sidestepping ancient reports that Pythagoras played the lyre and liked to sing and dance. Unlike most Greeks, he says, Pythagoras wore long trousers and dressed in white. Baldi says that in his own time Pythagoras was highly regarded for his expertise in magic and prognostication, as he had been in Antiquity, Druidic times, and the Middle Ages. In considering the controversy over whether or not Pythagoras left any writings, Baldi avoids vouching for any texts other than the *Golden Verses*, still famous in his time, and the significance of the letter "Y," made famous by the "prince of Italian philosophy."

Noteworthy is Baldi's assurance that Pythagoras very much liked architecture; indeed, the biography is riddled with references to Vitruvius. This is the first time (aside from the implications made by Vitruvius himself in Antiquity and those of Pacioli toward the beginning of the sixteenth century) that a biographer of Pythagoras discusses his influence in architecture. In summary, Baldi concludes, "Pythagoras was inferior to God, but superior to all other men."[88] Though Baldi's work was not published until long after his death,[89] it serves as a measure of the enormous amount of information known about Pythagoras in the late sixteenth century.

At century's close, Galileo Galilei (1564–1642) and Johannes Kepler (1571–1630), both learned mathematicians and astronomers, acknowledged their debt to Pythagoras. Though this might be deduced in the cosmographical pursuits of both, it is perhaps most poignantly stated in a letter of 1598 from Kepler to Galileo. Alluding to Galileo's practice of secrecy, Kepler says "and in this you follow Plato and Pythagoras, our true preceptors."[90] Kepler, an admirer of Cusanus, was especially proud to acknowledge the authority of Pythagoras in his works: Geometry, he declares, has two great treasures: "[o]ne is the golden theorem of Pythagoras. ... the other is the division of a line into extreme and mean proportion."[91] Speaking of the universe, he says: "Pythagoras teaches us its arrangement with five figures." By "figures" he of course means "bodies" or "solids." Kepler thus confirms that the five regular geometrical solids were not the discovery of Plato ("Platonic" solids) but of Pythagoras.[92] Writing at the end of the sixteenth century as the "scientific revolution" began, Kepler paid Pythagoras a stunning compliment: Had Pythagoras lived in the sixteenth century instead of long before, there is no doubt he would have made the same discovery as Copernicus and that this discovery would be as well known as his five solids.[93]

In the late sixteenth century practitioners of the occult sciences still existed, as Baldi had noted. One example is Giambattista Della Porta (ca. 1535–1615), a Neapolitan whose works were popular in France and Spain, where he traveled extensively. In describing the pedigree of famous sages who inspired the world of magic, he is but one of many who continued to express their regard for Pythagoras.[94] Such texts would continue to appear well into the seventeenth century.[95] In that century, a school of philosophy based on Ficino's view of an unbroken channel of esoteric wisdom that passed from Moses to Hermes Trismegistus to Pythagoras to Plato was to develop at Cambridge where strong interests in the occult would reappear.[96]

The acceleration of interest in Pythagoras in the sixteenth century was prodigious in its amount as in its quality. In their eagerness to proclaim the authority of Pythagoras, scholars continued to build on the effulgence of information accumulated from rediscovered antique sources in the previous century. Interest in Pythagoras was especially acute in the early 1500s, when a new depth of interest in him and his ideas is particularly notable in the works of writers from such diverse points of view as mathematics (Pacioli, Zorzi), Hebraica (Reuchlin), philosophy (Erasmus), and music (Gaffurio). Intellectuals who disagreed with each other on other matters (e.g., Clichtove with Erasmus) were in agreement about the importance of Pythagoras.[97] He held a high place in the thinking of scholars from Italy, Germany, France, Holland, and Spain.

Throughout the sixteenth century, Pythagoras was recognized above all for his influence and his discoveries, mainly those centering on universal harmony. There were no great controversies about his importance in the many fields with which his name was associated – including arithmetic, number symbolism, geometry, the reconciliation of contraries or the balancing of opposites, moral purity, the pursuit of virtue, music as medicine, musical proportion, the practice of silence, the use of enigma, vegetarianism, astronomy, and the immortality of the soul. He was also celebrated for his inventions, including the theorem of the right triangle, the concept of philosophy, musical proportion, and the letter "Y," which permitted humans to choose virtue over vice. He was universally recognized as the discoverer of the art of measurement and, by extension, proportion. It was this discovery that had led to the study of perspective and to the perfection of architecture (as Pacioli and Baldi claimed). It also inspired painters to achieve compositional harmony (as Lomazzo and Comanini suggested).

Above all, in the sixteenth century Pythagoras was known for his wisdom and his love of harmony. Intellectuals had come to believe that this exceptional wisdom derived from his connection, by then widely accepted, with Moses and the Kabbalah. Pythagoras's wisdom was embodied in his mathematics and in his discovery of the significance of number. Together these provided a key to the secrets of nature and the function of the universe; and they enabled harmony. The sphere of the universe contained within it the five solids that he had discovered. By century's end, as Postel's, Lomazzo's, Baldi's, and Kepler's authority would have it, these had come to be known as "Pythagorean" solids. At the same time, various discoveries attributed to Pythagoras from outside the intellectual world continued to survive in the domains of magic, prognostication, and alchemy.[98]

Familiarity with Pythagoras was so widespread (throughout Europe but especially in Italy and Germany) that authors alluded to him without even mentioning his name. He was such an easily recognized personality that some could even make lighthearted fun of him. Occasions for this were, however, few and were restricted to the subject of transmigration of the soul. All in all, everyone knew who he was. Though different people might have different reasons to admire him, the facts about his life and doctrines had become conventionalized.

Despite the scientific revolution and the new language of "rationalism," beliefs in the mystical and wondrous aspects of Pythagoras also survived well into the seventeenth and eighteenth centuries, when they came to be romanticized. A work published in London in 1695 describes Pythagoras visiting the royal palace of the king of India. In a letter attributed to him and addressed to this (unnamed) king, Pythagoras lectures him: Pythagoras's religion recommends abstinence from flesh; tyranny is unreasonable; admiration for hunting is wrong because it is against nature; Jewish doctors teach that Adam was the first human to eat herbs and fruit – flesh was not in his diet; the practice of magic requires that its practitioners be virtuous human beings; in order to keep

God's laws, it is important to study the sun, moon, and stars; and above all, one must be against violence and cruelty. In a second letter to the king of India, Pythagoras rhapsodizes: Unity is the origin of all number and contains every number joined together. He persuasively explains that proper practice and use of numbers will fortify humans against the temptations of evil demons and enable them to achieve concord in their lives.

Another English seventeenth-century work claims that the mystic philosophy of Pythagoras was communicated through the word of God and his good angels. While living in France in the same century, the Spanish writer Antonio Enriquez Gómez wrote a celebrated book, *El siglo pitagórico* (*The Pythagorean Century*), a testimony to Pythagoras's continued popularity.[99] In the next century, a French publication describes Pythagoras as one of the "greatest geniuses that nature ever produced." His authority lives on forever, it holds, because he was a profound and sublime genius.[100] This is not to mention the fact that the publication record of the *Golden Verses* of Pythagoras extends well into the eighteenth century. It was not until 1881 and the work of François Lenormant that romantic works about Pythagoras would decrease in their intensity and be replaced by serious studies such as those of Cumont and his contemporaries that would revive scholarly interest in Pythagoras and reassess his contributions to the history of civilization.[101]

Part Two:
The Many Faces
of Renaissance
Pythagoreanism

FOUR:

THE PYTHAGOREAN TRADITION
IN THE EARLY FIFTEENTH
CENTURY

The word "Pythagorean" was well known among Renaissance writers, for many of them, including Leonardo Bruni and Pico della Mirandola and their successors, used it. This chapter will consider the ideas of those who regarded themselves as followers of Pythagoras, as well as of those who appear to have subscribed to certain elements of the diaspora of his influence, some of which lingered from medieval times and some of which involved newly discovered knowledge from Antiquity. It will attempt to explain who may have been, in a general as well as a specific sense, attached to the legacy of Pythagoras. It is not easy – nor would it be wise – to offer a categorical definition of what it meant to "be" a Pythagorean in the Renaissance. Certainly, it was not a club that people joined. Nor was it an absolute ideology that required adherence to a catechism of tenets. For every thinker who credited Pythagoras as a source of inspiration, there were many more who did not, though all were beneficiaries of generally accepted notions that can be associated with the widespread legacy of his reputation.

As we have seen, even a casual glance at the many-sided aspects of Pythagoras in the Renaissance cannot fail to appreciate his popularity. Viewed through Renaissance eyes, the doctrines believed to have been taught by him were relevant to a wide variety of interests, from arithmetic to geometry to social justice to music to magic. While some may have been interested in a single "Pythagorean" subject, others might have been interested in several. It may be difficult for modern readers to understand the many links that joined what might appear to be "scientific" with "nonscientific" principles. These were incorporated in a different view of "wisdom" than is ours today – largely due to the influence of the precious works of ancient writers who had described Pythagoras as the wisest of all sages because he possessed superior knowledge in theological and scientific matters. For Renaissance thinkers wisdom included, in addition to systematized knowledge, "divine" knowledge that attached cosmo-logical mysteries to verifiable facts.

Most difficult for the modern reader to understand may be the associa-tion of these views with Christianity, most specifically their reconciliation with Christian doctrine. In this context, it must not be forgotten that Pythagoras had been admired by churchmen since Early Christian times. This foundation no doubt made it possible for devout Christians to be Pythagoreans; some of these were prelates, including cardinals, and possibly two were popes.

In addition to demonstrating their devotion to any one, or more, of the tenets associated with the teachings of Pythagoras, Renaissance Pythagoreans could choose to live their lives in accordance with Pythagorean teachings that they now avidly read about in the original Greek. These included such practices as frugality, silence, secrecy, asceticism, vegetarianism, and the sharing of posses-sions. Some Renaissance writers tell us that they were followers of Pythagoras. Others, who may have admired Pythagoras, do not claim to have been his followers. Yet others, perhaps less inclined to personally acknowledge Pythagoras, simply provide information about the general trends of Pythagorean interests.

This synthetic picture that lacks boundaries was complicated by the increas-ingly important presence of Plato in Renaissance thought – a presence, no doubt, behind the tendency of many modern writers to use the label "Neoplatonism" to designate the revival of Platonic studies without regarding its Pythagorean com-ponent. As we have seen, Plato's debt to Pythagoras came to be well known in the Early Renaissance and was used as an argument for making him acceptable to Christians. Because Plato was widely believed throughout medieval times to have been a follower of Pythagoras and the *Timaeus* to be his most Pythagorean work, he was considered to have been a disseminator of Pythagorean ideas. Among these were an arithmetical language that attributed special meanings to numbers; a geometric metaphor according to which shapes and volumes describe ideas; the basic concept that the universe is made up of contraries (such as odd and even, light and dark, good and bad); and the idea that a single god incorporates and manages all these in his person and in his creation of the universe. In addition, the enigmatic language with which Plato describes cosmic structure, the order-ing of the world, and the achievement of equilibrium doubtless exemplified, for his Renaissance devotees, the reticence of Pythagoras and his followers to express ideas directly for fear of their corruption by the uninitiated.[1]

Essentially, Plato's famous creation explained Pythagorean cosmology as, it was imagined, Pythagoras's first disciples had taught it. The cosmos was an admi-rable and beautiful firmament that contained seven heavenly bodies – five planets in addition to the sun and moon. The functioning of these bodies, all spheres, resulted in the invention of music and proportion, for cosmic tones resulted from the velocities of the planets as they moved in a fixed relationship to each other. This order and harmony was reflected in the significance of number, which, ultimately based on the four elements, could be added, subtracted, and otherwise compounded in different ways to explain the mysteries of the universe. At the center of all things was the monad, or number 1, which, being godlike, was the origin of all things.

Symbolic of the universal order that was central to the Pythagorean legacy was the lyre. With its seven strings it emitted cosmic music that could be used to heal the disturbed and enable them to contemplate the heavens and harmonize their behavior with society. The concept of universal order incorporated moral reform, which opposed war, litigation, excessive luxury, familial abuse and other forms of depravity; it urged frugality, self-restraint, communal friendship, the sharing of property, and the practice of piety and justice. Earthly behavior thus reflected universal order, enabling humankind to reach god.[2]

In order to demonstrate the development of this tradition and the variety of its faces for the Renaissance, this chapter will focus on individuals who, self-declared or not, appear to have been closely involved with the general movement of Pythagoreanism in the Early Renaissance. It will consider, in a peripheral way, general information provided by other Renaissance writers about Pythagoreans and their beliefs, habits, and lifestyles.

THE RESURGENCE OF PYTHAGOREANISM IN FLORENCE

There can be no doubt that Coluccio Salutati paved the way for the enthusiastic and self-confident eruption of Pythagoreanism in Italy. Mindful of the Pythagorean leanings of Petrarch, Salutati convinced his contemporaries in early fifteenth-century Florence of their importance. This was especially vivid in his major treatise, *De laboribus Herculis*. Here Salutati finds numerous occasions to recommend the Pythagorean "Y" as an inspiration to lead a moral life. Though this idea had received the attention of Saint Jerome, Servius, Ausonius, Martianus Capella, Isidore of Seville, and a host of others in earlier medieval times, Petrarch had been the first to comment extensively on it.[3] In his discussion of the conflict between loftiness and baseness in human life, Salutati takes his cue from Petrarch and links the "choice of Hercules," that is, the choice between virtue and vice, to Christianity. It is necessary, he says, to choose the correct branch of the Pythagorean "Y" in order to make the correct choice in moral matters and ascend from the underworld to return one's soul to God.[4]

The strength of Salutati's Pythagorean tendencies is evident in other aspects of this work. For example, in speaking at great length and in a technical way, about musical sequences, intervals, octaves, and tones, he quotes from Philolaus, Boethius, and Macrobius – all Pythagoreans. He also demonstrates a special interest in celestial harmony, explaining that the revolutions of the heavenly spheres are determined by the magnitude of their weight and the diversity of their motion. The Muses, who sang and played their music in union with Apollo, reflect the perfected celestial harmony that results. Though discovered by Pythagoras, he explains, this idea was disseminated to posterity by Plato and other Pythagoreans.

Salutati also finds occasion in this text and others to voice his strong support for the symbolism of number. He discusses the numbers of "mystical perfection" up to 10, as well as the Seven Liberal Arts, the trivium and the quadrivium, the monad, the triad, the seven-toned scale, and the power of unity and harmony that result from proper attention to number. Clearly, for Salutati as for most Pythagoreans since the time of Nicomachus in the first century A.D., numbers have a sacred, theological, side. Speaking of the student of number, Salutati says:

> He will find the numbers of mystical perfection. … He will learn to understand the infinite sacramental meanings of each mystic number, which are a part of theological learning and are necessary to a clear understanding of sacred literature.[5]

In this context, without mentioning Pythagoras by name, he advises Christians how much they have to learn from Antiquity: "Whence did the primitive Church learn how to express itself if not from the heritage of the heathen?"[6] He also expresses admiration for the cube, above all other geometrical shapes. This form, he claims, invites the contemplation of God. Very likely, he was a Pythagorean.

Salutati's enthusiasm for Pythagorean ideas appears to have been inherited by his younger contemporaries Pier Paolo Vergerio (who describes his familiarity with Pythagorean customs) and Leonardo Bruni (who advocates the practice of silence taught by Pythagoras "who among all peoples has a great name for wisdom"). Parallel to it was that of Guarino da Verona (1374–1460, an inspiring and learned educator who recommends Pythagorean discipline for training children), and Aeneas Sylvius Piccolomini (Pope Pius II, a learned humanist who advocates Pythagorean temperance, training in musical harmony, modesty, and moral conduct in the education of the young).[7] Above all, Salutati's fervor prepared Florence for the arrival in 1439 of the famous Greek philosopher and teacher Gemistus Pletho.

THE GREEK FACTOR: PLETHO AND BESSARION

Inspired by his hero, Plato, Gemistus Pletho was a strong advocate of Greek philosophy, which he describes as the culmination of a long tradition of wisdom that had been transmitted to Plato by Pythagoras. To demonstrate the importance of

Plato to the West, which had until this time – and even into the next generation – shown a marked preference for Aristotle, Pletho emphasizes the Pythagorean roots of Plato while decrying Aristotle as a spoiler who, despite having been a student of Plato, had founded his own sect, thus perverting the long tradition of (Pythagorean) philosophy.[8]

In his interpretation of the so-called *Chaldean Oracles*, a composite Roman text he (mistakenly) believed represented ancient Zoroastrian wisdom, Pletho presented a mini-anthology of Pythagorean doctrines. Among these were the immortality of the soul, metempsychosis (transmigration), and the divinity of numbers. Paying special homage to the number 7, he claimed that because it symbolized the seven planets it paved the way to paradise and the eternal harmony and concord of the universe.[9]

Surviving fragments of Pletho's major work, the *Treatise on Law*, underline his admiration for a number of Pythagorean doctrines, including transmigration, self-restraint, abstinence from meat, the sharing of property, and the achievement of virtue through leading a well-ordered life that avoids extremes and seeks moderation and unity. The tradition of wisdom behind these teachings was based on a cocktail of somewhat exotic doctrines that Pletho concocted from the Pythagorean writings of his predecessors in the Byzantine medieval world, especially Proclus and Michael Psellus. He enthusiastically declares that perfection is discovered through number. Referring to Apollo's tripod, he suggests it is a sacred triad that indicates a foreknowledge of the Trinity.[10] We are told that the universe is divided into three kinds of substance – the first eternal and unchanging, the second eternal and changeable, and the third historical and mortal. His discussion of the virtues of number does not stand alone. It is accompanied by a demonstration, in the organization and planning of his text, of the symbolic application of number. The text is divided into three books, surely a tribute to the significance of the triad. To the treatise are appended twenty-seven hymns intended for liturgical use. This number was invested with mystical meaning by Plato and the Pythagoreans for it was the first cubic number ($3 \times 3 \times 3 = 27$). In addition, each hymn is composed of nine (the sum of $3 + 3 + 3$ and the number of the Muses) verses.[11] In this light, it cannot be accidental that Apollo, whom Pythagoreans associated with the seven strings of the lyre and whose birthday was celebrated on the seventh of any given month in Antiquity, is the dedicatee of the seventh hymn. Apollo, Pletho explains, rules and governs with perfect unity; thus he inspires the law that creates harmony in the universe: Justice is the accord that results.

Such concepts led Pletho to share his passion for a Pythagorean principle that would come to be of primary importance for Renaissance architecture and art. All beauty, he reflects, is based on measure and proportion. These are achieved through number. Perfection is the result of the unified symmetry created by the interaction of measure and proportion. The balance between extremes plays, he continues, a vital role in obtaining beauty and perfection. This is because in their reconciliation the opposites achieve a perfect rapport with each other.

Affirming his belief in the Pythagorean doctrine of the immortality of the soul, Pletho admonishes those who would stray from the Pythagorean doctrines of Plato. The followers of Pythagoras and Plato have been guided, he explains, by the gods; this guidance differs from that of sophists and poets who, seeking to promote novelty, are immoral and deceptive. Only the teachings of Pythagoras and Plato are "the purest," he underlines, and deviation from them leads to ill.[12]

In maintaining the primacy of Plato's philosophy, Pletho had to defend himself against the argument, raised by Aristotelians, that Plato did not explain all the things that mattered to Christians. Pletho took the view that, as a Pythagorean, Plato practiced enigma and secrecy: For this reason, Plato discussed only important questions, without writing down all his ideas.[13] This defense shows that Pletho had a clear predilection not only for Pythagorean ideas but also for Pythagorean methodology.

Although Pletho does not apply the label "Pythagorean" to himself, he makes it clear that Plato, his passion and the subject of his main interest, was bonded to Pythagoras: "That is why we adhere to the doctrine of Zoroaster, following Pythagoras and Plato. It is superior to others in accuracy … . Other doctrines vary in merit in so far as they depart from it."[14] It is clear that Pletho regards Pythagorean principles as fundamental to the history of civilization. Using the highly regarded *Golden Verses* of Pythagoras as the example of example, he quotes from them frequently in his major works.[15] Because it was personally copied by him, a manuscript of the *Golden Verses* that found its way into the collection of Cardinal Bessarion underlines his regard for the importance of this work.[16] Surely, Pletho was a Pythagorean.

The personal impact of Pletho on contemporary Italians may well have been limited because as a foreign intellectual he may have appeared to be far more interested in paganism than in Christianity. Yet his personal acquaintance with several Florentine intellectuals suggests that they were stimulated by him. Prominent among these was Paolo Toscanelli (1397–1482), whom Pletho mentions by name.[17] Surviving evidence from the hand of this famous Florentine cosmographer, mathematician, and physician, who was a friend of the architects Filippo Brunelleschi and Leon Battista Alberti, is insufficient to maintain he was a Pythagorean, notwithstanding the claim (which appears to be unfounded) by a modern American writer that Toscanelli was a vegetarian.[18] However, our knowledge about his life does suggest that he did have a frugal lifestyle and that he did have Pythagorean mathematical interests.[19] The temptation to think of Toscanelli as a Pythagorean is not lessened by the fact that, aside from Pletho, his friends included Nicholas Cusanus, Ficino, and Pico della Mirandola, all of whom will be described as Pythagoreans in the pages that follow. It is all the more captivating because in the following century the eminent painter Giorgio Vasari would represent Toscanelli wearing a turban.[20]

The influence of Pletho was felt, as discussed in Chapter 2, by a number of scholars of the next generation. Among these were Cardinal Bessarion, Cardinal Nicholas Cusanus, and the architect Alberti. The younger Marsilio Ficino would soon own copies of Pletho's major works, some of which he would translate from Greek into Latin.[21] It was certainly owing to Pletho's stimulation that a striking new ambition was born in the mind of his contemporary Cosimo de'Medici, the ruler of Florence at the time of his visit, to support Platonic studies in that city. Although Platonism in Florence would attach itself to Christianity, a goal perhaps too prosaic for Pletho whose exotic appeal was limited to his personal revival of ancient Antiquity, Pythagoreanism would always hover in the background, as we shall see when considering the work of Ficino.

Among his many priorities (his theological writings, his translations of Greek works into Latin, his campaigns to recover Constantinople from the Turks, and the literary academy he founded in Rome), Cardinal Bessarion demonstrated his admiration for Pythagorean principles in his participation in the learned discourses of his time. Although he did not agree with what he regarded as the "excessive religious piety" of those who focused on pagan rather than Christian ends, he vouched, in many ways, for Pletho and his advancement of Platonic philosophy.[22]

Following the death of his teacher Pletho (in about 1452), Bessarion wrote a letter, remarkable for that of a Christian prelate, to Pletho's two sons. It suggests that their father was Plato reincarnated. In accordance with Pythagorean doctrine on the ascent and descent of souls, the learned prelate explains, the soul of Plato was sent on earth to enter the body of Pletho. Urging Pletho's sons not to cry but to rejoice in anticipation of the heavenward journey of their father's soul, Bessarion describes his own joy in having known their father, who deserves to be, he fervently declares, the most honored man of Greece. Thus does the most erudite and conscientious of Catholic prelates express the inspiration and consolation he imagined from the Pythagorean belief in transmigration and its connection with the immortal life of the soul, even if he did not belong to a doctrinal cult.[23]

That Bessarion was knowledgeable about Pythagoreanism is evident from the library he assembled. Aside from being the greatest Greek library of his time, it contained the major ancient works on Pythagoreanism (see Appendix A). Significance must also be accorded to the fact that he collected the manuscripts of Pletho (which he bequeathed as part of his legacy to the Library of San Marco in Venice, today the major repository of Pletho's works). Surely this reflected his appreciation for the education he had received from Pletho, even though they did not always agree.[24] Perhaps more important, Cardinal Bessarion was practicing what Pythagoreanism preached in seeking unity and harmony in all aspects of religion and scholarship. The major theme, or philosophy, that animated virtually all the writings of this erudite humanist was the reconciliation of opposites.

This theme was exemplified in the harmonizing of Hellenism with Christianity, a highly original aim quite different from the goals of any of his predecessors, including his teacher Pletho, who, in his pro-pagan angst, ignored Christianity. This goal of reconciliation is noted in Bessarion's inspiration to unite the Greek Orthodox and Roman Catholic churches, or East and West.[25] The active and distinguished role he played to this end can be seen in the magisterial discourse he delivered to the Greek delegation at the Council in Florence. Dissension is bad, he proclaimed; union brings peace. There must, he emphasized, be concord among Christians: Contrarieties must meet in a middle ground to achieve harmony. This pioneering aim would be shared by his colleague Cusanus and with the future pope, Aeneas Sylvius Piccolomini.[26]

As an erudite prince of the Church, Bessarion sought another type of reconciliation, namely, that between Hermetic teachings and the Christian religion. In endorsing and promoting the printing of works such as those of Apuleius, which included several fundamental texts of Hermeticism, he sought to promote a harmonious relationship between these texts and Christian revelation. His colleague Cardinal Cusanus joined him in attesting the worthiness of this goal.[27] Thus were two of the most respected and learned men of the Church deeply engrossed in exploring the sublime idea of the integration of ancient texts and ancient magical traditions with the Christianity represented by their red hats.[28] This union allowed not only the philosophy but also the occult wisdom of ancient Greek Pythagorean tradition to become absorbed, and legitimized, by Christian Renaissance scholars who would make out of this combination of ancient elements a new and modern civilization.

Perhaps most important, this influential prelate stepped boldly and decisively into a controversy that was to become the most significant philosophical debate of the mid-fifteenth century. This concerned the relative importance of Plato, whose works – except for the *Timaeus* – were still little known, and Aristotle, whose works had been widely known throughout medieval times when Dante regarded him as "the" philosopher. The influence of the Greek émigrés to Italy, and especially of Pletho, had inspired a new and disproportionately greater interest in Plato over Aristotle than had been exhibited previously. This, in turn, had led to disputations among the learned, some of them acrid, as to which of the two was more important. The Aristotelians held that Aristotle had been accepted by Christians and that Plato was incompatible with Christianity, while the Platonists maintained that Plato should be revered by Christians because not only had he put forward a belief in one God but he had also anticipated, in his reverence for the triad, the mystery of the Trinity. These were indeed tumultuous times.

The wise Bessarion entered the fray by writing a long and learned treatise that, showing that both were not only compatible with but vital to Christianity, aimed to reconcile the two philosophers and their philosophies. His *In calumniatorem Platonis*, the most significant work of his later years, offered a reconciliation in the war between the Platonists and the Aristotelians. His visionary approach considered the major doctrines of each and advocated a middle ground that joined both. This work sought to establish equilibrium and harmony not only between Plato and Aristotle but also, in a more general way, between Greeks and Latins and between ancient wisdom and Christian thought. In suggesting that Plato had anticipated Christianity, Cardinal Bessarion was making Plato acceptable to Christians, for he regarded Pythagoras, Plato's teacher, as a prophet of Christianity. Pythagorean in its inspiration and methodology, this work would influence the enormous diffusion of interest in Plato that took place in late fifteenth-century Italy; its many subsequent printings in the next decades pay tribute to the significance of Bessarion's influence.[29]

The role played by this work in making Plato and his works better known in Italy gave center stage to Pythagoreanism. Plato was a Pythagorean, Bessarion exults, for not only did he receive an education in Pythagorean mores, but he adhered to Pythagorean precepts. In valuing secrecy and refraining from divulging esoteric doctrines to the public, Plato was concealing a sublime theology in his works. His use of language, metaphor, and enigma shows, Bessarion argues, how much Plato valued the oral tradition of Pythagoreanism and how much he respected the supreme mysteries of the philosophy from which he derived his own. The importance of Pythagorean mathematics to Plato was great, Bessarion observes. Plato's high esteem for number was especially evident in his regard for numbers 3 and 4. Grounded in Pythagoreanism, he believed in the importance of the doctrine of harmony that was obtained by reconciling contraries. His ideas were basically in agreement with those of Aristotle, who had been preferred by Christians in the past only because Plato had been insufficiently known to them. Bessarion was not the first to balance the two as contraries (Saint Augustine and Petrarch had contrasted them by citing Aristotle's earthly authority, *in naturalibus*, as opposed to the spiritual authority of Plato, *in divinis*).[30] Bessarion concludes that the ideas of Plato and Aristotle had common ground in the diffusion of Pythagoreanism because Plato was a follower of Pythagoras and Aristotle had been Plato's pupil.

The powerful urge of Cardinal Bessarion to reconcile opposites can perhaps best be illustrated by the intuition of Lorenzo Valla, a fellow humanist who was well acquainted with him. Lorenzo observed that in Constantinople Bessarion was "more Latin than the Greeks, while at Rome he was the most Greek of the Latins."[31] Not un-Pythagorean was the lifestyle of this "wise, ingenious, and divine man," Bessarion. As opposed to the demonstrative munificence practiced by most of his fellow cardinals, he was decidedly frugal. His contemporaries tell us that he avoided luxury and lived a life of extreme simplicity. The only necessity he regarded as important was to have sufficient funds to enable him to have manuscripts copied and to purchase books for the great personal library he would, eventually, bequeath to the city of Venice.[32] Bessarion was certainly, at heart, a Pythagorean.

INTERTWINED THREADS OF BALANCE, PERFECTION, AND FRUGALITY: GERMANY, FLORENCE, AND ROME

The German cardinal Cusanus shared, as suggested earlier, a wide range of interests with his Greek colleague in Italy, Cardinal Bessarion. In his early career, Cusanus was acquainted with Pletho, whom he had met in Constantinople, and involved with the Council of Florence. He also knew Toscanelli, whom he had met in Padua.[33] During this time he issued, in a work entitled *De concordantia catholica* (*Catholic Concordance*), an impassioned plea of his own for concord and the reconciliation of differences that had arisen within the Catholic Church.[34] Speaking as a canon lawyer, Cusanus makes numerous practical suggestions for replacing dissension with synthesis. Only in this way, he maintains, could the harmony necessary to unify opposing points of view be obtained. His hope for a harmonious universe reflects his familiarity with the Pythagorean-Platonic worldview expressed in Plato's *Timaeus* and in the works of Dionysius the Areopagite. The arguments Cusanus presented served well, also, to suggest how the rule of law might be applied to find common ground in the bigger picture of the struggle between Eastern and Western churches. He argues that a harmonious universe ruled by the moderation of a mutually agreed upon order would eliminate dissension.[35]

Before the Council of Florence was over, Cusanus was already at work on his most famous text, *De docta ignorantia* (*On Learned Ignorance*).[36] In this work, completed in 1440, he speaks primarily as a mathematician. It is here that his admiration for Pythagoras as the ultimate source of number was, as previously described in Chapter 2, most succinctly expressed. A considerable part of this text is devoted to translating that admiration into the practicalities of using number to denote symbological meaning. In praising indivisible oneness ("Maximality") as absolute and infinite for it absorbs all universal capabilities into one being and one end, Cusanus is conspicuously remembering ancient Pythagorean praises of the monad as the ultimate cause of all things. Texts such as those of Diogenes Laertius and Iamblichus, well known in Italy and certainly to him, affirmed the Pythagorean belief that the principle of all things is in the absolute and eternal monad, the stable basis of all number that, self-sufficient and everlasting, maintains and preserves everything in the universe in such a way that it coincides with God.[37]

Whereas the number 1, the monad, is union, the number 2, the dyad, Cusanus argues, is the cause of separation, duality, and dissension. Again, this echoes Pythagorean texts, for example:

> When the monad manifests unification, the dyad steals in and manifests separation. … The monad is the cause of things which are altogether similar and identical and stable. … the dyad is the cause of things which are altogether dissimilar.[38]

The number 3, Cusanus continues, is oneness just as oneness is threeness, an obvious reference to the Trinity, which, he asserts, is a triangle consisting of three equal right triangles.[39] The triad is beautiful beyond all numbers because it is the first to make actual the potentialities of the monad, including perfection and unification; it is represented by the plane figure of the triangle, as ancient Pythagoreans had argued:

> The triad ... is called perfect by some, because it is the first number to signify the totality – beginning, middle and end. ... Triangles both reflect and are the substantiation of being plane. ... The triad is the form of the completion of all things, and gives all things equality.[40]

While paying tribute to Pythagoras's favorite forms – the circle, as the most perfect surface figure because, consisting of an infinite line, it is infinite, and the sphere, as the most perfect corporeal figure because it is compounded from the circle – Cusanus extols the triangle as the most perfect rectilineal figure because, for him, it symbolizes the Trinity. Thus he is again "remembering" Pythagorean beliefs as, this time, he admits: The most perfect forms, he says, are the sphere, the circle, and the triangle, "that trine Oneness which Pythagoras, the first philosopher of all and the glory of Italy and of Greece, affirmed to be worthy of worship."[41]

Cusanus states his belief in the doctrine of the essentiality of all the numbers up to 10, a doctrine undeniably Pythagorean. Like Pythagoreans, he views the number 10 as the most powerful number and suggests, through a complicated argument, that its perfection can be illustrated by the pyramid. Citing Boethius as "the most learned of the Romans," and Pythagoras as the first to investigate truth "by means of numbers," Cusanus allies himself with both in asserting that number is basic to everything. Accordingly, "number encompasses all. ... Therefore number ... is present not only in quantity but also in all things. ... Perhaps for this reason Pythagoras deemed all things to be constituted and understood through the power of numbers." The Lord, he repeats, created all things in number, weight, and measure. Mathematics, he adds, "assists us very greatly in apprehending various divine truths."[42]

Among these truths was the action of God who, as an artisan, created the perfection of a universe governed by geometry and proportion. In describing God's sense of order, Cusanus's Pythagorean language is unmistakable: God created everything with arithmetic, geometry, and music. Through arithmetic God united things by number; through geometry he shaped them; and through music he gave them proportion. God so valued proportion that in establishing the interrelationship of parts he allowed for each part to have an immutable relation to the whole. Thus is everything unified in perfect harmony. The harmony of these elements will continue forever, Cusanus explains, unless it is destroyed; when the harmony is destroyed, all things will be dissolved. Pythagorean also is his terminology in referring to God as the coincidence of, or balance between, opposites. He suggests that God can be evoked by geometrical forms such as the triangle (God is the beginning, middle, and end, at the same time) and the circle (God is the center and circumference of everything).[43] In speaking (mathematically) of transforming a triangle into a circle he suggests that it can also be made into a sphere. This, he suggests, would be an example of perfect harmony.[44] (As will be seen later, such ideas were to fascinate certain Renaissance painters, in particular Leonardo da Vinci.) Indirectly, Cusanus admits to his Pythagoreanism:

> Did not Pythagoras … consider all investigation of truth to be by means of numbers? The Platonists … and Boethius affirmed that. … I concur with them and say that … the pathway for approaching divine matters is opened to us only through symbols. …[45]

A few years later, in a work entitled *Idiota de mente* (*The Layman on Mind*), Cusanus repeats himself: "Speaking symbolically, the wise said that number is the exemplar of things." Number has, he continues, a "marvellous nature."[46] Speaking again as a mathematician, he says: "I don't know whether I am a Pythagorean or something else … however I deem the Pythagoreans – who … philosophize about all things by means of number – to be serious and keen." They were, he explains, "speaking symbolically and plausibly about number that proceeds from the Divine Mind."[47]

Hardly had this work been completed than Cusanus embarked, this time speaking as a theologian, on a work that attempted to bring together the divisive elements of contemporary religion (Christians and Turks) into a peaceful harmony of common consent. Uninformed faith, he argues in *De pace fidei* (*On Religious Harmony*), produces conflict, whereas through the reconciliation of conflicts, true faith (or peace) emerges. In asserting that a multitude cannot exist without diversity, which leads it into conflict, he pleads for the harmony of concord. This harmony, he urges his readers to believe, leads to the singleness and unity of divine truth: There is no plurality in God, who is a unity. In a way, he is "remembering" the old Pythagorean devotion to Apollo, whose name means "without multiplicity."[48] These thoughts lead him to repeat what Pythagoras was believed to have said long before, that philosophy is the love of wisdom.[49]

In a later work completed in 1463, *De ludo globi* (*The Game of Spheres*), Cusanus speaks as a cosmographer. In this dialogue between himself and a succession of friends, he anticipates Copernicus by observing that the world is round and that as an infinitely turning sphere it takes its place in a universe whose center is the sun. He describes this arrangement in terms of a cosmic numerology in which the number 10, which for him signifies perfect order, has a special status.[50] The idea that the sun (or fire) was in the center of the universe was familiar through quotations from Philolaus (called "Philolaus the Pythagorean" by ancient sources well known by this time such as Nicomachus, Plutarch, and Boethius, as well as by contemporaries such as Salutati). Similarly, in Pythagorean doctrine, the number 10 was associated with the cosmic wholeness of the universe whose harmonious structure was based on number and proportion. (Because it symbolized the *tetraktys*, the triangular array of the first four numbers that, added together, produce 10, it was the most perfect of the perfect numbers.)[51] A plea for the universal symbolism of the monad closes the dialogue, as Cusanus speaks:

> [C]ommit to memory this specific point: there is but one true and precise and most sufficient form forming all things, shining forth variously in various signs, and variously forming, determining, or putting into act formable things.[52]

In organizing his text, while writing about the hunt for wisdom, Cusanus takes the symbolism of number into account. He identifies three regions of wisdom and ten fields most appropriate to the hunt for wisdom. Not surprising to a person familiar with Pythagoreanism, the tenth field represents (not unlike the *tetraktys*) absolute beauty and perfect order.[53] It is a tribute to Cusanus's Pythagoreanism.

The order Cusanus sought in the universe was reflected in his personal life, which might well be described as Pythagorean. He was noted for his extraordinary patience, honesty, and altruism, as well as for a special interest in helping others to achieve good health. An example of the latter is the hospital that Cusanus founded at Cues (or Cusa), his birthplace, and where his heart was eventually buried. Parenthetically, he is described by his biographers as one who characteristically and perhaps intentionally used enigmatic phraseology in his sermons.[54]

Bessarion and Cusanus counted, in their circle of colleagues, a number of mathematicians. Among these perhaps the most outstanding was Regiomontanus (1436–1476), a German whose real name was Joannes Müller and whose Italian name (conferred on him during his sojourn in Italy in the 1460s) was Giovanni di Monteregio.[55] Although his extant writings do not permit us to deduce that he was a Pythagorean, he did admire Pythagoras as the founder of mathematics and the inventor of the study of number; his fascination with the triangle, a subject on which he wrote an entire treatise, suggests an extension of this admiration.[56] Among other friends of the two cardinals were Toscanelli, who, as suggested earlier, may have been a Pythagorean, and the architect Alberti, who surely was one.[57]

Had Alberti not affirmed his accord with Pythagoras, as described in Chapter 2, describing his Pythagoreanism might have been a more challenging task. Because he did, his relationship with Pythagoreanism is invitingly provocative. Viewed against the background that he was, among other things, a learned humanist and mathematician, Alberti's familiarity with such works as those of

Nicomachus that purported to explain Pythagorean principles concerning number, harmony, and proportion can be assumed. He must have known well the long medieval tradition that claimed that harmony had been invented by Pythagoras and developed by Macrobius and Boethius.[58] In a youthful work that credited Pythagoras with excellence for his precepts, Alberti attempted to imitate them with some of his own.[59]

However, Alberti set out on a more significant new enterprise. He became the first Renaissance architect to theorize on how "modern" buildings should be designed and constructed. This subject dominates his major text, the *De re aedificatoria*, composed during the 1450s. Though it may appear to be contradictory, the modernity of his ideas was largely inspired by his reading the ancient writer Vitruvius. Knowledgeable in the technical advances of his time, Vitruvius was conditioned by his own admiration for the past, especially for Greek Antiquity and Pythagorean ideas.[60] The only surviving work on ancient architecture, Vitruvius's *De architectura* was divided into ten books. In this he was followed by other Pythagoreans after his time – such as Theon of Smyrna, Anatolius (a third-century bishop, probably the teacher of Iamblichus, and the author of *On the Decad*), Iamblichus, and Boethius.[61] As the number most highly regarded by Pythagoreans, the decad was the paradigm for the perfection in God's organization of the universe, which was fitted together with impeccable harmony as exemplified by the *tetraktys*. Imitating this order, books could be perfectly organized. A perfectionist if ever there was one, the modern Alberti, taking his cue from the past, divided his masterpiece too into ten books.

Describing the ideal education of the modern architect (as opposed to the practical preparation traditional architects received as skilled builders in his time), Alberti looks back to Vitruvius's recommendations respecting the education of the architect. In addition to history and philosophy, the architect must understand geometry, music, medicine, justice, and astronomy, qualities markedly similar to those cited by late-Antique writers on Pythagorean education.[62]

Alberti writes with admiration about values of frugality and parsimony, suggesting that, based on the dictum of Pythagoras, these values ought to be applied to domestic architecture as well as to religious architecture.[63] In the case of domestic architecture, he says he is following the moral values of the "most prudent and modest of our ancestors" who in their lifestyles practiced frugality. His expert from Antiquity on this subject is Plato. "Extravagance I detest," Alberti declares in one of his few emotional statements.[64] His anti-the-excesses-of-adornment position leads him to praise simplicity and plainness as beautiful and ennobling virtues that apply to architecture in general. Though it does not appear he knew the ancient Pythagorean basilica at Porta Maggiore in Rome (which had not yet been excavated), it is noteworthy that his taste for simplicity and purity in architecture corresponds with the restrained interior adornment of the only Pythagorean building from Antiquity known to us.[65]

Beauty, Alberti asserts, using by now familiar Pythagorean language, results when parts of the whole are consonant with each other according to number, form, and proportion. He discourses on each of these in turn. It is in his elaboration of the importance of number that Alberti's Pythagoreanism can best be felt.

Separating odd from even numbers (as Nicomachus had done), Alberti defines number 1 as perfection. It is the perfect cube ($1 \times 1 \times 1 = 1$) that, because its root is 1, is consecrated to God. He also describes the pervasiveness of number 3, the divinity of number 4, the comprehensive nature of number 5, the perfection of number 6, the heavenliness of number 7, the equilibrative powers of number 8, and the circulatory nature of number 9. He reserves his greatest praise for number 10, the most perfect number of all, he rhapsodizes, "because its square equals the cube of four consecutive numbers."[66] Though he does not mention Pythagoras by name in his discussion of number, Alberti appears to assume that his reader is aware of the underlying Pythagoreanism of his numerical associations, for it is this discussion that leads him to say, "I affirm *again* [italics mine] with Pythagoras. . . ."[67]

For Alberti, the epitome of architectural form is the ideal church, which is based on the purest of all forms, the circle. The circle and forms associated with it (the "Platonic" solids, which could all be fitted into the sphere) were organically beautiful, he argues, because the conformity of ratios and the correspondence of all parts could be realized in the centralized plan. In viewing a circle, the beholder's glance sweeps around instantaneously and unstoppably because this form, having no beginning and no end, is free of interruption or obstacle, a comment that brings to mind Pletho's description of the circle as an infinite line. Only in this ideal plan, suitable for the church as the noblest ornament of a city, does a building become perfect, that is, absolute and immutable while at the same time static and lucid. This must be emphasized by standing the church on elevated ground, surrounded by beautiful clear air and isolated from the surrounding daily life by a large pedestal that is the basic substructure for the large central dome that crowns the building and provides its cosmic significance.

Alberti's discussion of proportion, which follows that of form, is unmistakably Pythagorean: In the balancing of opposites, it is important to find the mean. The mean may be found arithmetically, geometrically, or musically. Numbers define it perfectly and thereby establish the proportions. In the rational integration of all carefully measured parts of the building, each part will have its fixed size and shape so that nothing can be added or subtracted without destroying the whole. Together numbers, form, and proportion constitute a harmonic relationship that echoes the harmony of the universe. To this, Alberti stresses, the architect must be sensitive.[68] His discussion of *concinnitas* (concinnity), or harmony, as an ordered arrangement similar to a concord of sounds locked together by the relationship expressed between consonant strings, is based on ancient descriptions of harmony as the greatest discovery of Pythagoras.[69] Thus was Alberti, taking his cue from the past, proposing something very modern: the first Renaissance canon of proportion for architecture. He proposed similar canons of order for sculpture and painting, most notably, a system of artificial perspective that would relate all parts of the composition, by means of coordinates, to a central point.[70] In all cases, these canons were based on geometry – the square, the cube, the triangle, and the pyramid.

Although no document tells us that Pope Sixtus IV was a Pythagorean, his commission in the 1470s to the humanist Lilio Tifernate to translate the complete works of Philo of Alexandria from Greek into Latin made an enormous contribution to the development of Pythagoreanism in the second half of the fifteenth century and the first half of the sixteenth. A first-century Jewish Greek author, Philo was well known as a Pythagorean in late Antiquity, when he was called "Philo the Pythagorean." His attention to the symbolism of number was widely acknowledged. Among the works by Philo that were translated for Sixtus IV was his monumental *Life of Moses*, a work that strongly influenced the Pope in planning the decoration of the walls of the Sistine Chapel.[71] The resulting renewed interest in Moses would pave the way for successive generations of humanists to believe what older Antique authors had suggested long before – that Pythagoras had studied at the feet of Moses. As will be discussed in the next chapter, the inspiration for the commissioning of this cannon shot so important for Renaissance Pythagoreanism most likely came from the librarian of Sixtus IV, Platina, who may have been a Pythagorean.

Early fifteenth-century humanists knew a great deal about the teachings of Pythagoras not only from their medieval inheritance but also from the influx of new information that came to them directly from Antiquity. Much of this new information came from followers of Pythagoras. In extracting lessons from their admired works, which they were now able to read in the original, Italian humanists began to imitate the various paths of thought and behavior suggested by ancient classical authority. In so doing, they created a new worldview that from the beginning put a high value on moral and intellectual principles believed to have been taught by Pythagoras himself. Thus did humanist learning exert a deep and fruitful influence on areas that included moral behavior and the place of humankind in the universe.

Largely enabled through the impact of the teachings of Greek émigrés who arrived in Italy early in the century, the Platonist revival that took place in the first part of the fifteenth century provided the gift of an extraordinary legacy to the Italians. The long history of Pythagoreanism in Antiquity was now studied in scholarly ways that accelerated its importance to the point that it exerted a marked influence on intellectual and educational discourse. Though the center of this discourse was in Italy, some leaders of the Pythagorean group that gathered there came from other countries, notably Greece and Germany.

Fundamental to the first appreciation of Pythagorean ideas in the early Renaissance was the Chancellor of Florence himself, Coluccio Salutati. Inheriting Petrarch's admiration for Pythagorean authority, Salutati appreciated the long line of thinkers who had followed the doctrines of Pythagoras to his day. His enlightened rule of Florence fulfilled the Pythagorean ideal that he preached – making sound moral choices and promoting social justice.

As a Greek intellectual on Italian soil, Gemistus Pletho emphasized the multifaceted significance of Pythagoras's teachings for Plato, who might, because of his dependence on Pythagoras, who was already admired by Christians, be similarly admired by Christians. Pletho's arrival in Florence provided a spirited impetus to his Italian contemporaries to engage in philosophical, theological, and cosmological speculation that was rooted in the importance of Pythagorean doctrines. His masterpiece, a treatise on law, pointed the ways in which the vast *harmonia* of the universe might be reflected in the well-ordered and morally responsible lives of his readers.

As princes of the church, the Greek Bessarion and the German Cusanus held in common a Pythagorean approach. They both had great respect for the symbology of number, and they both saw God as the great balancer of opposites. Bessarion's letter to the sons of Pletho showed his sensitivity to Pythagoreanism, while Cusanus, who thought he might be a Pythagorean, proclaimed a Pythagorean mystery in declaring that the perfection of the number 10 is illustrated in the pyramid. He also praised the ideality and integrity of the triangle, the circle, and the sphere.[72] Their contemporary, Alberti, openly suggested he was a Pythagorean. Through him, the ancient ideas of Vitruvius, a Pythagorean of Antiquity, provided an avenue to modernize architecture by giving it a language of its own.

Bessarion, Cusanus, and Alberti all appear to have expressed their Pythagoreanism in practicing frugality and social responsibility, as well as in intellectually showing their intense respect for symmetry, measure, and proportion. They all aimed at the achievement of harmony, according to which all elements in matters of world order, spiritual relations, and individual creations could be balanced or reconciled. Arranging numbers in geometrical shapes and finding symbolic value in doing so, they established that the same God who had created a perfect universe, and who governed by geometry and proportion, could also inspire the ultimate creation of order. In this vast body of learning and practical applications, the circle and forms associated with it began to reign supreme because, reflecting the order of the cosmos, they exemplified the harmony of concord. That quest for harmony was to result, as we shall see in considering the visual arts, in the creation of a "purer form, more beautiful and more divine," which reflected the perfect knowledge of "heavenly matters" attributed to Pythagoras by his followers in Antiquity.[73]

FIVE:

THE STRENGTHENING AND DEEPENING OF PYTHAGOREANISM IN THE LATER FIFTEENTH CENTURY

The investigation of "heavenly matters" was a primary concern of Marsilio Ficino, for whom philosophy and theology were one and the same thing. As a devout Christian and ordained priest, this influential Florentine philosopher openly proclaimed himself, as we saw in Chapter 2, to be a follower of Pythagoras.[1] Ficino's life and works offer a complex of supporting documents concerning his Pythagoreanism. Much is known about his personal life, from the testimony of his own letters and from the biography of a contemporary written by Giovanni Corsi in 1506, seven years after his death.[2] Ficino's original texts also reveal a great deal about his Pythagorean beliefs. These would, through their dissemination and influence, stimulate many of his contemporaries and descendants in Italy and north of the Alps.

FICINO'S PYTHAGOREANISM AND HIS PROSELYTIZING

The letters of Ficino aroused great interest in their time, primarily because his correspondents were, for the most part, famous and influential statesmen, prelates, and noted humanists, such as Lorenzo de'Medici, Cardinal Bessarion, and Angelo Poliziano. Early on, his friends and acquaintances learned about his abiding belief that the sun represented the unity of God as the unity of unities (the monad). Later letters show that, if anything, this belief intensified as Ficino matured. He held up harmony as the most important concord of concords, orchestrated by a monadic God (the "supercelestial One") who, as the sun, "set his tabernacle in the sun."[3]

His descriptions of Plato's underground cave, from which men could emerge into the dazzling light of the sun, suggest the oldest surviving Pythagorean temple in Rome (mentioned earlier in the introduction and in Chapter 2, as having not yet been excavated in his time), which was lit by a shaft of sunlight penetrating into its underground space. The recipients of his letters learned of his approbation for the harmony of earthly law, which, emanating from divine law, reflects the marvelous harmony of the divine spheres; they also learned of his trust in the power of harmony to soothe the soul, as well as of his respect for Pythagorean enigma.[4]

Ficino's letters assert frequently his conviction of the necessity to be frugal, to avoid excess, and to share all things in common: "For us [speaking of himself] as for the Pythagoreans, all things are held in common: what I wish, all wish; what everyone desires, I desire."[5] He makes clear his personal opposition to material abundance, which he characterizes as "shackles." He finds many opportunities to remind his correspondents of his own lifestyle, which he describes as governed by poverty, modesty, and humility – for example: "I am certainly content with few possessions, even though I am often held in contempt by many."[6]

In a letter to Poliziano, Ficino clearly lays out his Pythagorean interests. The list he provides of his translations and commentaries on ancient Pythagorean texts includes such titles as "Four Books from Iamblichus' *On the Pythagoreans*" (a work now believed to be lost); the "Mathematics" of Theon of Smyrna; the "Platonic Definitions" of Speusippus; the *Golden Verses* of Pythagoras; the *Symbola* of Pythagoras; and Porphyry's *On Abstinence from Killing Animals*.[7] Other works he lists, though ostensibly about Plato, are largely Pythagorean in their subject matter (e.g., "Magnanimity, Happiness, Justice, Divine Frenzy" and "Theology on the Immortality of Souls," otherwise known as his *Platonic Theology*, and *De numero fatali* or *On the Fatal Number in Plato's Republic*). Ficino also translated, as mentioned in Chapter 2, the corpus of Hermetic texts, including the *Pimander* and *The Mysteries of Egypt*, occult works that invoke the name of Pythagoras. In his commentaries to these texts he rhapsodized that a "wonderful" system of philosophy had been formulated by Pythagoras, an unimpeachable ancient theologian, and his followers the great philosopher-prophets Philolaus and Plato.[8] Accordingly, Ficino's letters extend particular praise for the well-known Pythagorean concepts of proportion, number, measure, and the balancing of contraries. Ficino also advocates practicing the rule of silence.[9]

In his letters, Ficino adulates Pythagorean expertise in medicine and music. Referring to Pythagoras's fame for calming the violent agitation of untamed youths through music, he advises Lorenzo de'Medici to turn to Apollo for assistance in calming the frenzied behavior of his subjects. Plato, he says, understood from Pythagoras the benefits of solemn and calming music for body and soul. Ficino assures his reader that temperate behavior can be achieved and regulated by the curative benefits of Apollo's lyre, an instrument Pythagoras was believed to have played. The authority of the lyre is praised in many of his letters, perhaps most poignantly in a poem he included in a letter to the Venetian nobleman Bernardo Bembo in which he says he himself played and sang to this instrument. The lyre, Ficino says, symbolizes the music of the spheres. He explains that its seven strings represent not only the divinity of music but also the salvation of humankind. Divine love, as love between creatures, is also symbolized by the lyre: "Even strings seem to respond to strings that are similarly tuned, and one lyre resounds in answer to another."[10]

To Ficino, harmony was of special importance. Of this, the universe was a perfect example. God's ingenious arrangement of the spheres so that their movements were perfectly regulated in relation to one another was, Ficino tells us, the discovery of Pythagoras.[11] This perfect organization depends, he explains, on proportion and number. The importance of number is exemplified in his discussion of Plato's birth date in a letter to a fellow philosopher. Because Plato was born on the seventh of the month and died on his own birthday (also the birthday of Apollo, the god of Pythagoras), the Magi reckoned that he lived a special life, a fact not diminished by his having lived to be eighty-one, which, as Ficino carefully points out, is thus, as the product of 9 x 9, a "most" perfect number.[12]

Ficino's letters provide ample evidence of his special interest in the healing arts and magic. Although he did not personally enjoy good health, Ficino engaged in healing his sick friends. He claims that the "Academy" (no doubt his private studio) was actively engaged in providing ointments and poultices to soothe pain. Speaking of the system whereby he prescribed medicine "which follows Platonic medicine," he says: "Indeed, I use this myself more than anything else, and I make it available to all who are dear to me." He describes his models as Pythagoreans who, taking their cue from Apollo, the "source" of medicine, were masters in the art of healing through chants and diet, as well as in calming with lyre and song.[13]

In another letter Ficino describes his love of justice and urges brotherly love, humility, and emotional restraint. Still others present views on how the immortal soul is fed by virtue. Admonishing one of his readers to "Do your utmost to live in harmony," Ficino urges him to adopt a Pythagorean way of life.[14] Entreating others to follow Pythagorean tenets, he puts forward his own example while using the art of persuasion. Living a Pythagorean life is not, he elucidates, incompatible with Christianity. Conflating Christ with Pythagoras, he describes the food provided by Christ at the wedding dinner at Cana and at the Last Supper as made up of bread and fish; these meals were, he imagines, accompanied by melodious sounds. He adds that he abhors extravagant meaty banquets. Admitting to his love of good wine, he finds many occasions to describe the virtues of vegetarianism, for example: "[W]e do not want by any means to lack the Pythagorean fruits, cabbages and apples, for there is no easier nor healthier table than that."[15]

Writing to the Archbishop of Amalfi, Ficino affirms his belief that a Christian prelate can also be a Pythagorean. After describing what he says is the Pythagorean view that Plato was a follower of Moses, he explains: "Why all these words, Revered Father? They are for you to read … so [you] may now cease to be surprised that, although Marsilio is a priest, he has such frequent recourse to philosophy." His advice to a fellow philosopher is clear: "Imitate then, as you have so begun, Pythagoras. … persevere in your conduct."[16]

Corsi's *Life of Marsilio Ficino* is a valuable document for it corroborates much of the information contained in Ficino's letters. As one who knew his subject only by reputation, Corsi confirms the Pythagorean character of Ficino's personal lifestyle and interests. He cites Ficino's dedication as a practitioner of the healing arts, mentioning that he cured his friends free of charge. Corsi tells us that Ficino was reputed to possess divine skill in the practice of magic (a skill not unlike that reputedly associated with Pythagoras in Antiquity). He also cites Ficino's reputation for making great efforts to reconcile feuding friends and underlines Ficino's aversion to all extravagance, sensual pleasures, and material wealth.[17]

A longer biography of Ficino, written some years later by an author thought to be Piero Caponsacchi, stresses the pleasure Ficino took in playing the seven-stringed lyre and promulgating the doctrines of Pythagoras, including the practices of simplicity, vegetarianism, and healing. In its general content, this biography essentially confirms the information provided in Corsi's biography, which in turn corroborates that provided by Ficino himself.[18]

Many of Ficino's Pythagorean views are laid out in his text on lifestyle and health, *De vita*. Immensely popular during the Renaissance, this work stresses the importance of harmony and concord throughout the universe and their effects on the well-being of humans, especially scholars (Ficino's primary audience). His approach, enigmatic throughout, incorporates and blends together Christian ideas respecting the Trinity and Pythagorean notions of the triplicity of the universe (supercelestial, celestial, and sublunar). The fact that this text is divided into three books appears to be no accident but, rather, a tribute to the symbolism of the triangular number 3.

On the authority of "the Pythagoreans," especially Plotinus and Porphyry (famous Pythagorean-vegetarians of Antiquity), this text recommends, as do Ficino's letters, abstaining from meat as a primary avenue to achieving good health. Human beings, Ficino stresses repeatedly, lived well when, before the Great Flood, they did not eat animals; so they should expect to live long lives without having to harm animals.[19] Accordingly, Ficino's manual recommends the preparation of food made from plants. It also suggests other practices that promote good health. One of these is chanting songs whose tones are coordinated to the music of the spheres, the influences of the stars, and other cosmographical emanations. Such songs, he assures us, can cure certain diseases, mental and physical, as the Pythagoreans and Platonists so well understood.[20] Ficino's hands–on approach to helping his fellow intellectuals to achieve good health is clear:

> Hail, intellectual guest! Hail to you too, whosoever you are who
> approaches our threshold desiring health.… I will give you, please God,

the health I promised you. … The shop of your friend Marsilio is a bit larger than what you see here, enclosed only in those boundaries. … The whole forms an epitome of Medicine which will assist your life as much as possible, that it may be both healthy and long; and it employs … the resources of doctors, aided by the heavens.[21]

Together with his assistants, the Muses, this text reminds its readers, Apollo is the ultimate guide in matters of health. In his honor, Ficino recommends the playing of the seven-stringed lyre in the morning while facing the rising sun; he also advocates hearing, smelling, and imagining solarian things: "Move among solarian men and plants and touch laurel constantly."[22] He recommends wearing a special gem that he associates with Apollo on a golden necklace hung from the neck by saffron-colored threads. The Magi too had practiced magic, he reminds us, for they brought frankincense to the sun king, Christ. For Ficino practical (or "white") magic was primarily based on numbers such as 4 (referring to the four elements and the four "qualities"), a number that helps us to attract good celestial influences in daily life. Taking into account the divine nature of the number 7 and its relation to the seven planets, he offers seven steps that evade disorder and lead to a "heavenly" life.[23] His strong interest in the number that symbolizes the Pythagorean music of the spheres is corroborated in his own commentary on the work of Macrobius, a late-Antique author who studied the music of the spheres and, specifically, the role of number.[24]

Ficino's attachment to number is nowhere more evident than in his *Commentary on Plato's Symposium*. This work celebrates the symbolism of the number 7, a symbolism, he reminds us, that is conveyed in the fact that Plato both was born and died on the seventh of November. In urging Lorenzo de'Medici to honor this day, Ficino invokes the importance of the components of the number 7, the number dedicated to Apollo, for Pythagoreans: Number 3, referring to three worlds in one, is the measure of all things, while number 4, which governs all divine matters, leads to the universal number ($1 + 2 + 3 + 4 = 10$).[25] Not surprisingly, this text contains seven chapters. In *De amore* (*About Love*), a commentary on Plato, Ficino reasserts his belief in the symbolism of number by writing that God governs all things by threes. Modern scholarship has established the importance of number, especially the triad, for Ficino.[26] In his other works, particularly those that discuss music, Ficino reminds us of the primacy of the *tetraktys*, that is, of the universality of the number 10, which takes into account the principles of musical harmony.[27]

Ficino's indebtedness to Pythagoreanism is reflected in the commentaries he wrote on the various Pythagorean texts he translated. Most significant of these, perhaps, is one on a work thought at the time to be part of Iamblichus's *Secta pythagorica* (*The Pythagorean Way of Life*), a work now lost. Ficino's text rapturously endorses Pythagorean doctrines, including the contemplation of divine things, the significance of mathematics for understanding divinity and harmony, the importance of secrecy and enigma, and the respect due the rising sun.[28] Similar Pythagorean teachings are described in his commentary on a text on Pythagorean symbols, as well as in one on the *Golden Verses* of Pythagoras.[29] The intensity of his interests in Pythagoreanism is evident in his translations of the works of Plotinus, an important Pythagorean of Antiquity (whom Reuchlin would soon after identify as "the distinguished Pythagorean"), as well as in the fact that his library contained works by William of Conches, a notable Pythagorean of medieval France.[30]

The belief that both Moses and Pythagoras had received their educations in Egypt provided a reason for Ficino to link them and therefore to "prove" the affinity of Mosaic and Christian doctrines through the mission of Pythagoras, who had impeccable credentials as a religious philosopher. (In the fifteenth century, Egypt was regarded as the land of ancient wisdom and the birthplace of study in mathematics, law, medicine, and astrology.)[31] Because Pythagoras had received his instruction from Moses, Ficino tells us, Plato was inspired to pave the way for reconciling Christian theology with Mosaic truth.[32] Plato's belief in the immortality of the soul was another doctrine that, central to the Pythagorean legacy, anticipated Christianity. Ficino saw to it that this doctrine above all played to his audience so as to encourage Plato's standing with Christians.

The soul's immortality constitutes the backbone of Ficino's greatest work and masterpiece, the *Platonic Theology*. In constructing his argument, he equates Pythagorean and Platonic views of the soul.[33] The immortal soul, discovered by Pythagoras and described by Plato, is, he rationalizes, a "spiritual sphere," for it moves in an unending circular manner that continuously renews itself.[34] Plato's doctrine of the balancing of contraries was also, he tells us, derived from Pythagorean thought: Contraries form harmonious beauty when they are balanced. As the universal moderator who reconciles contraries, God can be described, we are told, in geometrical terms. He is a circle that is without beginning and end and is never at rest. It is he who set the sphere of the universe in motion. Such concepts cannot but remind us of the importance of the circle and the sphere for Pythagoreans.[35]

Ficino is also attracted to the triangle, a geometrical form traditionally associated with Pythagoras, who was believed to favor triads in general. Ficino asserts that Pythagoreans highly regarded triangles because this form suggests the wide world of souls, with Unity (or Apollo) presiding at the apex. He also affirms, in an obvious reference to the triangle, that God's governance is symbolized by the number 3 because all its parts are equal.[36]

The Platonic view of the triangle, Ficino suggests, embodies all triangles. Triangles were important to Platonic thought, we learn, especially the isosceles (which has two equal sides), because it was governed by balanced measurements, and the equilateral, because it inspired the greatest triangle of all, the Trinity.

In Platonic thought, he tells us, the right-angled triangle was regarded as the "beautiful" triangle.[37]

Ficino's view of the Pythagorean tradition is deeply embedded in his presentation of the doctrines of his hero, Plato. The profound impact that Pythagoreanism had on Plato, Ficino tells his readers in the *Platonic Theology*, is exemplified by Plato's teachings on mathematics. Like the Pythagoreans, he considered number to be the guiding principle of the universe.[38] Plato identified a monadic God who was the "One," a doctrine he learned from his Pythagorean teachers who associated it with Apollo. This principle, Ficino tells us, was passed on to Christian theologians. Plato's doctrine of three primordial causes was based on the Pythagorean systematization of the world that anticipated the doctrine of the Trinity, a doctrine that would be taken up and perfected on behalf of Christianity by Saint Augustine. In explaining the theological importance of the four elements that constitute the basis of the universe Plato was also basing his idea, we are told, on Pythagorean doctrine. The number 4 (which leads to the *tetraktys*, or the universe) is reflected in the fourfold fountain invigorated by four streams that is, according to Ficino, the soul.[39]

One of Plato's most striking formulations, Ficino tells us, was his description of God as the architect of the universe. This concept, he says, was gleaned by Plato from the Pythagorean Parmenides and is exemplified in the product of God's masterpiece, the music made by the revolving planets.[40] The celestial harmony made by the music of the spheres enables the soul, or the spirit, to contact the divine. Most important for Plato's concept of the universe was the great source of light, the sun, which Ficino, like Pythagoras, venerated.[41] A text by Ficino entitled *Librum de Sole* (*Book about the Sun*), opens with a reference to the Pythagorean notion that the sun is the light of God that inspires the mind.[42] He does not hesitate to credit Plato's Pythagorean inspiration for such doctrines:

> [J]ust as Plato includes in the *Parmenides*, to the extent that he can, all the classes of things divine, so he embraces in the *Timaeus* everything in the realm of nature; and in each dialogue he is principally a Pythagorean speaking a Pythagorean part.[43]

Ficino's search of the past led to a bold modernization of the old idea that Plato was a Pythagorean. Though his primary subject is Plato and though he consults other ancient authorities, it is, Ficino holds, the followers of Pythagoras, the early Pythagoreans, who paved the way for Plato, who in turn paved the way for Christianity. Thus did Ficino – as an influential intellectual whose works interlaced Pythagorean cosmology, philosophy, numerology, medicine, music, and magic with Christian theology, and as a canon of the Cathedral of Florence whose sermons were popular and authoritative – ingeniously create an avenue to induce his fellow Christians to accept Plato.

Whether Lorenzo de'Medici ever attended any of the lyre recitals given by Ficino in which Ficino is reputed to have achieved trancelike, enraptured states, we may never know. Although because of his abuse of power and luxurious lifestyle, Lorenzo can hardly be considered to have been a Pythagorean, Ficino undoubtedly tried to make him one. A poem of Lorenzo's, echoing Ficino's view of God as the great architect of a universe based on symmetry and the four elements, suggests that he might have taken a fashionable dip into the waters of Ficino's brand of Pythagoreanism. It describes the ascent of his soul toward the supreme good of the sun.[44] Perhaps, because the name Lorenzo is derived from *laurus*, the Latin for laurel, and he shared this emblem with the god of Pythagoras, Lorenzo was drawn to the idea that Apollo was an appropriate "guardian" for him (as indubitably advocated by Ficino).[45]

PICO'S VERSION OF PYTHAGOREANISM

Among the first to feel the influence of Ficino and the attraction of his beliefs was the young Pico della Mirandola, who arrived in Florence in the mid-1480s. Though he would spend most of his brief, albeit tumultuous, life there, it was shortly afterwards in Rome that he first showed off his intense Pythagorean inclinations, doubtless inspired by some of the books he was beginning to collect for his fabulous library (described in Appendix A), in an enthusiastic display of his already extraordinary learning.

In his *Oration*, which he prepared for delivery in Rome in 1486, Pico repeatedly expresses his admiration for a variety of Pythagorean doctrines. Advocating poverty and frugality, he advises his hearers that it is only by spurning earthly goods that one can reach the divine. Just as Plato had suggested in the *Timaeus* and as Ficino was currently describing, God was for Pico a perfect monadic being who, as a divine craftsman or master builder, had designed an impeccably functioning universe. Like Plato and Ficino, Pico also praises the light of the sun, because it enables immortal souls to achieve the same "knowledge of divine things" that so captivated Ficino. This concept was, for Pico, the most worthy ambition of humankind; an important part of his own vision, it was one to which he would frequently return.[46] Relying on Empedocles, Pico explains that the dual nature of the soul is the cause of all discord and can be "cured" only by the light of monadic theology that, alone, can reconcile its opposing (heavenly and earthly) tendencies. Speaking of concord, he praises the Pythagorean love of peace and friendship, using words paraphrased from Iamblichus's biography of Pythagoras.[47] Pico illustrates the enormous prestige of the more traditional Pythagorean doctrines by citing their influence not only on Christians but also on Muslims, including, he claims, on Mohammed himself.[48]

Among the most sacred characters in his *Oration* are Moses, the great teacher of Pythagoras; Apollo, the great illuminator; and Pythagoras himself.[49] Pythagoras's doctrines, Pico explains, require that we practice diligence, that we contemplate the omnipotence of the sun who is God, that we practice continence, and that we achieve harmony in our lives. Pico puts his stamp of approval on these doctrines by calling them "compelling" and "inspiring." Paying his respects to geometry, he observes that the triangle is an important symbol of harmony, for it is so harmonious that it obliterates discord. He would later continue this line of thought in describing the universe as a sphere and God, heaven, and the soul as circles.[50]

Maintaining the "oneness" of philosophy, Pico argues for concord throughout his *Oration*. The reconciliation of Platonists and Aristotelians is, he maintains, a necessity for intellectual unity; it leads to the discovery of divine truth. Pico expresses his esteem for the "ancient" Pythagorean system of "philosophizing through numbers." Pythagoras's secret doctrine of number is not only sacred but even, he fantasizes, sublime.[51] Pico speaks of the threefold character of philosophy, the four rivers of God, and the seven lights of Moses. Pointing to the exemplary role of Salmoxis, the slave of Pythagoras who taught his master's doctrine, Pico advocates divine magic as medicine for the soul. For him the mysticism of number was supernatural, for it connected his world with the world of classical and Hebraic Antiquity. His greatest admiration is, however, reserved for the concept of enigma and mystery. The contemplation of these, he asserts, brings us from darkness (the cave concept of Plato's *Timaeus*) into light (the sun, as the wisdom and knowledge of God).[52]

Naming those who most inspired his thoughts for the *Oration*, Pico includes Empedocles, Plato, Boethius, Plotinus, Iamblichus, Porphyry, Democritus, Dionysius the Areopagite, and Saint Augustine – all Pythagoreans. He was also, he says, impressed with Kabbalistic texts, as well as with the works of Philo (whose complete Greek works elucidating among other things Pythagorean number symbolism had just been translated, as noted in Chapter 4, into Latin). Through these works the holy teachings of Pythagoras were revealed, Pico rejoices, and bequeathed to Christians in the form of concepts such as that of the Trinity.[53]

In the publication of the *900 Theses* that accompanied his *Oration*, Pico offers written support for his ideas. His list of what were to him the most significant contributions of the various ancient philosophers clearly reveals his Pythagorean beliefs. Of these, the idea of concord and harmony – an oft-repeated goal in Pico's writings – is by far the most important. Associated with Pythagoreanism since Antiquity, this aim meant, for Pico, bringing together and reconciling Greek philosophy with Hebraic and Arabic written traditions to form a single and fundamental basis for Christianity. This he supports with an abundance of propositions borrowed from ancient Pythagorean authorities, Hermes Trismegistus, and the Kabbalah. Pico's Pythagoreanism is encapsulated in his advice to those who wish to discover the concord inherent in all philosophical works: Master number symbolism, enigma, and secrecy.[54]

Perhaps the most critical Pythagorean characteristic of the theses presented in this work is their dependence on the application of numerical symbolism. Repeatedly, Pico invokes the authority of Pythagoras in maintaining that the universe is organized according to number. "The number of Orphic hymns is the same as the number with which the threefold god created the world, calculated according to the method of the Pythagorean quaternarius [*tetraktys*]," he declares.[55] He invokes reverence for the mystical significance of the triangle, for its shape symbolizes the unity of the Trinity and advocates triplicity in its various forms. One of these is what he enigmatically calls "Pythagoras's threefold proportion," and defines as mathematical, geometric, and harmonic. A section on Proclus (a Pythagorean of late Antiquity) speaks again and again of the importance of triads. "Perfect" numbers like 6, 10, 28, and 40 (which contains the essential numerical components of the *tetraktys*, 4 x 10) are special, as are the "divine" numbers 3 and 7. The Kabbalah, he notes, is an important source for Christians because of its symbolic use of number. Concerning it, he offers several mysterious observations, among which is the claim that no science offers as great assurance of the divinity of Christ as do mysticism and the Kabbalah.[56] Defending this point of view, he adds: "What the Cabalists say, that the light restored in the seventh shines more than the light left behind, miraculously agrees with Pythagorean arithmetic."[57] Thus does Pico use number in symbolical ways that attend to his mystical goals.

Moreover, as modern scholarship has pointed out, the structure of the *900 Theses* was precisely thought out so as to conform with Pico's individualistic interpretation of how Pythagorean number symbolism might be applied to suggest secret pathways that lead to the discovery of truth.[58] Truth is proved by numerological patterns. For example, Pico offers seventy-two (the number of letters in one of the most recondite Kabbalistic names for God) explanations that describe the Kabbalah. The overall number of nine hundred theses was selected, he confesses, because it was of mystical value in his personal doctrine of number. He reassures us: "If my doctrine of numbers is correct, this [speaking of the number 900] is the symbol of the excited soul."[59]

Another noteworthy aspect of the *900 Theses* is the undercurrent of enigma and secrecy that protect divine mysteries from being "fully revealed." Almost invariably, Pico's statements refer to cosmic principles that are useful in decoding mysterious sacred texts. For example, he uses terms like "the creative mind," "the angelic mind," "the world soul," and the "intellectual nature of the soul." Speaking of the place of Orphic Hymns in his worldview, he says, "Anyone who does not know how to intellectualize sensible properties perfectly through the method of secret analogizing understands nothing."[60] By speaking this slippery language Pico attempts to unite technical terms from a wide range of religious traditions, suggesting that they inevitably lead to concord and harmony. Not only was Pico's dramatic Pythagorean-inspired defense against all comers at Rome brilliant and original, it made him instantly famous and, notwithstanding his noble birth and youthful attractiveness, infamous.

Written in the following year (1487), Pico's *Apologia* was designed to dispel the theological worries that his nine hundred theses had caused for papal authorities. Here Pico sums up his personal philosophy: He has tried, he explains, to search out the important ancient philosophies – of Hermes Trismegistus, the Chaldeans, and Pythagoras – and to reassemble them, uniting them with the secret mysteries of the Jews. Clearly, it was not only unifying these philosophies that mattered to him but, as well, arranging their doctrines in an order that demonstrated their contributions to Christianity. This desire to put order in the theological world is not dissimilar to the Pythagorean longing to put order in the universe.

In the *Heptaplus*, whose main concern is the relation of Kabbalistic mysticism to Christianity, Pico underscores the importance of ancient Pythagorean doctrines for the Kabbalah and Christianity.[61] This work is organized into seven books, each of which consists of seven chapters that, Pico assures us, were specifically planned around the symbolism of the number 7.[62] As he knew from Nicomachus, Iamblichus, Philo, and other Pythagoreans of Antiquity, the heptad was not only God's instrument for the creation of the universe. It was also the number of primary concord, because it is the sum of 3 (the first perfect number, for it signifies beginning, middle, and end) and 4 (the basic number of the *tetraktys*): $4 + 3 = 7$. In addition, he considered 7 the number of divine concord, because it refers to the number of celestial bodies and the seven strings of the lyre that symbolize the music of the spheres.[63] No doubt, Pico was following the example of Pythagorean writers of the past, such as the ancient Roman Marcus Varro and the medieval philosopher Thierry of Chartres, in organizing his text around the symbolism of this important, and divine, number.[64]

Further pursuing the symbolism of number, Pico describes 3 "worlds" of the universe (angelic, celestial, and corruptible or earthly), 4 worlds of humankind, 10 spheres of the heavens, 9 choirs of angels, 7 planets, and 7 lights, all brought to light by Pythagoreans, he says. He pays particular attention to other Pythagorean discoveries, such as the "fullness" of the number 4, which leads to the *tetraktys* and (enigmatically, perhaps) to the indivisible nature of the Trinity. Summarizing his discussion of number, he says, "Let us apply these notions to divine things, after the Pythagorean custom."[65]

Using the example of Moses, Pico reaffirms his previous exaltation of Pythagorean secrecy and enigma. Moses, he explains, "did not even reveal everything" to his followers, "since they were not fit for everything, and there were many things which they could not endure until the coming of the spirit taught them all truth." It was only after he received the light of the divine sun, Pico says, that Moses knew wisdom, but Moses, too, kept the light screened from those who were not initiated.[66] Pythagoreans saw the sun as the elemental fire of the universe, Pico reports, and it is the sun that leads to the primal (or monadic) unity of God. Like Ficino, Pico explains that because Christ is the sun, he placed his tabernacle in the sun.[67] The idea that wisdom is available only to the elect was understood, he continues, not only by Moses but also by early Christians, for example, Saint Paul.

Suggesting that the Christian practice of prayer originated with the Pythagoreans, Pico's exposition ends with a grand finale that demonstrates, through a complicated numerological and symbological argument, the mutual harmony between the religion of Moses and that of Christ. The reconciliation of these opposites, he concludes, leads to the truth.

By upholding Pythagorean values and using Pythagorean techniques such as those just described, Pico is inspired to press onward, and so he does. His next, and what was to be his major, project was to propose the concord of Plato and Aristotle, or the reconciliation of the two major philosophies of the classical world. At the time of his premature death in 1494, he was working on a vast *Concord of Plato and Aristotle*. Its only remaining fragment, known as *De ente et uno* (*On Being and the One*), reveals the fundamental principles of his approach. These center on a form of applied Pythagoreanism. Plato and Aristotle were, he argues, in basic agreement on the unity of God. They both understood, albeit in different ways, that unity (the monad) is the basis of all number. Using different terms, they both agreed that God is intellect and intelligible. This point leads him to ramble, in speaking of God as the emanation of the number 4 (he is one, good, true, eternal). Before his text drops off, Pico makes a bewilderingly Pythagorean statement: "If I am not mistaken, this is that *tetraktys*, that is, quaternity, by which Pythagoras swore and which he called the principle of ever-flowing nature. We have demonstrated that these things, which are one God, are the principles of all things."[68]

Pico's individualistic application of Pythagorean ideas can be seen in other works he composed. In a short work on love, for example, he focuses on the unity of God that supervises all creation, including the 4 elements of which the body is composed, the 3 parts of the world, the 8 heavenly spheres, the 7 planets, the 9 muses, the 3 degrees of knowledge, and the 3 virtues.[69] All these are distinguished by contrarieties that, he says (at his enigmatic best), when unified, produce harmony, the basis of beauty and love. Only God, we are told, is a pure uncompounded unity.

Though he jubilates when he speaks of "the Pythagoreans," Pico refrains in his formal works from declaring himself to be a Pythagorean – perhaps because his aim to promote an all-inclusive concord between religions and philosophical systems might have been compromised if he appeared to be one-sided. Doubtless, this reticence lent the appearance of objectivity to his admiration for the antiquity, secret teachings, and tenets of Pythagoreanism. To his friend and colleague Ficino (a declared Pythagorean), however, he came out of the closet: "I am a

Pythagorean, for whom nothing is more revered than friendship, and if there is anything which could diminish or weaken that [friendship] between us, then let it, as they say, to the winds."[70] The strength of his Pythagoreanism poignantly leads him, he says, conflating Pythagoreanism and Christianity, to God:

> O Gracious God, God of the secret Pythagorean teaching as well as the open teaching of the ancient philosophies, a powerful prayer has suddenly invaded my breast, to be able to read and make a thorough study of these books by myself, without any inter-mediary. And this I am now doing … . This is my desire, Marsilio, these are my fires, which are no longer promising me a fleeting and empty delight, but are offering me a delight that is firm, a true image of the "glory which shall be revealed to us."[71]

The nephew of Pico, Giovanni Francesco Pico della Mirandola, corroborates his uncle's Pythagoreanism in his biography of Pico: Pico's birth, he says, was attended by a miracle in which a circular garland of light hovered over his mother; as a beardless young boy, he was considered to be a divine philosopher; after an early period of "wantonness," when he "set many women afire," he changed his life to one of continence and piety; he came to be known for his virtue, wisdom, and diligence. Most significant, the bulk of his nephew's report describes Pico as disdaining all earthly things and sharing generously with others. He gave his riches, which he scorned, to the poor, including his silver dishes and utensils. Of his vast properties, he kept only a small piece of land, just sufficient for himself and his household, giving away the rest. He was content with simple fare at home and, like Ficino, was a vegetarian. He exhorted his friends to disdain earthly things and, following his example, to dedicate their lives to piety.[72]

OTHER LATE-CENTURY PYTHAGOREANS IN TUSCANY

Interest in Pythagoreanism was shared by other members of Ficino's and Pico's generation. Although it might be imagined that the pleas of the Florentine humanist Alamanno Rinuccini (1426–1499) for citizen equality and freedom from tyranny reflected the ancient tradition that Pythagoras, himself an enemy of tyranny, had taught in stressing social equality and justice, Alamanno does not tell us this. However, an enthusiasm for Pythagoreanism on his part is suggested by the fact that in 1488 he translated Philostratus's *Life of Apollonius of Tyre*, a long work considered from the time of its creation (in late Antiquity) to the Renaissance to provide a model of the Pythagorean life, if not of the life of Pythagoras himself.[73]

A stronger case may be made for Angelo Poliziano, who was a friend to both Ficino and Pico. He writes of the pleasurable sounds evoked in him by the music of the lyre, of his reverence for the "sanctity" of the Pythagorean science of number, and of his interest in prognostication. His commentaries on Ovid's *Fasti* and his *Panepistemon* (*All Knowledge*) betray his strong interest in Pythagorean maxims, as well as in the writings of Nicomachus, Martianus Capella, Macrobius, and Vitruvius, and in Cicero's *In somnium Scipionis* (*The Dream of Scipio*), the work in which Cicero elucidated the harmony of the spheres.[74] Perhaps not surprising, regarding this humanist poet who wrote about the life of Pythagoras and his discoveries in geometry, proportion, and harmony, is the fact that his curiosity was stimulated by Sappho. In 1481 he composed a commentary on Ovid's then recently discovered epistle of Sappho to Faon. In one of the *Heroides*, Ovid's work (which had been lost during the Middle Ages) described the suicide of this early Greek poetess. In plunging from the top of a cliff crowned by a temple to Apollo, Sappho dedicated her plunge and her lyre to Apollo because, in saving her, Apollo would grant her eternal life, demonstrating the immortality of her soul. In her love of Apollo and of her lyre, as well as in her wish for immortality, Sappho may possibly have been the first Pythagorean.[75] The only surviving Pythagorean temple from Antiquity, the Subterranean Basilica at Porta Maggiore in Rome, makes much of Apollo's rescuing Sappho from her leap. This scene was so meaningful for Pythagoreans that not only did it constitute the only large sculptural adornment of the temple, but it was placed over the altar. Though there is no evidence to suggest that this underground temple was known to Renaissance archaeologists, it would seem that in some way Poliziano had understood the association between Sappho, Apollo, and Pythagoreanism, a subject which has been discussed elsewhere.[76]

URBINO AND THE MATHEMATICAL ANGLE

Modern scholarship has shown that the court of Federigo da Montefeltro, as well as that of his son and successor, Guidobaldo, was impregnated with reverence for Plato and respect for Pythagorean principles. Our principal source on the library built by Duke Federigo (1422–1482) informs us that it was one of the most wide-ranging and complete private libraries of the fifteenth century and one that focused on Platonic and Pythagorean works.[77] Federigo's rapport with Florentine intellectuals began when he established a friendship with Alberti who, as discussed earlier, was surely a Pythagorean.[78] This rapport developed further under the influence of Ficino, who, proud to be a Pythagorean, corresponded with Federigo and dedicated four of his works to him.[79] The influence of Ficino can be seen in the library at Urbino, which contained numerous works by ancient Pythagorean writers, as well as several thought at the time to have been authored by Pythagoras himself, including the *Golden Verses* and the *Sententiae multae* (*Maxims*).[80] Federigo was also friendly with Cardinal Bessarion (very likely, as already described, a Pythagorean). Bessarion visited his court as did probably also Alberti.[81] It was to Federigo that the previously mentioned Florentine humanist Alamanno Rinuccini dedicated his translation of the ancient Pythagorean work, the *Life of Apollonius of Tyana*.[82] A tribute Federigo approved, in the form of an inscription in the courtyard – or nucleus – of his palace at Urbino, speaks of the Duke's "justice, mercy, generosity, and piety," suggesting that he was anxious to make up for his fame as a man of war by vaunting his Pythagorean qualities.[83] Shortly after Federigo's death, one of Bessarion's close friends, Lilio Tifernate, the translator of Philo's works for Sixtus IV, came to work at the court of Urbino.[84]

Vespasiano da Bisticci, the Florentine bookseller who obtained most of Federigo's precious manuscripts for him, tells us a great deal about the Duke of Urbino. Federigo was a skilled mathematician and geometrician, and his library included a large number of mathematical works, including "all the Greek works on geometry, arithmetic, and astrology." His interest in astronomy was nourished by astronomical observations (in which he actively participated) made from the golden-sphered *torricini* (turrets) of his palazzo. It was Federigo who attracted to Urbino the famous Flemish mathematician Paulus de Middelbourg (1445–1533), who was to become a noted astrologer at his court.[85]

Thus began a long tradition of the patronage of mathematics at the court of Urbino.[86] Bernardino Baldi, the first biographer of Paulus and himself a mathematician, describes the reputation Paulus had earned before his arrival at Urbino, first at Louvain and subsequently at the University of Padua, as that of an "extremely acute arithmetician and great astrologer." According to him, Paulus arrived in Urbino in about 1479, apparently the result of Federigo's ardent wish to surround himself with northern mathematical wise men, or *sapienti*. These included Giacopo da Spira (Jacob of Speyer), whom Paulus himself acknowledged as "king of astrologers," and the famous astrologist *convertito* Guglielmo Raimundo Moncada (Flavius Mithridates), teacher of Kabbalah to Pico della Mirandola. Not only did Paulus become the personal medical doctor and astrologer of Federigo, but he also entered a world where astrology, mathematics, and music were revered.[87]

Paulus was well appreciated by the court of Urbino, as we know from a long poetic work composed by Giovanni Santi (the father of Raphael), a member of Federigo's court. Writing in the 1480s, Giovanni describes Paulus as a man of "acute" intelligence and of the "highest" achievement in the sciences, particularly in algebra and arithmetic. This "most excellent of men" knew secret things that other men did not know, Giovanni says. His expertise included the measurement of the heavens and the influence of the stars and planets on earth.[88] Correspondence between Paulus and Ficino establishes not only their acquaintance but also Ficino's high regard for his collaboration in restoring "ancient knowledge" and Platonic teachings.[89] Considering its source, this statement speaks volumes respecting the likelihood of Paulus's dedication to Pythagorean doctrines.

Because most of Paulus's surviving writings prior to 1513 are prognostications, we cannot know the specifics of his thought. However, given Plato's standing (not to mention Ficino's) as a Pythagorean, the conclusion that Paulus was a Pythagorean is inescapable.[90] His advice was no doubt influential in Federigo's commissioning, for the Montefeltro palace, architectural projects with Pythagorean schemes. These will be discussed in Chapter 8.

Following the death of Federigo, Paulus continued to serve the court of Urbino under Guidobaldo da Montefeltro as mathematician, astrologer, and prognosticator. It was there that he came into contact with other mathematicians, for example, Luca Pacioli, who in turn was in contact with artist-mathematicians such as Piero della Francesca and Leonardo da Vinci – all of whom had, at the very least, strong Pythagorean leanings. The influence of both Pacioli and Piero, if not of Paulus himself, was in turn passed on to two sons of Urbino who, growing up at the time of Paulus's great influence at the court, would put their mark on the visual arts of the sixteenth century – the future painter-architects Bramante and Raphael. By the turn of the century the acceleration of interest in "old" ideas launched in Urbino would experience a dazzling development that would, paradoxically, energize, through their work, the modernization of Renaissance art and architecture. (The Pythagoreanism of Bramante and Raphael will be discussed in Chapters 8 and 9.) When both were in Rome in the service of Pope Julius II in the early 1500s, Paulus was invited to serve the papal court – raising the possibility that it was at their suggestion that he was invited.[91]

Thus does an era open in mid-fifteenth-century Urbino, fed by Florentine intellectuals, in which mathematics and art enriched each other through Pythagorean inspiration. Stimulated by his passion for mathematics, Federigo took an active interest in architecture. Among the architects he attracted to Urbino were Luciano Laurana (1420–1479) and Francesco di Giorgio Martini (1439–1501). The former was charged with the redesign of his ducal palace, while the latter was engaged to rebuild his fortifications, construct a number of monuments, and complete the ducal palace after the departure of Laurana in 1472. Both were likely Pythagoreans. Though not much is known about Laurana, who left no writings, the fact that he was deeply influenced by Alberti may have inspired Federigo to select him to design the Grand Courtyard of his palace. The contract presented by Federigo to Laurana expresses his view that architecture is founded upon the arts of arithmetic (numbers) and geometry, which are, he says, much esteemed at his court.[92] The Pythagorean character of this courtyard will be discussed in Chapter 8.[93]

A great military engineer as well as an architect (and a painter), Francesco di Giorgio Martini was also a serious and original writer on the subject of architecture. Though his major works do not speak of Pythagoras or Pythagoreanism as such, his Pythagoreanism is quite clear in the mixture of Vitruvianism and Platonism he proposes. Written in Urbino in the 1480s, his *Trattato di Architettura*

(*Treatise on Architecture*) is very dependent on Vitruvius. Throughout the manuscript, Francesco lends authority to his ideas by introducing them as though they were approved by Vitruvius: "As Vitruvius says. ..." Indeed his ties to Vitruvius are stronger than a superficial reading of his anecdotes and references to this great Pythagorean architect of Antiquity would suggest. Vitruvius is his primary guide and main authority, especially for measurement and proportion. As though to underline this dependence, Francesco made a translation of Vitruvius's text from Latin into Italian during the time he was composing his magnum opus.[94]

Essentially a humanist discourse, perhaps inspired by his patron Federigo, Francesco's *Trattato* lauds number, proportion, and geometry as the primary avenues to attaining his goal, harmony. Yet he is less philosophical and more down to earth and pragmatic than was Alberti (who had died in the previous decade). Comparing architectural measurement to the proportions of the human body (doubtless inspired by Vitruvius), he declares that the eight interlocked parts of the body correspond to the proportionate measurement that an architect must understand so as to be able to construct a building in which nothing can be added or subtracted without dislodging the harmony of the whole. "The ancients" (obviously referring to the Pythagorean *tetraktys* as the symbol of perfection in the universe), he says, declared that the number 10 is perfect. The proof of this, we are told, is that we have ten fingers on our hands. Francesco discusses the "perfect" numbers, praising 16 (6 and 10) as the "most" perfect. Here he is paraphrasing Vitruvius.[95] He also has high praise for the number 4, as he does for the geometric forms of the square, the cube, the circle, and the equilateral triangle. Discussing building types, Francesco proposes that the square is basic. The square engenders descendants, including rectangles, that allow the architect to change relationships and thereby create the desired proportions. In Francesco's system of proportions, the ideal form is a numerical and geometrical cube that, as George Hersey demonstrates, derives from Vitruvius and is clearly Pythagorean.[96] The drawings accompanying Francesco's treatise suggest that for him drawing was not merely a form of mechanical illustration but a speculative endeavor requiring a knowledge of arithmetic and geometry.

Also during the 1480s, an event of great moment occurred. In 1486, the first printed edition of Vitruvius (the editio princeps) was issued in Rome by the humanist and mathematician Giovanni Sulpizio da Veroli (b. ca. 1430).[97] This edition would supersede all the precious manuscript editions of this work and would itself inspire future printed editions, such as the magnificent one edited by Fra Giocondo that would be printed in Venice in 1511. Significant, no doubt, for those interested in Vitruvius was Giovanni Sulpizio's prior visit to Urbino. At that time, in 1476, Federigo da Montefeltro was still alive, building his library and surrounding himself with mathematicians. Giovanni Sulpizio recorded his trip in an epigram that honors his host and his host's palace in Urbino.[98] It is thus not unlikely that Giovanni Sulpizio made his trip there for research and consulation and that the legacy of his influence there was strong. Perhaps it was this circumstance that inspired the Duke to appoint Paulus de Middelbourg, who arrived in Urbino in 1479 as court mathematician to study "heavenly measurements."[99] However, it was very likely that Sulpizio's visit to Urbino inspired Francesco di Giorgio Martini to write his Vitruvian treatise on architecture (composed in Urbino in the 1480s). Indeed, Urbino was a hotbed of Vitruvianism.

The circumstances just outlined make it probable that Giovanni Sulpizio also met the artist Piero della Francesca (1416?–1492) in Urbino. About sixty at the time, Piero was painting, though he was also an active mathematician engaged in the study of measurement. Piero's interest in Vitruvius begs the question whether he was a Pythagorean; regarding this, he leaves us several positive clues.

Piero's principal mathematical writings consist in three treatises, the *Trattato d'abaco* (*Treatise on the Abacus*), *De prospective pingendi* (*On Perspective in Painting*), and *Libellus de quinque corporibus regularibus* (*Book on the Five Regular Bodies*).[100] The first of these, like other abacus arithmetic texts, had a commercial purpose in that it laid out basic arithmetic useful for solving practical problems. However, it was unusual in that though its problems are set in numerical form, they show a strong interest in geometry. The problems this text contains involve calculations regarding the measurement of triangles, squares, circles, cubes, and spheres, as well as their proportionate relationships to each other – for example, how to inscribe a circle in an equilateral triangle. The text also includes a method for expressing proportion by dividing a line into its mean and extreme ratio, allowing the smaller section to be in the same proportion to the larger as the latter is to the entire line (the "golden section").[101]

The intended subject of his second treatise, *De prospectiva pingendi*, was, we are told by Piero himself, proportion. For him, proportion (*commensuratio*) meant perspective. This work largely consists in establishing how proportion can be achieved through the application of mathematics. For example, Piero demonstrates how to transform a square into a cube and the relation of a domestic dwelling (a house drawn in perspective) to a cube. He also demonstrates his historical awareness by referring to Pythagorean predecessors such as Vitruvius and the thirteenth-century mathematician Leonardo da Pisa (also known as Fibonacci), who, despite his innovations, worked in the tradition of the ancient Pythagorean Nicomachus.[102]

The *Libellus de quinque corporibus regularibus* is, on the other hand, devoted entirely to geometry, with a twist: The problems are posed in numerical form. Grounded in Plato's *Timaeus* and Euclid's *Elements*, they consist primarily of exercises in constructing the tetrahedron (four-sided pyramid), cube, octahedron, icosahedron, and dodecahedron. The five solids had a symbolic value for they were associated with the four elements and the cosmos – the cube with earth, the icosahedron with water, the octahedron with air, the tetrahedron with fire, and the dodecahedron with the cosmos. Piero imagines elaborate constructions in which these solids may be truncated in various ways so that they may be unified by fitting one into another.[103]

Not only did Piero study individual solid bodies and solid bodies inscribed in spheres, he also meditated on plane geometrical figures and irregular bodies.[104] Thus is his main subject the way in which forms are related to one another proportionately. In dedicating this volume, written between 1482 and 1492, to Guidobaldo, Duke of Urbino, Piero intimates his Pythagorean leanings, for he paraphrases Vitruvius, indicating his respect for this Pythagorean architect of Antiquity.[105]

Although Piero has little to say about the history of mathematics per se and nothing to say about Pythagoras specifically, it could be argued that his interests, including especially his fascination for the five regular solids or polyhedra and his concern with the measurement of three-dimensional bodies such as architects use, suggest that he had a more than passing interest in Pythagorean mathematics. The possibility that his inspirations were Pythagorean is underscored by his friendship with Alberti, as well as by his respect for Vitruvius. It is also suggested in the fact that his contemporary, the mathematician Luca Pacioli, an admirer of Pythagoras, would print two of his works and include them within his own.[106]

The humanist Polydore Vergil, who knew a lot about Pythagoras, as discussed in Chapter 2, had a more than casual interest in Pythagoreanism. This is no surprise, for Polydore too came from Urbino. According to his explanation, the two sources of philosophy ("scientific" and "Pythagorean") derived from Anaximander the Ionian and Pythagoras the Italian.[107] No doubt he was referring to the division between natural philosophy and mystical philosophy that had been explained in Antiquity by Diogenes Laertius. Polydore appears to have preferred the latter, probably because of the importance of the symbolism of number for mathematicians at Urbino. Perhaps it was just such a discussion that inspired his fellow Urbino native, the painter and future architect Raphael (for whom Polydore has great praise), to represent Anaximander and Pythagoras playing their opposite roles in the *School of Athens*, as will be discussed in Chapter 9.

OTHER MATHEMATICAL CONSIDERATIONS

Mathematics figures conspicuously in other parts of Italy too. Interlocked with humanism, it formed the pursuit of Giorgio Valla (1430–1500), a prominent scholar of late fifteenth-century Venice. A distinguished professor of mathematics, Giorgio acquired a large number of manuscripts that formed the basis of his renowned private library, a collection very strong in Greek mathematical works.[108] His mathematical writings came to be as celebrated as his library, both of which attracted important visitors to his house in Venice. Although we do not know the identities of all those who visited him, it is thought that they included Leonardo da Vinci, who visited the Adriatic city in 1499. The young Copernicus, however, who came to Padua two years later, was too late to meet him. Nevertheless, both men are known to have been familiar with Giorgio's writings.[109] Copernicus was no doubt attracted to Giorgio's geo-heliocentric cosmological theory, a theory that owed a debt to Pythagoreanism.[110]

In a series of letters to humanist friends written during the 1480s and 1490s, Giorgio expressed his belief that the discipline of mathematics belongs to the greater field of philosophical studies, a traditional view as well of ancient Pythagoreans. Accordingly, in a letter to the Platonist (and possible Pythagorean) Jacopo Antiquario in Milan, Giorgio traces the history of mathematics from its beginnings with Pythagoras through its development with Plato in the *Timaeus*.[111]

Giorgio's intellectual interests are reflected in his major work and masterpiece, *De expetendis et fugiendis rebus* (*Concerning What Ought To Be Desired or Shunned*), a monumental humanist encyclopedia compiled from classical sources that was published in 1501, a year after its creator's death.[112] Though this work remains insufficiently studied in modern times, there is little doubt that it was groundbreaking at the time, for Leonardo and Copernicus eagerly consulted it.[113] Its division into forty-nine books surely reflects Giorgio's Pythagoreanism, for 49 is the square of 7 (7 x 7 = 49), the most revered number of the Pythagorean decad and the number that brings together music and astronomy, or the music of the spheres, a subject central to his mathematics. Pythagorean in its fusion of mathematics and philosophy and in its celebration of numbers, this text establishes the fundamental role of mathematics in the long intellectual journey to the lofty realms of universal theology. Thus mathematics is its opening subject. In three books Giorgio covers the history of ancient arithmetic by translating, paraphrasing, and commenting on the works of Nicomachus, Anatolius, and Boethius – all Pythagoreans.[114] The finishing touches in this section are provided by his references to Maximus Planudes, a medieval monk and mathematical theologian from Constantinople who appears to have been a Pythagorean.[115]

Book III of Gorgio's encyclopedia is the most interesting, for it expresses what has by now become the traditional Pythagorean view of arithmology, or the theology of arithmetic.[116] Here Giorgio dedicates twenty chapters to a discussion of figurate numbers (i.e., numbers that can be fitted into a regular geometrical arrangement of equally spaced points). His discussion considers what patterns of units can be fitted into what geometric shapes (such as triangles and squares, as Nicomachus had first explained), and the symbolism and properties of each number up to 10, the universal number of Pythagoreans. From here on, he proceeds to collate human knowledge from classical sources. Grouped into three categories, these chapters include discussions of arithmetic proportion, geometric proportion, and harmonic proportion. The important subject of proportion leads to a consideration of cosmological music and the music made by the seven planets,

that is, the music of the spheres, the by now time-honored Pythagorean interpretation of the cosmos. This in turn leads to sections on geometry and physics,
astrology, medicine, rhetoric, poetry, economics, and physiology. The conclusion
reinforces his view that all these disciplines, starting with mathematics and ending
with the study of history, form the domain of philosophy, the discipline invented
by Pythagoras.[117]

Giorgio Valla's interest in the relation between mathematics and music
is underlined in a small volume on musical harmony he published in 1497.[118]
Essentially a commentary on an ancient work on harmonic theory by Cleonides,
a follower of the ancient Greek philosopher and musical theorist Aristoxenus,
Giorgio's text opens with an acknowledgment to the influence of Pythagoras
and Plato:

> The opinion of the Pythagoreans and the Platonists from ancient
> times is that nothing is preferable to the promotion of the idea that all
> things in nature possess harmony. ... The operations of heaven safe-
> guard those eternal revolutions from which our weak and mortal bod-
> ies profit, guiding them constantly, above all our souls.[119]

A clue as to how Giorgio came to be inspired to revive Pythagorean mathematics can be found in the funeral oration given on the occasion of his death
by one of his former students, Bartolomeo Zamberti.[120] Zamberti informs us that
in Milan Giorgio had studied with Constantinus Lascaris. (The author of the
first Renaissance biography of Pythagoras as well as of an edition of the *Golden
Verses* that saw many future printings, Constantinus was, as noted in Chapter 2,
surely a Pythagorean.)[121] This oration tells us more: Giorgio's aim was to make
ancient mathematics live again, and especially "Platonist" mathematics, which, as
he suggests, conjoined mathematics with philosophy. Giorgio's Pythagoreanism is
confirmed by his adopted son, Giovanni Cademosto, who wrote a biography of
his father.[122] According to his testimony, Giorgio gave lectures on Vitruvius while
at Venice in the 1490s. Not surprisingly, we also learn from Giovanni that Giorgio
was an ardent supporter of the poor and that, in disdaining his own worldly
riches, he practiced extreme generosity to those in need.

Parallel to the pioneering theoretical interpretations of mathematics practiced in the fifteenth century by Paulus de Middelbourg, Francesco di Giorgio,
Piero della Francesca, and Giorgio Valla, the Renaissance inherited from the
Middle Ages a long tradition of interest in the works of Pythagorean mathematicians. This resulted, after the invention of printing, which occurred in the 1460s,
in the proliferation of works by Nicomachus, Boethius, Martianus Capella, and
others. The popularity of their texts, which were among the manuscripts and early
printed books widely known to mathematicians in the fifteenth century, constituted a tradition that would continue well into the next century.[123] This tradition,

not to mention one of Cicero's *In somnium Scipionis* and Macrobius's commentary on it, constituted the fundamental reading for those interested in studying the harmony of the spheres, an important preoccupation of Pythagoreanism.

There also existed a tradition that studied late-medieval interpretations of these works. In concentrating on the theory of numbers and the geometry of the square and the cube, such works – which had a huge publication record in the fifteenth century – contributed in their own way to the dissemination of the Pythagorean tradition that they openly acknowledged. Books of this type included editions of works by Thomas Bradwardine (1290–1349), an English cleric, and Jordanus Nemorarius (fl. 1380s), a German scholar. After the invention of printing, both, who were Boethian mathematicians, came to be better known in the Renaissance than they had been in their own medieval times. Both concentrated on the theory and symbolism of numbers. Following Boethius and many other Pythagoreans of Antiquity, Jordanus divided his main work into ten books.[124]

The invention of printing also responded to the needs of those engaged in the rapidly developing commercial world by providing practical arithmetic texts, a practice that began in the late fifteenth century. These, usually small, compendia of commercial or applied arithmetic often openly acknowledged the debt of arithmetic to the Pythagorean tradition. One such example is Filippo Calandri's *Aritmetica*, the first printed Italian arithmetic text with accompanying woodblock illustrations that provide multiplication tables and examples of long division in the modern form. Most of the problems it presents are conceived in terms of practicalities, such as money to be gained or lost, but its frontispiece is an illustration of Pythagoras at work that carries the inscription "Pictagoras arithmetrice introductor" (see fig. 5).[125] This of course makes its clear that arithmetic is a Pythagorean discipline.

Brief mention should be made of the fact that fifteenth-century astrological literature, a branch of mathematics, was not without its Pythagorean influences. In interpreting the universe mathematically, the literature of astrology focused on the belief that the heavens governed all, a form of divination that held that the stars and planets influenced terrestrial events and human affairs.[126] This subject, though also associated with the ancient astronomer Ptolemy, has a long tradition in doctrines identified with the followers of Pythagoras.[127] It can be traced back to the third century A.D. when Iamblichus affirmed that Pythagoras himself had been well versed in divination and had studied the heavens.[128]

Despite its relations to the widespread intellectual stimuli of the Kabbalah, hermeticism, and other forms of esotericism, astrology had its own life in the early Renaissance as a discipline that, continuing from medieval traditions, gave rise to treatises that were, by and large, highly technical. Demonstrating an awareness that the history of this occult science is based on mathematics, many of their authors express a debt to Pythagorean ideas. Lorenzo Bonincontri (1410–1491) will serve as an example. Writing in the 1480s, he affirms his adherence to Pythagorean teachings. As he puts it, Pythagoras, Empedocles, Plato, and Hermes had explained that the soul lives in heaven, where it is fed heavenly nutrients, before it is sent to dwell in a given body, a doctrine he professes to endorse.[129]

GAFFURIO AND THE *HARMONIA* OF MUSIC

In the world of music, where the tradition of Pythagorean tuning had been generally accepted since late medieval times, a distinctly Pythagorean movement developed in Italy toward the end of the fifteenth century.[130] One of the earliest and most complete practitioners of this trend, which would come to be pan-European in the sixteenth century,[131] was the Italian Franchino Gaffurio. Discussed in Chapter 2 as an admirer of Pythagoras, Gaffurio was working in Milan (the city where Pythagoras was hailed as a "priest of music") as choirmaster of the cathedral and court musician to the Duke in the late 1400s at the same time that Leonardo da Vinci and Bramante were there. Though Leonardo will be treated in the next chapter, Gaffurio will serve to close this chapter, as his major works were published in 1492 and 1496. The exuberance of Gaffurio's praise for Pythagoras as the inventor of harmonic theory was accompanied by his affirmation of the abundance of inspiration he received from Pythagorean traditions. This inspiration can be discerned in three areas.

First, Gaffurio is primarily concerned with explaining music theory in terms of "sacrosanct" number that enables the construction of celestial harmony. Referring to this as Pythagorean methodology, he says, "Music chose to borrow as suitable means the numbers of arithmetic and the quantities of geometry. Their employment is recognized as proper for an accurate relationship of sounds."[132] He defines instrumental music, tonal systems, the proportions of intervals, and harmonic proportionality in terms of numbers, exhibiting a particular fondness for the numbers 3, 4, 6 (a perfect number, he tells us), 7, and 10.[133] Gaffurio's Pythagoreanism is also reflected in the fact that he commissioned the first Latin translation of the Greek treatise on harmonics of Manuel Bryennius, a Byzantine music theorist who had revived, in about 1300, ancient Greek tonal systems that he credited to Pythagoras.[134] Surely these views explain why, since 5 was regarded by ancient Pythagoreans as the number of perfect concord because it encompasses the first even number (2) and the first odd number (3) and because, when squared it always encompasses itself (5 x 5 = 25), he divided his work into five books.[135]

A second area of Pythagorean inspiration can be seen in Gaffurio's interest in the music of the spheres, which he refers to as the harmonization of the seven modes and planets. His investigations suggest that some of the heavenly bodies emit "masculine" sounds, while others emit "feminine" sounds. He concludes that heavenly sounds, as proposed by Pythagoras and Plato, are inaudible to baser people, who live like beasts, whereas they can be perceived by those who "reach the summit of virtue" and have acquired knowledge and wisdom that enables them to hear the elusive harmony.[136] This, of course, parallels the traditional view of Pythagoreans that their teachings, thanks to enigma and secrecy, are comprehensible only to the initiated.

A third aspect of Gaffurio's Pythagoreanism lies in his approach to the purpose and benefits of music, which are, he reminds us, to soothe body and soul. The body grows weak and the soul feint when not stimulated by musical harmony, for both body and soul are built of the same numbers out of which harmony is made.[137] Thus, Gaffurio concludes, can music influence the psychic state of its listeners and offer through its enchanting harmonies a cure for those who are disoriented.

Gaffurio was as ardent a follower of Boethius (his "leader") as he was of Pythagoras, for he invokes the names of both in explaining his overall theory of the importance of concord in any harmonious mixture. His Pythagoreanism is confirmed in a poem by one of his contemporaries:

> Here is witness to the beautiful book of Gaffurius ...
> He withdrew inwardly to the mysteries of the heavens,
> Investigating thoroughly the teacher Pythagoras,
> Arising he brings forth those originally distinguished in the art
> He reveals more recondite matters. ...[138]

Also Pythagorean was Gaffurio's invention of a scheme that attempted to explain the harmony of the spheres in terms of the Pythagorean triads that, it was believed, had so influenced Plato. Gaffurio's illustration placed the triad of the Three Graces and the triad of Serapis (triple-headed god of the underworld) at opposite ends of the great cosmic scale connecting heaven and earth. The trinity of the graces made celestial music in the heavens under the guidance of Apollo, while that of Serapis produced subterranean silence. Thus was the whole universe balanced, permeated, and harmonized from top to bottom by triadic rhythms that constituted a universal symmetry in which the seven planets took their relatively audible places (exemplifying the music of the spheres) under the guidance of Apollo with his seven-stringed lyre.[139]

THE ROMAN CONNECTION

Pythagorean beliefs, as we have seen, came in many forms in the fifteenth century. While there were, doubtless, pseudo-Pythagoreans who did not participate in the depth of the movement, certainly there were also many who, though they did not conform to every Pythagorean maxim, nonetheless were important exponents of various Pythagorean points of view. One such person was Bartolomeo dei Sacchi, better known as Platina (1421–1487) who, as a prominent member of the

Roman Academy (the future University of Rome) and the librarian of Sixtus IV, held a position of great influence. (Very likely, it was at his suggestion that Sixtus commissioned the translation of Philo's works.) Aside from being an important scholar, Platina was, like Ficino, a great believer in the healing arts, which suggests his Pythagoreanism.

Published in 1475, Platina's *De honesta voluptate* (*On Genuine Pleasures*), offers a remarkable parallel to Ficino's *De vita* except that Platina appears to have approved of eating meat.[140] Platina's work is far more than a cookbook. It offers recipes for daily life as well as for the consumption and preparation of food. Platina advocates simplicity and frugality. He admonishes those who require dazzling events and heavy banquets in order to enjoy life. He speaks of love and respect for others, and he offers advice on relations between the sexes. The latter should be few and far between, he explains at length, and restricted to the winter months. An excess of sexual indulgence turns enjoyment into lust, which is destructive to the human body. These and other counsels that he offers appear to paraphrase the mantras on behavioral moderation of numerous ancient Pythagoreans, such as those reported by Diogenes Laertius. Pythagoras himself, Diogenes had reported, advised moderation in daily life, as well as in eating and drinking and certainly in sexual indulgence, which, he said, was appropriate only to the winter months and was otherwise generally harmful.[141] Platina cites Pythagoras as one of the authorities for his volume, which, incidentally or not, was in the library of Leonardo da Vinci – whose possible Pythagoreanism will be discussed in the next chapter.[142]

Pythagoreanism, as it was combined with Platonism, experienced an effulgent development in the fifteenth century. While on the one hand it appealed to philosophers, mathematicians, and astronomers, on the other it fascinated religious thinkers who saw in this direction of thought confirmation of the antiquity and profundity of Christian beliefs. In the Renaissance all these "consumers" could be one person, for mathematics and astronomy were considered, by Pythagoreans at least, a part of philosophy. This person, most likely, was a Christian, perhaps a cleric. While scholars generally considered Plato to have been a follower of Pythagoras, if not a Pythagorean himself, they viewed his masterpiece, the *Timaeus*, as exemplifying Pythagorean mathematical philosophy. Thus the teachings of Pythagoras lurked in the background of Platonism.

There were three major core areas where Pythagoreanism experienced a particularly concentrated and rapid growth in the second half of the first century of the Renaissance. First among these was Florence. Here the fermentation of Pythagorean ideas is steady, strong, and clear. In the later fifteenth century, both Marsilio Ficino and Pico della Mirandola emphatically embraced Pythagoreanism. They even lived the lifestyle of ancient Pythagoreans who, like Plotinus, were associated with vegetarianism, frugality, and the sharing of earthly goods.

Ficino's extensive work on Plato had made ever more clear the Pythagoreanism of his hero. He persuaded his contemporaries to respect Plato's doctrine of the immortality of the soul because Plato had followed Pythagoras; he rejoiced in propounding Plato's appreciation of the triangle, also derived from Pythagoras, as symbolic of the triple powers of the soul. Ficino honored not only the triangle, but also the circle and the sphere. His Pythagoreanism reached the point of religious fervor in his zeal for playing the lyre and practicing the healing arts. His admiration of Plato was reflected in his acquisition, for his studio in Florence, of a bust of Plato from Athens. Before this bust a flame was kept burning night and day.[143] Pico della Mirandola discovered an affinity that linked the Platonists and Christians with Mosaic law in the hidden meanings of the Kabbalah, making it possible, through the example of Pythagorean mystery and enigma, for the initiated to grasp the harmony that gave them all a common depth and language. The philosophies of Pythagoras and Plato were so akin to the Christian faith, Pico argued, that Saint Augustine had thanked God for them.

Despite their many differences, both Ficino and Pico viewed the triad, which derived from Apollo, and the triadic rhythms of the universe as all-important invitations to celestial meditation and the Trinity.[144] Both expounded the reconciliation of opposites as the universal system through which moderation was achieved. Both advocated veneration of the sun as the light of Christ. Both enthusiastically suggested putting the altar of Christ in the sun. Both speak of the importance of the "knowledge of divine things," and of God as the great craftsman who designed the universe. Thus were the primary concerns in Florence for Pythagorean unity of philosophy and religion.

A second area was Urbino, a center of mathematics. Here the patronage exerted by Duke Federigo involved Paulus de Middelbourg, Francesco di Giorgio, and Piero della Francesca, among others. In addition to these, Polydore Vergil would inspire the young Raphael before leaving for England, where he no doubt brought his knowledge of *urbinate* humanism. Especially with the much admired Canon of Florence Cathedral, Ficino, as his guide, Federigo da Montefeltro showed a remarkable deference to and preference for Pythagorean mathematics, astronomy, and architecture, a deep-seated regard that was bequeathed to the next Duke, his son Guidobaldo.

A third center where Pythagorean ideas were actively developed was Milan. There, toward century's end, Gaffurio wrote his celebrated treatise on the importance of number for musical harmony. Also there was Leonardo da Vinci who, undoubtedly, had arrived imbued with a knowledge of Florentine Pythagoreanism. The young architect Bramante, from Urbino, where he surely had acquired familiarity with Pythagorean mathematical ideas, was also a new arrival. Also there was the diplomat Jacopo Antiquario, a Platonist in close touch with both Pico and Ficino as well as with Giorgio Valla who, though living in Venice, was a native of the Milan area. Another interesting character in this *mise-en-scène* was Pacioli who, well known at the courts of both Urbino and Milan, will be considered in the next chapter.

In Venice a fourth center began to take shape, primarily in the work of the mathematician Giorgio Valla. A professor in Venice, Valla was deeply interested in the symbolism of numbers as well as in proportion and geometry, disciplines traditionally associated with Pythagoras's teachings. In Rome, meanwhile, a fifth center was emerging under the influence of Platina and Pope Sixtus IV.

The ideas that bound these centers together in a general philosophical commonality were harmony, concord, number, and cosmology. One and the same concept of harmony presided over all these centers: Subject to the laws of number, it included physical and spiritual matter, spoke the language of geometry and music, and could, as a philosophy, be applied to all disciplines.

By century's end, this movement – stimulated by the invention of printing and the increased availability of the works by eminent ancient Pythagoreans such as Boethius and Vitruvius, not to mention those attributed to Pythagoras himself – had touched many fields. Now accepted by Christians, Plato was appreciated for his interest in the mysticism and science of number, both of which demonstrated his assimilation of Pythagorean ideas. At the same time, a culture of Pythagoreanism existed in the world of astrology (which though historically akin to astronomy was feeling the pangs of separation from its twin as philosophers debated its worthiness), frequently a preferred occupation of mathematicians. It also existed in the world of music, where mathematics counted, for number was an important element of music, and in the world of politics, where it was remembered that Pythagoras was a friend of liberty and an enemy of tyranny. Meanwhile, the long-lived medieval undercurrent of Pythagorean tendencies in the world of magic and alchemy continued to have a life of its own. Ficino himself, applying the magic of number to practical issues, found creative avenues to give cosmological guidance to his advisees. Thus could they look to the stars and planets to modify their behavior or improve their health.

There is no definition of what Pythagoreans looked like or exactly how they behaved in the first century of the Renaissance. There were, apparently, no Pythagorean cults or communes as had existed (according to Cicero) in the first century B.C. The influence of Pythagoras had become so broad and so diverse that his doctrines (or supposed doctrines) were revered by many, seriously investigated by some, and merely applied by rule of thumb by others. Pythagoreans of the early Renaissance saw an overarching importance in ideas of symmetry, proportion, and harmony. At the same time there were certainly those who appropriated one or another Pythagorean idea in a conventionalized way without crediting, or perhaps even realizing, the source from which it came.

Turn-of-the-century Pythagoreans tended to live well-ordered lives, as they had in Antiquity. The Pythagorean tenets were well known to them through the *Golden Verses*, *Symbola*, and similar works, as well as through commentaries on them. Though they did not necessarily dress in white their way of life was expressed in disdaining riches, sharing material goods, believing in the immortality of their souls (which corresponded with their Christianity), contemplating the divine, and, sometimes, practicing vegetarianism. As the sixteenth century dawned, none of these things changed. Rather they continued much as before, becoming – if anything – ever more deeply embedded in the culture of the Renaissance.

SIX:

THE MATURATION AND VICISSITUDES OF PYTHAGOREANISM IN THE SIXTEENTH CENTURY

As the sixteenth century dawned, Pythagoreans thought of the cosmos, or universe, as beautifully ordered. That order was expressed primarily in terms of numbers that had mysterious significances that had been discovered by their ancestors. Thus their attention was directed to numbers in geometrical, as well as in arithmetical, terms. Numbers could be arranged in geometrical formations, as in the case of figurate numbers. The offspring of these numerical systems were the musical tones that regulated the harmony of a well-ordered universe that had been created and arranged by a single God around a central fire. Thus did Apollo and the sun, whom Pythagoras and his followers had worshipped in Antiquity, come to be conflated with God the father and God the son (symbolized by the sun) and, thanks to Ficino and Pico, Christianized. Indeed, by the late fifteenth century, Pythagoras had become an honorary Christian.

Christians were not the only inheritors of Pythagorean thought. The idea that Pythagoras had studied at the feet of Moses resurfaced, especially after the translation and availability in the fifteenth century of the first-century works of Philo, who had explicated Jewish scripture in terms of the theological significance of number. First expressed in late Antiquity by Hermippus, Aristobulus, Numenius, and others, the idea that Pythagoras had studied with Moses, revived by Ficino in the late fifteenth century, was to experience a virtual explosion in the early sixteenth, as will be seen in the pages of this chapter. In this sense, Pythagorean thought was a great unifier that bound together pagan and Jewish Antiquity as the pedestal of Christianity. Delving into the literature of Pythagoras's followers was a way of strengthening Christianity and "proving" its continuation from, and perfection of, ancient pagan and Jewish thought. Nor had interest in Pythagoras and his teachings ever died in the Arab world.

The mysteries of theology, philosophy, mathematics, astronomy, and music, related disciplines that together formed the unity of wisdom, could be apprehended through education and study. The contemplation of divine principles was key. Revealed by enigmatic allusions that could be understood by the initiated, the answers to questions, whether demonstrative (as in geometry) or contemplative (as in philosophy), lay in one word: harmony. Harmony was divine. Yet it could be grasped by the senses as well as by the intellect. Even the more popular elements of Pythagoreanism in such areas as astrology, alchemy, and medicine used enigmatic language to explain the mysteries of nature and discover divine order. As in the case of Apollo, the god of Pythagoras and the great unifier, the teachings of Pythagoras addressed the contemporary sixteenth-century world by promoting, as Pico della Mirandola had dreamed, the unity inherent in harmony.

PACIOLI, LEONARDO DA VINCI, AND THEIR FRIENDS

Active intellectuals in early sixteenth-century Italy exhibited more than casual familiarity with Pythagorean thought. Because this tradition had come to them from ancient authors under the enthusiastic chaperonage of Ficino, Pico, and others, they became "Pythagoreanized" (or "modern") in their intellectual approaches. However, they did not necessarily admit to such a label.

Luca Pacioli saw in Pythagoras much more than the wise man and mathematical intellect he praised. In many ways, the work of this Franciscan intellectual demonstrates his enthusiasm for the methodologies of Pythagorean mathematicians of the past. These became his models. Strong Pythagorean tendencies are demonstrated in his *Summa arithmetica*. It is, perhaps, in his dedication of this work that Pacioli most clearly reveals them. The elaborate bow he makes to Guidobaldo, Duke of Urbino (a center of Pythagoreanism), compliments the Duke on his library and cites the preeminence of Urbino in mathematics. Pacioli's dedication opens by praising three intellectuals whom, he says, were most venerated in Urbino: Paulus de Middelbourg (who in return greatly admired Pacioli) for his accomplishments in astrology;[1] Vitruvius, for his demonstration of the practicalities of proportion; and Alberti, for writing the "perfect" book on architecture. All were Pythagoreans. The list of favorite artists he attaches praises above all Leonardo da Vinci, whose interest in Pythagoreanism will be discussed later.

Pacioli's dedication draws attention to music, astronomy, and architecture as the beneficiaries of arithmetic, for all incorporate number, proportion, and proportionality, or harmony.[2] Architecture, Pacioli suggests, was such a beneficiary. Like a good Pythagorean, he affirms that everything has number and measure. In a second dedication he informs his reader (the Duke) that Boethius had been the first to explain number and its significance — a significance that he demonstrates in the long section on numbers that follows. Perhaps because it was common knowledge, he omits tracing the ancestry of numbers back from Boethius to Nicomachus to Pythagoras.

In the opening section of this work, on arithmetic, Pacioli, reflecting the traditional Pythagorean views of Boethius, whom he frequently paraphrases, makes it clear that he views number as the first and most important principle of the universe. Taking this concept further, he demonstrates the use of number in a way previously unknown. A woodcut illustration shows the various positions of the hand and its fingers in demonstrating given numbers.[3] While the single-digit numbers can be readily understood pictorially (1 = 1 finger folded, 2 = 2 fingers folded, etc.), the designation of numbers up to 9,000 requires some imagination. What is significant is that after the number 10 (it will be remembered that the decad was a perfect and universal number for Pythagoreans), Pacioli lists all successive numbers in terms of tens (or 10 x 10, 100, and 10 x 100, 1,000).[4]

His demonstration of the "how to" of multiplication is accompanied by an illustration of a multiplication table that also is governed by the number 10. This table, called the *mensula Pythagorae*, is copied from Renaissance editions of the *De arithmetica* by Boethius.[5] Pacioli's table is laid out in "latitudes" and "longitudes" that refer to a system of numbering across and down. One through 10 across the top constitutes the "longitudes," while 1 through 10 in the first descending column constitutes the "latitudes." Thus is a grid constructed based on the number 10. In multiplying two numbers, the reader finds that their point of intersection is the product of the value of the number at the top and the number in the first descending column. (Thus 3 across multiplied by 3 down yields 9, while 3 across multiplied by 4 down yields 12.)[6]

Other topics in this section include the operations of numbers, combinations of numbers, proportionate relations of numbers, classes of numbers, and — most important — the symbolism of numbers.[7] Though the symbolism is somewhat Christianized, the concept that numbers have theological significance has a long history in the Pythagoreanism of Antiquity and the Middle Ages. Accordingly, the number 1 (the monad) is perfection, while 2 refers to opposites, such as hot and cold, good and bad, hunger and satisfaction. Number 3 is perfect, while it also represents the theological virtues (Faith, Hope, and Charity), as well as the principal sins (luxury, pride, and avarice) and the grades of penitence (contrition, confession, and satisfaction). Examples of the symbolism of the important number 4 include the 4 elements (derived, Pacioli says, from Plato's *Timaeus*), the 4 directions, the 4 seasons, and the 4 sensations (hot, cold, humid, dry). A mysterious plate illustrating special uses of number is composed of thirteen tables, all of which contain series of numbers ending in 30.[8] The importance of arithmetic in achieving harmony is demonstrated in another plate containing a table that equates arithmetic and proportion. If one follows only one route, within arithmetic, it seems to suggest, this would lead to "discontinuity," and "irrationality." Arithmetic functions best, according to this chart, in terms of its function of measurement and its association with geometrical proportion, which produces "continuity" and "rationality." Together, arithmetic and geometry make for balance and symmetry and the ultimate goal of number, harmony.

In the section on geometry, Pacioli presents the Pythagorean theorem (though he does not call it that) and illustrates its geometrical proofs. This is followed by practical advice, derived largely from Vitruvius, showing the utility of the theorem in constructing steps and in leaning ladders against walls. In the section on proportion, Pacioli illustrates not only triangles, pyramids, squares, and circles but, as well, these forms inscribed within each other. He also illustrates the five regular solids, widely known, he says, through Plato.[9] Euclid is important for Pacioli in the sections on geometry, but his frequent allusions to Boethius and Vitruvius throughout the text suggest that these are his true heroes. Though he also borrows from others (e.g., the medieval mathematician Fibonacci) he does not always credit them.[10]

In his *De divina proportione*, a text on which he had been working since 1496 when he met Leonardo da Vinci, his housemate in Milan, Pacioli demonstrated his interest in Pythagoreanism.[11] This work was devoted to showing that the quadrivium (first described in Antiquity by Archytas, a possible pupil of Pythagoras, and known throughout the Middle Ages through Boethius), or four disciplines of arithmetic, geometry, astronomy, and music, could lead the philosopher out of darkness and into the light of truthful sensory perception. This "truth" was reflected in the visual arts, he maintained, including perspective, painting, sculpture, and architecture, which are based on geometrical forms such as the pyramid and sphere that he discusses at great length. The visual arts are listed, together with "secret sciences," in the subtitle of this treatise, which was dedicated to the Duke of Milan.[12] Its perspective illustrations were drawn by Leonardo da Vinci, who as an engineer and mathematician (not to mention painter, architect, and sculptor) in the employ of the Duke was his collaborator. Whether contrived by Pacioli himself or by Leonardo, the fifty-nine large stereometric representations of regular and irregular bodies drawn in perspective in the *De divina proportione* demonstrate an enormous inventory of the possibilities inherent in the truncation of the five regular solids so as to give shape to new and more "perfected" forms, many of which can be circumscribed within a sphere and all of which are centralized.[13] It is no wonder, then, that Pacioli so frequently refers to the *Timaeus* in this text and that he considers the dodecahedron to be the most divine of forms ("nobilissimo") for it contains the proportions of the cosmos.[14]

Pacioli's Pythagoreanism, as demonstrated in this work, can perhaps best be summarized by his castigation of contemporary architects (surely referring to those who were at the time building the enormous cathedral of Milan in the northern Gothic style) who knew nothing of Vitruvius:

> We call architects those who have never even seen the cover of the excellent book by the learned and great mathematician Vitruvius, who wrote about architecture with the greatest wisdom. ... Those who deviate from his teachings ... are a disgrace to the discipline and therefore will never know the joy that Pythagoras experienced when he discovered the true proportion of the straight lines of the right triangle. This angle is of such excellence that ... without understanding it, it is impossible to understand proportion. ... In deviating from Vitruvius's advice, these architects make torturous and deformed buildings.[15]

This paragraph says it all. Pythagoras and Vitruvius are interlocked and whoever deviates from their (mathematical) teachings not only is wrongheaded but is also unable to obtain true proportion. It also makes it clear that Pythagorean doctrine is the arbiter of perfect proportion. The fact that his work is about the divinity of proportion is in itself a Pythagorean concept, for it recalls an old Pythagorean concept well known in Antiquity – the theology of arithmetic. Indeed, Pacioli explains that perfect harmony was first explained in the mathematics of the "divine" Plato, who understood the discovery of Pythagoras, and was subsequently explained in the *De arithmetica* of Boethius.

Pacioli's travels brought him from Milan to Venice in 1494 (at a time when Giorgio Valla, his colleague in mathematics, was a professor there) on the occasion of the publication of his *Summa arithmetica*.[16] He visited the Adriatic city again in 1508. The occasion of his presence in Venice at this time was to deliver a special honorary inaugural lecture celebrating Euclid. In that lecture, on 11 August in the church of San Bartolomeo di Rialto, Pacioli made certain to exalt Pythagoras and Nicomachus as the Greek founders of the science of number, and Boethius and Apuleius as their Latin followers.[17] Though Giorgio Valla was already dead at the time, other mathematicians and cosmological humanists were present, in addition to a number of Spanish theologians and numerous philosophers and medical doctors. Also in attendance was the great Venetian humanist printer Aldus Manutius and the great Veronese humanist mathematician Fra Giocondo, whose first illustrated edition of Vitruvius's *De architectura* would be issued in nearby Verona in 1511.[18] Thus were Milan and Venice linked in the world of early sixteenth-century Pythagorean thought in Italy, in part through the activities of Pacioli.

Pacioli's Pythagoreanism is underlined by his high esteem for Nicholas Cusanus (who, it will be remembered, espoused Pythagorean ideas). In this light, the admiration he expresses for Leonardo da Vinci suggests that Leonardo too may have been attached to Pythagorean ideals.[19]

Leonardo da Vinci (1452–1519) was a character of the utmost canniness. He does not tell us much about himself. But we can deduce his admiration for Pythagoras because he studied his theorem; this admiration is also suggested by the literary works he owned and by those contemporaries with whom he associated.[20] Though he does not tell us that he was a Pythagorean, what is known of his reading, acquaintances, interests, and personal habits strongly suggests he was.

For Leonardo, Plato was the most important author of Antiquity. Though he certainly knew the *Timaeus*, he appears to have known, as well, Ficino's translations of Plato's many other works that appeared in Florence during the late 1470s and 1480s. Leonardo's great respect for Plato, with whom he was not always in agreement, can be seen in an extensive passage in which he discusses Plato's teachings on the four elements and their relation to the universe, and in his discussions of the 5 regular solids.[21]

Leonardo's familiarity with Boethius is revealed in a comment he wrote to accompany his illustration of the rules of acoustics: "In these two rules, that is of the blow and of the force one may employ the proportions which Pictagoras made use of in his music."[22] This observation indicates his interest in an important musical discovery attributed since late Antiquity (in the writings of Boethius) to Pythagoras – namely, the dependence of the musical intervals on arithmetical ratios. Perhaps Boethius's sixth-century ideas were introduced to Leonardo by the learned (Pythagorean) musical theorist Gaffurio.

The probability that Leonardo and Gaffurio, who shared a strong interest in music and mathematics, were in personal contact is suggested by the fact that they were the same age (Gaffurio was born in 1451, Leonardo in 1452) and by the coincidence that they were both in Milan, and both in the service of the Duke, at the same time, in the 1490s. This connection may account for Leonardo's frequent references to musical harmony, which, he maintained, like polyphony, produces beauty. Leonardo's interest in Pythagorean music theory is underlined by his own musicianship. Not only did he play and sing "divinely" to the lyre (Apollo's, Pythagoras's, and Ficino's instrument), he constructed a beautiful one of his own invention, made of silver. He brought this precious instrument with him to Milan in 1483.[23]

Indubitably, Leonardo's interest in Boethius was solidified by his friendship with Luca Pacioli. It was in Milan during the time he, presumably, knew Gaffurio that Leonardo met Pacioli. The latter was called to the court of Lodovico Sforza in 1496 while Leonardo was at work there. From Leonardo's several mentions of Pacioli in his manuscripts it is evident that they formed a firm friendship, most likely based on their mutual interests in perspective, mechanics, architecture, and, above all, mathematics.[24] In one instance, Leonardo refers to Pacioli as his teacher, for he says he is learning the multiplication of roots from Maestro Luca.[25] In this light, it should be remembered that the multiplication tables presented by Pacioli in his *Summa arithmetica*, copied from Boethius, were called "Pythagorean" multiplication tables. Certainly, the influence of Pacioli reinforced Leonardo's interest in the works of Boethius. While Leonardo was undoubtedly familiar with Boethius's *De arithmetica*, it was more than likely that Boethius's *De musica* was of greater interest to him. Boethius's interest in harmony must have been particularly attractive to Leonardo. Possibly it provided the inspiration for Leonardo's construction of a monochord like the one used by Pythagoras, described in the text of Boethius.[26]

It was, however, their collaboration in Pacioli's *De divina proportione* from 1496 to 1498, for which Leonardo produced the illustrations, that brought them closest and stimulated Leonardo's great respect for Vitruvius.[27] Pacioli's verdict that architects who deviated from the "true" teachings of Vitruvius were in error was surely linked to his view that perfect geometric proportion was dependent on the right angle of the square, the discovery of Pythagoras that so elated him. Leonardo's interest in solving problems of arithmetic incommensurability (i.e., elements that are seemingly irreconcilable because they lack a common standard of comparison) by geometrical means, which he identified with discovering "divine harmony," was surely stimulated by his contact with Pacioli. In a famous drawing of about 1496, Leonardo demonstrated that by inscribing a figure in a circle he could establish commensurability (i.e., he demonstrated that both could share a common measure) geometrically. In this sense, both Leonardo and Pacioli were inspired by Vitruvius, for Vitruvius had praised the Pythagoreans for solving problems of incommensurables by geometric methods.[28] Thus did Leonardo and Pacioli share the belief that true proportion is predicated on geometry.[29]

Leonardo's admiration of Vitruvius may have been activated by his friendship with Francesco di Giorgio who, as discussed in Chapter 5, was a Pythagorean whose historical mentor was Vitruvius.[30] This is reflected in the conviction shared by both regarding the importance of drawing for conceptualizing and illustrating scientific problems. This connection is underlined in the fact that Leonardo acquired and annotated an early version of Francesco di Giorgio's treatise on architecture, one of two works he owned by this author, a work based on the authority of Vitruvius.[31] Leonardo's interest in Vitruvius is evident not only in the fact that he apparently cherished his own copy of Vitruvius's *De architectura*, but also because he quoted extensively (a rarity for Leonardo) from Vitruvius.[32] He refers to Vitruvius's methods of measurement, his interest in the triangle, and his studies of motion including the revolutions of wheels and the functions of other mechanical constructs. Even if his own investigations yielded different results, Leonardo is always careful to cite the authority of Vitruvius with respect.

While it is unlikely that Leonardo could have known Alberti, who died shortly after his arrival in Florence as a young man, it appears that he admired Alberti enormously. A number of passages in his writings make it clear that he had studied Alberti's written works, two of which he owned.[33] Leonardo refers to Alberti's studies of proportions and weights in a work intended for Sigismundo

Malatesta, lord of Rimini; elsewhere he cites precise information on the same subject that he says he read in Alberti's *Ludis rerum mathematicarum* (*The Discipline of Mathematics*).[34] In his notes, Leonardo calls attention to Alberti's studies of balance in relating the power of wind and the depth of water to the motion of ships. This is almost certainly derived from a work, now lost, by Alberti that was well known at the time.[35]

Probably also inspired by Alberti, Leonardo's views on painting strongly assert its scientific nature. His complimentary discussion of painters who "described and codified their art as science" undoubtedly refers to Alberti's precedent. So also does his description of painting as dependent on arithmetic and geometry, from which perspective was born, vividly bring to mind Alberti's *Della pittura*, a work that, first published in Florence in 1435, codified the scientific approach to constructing a unified space. Perspective, Leonardo elaborates, is dependent on the visual rays of astronomy that calculate distances and dimensions with number and measure. His further assertion that painting is a harmony similar to music also echoes Alberti's discussions of painting and architecture.[36] In discussing proportion, Leonardo's declaration that "Every part of the whole must be proportionate to the whole" brings to mind Alberti's insistence, in his treatise on architecture (a work Leonardo owned), that beauty consists in the relation of each part to the whole, a relation that produces harmony from which nothing can be added or subtracted without unbalancing the whole.[37] Clearly also, Leonardo refers to Alberti in stating that "[A] building should always be detached on all sides so that its form may be seen."[38] Such observations provide evidence that, like Alberti, Leonardo believed that the key to correct proportion lies in the essence of concord that, produced by musical harmony, promotes perfect unity.

In addition then, to the Pythagoreanism of his preferred sources, Plato, Vitruvius, Boethius, Giorgio Valla, Gaffurio, Pacioli, and Francesco di Giorgio – all of whom can be associated with Pythagorean ideas – Leonardo's admiration of Alberti strongly suggests his own interest in Pythagoreanism.

A Florentine who may have been familiar to Leonardo (as his frequent references to "maestro Pagolo medico" imply) was Paolo Toscanelli. Though as suggested previously Toscanelli may have been a Pythagorean, Leonardo's attraction to this older intellectual (who died in 1482, approximately eleven years after Leonardo's arrival in Florence and just before his departure for Milan) was surely based on the vastness of his scientific knowledge and the experimental nature of his investigations. This association may have inspired a pursuit that they appear to have held in common, mathematics. This is suggested by Leonardo's insistence that the conflation of arithmetic, geometry, and music enables the artist to discover the interrelationship of parts that leads to perfect harmony.

Though he probably met Giorgio Valla in Milan in the early 1480s, Leonardo had an opportunity to see him again in Venice in 1499. In any case, Giorgio's vast Pythagorean encyclopedia, *De expetendis et fugiendis rebus*, was probably well known to Leonardo, for it appears that he owned a copy of it.[39] Leonardo's writings show that, in his attempts to conflate the practical sciences of mathematics, cosmography, navigation, and astronomy in the interest of discovering the harmony inherent in the celestial bodies, he was influenced by Giorgio's major work.[40] The interlocked intellectual interests of Leonardo were not distant from those of Giorgio Valla. Nor were they distant from those of Gaffurio. Giorgio's polymathic interests in cosmology, arithmetic, and proportion, were Pythagorean in that they were based on Nicomachus and Boethius. They paralleled Gaffurio's investigations of celestial sounds and harmonic proportion that revered the same ancient Pythagorean predecessors. Both Giorgio Valla and Gaffurio were Pythagoreans and both were surely personally known to Leonardo. Leonardo would have been among friends when he discussed Pythagorean topics such as harmony and mathematics, not only with Pacioli but also with them.

Whether first inspired by Pacioli, Giorgio Valla, Gaffurio, or all three, Leonardo's interest in harmony extended to the reconciliation of opposites, an idea associated with Pythagoreanism since Antiquity.[41] Leonardo speaks of pleasure and pain, tribulation and repentance, envy and gratitude, tolerance and intolerance: "They are back to back because they are opposed to each other; and they exist as contraries on the same body, because they have the same basis"[42] He also speaks frequently of the unifying power of the circle and of the five regular solids, each of which, he believed, could be circumscribed by a sphere.[43]

The likelihood that Leonardo was a Pythagorean is underlined by his views respecting animals. One comment among the sixty-five hundred various surviving sheets of text and drawings left by Leonardo demonstrates his familiarity with the Pythagorean doctrine of transmigration, for it discusses the peregrinations of souls, which, he suggests, animals have. However, since it forms part of a humorous jest, it does not reveal anything specific regarding his thoughts on this subject.[44] More important is the fact that he was a vegetarian. Though some modern writers have assumed this in putting forward their interpretations of Leonardo's personality, they have offered no proof.[45] Leonardo, however, speaks for himself.

Leonardo's Pythagorean tendencies are spelled out in the large number of comments he makes relating to the subject of vegetarianism that are clearly linked to his deep sympathy for animals. The passion and phraseology with which he expresses his anger over the killing of animals is reminiscent of Ovid's description of Pythagoras's view as described in the *Metamorphoses*, a work that Leonardo owned.

Writing about food that has been alive, Leonardo says:

A large part of the bodies which have had life will pass into the bodies of other animals, … ministering to their needs and bearing away … waste; the life of man is made by the things which he eats, and these carry with them that part of man which is dead.[46]

A note entitled "Of Sheep, Cows, Goats, and the Like" reads: "From countless numbers will be stolen their little children, and the throats of these shall be cut, and they shall be quartered most barbarously."[47] In another, entitled "Of Asses Which Are Beaten," Leonardo expresses his sympathy for animals that are beaten:

> I see thy children given into slavery … without ever receiving any benefit, and in lieu of any reward for the services they have done … they are repaid by the severest punishments, and they constantly spend their lives in the service of their oppressor.[48]

Another, entitled "Of Asses," reads: "The many labours shall be repaid by hunger, thirst, wretchedness, blows and goadings."[49] Yet another, entitled "Of Things Which Are Eaten Which Are First Put to Death," reads: "Those who nourish them will be slain by them and scourged by barbarous death."[50] In "Of Eggs Which Being Eaten Cannot Produce Chickens," he laments: "Oh! How many will those be who will never be born."[51] In "Of Fishes Which Are Eaten with Their Roes," Leonardo observes: "Endless generations will perish through the death of the pregnant."[52] In "Of the Beasts from Whom Cheese Is Made," he says "The milk will be taken from the tiny children." Concerning the stripping of horns from rams, Leonardo says: "In the horns of animals shall be seen sharp irons, which shall take away the lives of many of their species."[53] Of bees, Leonardo says: "They live together in communities. They are drowned in order that their honey may be seized."[54] A remark about animals in general reads: "All the animals languish, filling the air with lamentations," while one about dolphins and tuna cites their frightened demeanor before those who pursue them with "insensate fury," terrifying the fishes that become the spoil of people.[55]

In a statement on the cruelty of humans to animals, Leonardo comments further:

> There shall be nothing remaining on the earth or under the earth or in the waters that shall not be pursued and molested or destroyed … and their own bodies shall be made the tomb and the means of transit of all the living bodies which they have slain.[56]

In a letter he describes a bodyguard as "abusive" because the guard goes about with a gun, killing birds.[57]

These and other surviving comments provide abundant testimony to Leonardo's vegetarianism. This is only emphasized by numerous remarks Leonardo makes concerning his respect for animals. Animals, he says, are incapable of wrongdoing, as opposed to human beings, who often are – especially in their treatment of animals – evil: "Man has much power of discourse which for the most part is vain and false; animals have but little, but it is useful and true, and a small truth is better than a great lie."[58] Leonardo's disdain for "human stupid-ity" is expressed in speculating that their self-absorption alienates humans from nature; thus, in times of great snows helpless beasts, who lack such conceits, come to the houses of human beings to beg alms as from their masters. Ironically, he speculates, "The masters of estates will eat their own labourers."[59] Human beings, when they are satiated, have no greater desire than to see to it that "Nothing will remain on earth, or under the earth, or in the waters, which will not be perse-cuted, disturbed, and spoiled."[60]

According to Leonardo, animals understand justice, fidelity, loyalty, humility, and chastity (all notable Pythagorean virtues), whereas humans who use animals as a vehicle for food "are much below beasts." He disdains such people as being noth-ing other than passages for food and manufacturers of excrement because they produce nothing but "full privies."[61] The elephant, for Leonardo, embodies virtues seldom found in human beings: "[It] has, by nature what is rarely found in man, that is, Honesty, Prudence, Justice, and the Observance of Religion."[62] Elephants, he says, are merciful, give assistance to each other, and are reluctant to fight.

The moral code implied by Leonardo's many various surviving notes con-cerning life and conduct suggests that his life was governed by temperance as opposed to lust, abstinence as opposed to gluttony, chastity as opposed to promis-cuity, simplicity as opposed to avariciousness, and other lofty principles familiar to those who knew the Pythagorean maxims. He advocates light exercise and strict rules for sleeping, refraining from "wantonness," and observing a "strict diet." In addition, in a number of passages he expresses his reprobation and harshest con-tempt for humans who do nothing useful but strive merely for riches. In several letters, he apologizes for having to earn a living. Elsewhere he laments the misery of humankind for it is the slave of money.[63]

Leonardo's views on nature reveal a man who was deeply committed to animals, as Pythagoras was known to have been in the literature of Antiquity. Pythagoras was described by one of his own contemporaries as having saved a little dog from being beaten; from this incident, a long tradition describing Pythagoras's opposition to killing animals became well established in ancient literature in works familiar to Renaissance readers.[64] Similarly, Leonardo's views on morals suggest recurrent themes first expounded by ancient Pythagoreans, who were governed by strict rules in conducting their personal lives. These themes survived in works such as the *Golden Verses*. Praising such virtues as justice, fidelity, friendship, continence, abstinence, and piety, these maxims were still, after a long life in the medieval world, well known and highly regarded in Renaissance Italy.

Leonardo's empathy for others and disregard for the accumulation of riches is complemented by the attention he pays, in his last will and testament, to his servants. To them, he thoughtfully bequeaths clothing, money, and land. His inter-est in numbers is evident here, for he decrees that at his funeral sixty torches be carried by sixty poor persons. The torches, he stipulates, were to be divided among four churches, with each church to receive ten pounds of wax for candles.[65]

While, owing to the complexities of his notations and to their fragmentation, it is difficult to determine the full extent of Leonardo's commitment to any single ideology, his interests, personal associations, and views on the practicalities of life all make it clear that his intellectual outlook and personal habits were decidedly Pythagorean and that in this respect he shared much with Ficino and Pico. Although Leonardo, perhaps the most dazzling intellect of his time, did not cast himself as a "Pythagorean" in the clear language that Ficino, for example, had, it appears that he functioned as a spiritual epicenter of Pythagorean thought in northern Italy. When he moved to France in about 1516, his interests could continue for it appears, as will be discussed later in this chapter, that Pythagorean mathematical thought was well established in northern Europe at this time.

These were years of strong activity on behalf of Pythagoras among mathematician contemporaries of Pacioli and Leonardo at the international level. Among the many non-Italian mathematicians who published texts on the philosophy of mathematics was Gregorius Reisch (d. 1523), a German Carthusian monk and confessor to Emperor Maximilian I. In his magnum opus, *Margarita philosophica tractans* (*Philosophical Pearl*), published in Strasburg in 1503 and the first modern encyclopedia to be printed, he paid tribute to the long-lived medieval idea that Pythagoras invented the trivium and the quadrivium. He provides a compendium of both and describes, in addition, the moral and natural sciences as well as occult knowledge (sleep and wakefulness, respiration and inspiration, life and death, the usefulness of letters and number in Hebrew lore, etc.), a subject that will become increasingly important in midcentury Germany. Prominent in his discussion of arithmetic is a summary of Boethius's *De arithmetica*. A large woodcut representing the Liberal Arts as a female figure shows her flanked by Boethius and Pythagoras.[66] This image will be discussed in the next chapter (fig. 7).

Another prominent mathematician of those years is the Swiss Johannes Blasius (d. 1550). In a work entitled *Liber arithmetice practice astrologis* (*Book of Arithmetic for Astrologists*), published in 1513, Blasius makes his Pythagoreanism clear by anointing the ardent Pythagorean to whom his treatise is dedicated as the high priest of mathematics:

> That famous Pythagoras, who first laid claim to the name of philosopher, among not a few who recommended most salutary pursuits to the human race, especially warned that good must be cherished with reverence and that the soul must be made beautiful with learning. You, a most diligent observer of Pythagorean doctrine, are so strong in learning and so illustrious in erudition that you deserve easily to be chosen high-priest in the registry of the most famous. Your office is of such distinction that all may call you a priest of great honor.[67]

The bulk of his text is devoted to number theory derived from the ancient Pythagoreans Nicomachus and Boethius.

Thus was Pythagoreanism clearly appealing to mathematicians and scientific philosophers of the early sixteenth century not only in Italy but also in northern Europe. But not all Pythagoreans were mathematicians. Baldassare Castiglione is a good example of someone who shaped his literary response to the question of what constitutes the perfect courtier according to Pythagorean principles. Throughout his masterpiece, *Il Cortegiano* (*The courtier*), written in 1514 and first published in 1528, he praises moderation, unity, the balancing of opposites, proportion, and the value of music in the development of the harmonious personality. His courtier is a man of moderation who seeks the middle ground, where perfection lies.[68] Not surprisingly, Castiglione was a member of the court at Urbino.

ROMAN PERSPECTIVES

Early sixteenth-century Rome was unusual in two respects. First, most humanists active there were connected with the papal court, and second, most of these humanists were not home grown but came from elsewhere in Italy or, even, Europe. One of these was Filippo Beroaldo Senior of Bologna, the publisher of the *Symbola Pythagorae* discussed in Chapter 3. Although this work (see Appendix B) is primarily dedicated to publishing the moral doctrines attributed to Pythagoras, Beroaldo makes clear his own Pythagoreanism in recommending to his readers that they live according to the teachings of Pythagoras: "Our welfare lies in imitating Pythagoras," he says, and "following continually his teachings." These teachings, he insists, instruct us to "shake off sloth and torpor" and to keep away from the excesses of "wanton behavior."[69]

Another such humanist was Tommaso Inghirami (1470–1516), an electrifying orator, who as Canon of St. Peter's and papal librarian to Popes Julius II and Leo X was in a highly influential position both in Rome and at the Vatican. A native of Volterra, he had been raised in Florence, and there is good reason to believe that he knew Pico della Mirandola and admired him to the extent that he influenced the then pope, Alexander VI, to lift the ban on Pico. Tommaso's admiration for Pico is evident in the fact that he paraphrased Pico's writings in his orations.[70] Early on, Tommaso was connected with Vitruvius for as an actor he played the lead role in a play performed to inaugurate the theater in the newly rebuilt Palazzo della Cancelleria that boasted the first (modern) Vitruvian architectural setting. This special event took place in Rome in 1486, and the performance was memorialized in the dedication by Giovanni Sulpizio da Veroli (who it will be remembered visited the court of Urbino) of his groundbreaking work, the first printed edition of Vitruvius's *De architectura*, published in that same year. Tommaso was also well connected with the court of Urbino.[71]

Tommaso had another important connection with Pythagoreanism. As a highly regarded expert on Cicero and the most famous Ciceronian in Rome, he was well acquainted with Cicero's penchant for Pythagoreanism. He surely knew that Cicero regarded Pythagoras as a divine authority, and that Cicero had made a pilgrimage to Metapontum to visit the house of Pythagoras, which had become a shrine in his time. Also certainly known to Tommaso was Cicero's admiration for Pythagoras as a mathematician and his regard for Plato's Pythagoreanism, which had influenced his own view that number – manifested through arithmetic and geometry – produces harmony and affects all branches of knowledge. Nowhere was this more brilliantly expressed than in the first description of the harmony of the spheres by Cicero in the *In somnium Scipionis*, the only section of a much larger work, the *De re publica* (*On the State*), to survive in medieval times. Because of this special importance, its lost parent work, which provided the background to Cicero's exposition that numbers governed the "symphony" of the heavens, had long been eagerly sought. It was the young Tommaso who found this work. The discovery of this precious text, the only one of Cicero's still not accounted for in the last decade of the fifteenth century, made the Ciceronian corpus complete.[72] Last but not least, Tommaso Inghirami would have been aware of something that other intellectuals also knew well – that Cicero's most revered personal friend in the first century B.C. was Nigidius Figulus, an ardent Pythagorean. Nigidius was important to the Rome of Cicero's time for he had worked hard to keep Pythagoreanism alive in the city.[73]

Though Tommaso did not say so in writing, this influential clergyman, who was a friend of the painter Raphael and was his humanist advisor in the painting of the Stanza della Segnatura, appears to have been, like his hero, Cicero, strongly inclined toward intellectual Pythagoreanism. Yet despite the agglomeration of circumstantial suggestions to this effect, he appears to have rejected the practical values of Pythagoreanism, largely because he was known to be a bon vivant or gourmand.[74]

Another person of interest in early sixteenth-century Rome is Marco Fabio Calvo (ca. 1440–1527). A native of Ravenna and a medical doctor, Fabio apparently spent most of his adult life in Rome, where he was known as a Pythagorean and a vegetarian. While in Rome, he indulged his major interests, which were ancient medicine and mathematics (both, it should be noted, fields in which the authority of Pythagoras was strong). There he published the first complete Latin edition of Hippocrates (the *Corpus hippocraticum*), as well as two works on Galen. Because Hippocrates's work had been preserved in a piecemeal way, Fabio took the liberty of inserting commentaries that included antiquarian astrological and meteorological information. A note he inserted into this text expresses his regret that he was unable to include all the information on the science of number he would have wished.[75] A contemporary letter describes Fabio not only as a very learned man, but also as an ascetic who never touched wine and who ate only one meal a day. Another such letter describes him as a virtuous and holy man who scorned money and who, as a strict Pythagorean, lived very simply, eating primarily cabbage and lettuce.[76] It was perhaps inevitable that Fabio, as an expert on the topography of ancient Rome, should become friends with Raphael. As he himself says, he made a special translation of Vitruvius in *volgare* (Italian) in Raphael's home expressly to please his friend. Raphael, in return, expressed his love for Fabio by personally caring for him, like a father, during Fabio's serious illness.[77]

Though Raphael has not left us any Pythagorean texts, this care and devotion, beyond his desire for a Vitruvius text of his own, speaks louder than any written word. The accounts of Pythagoras by ancient writers well known to the Renaissance offer abundant descriptions of Pythagoreans caring for each other when they were ill; Pythagoras himself had exemplified this care in personally nursing the sick.[78] As we shall see, Raphael's Pythagoreanism will be evident in his paintings.

VENICE: THE *HARMONIA MUNDI* OF FRANCESCO ZORZI AND PYTHAGOREAN MUSICAL TRADITIONS

The theme of harmony so prevalent in early sixteenth-century Pythagoreanism continued to be important in Italy in later decades, especially in Venice where it had been born in the work of Giorgio Valla. There too the Venetian theologian-philosopher Francesco Zorzi (also known as Francesco Giorgio) established his wide knowledge and culture in the publication of his major work, the *De harmonia mundi*, in 1525.[79] The many subsequent editions of this work published not only in Italy but also in France, Germany, and elsewhere in Europe testify to its enormous popularity and influence.[80]

Heavily influenced by Ficino's Pythagorean ideas concerning the concord and unity of all knowledge, Zorzi's description of *harmonia mundi* is essentially a well-ordered and poetically conceived manifesto of Pythagorean cosmological themes. Its division into three parts clearly signifies Zorzi's admiration for the mysticism of number, to which he pays tribute throughout the volume. The number 3 is the ultimate symbol of harmony, he explains, for it reflects the divine Trinity and is exemplified in the perfection of the triangle that is the beginning, middle, and end of everything.[81] The proem to this work cites the authority of ancient Pythagoreans who wrote about the mysteries of "true philosophy." We can hope to understand these perplexing enigmas, we are told, through the use of numbers that are venerated by all Pythagoreans. Zorzi elucidates on number as the foundation of all things and as the key to understanding how reciprocal harmonies balance each other. The mutual agreement of cosmic harmonies is reflected, he assures us, in the harmonies contained within a human being, as well as in those contained in music.[82] Making a special argument for the virtues of number 6, Zorzi elaborates on the symbolism of various other numbers and their relation to the well-being of the universe.[83] He rhapsodizes on Plato's ascription of geometrical form to the four elements, especially on the perfect stability of the cube of the earth and on the pyramid, because they have four bases and four angles. He recommends the use of music in singing hymns to the creator and unifier of all divine things, as well as its use, by changing its modes, in practical areas such as preventing social ills by restraining people from wanton behavior.[84]

Zorzi criticizes the impious (those who do not respect Plato, Porphyry, Iamblichus, Boethius, and other Pythagoreans), who are the cause of dissonance. His primary goal is to demonstrate the importance of the divine monad. This principle is God, the architect of the universe, who, after having created all things, brought them back to form an orderly and perfect unity. Speaking in Vitruvian terms, Zorzi views the harmonious universe as an example of perfect architecture and perfect music.

The "perfect" music was, of course, the harmony of the spheres, a subject of great importance in Gaffurio's Milan and also a significant element in Zorzi's thought. This subject would continue to fascinate music theorists throughout the sixteenth century, remaining, despite some special effects (such as "secret harmonies" practiced by Jewish and Muslim mystics, and "alchemical music" practiced by esoteric craftsmen),[85] essentially tied to the classical music of the spheres first described by Cicero and elaborated by Macrobius and Porphyry, who had declared that the only mortal who could hear this music was Pythagoras. This fascination can be seen in the work of the Venetian Gioseffo Zarlino (1520–1590), who claimed to carry on the Pythagorean tradition established by Boethius in explaining harmony through number; the Florentine Vincenzo Galilei (d. 1591), who was interested in modifying medieval traditions of the scale and likewise sought to rediscover the purity of ancient music through number; the Dalmatian philosopher Francesco Patrizi da Cherso (1529–1597), who, openly declaring his Platonism while occupying the chair in Platonic philosophy at the University of Ferrara, viewed the music of the spheres as a model for understanding the universe; and in that of the Spanish lyre player and musical theorist the blind Francisco de Salinas (1514–1590), who, in his seven books on music organized to correspond with the seven planets, cited the usefulness of Nicomachus and Boethius for his compositions of concordant numbers designed to produce the sweetest harmony.[86]

ESOTERIC PYTHAGOREANISM: REUCHLIN AND HIS CONTEMPORARIES IN GERMANY, ITALY, ENGLAND, AND THE NETHERLANDS

Whereas the theme of harmony entranced Pythagoreans through the first decade of the sixteenth century, Pythagoreans of the next decades began to turn their attention toward the mysteries of the universe. Johannes Reuchlin, who, it will be remembered, had met Pico della Mirandola, was one such person. Imbued with the Pythagoreanism of his Italian colleagues, his abiding fascination for the relation between Pythagoras and Hebraic culture provides ample evidence of his active Pythagoreanism even in the face of his persecution.

The correspondence between Reuchlin and various of his friends, admirers, and defenders makes this clear. In an undated letter to Philip Melanchthon, he describes his admiration for Pythagorean discipline. Another, addressed to a lawyer, praises Pythagorean silence, while yet another, to a friend in Ror, cites Pythagorean moral example. A letter of 1515 to Pietro Galatino refers to the vivid contemporary interest in the relation of Pythagoras to the Kaballah. One from Erasmus to Reuchlin praises Reuchlin as the one who comes closest of anyone else to Pico.[87]

The dedication of Reuchlin's magnum opus, the *De Arte Cabalistica*, is unambiguous concerning his purpose, which was, he tells his dedicatee (Pope Leo X), to bring "to light the beliefs of Pythagoras." He explains: "I have therefore written of the symbolic philosophy of the art of the Kabbalah so as to make Pythagorean doctrine better known to scholars."[88] The division of this earthshaking Pythagorean text into three books suggests that the Pythagoreanism he displays and defends throughout for the number 3, the number known to Pythagoreans as the all-inclusive "perfect" number that comprises the beginning, middle, and end of all in one, was a symbol for him of the tripartite division of the universe.[89] As one who was a convinced believer in the power of number symbolism as a means of enigmatic communication, Reuchlin does not fail to weave various meanings by referring to number throughout his text. While his greatest praise is reserved for the number 7, the most revered of all numbers, he explains that the number 4, borrowed by Pythagoras from the Jewish Tetragrammaton to form the basis of the *tetraktys*, is even more important because it unifies Pythagoreanism with ancient Hebraic culture: "Kabbalah and Pythagoreanism are the same stuff."[90]

Reuchlin does not ignore geometry in his investigation of the history of Pythagoreanism. He speaks about circles, which, though they can be divided into parts, are examples of consummate harmony. A circle is harmony, he declares, and the lyre, with its seven strings, refers to the harmony of the universe that is represented by the circle. This "circular" argument is buttressed by references to the balancing of opposites, or contraries, by which the universe is harmonized. Through moderation, humankind too may attain such a harmony, he tells us. In holding aloft the Pythagorean "Y," as the choice of Hercules that provided human beings with the means to chose virtue over vice, Reuchlin proclaims that this letter enables humans to achieve a harmony reflecting that of the universe. He credits, as well, the roles of geometric forms in the structure of the universe. In joining their four sides, the marriage of the pyramid and the cube make a dodecahedron that Pythagoreans, he says, recognize as the universe. His reasoning is ultimately tied to Hebraic lore as he constantly reminds his readers of the importance of Moses for Pythagoras and Plato.[91]

Although, as discussed in Chapter 4, Reuchlin had his detractors, the intellectual world was decidedly on his side. He influenced nonintellectuals as well. This can be seen in the conversion of a German soldier to Pythagoreanism: A letter from the commanding general of the army of Duke William of Bavaria to Erasmus concerning the protection of Reuchlin's house when the army invaded Stuttgart suggests that at least one of the unsung heroes of Pythagoreanism could be found in the military. The letter commends a lieutenant, a Franz von Sickingen, who personally saved the aged and frightened Reuchlin from harm. This lieutenant had learned from Reuchlin to "zealously imitate" Antiquity, admire wisdom, and never say or do anything ignoble. Germany has gained much from the example of Reuchlin, the general says, and the worthy soldier who admired and saved him "deserves to be handed down to posterity."[92]

Another unsung hero of German Pythagoreanism was Conrad Mutianus (Conradus Mutianus Rufus, 1470–1526), a priest from Gotha, a small town near Erfurt. Infused with Pythagoreanism as a result of his Italian education, he was an ardent defender of Reuchlin. Though he was reputed to have a vast knowledge of ancient texts, he communicated only with friends he knew to be loyal and only by letter. These letters suggest his links with Pythagoreanism, for they affirm the value of enigma and silence: "Pythagoras taught his students to be silent. Therefore, like a Pythagorean, I held my tongue."[93] Perhaps this is why, like Pythagoras and like Christ (he suggests), he never published a word.[94]

The influence of Cardinal Egidio da Viterbo, who was a far more prominent defender of Reuchlin, was great – not only in Rome, where he was a prestigious preacher, but also in the north of Europe, where his *Scechina*, (*The Dwelling of God*), published after his death in 1532, came to be well known.[95] Referring to Pico, the initiator of the "Christian" Kabbalah, and to Pico's successor Reuchlin (whose *De arte Cabalistica* he owned and with whom he corresponded), Egidio was convinced that the unity of humankind and the future life of the church depended on incorporating "Kabbalistic truths" into the Christian religion. These truths he found primarily in the symbolism of number. Well known in the sixteenth century as an erudite and eloquent work, the *Scechina* treats the symbolism of each number up to and including 10, the universal number first established, Egidio says, in Aramaic and Hebrew culture and then expounded by Pythagoreans and Platonists. Aside from 10, the most sacred of all numbers, 3, 4, 7, and 8, were of special importance to Egidio. Speaking to the Pope (Clement VII, to whom his text is dedicated), Egidio points out that the first of these, the number of the triad and the Trinity, can perhaps best be understood in the triple crown of the papal tiara.[96] The Pythagorean implication is obvious, though Egidio refrains from pointing this out. Nowhere does Egidio declare himself to be a Pythagorean; yet it is clear that, like his spiritual guide, Saint Augustine, he was smitten by the esoteric doctrines of Pythagoras.

England was not immune to these new interests. On the contrary. Perhaps of all those who demonstrated interest in Pythagorean views the most prominent was John Colet (ca. 1468–1519), a rather unlikely person to be seduced by esotericism of any sort, for as a strict-minded churchman and Dean of St. Paul's he was involved in condemning heretics. Colet's early education in Italy (under the spell of Ficino and Pico, both of whom he knew personally) had, however, instilled in him the broad horizons of Florentine humanism and especially those of Pythagoreanism. No doubt it was this experience that inspired him to compose two treatises on the writings of Dionysius the Areopagite, whose works had been translated into Latin by Ficino.[97] While Colet's commentaries show that he had read the works of his Italian mentors and suggest that he was trying to imitate them, they give the impression of a writer more concerned with proving preexisting scriptural issues than with investigating a new philosophy. Another work of his, *De Sacramentis Ecclesiae* (*On the Sacraments of the Church*), is divided into seven chapters, which he relates not only to the seven sacraments but also to the symbolism the number 7 enjoyed in the mystical (Pythagorean) view of the universe. He also gives ample attention to Moses and to the three divisions of the universe so enthusiastically argued by both Ficino and Pico. Colet's letters, too, echo the then "established" idea that Pythagoras and Plato had "lit their tapers at the lamp of Moses."[98] Although he appears to have had Pythagorean aspirations, his work is characterized by an austere morality that lacks the passion inherent in the sources that inspired him.

Although Sir Thomas More (1478–1535) was also interested in Florentine "Platonism" (or Pythagoreanism), as well as in Hermeticism, he resisted the syncretic impulse of his Italian contemporaries. His publication of the *Life of Pico* written by Pico's nephew Giovanni Francesco Pico shows his own interest in Pico. Though both Colet and More were affected by the tremendous influence of the Pythagorean movement from Italy, they both show that the developing Puritanical point of view was too restrictive to allow them to indulge in the "eccentricities" of Pythagoreanism. One such eccentric was a younger compatriot, Robert Fludd (1574–1637), who would entertain ideas about the Kabbalah and numerical symbolism in the seventeenth century – a time that is beyond the bounds of this study.[99]

Notwithstanding the fact that he was called a "second Pythagoras" by one of his colleagues (as noted in Chapter 3), the Netherlander Erasmus carefully shields himself from any hints that might confirm his Pythagoreanism. However, at times, he suggests he was one. Speaking of his contemporary theologians, he says:

> They are satisfied with Aristotle alone and banish the Platonists and Pythagoreans from the schools. But Augustus preferred the latter two, not only because many of their ideas are perfectly consistent with our religion, but also because their figurative mode of expression … and frequent use of allegory are very close to the language of Sacred Scripture.[100]

He seems, also, to agree with the ancient Pythagorean, Archytas:

> [H]ear the verdict of a philosopher who is pagan though his thoughts are clearly worthy of a Christian. … The Pythagorean Architas [said] … that nature had given man no more fatal disease than the passion for pleasure. The burning desire for pleasure is aroused, grasping for control rashly without restraint. Hence (he used to say) countries are betrayed, governments overthrown, and secret parley held with the enemy.[101]

For the most part, Erasmus repeats facts well known in his time about Pythagoreans, referring to their maxims with respect and admiration. He admires their learning and their culture of caring for the sick, as well as their moral practices, including loyalty, friendship, chastity, and vegetarianism. Perhaps, his deep preoccupation with religious matters during the turbulent years he witnessed distracted him from being more transparent on the question of his own views. On the other hand, this lack of transparency may have been because he was practicing the use of enigma. In any case, as a quintessential humanist, Erasmus remained tied to the classical tradition and refrained from straying into the various paths of esoteric thought that his contemporary Pythagoreans were exploring. As an ideal scholar, he could praise Pythagoras as the "fountain of wisdom" and he could support Reuchlin with vivid energy, but as a writer of original texts, the closest he came to demonstrating his own Pythagoreanism was in his promotion of the idea of concord.

INTERNATIONAL PYTHAGOREANISM AND MAGIC: FRANCE, GERMANY, ENGLAND, AND ITALY

The importance of mathematics as a key to understanding not only the creation of the universe but all its vicissitudes became, increasingly, an international phenomenon in Europe. For many Pythagoreans the mutations and fluctuations of nature invited interest in the realms of magic. This does not refer to practitioners of "black," or demonic, magic who continued to exercise their craft through such traditional works as the *Turba philosophorum* that were concerned with spells and incantations, but to a new generation of practitioners of "white," or natural, magic. Inspired by Ficino, the latter aimed to survey nature in order to discover mysteries that might be solved by the application of Pythagorean "systems," based on number, measure, and harmony. One such system found mysticism in letters rather than numbers. After two trips to Italy, Geofroy Tory (1480–1533), a distinguished Paris printer, found inspiration in Vitruvius for designing each letter of the alphabet with emphasis on its geometric proportions. He paid special attention to the

Pythagorean "Y," being the first to designate the right branch as "virtue" and the left as "vice."[102] Other systems, based on a cosmic view of nature, form a persistent theme in the development of French sixteenth-century Pythagoreanism. While the sense of cosmic correspondence is implied in the revival of the ancient title "La Pleiade" assumed by a "constellation" of seven French Renaissance poets, this cosmic view of nature is exemplified in the work of a number of French intellectuals active from the 1520s to the 1580s. We thus return to Jacques Lefèvre d'Étaples, Josse Clichtove, and Guillaume Postel, all discussed earlier for their interest in Pythagoras himself, and introduce Oronce Fine.

A professor of philosophy who visited Italy, Lefèvre d'Étaples wrote texts in the traditional Pythagorean vein, as well as works that ventured into the occult. Examples of the former include a text on music theory describing the elements of harmony and a commentary on the *De arithmetica* of the "divine" Boethius. His interest in natural magic is evident in two Hermetic works (first translated from Greek into Latin by Ficino) that he edited.[103] His disciples published many editions of such occult works, in addition to others on natural medicine and prognostication.[104] The more influential Josse Clichtove was, however, more mystical in his inclinations. Among the numerous publications of this theologian and enraptured admirer of Pico were various commentaries on works by several medieval French Platonist-Pythagoreans and an impressive volume on number mysticism.

In the preface to the latter, Clichtove describes the Pythagorean doctrine of numbers – which designate concepts such as justice, unity, and purity – and its influence on all natural things. The most sacred number, as would be expected, is 10.[105] Speaking of Pythagorean number symbolism, Clichtove reminded an academic colleague at Paris that Pythagoras was "the most prestigious and important authority" on the central role of mathematics in music, astronomy, and "all subjects of divine contemplation." The study of his system of number is especially important, he asserts, for the "serious" investigation of circles, spheres, triangles, and pyramids. In another letter he explains that "divine Pythagorean instruction" on numbers can best be understood by studying "the godlike Severinus Boethius." This is necessary "so that the mind will be adequately prepared for deeper learning, just as experienced doctors prescribe medicines to strengthen the health of the infirm, or as Pythagoreans undertake certain rites of preparation."[106] Together, Lefèvre and Clichtove represent the adaptation to the French educational world of ideas borrowed from Italian humanism.

Postel was a well-traveled and respected scholar; yet he was a man of peculiar views. Perhaps because his professorships of mathematics and philosophy at Paris and Vienna were terminated, he had time to travel, first to the Orient and then to Italy. In Constantinople he learned Arabic and collected Arabic manuscripts on astronomy that he studied closely, as his surviving annotations suggest. His Latin translations of several Kabbalistic texts provide ample testimony to his knowledge of Hebrew.[107] Both these languages were useful in the development of his unique concept of natural philosophy as incorporating interests in arithmetic, music, astronomy, and, especially, number.

Postel's conception of the universe appears to have been fundamentally indebted to the Pythagorean notion of unity and syncretism. Though difficult to understand because of his idiosyncratic writing style, it is clear that he holds dear the most important tenet of Pythagoreanism – harmony. Harmony and its accomplice, light, Postel asserts, are Pythagorean as well as Platonic concepts, and both were instituted by God.[108] Perhaps it was his strong desire for harmony that motivated his strangely syncretic proposal that the world be united under the French king.[109]

The theme of unity dominates virtually all Postel's writings. For him the universe is a grand structure of correspondences that share a dynamic, if not spiritual, relationship. Plato, whose *Timaeus* had explicated this idea, was, for Postel, "the god" of all philosophers. Postel describes himself as deeply indebted to Plato, as Plato was to his Pythagorean education.[110] Nowhere is this more evident than in a text Postel published in Venice, his second home, in 1549 – shortly after the death in that city of Francesco Zorzi, whom he may well have known.

Postel's introduction to this text, entitled *De admirandis numerorum platonicorum secretis* (*On the Admirable Secrets of Platonic Numbers*), invites the reader to discover the "truth" impregnated in Christian doctrine as it was formed from the tenets of Pythagoras and Plato, who relied on Mosaic – and, he adds, "oriental" (meaning Arabic) – texts. Indeed, it would seem that the dream of Ficino to Christianize Plato was more than realized in the words of Postel, who declares that Plato was a Christian long before Christ.[111]

The number theory Postel lays out in this volume is far more complicated than the traditional Pythagorean system based on the *tetraktys*. Though the numerical significances he proposes start out in a traditional way – 2 as the binary number, 3 as Plato's triples, 4 as the key to history and the universe, 7 as the number of days of the creation – they are developed into deeply enigmatic propositions whose symbolisms are not always clear. An illustration of this is Postel's admiration for the number 72 as one that had divine meaning for Moses. This may refer to an imaginary analysis (which he does not provide) whereby as the product of 9 x 8, 72 is the product of two cubes (8) and 3 squared (9), or 2^3 x 3^2. Even more obscure are his suggestions, based on his understanding of Book VIII of Plato's *Republic*, that other numbers have secret symbolisms. One such number is 666, which, suggested to him by the *Book of Revelation*, may refer to a type of anti-Christ. Though he refrains from explaining how to analyze such puzzling numbers, he claims that 666 (which might be analyzed as being equal to the sum of its digits plus the cubes of its digits [$6 + 6 + 6 + 6^3 + 6^3 + 6^3$]) "proves" the unity of God.[112] Though, clearly, Postel held the Pythagorean values of order, unity, harmony, and number all in deep esteem, not to mention his preference for secrecy and enigma, it appears that he preferred to be thought of as "original."

Although he was not as indebted to Pico and Ficino as he was to the ancient Pythagoreans Theon of Smyrna and Boethius, another French mathematician, Oronce Fine (1494–1555), shared the Pythagorean concerns that had become important in the French mathematical world. He defended his interest in astronomy by imagining that this discipline was so ancient that it had been invented by Hebrews as far back as the sons of Seth. Though Fine professed to disapprove of astrology, he did not hesitate to treat subjects such as signs that might be derived from the planets respecting favorable times for bloodletting, administering medicines, and planting seeds. These interests suggest his solidarity with the medieval Pythagorean Sphere, which was still used for prognosticating. He also wrote a text on the squaring of the circle, an ancient Pythagorean preoccupation.[113]

Meanwhile, in Germany, two equally "original" Pythagoreans had been at work over the past decades, Agrippa and Paracelsus, both of whom were mentioned in Chapter 3. The inventive capacities of both were so novel that they may be considered whimsical if not totally submerged in the occult. The eccentricities of their work were matched, if not superseded, by that of Giambattista Della Porta in Italy, also mentioned previously.

Agrippa's *De occulta philosophia* (*On Occult Philosophy*) is clearly Pythagorean in its inspiration to present a unified methodology stamped with the authority of ancient Pythagorean lore about the soul, as in much of its content. However, drawing from Egyptian, Greek, Roman, Arabic, and Hebraic sources, it passes beyond traditional Pythagoreanism in its aim to promulgate methods to practice and experience magic and other occult arts.

Agrippa first describes the necessity for mathematical learning; the doctrines of number put forward by Plato, Theon of Smyrna, and Boethius; and the importance of unity (which, he notes, the Pythagoreans called "Apollo") and concord. Throughout these books, he duly credits his Pythagorean sources, especially in his lists of the various meanings of each number. To the numbers' traditional Pythagorean meanings he adds more to back up his claim that numbers have different manifestations in the different Pythagorean "worlds" – infernal, elementary (based on the elements), celestial, and supercelestial. He then introduces new Hebraic significances for number as well as numerical values for Hebraic letters. The attention he lavishes on mystical "Hebraic" number symbolism suggests that the legacy of Reuchlin was a powerful influence on him. He declares that Pythagorean proportion, measure, and harmony are fundamental to occult studies because such studies share with Pythagoreanism the desire to find accord and to understand planetary forces.

In the last section of this work, Agrippa leaves the Pythagoreans far behind as he elatedly enters the world of dark magic. Pythagoreans have inspired him and they have provided his language and imagery, but they no longer figure in the directions he provides for incantations to good and bad angels, the evocation of good and bad spirits, the summoning of souls of the dead, fumigations, and other occult practices.[114] It must be admitted that even so he did not forget his Pythagorean base. Many of the "arrangements" he concocts, such as the hostility of bad demons versus the protection of good demons, suggest the reconciliation of opposites. In the end, both must be propitiated in order to find calm. Similarly, he describes the "magical" workings of prognostication by calculating numbers in a way strikingly similar to that of the Pythagorean Sphere, still popular in his time.[115] Earlier on, Agrippa had said that Pythagorean "mysteries" resulted from dreaming about number.[116] Perhaps he was now dreaming "Pythagorean" dreams.

Agrippa was not the only member of his generation to be seduced by the occult philosophy and its association with magic that Pythagoreans knew had been embraced by Pythagoras and his followers in Antiquity. Ideas similar to his were advanced by several of Agrippa's German contemporaries, such as Michael Neander (who edited Pythagoras's *Golden Verses* and wrote a book on the holiness of the Hebrew language) and Matheiss Passinger von Iniching, as well as by the Spanish medical doctor and philosopher Gómez Pereira.[117]

The wide-ranging unsystematic writings of Paracelsus show that he too had strong Pythagorean leanings. However, because of their mystical character, his might be described as a kind of visionary Pythagoreanism. Influenced by Ficino's idea of cosmological-theological medicine, this itinerant medical doctor proposed that physicians should be astronomers, cosmographers, philosophers, and alchemists.[118] He was also indebted to Ficino for his ideas on the soul, which, he held, was subject to the influence of the sun and the stars. At the same time, following Reuchlin, his ideas were deeply attached to Hebraic mysticism. Medical practice was rooted, he argued, in Hebraic Antiquity. Outdoing Reuchlin, he proposed that the esoteric wisdom of astronomy could be traced back long before Moses, to Abraham and Adam; from them it went to Moses, to Pythagoras, to Europe, and, particularly, to Germany.[119]

Paracelsus's dependence on Pythagorean number symbolism is evident throughout his works, especially in his discussions of alchemy where he proposes a substitution of three elements – sulphur, mercury, and salt – for the traditional four.[120] Speaking of the first ten numbers, he refers to Pythagorean learning: "The Ternary with the magical Quaternary produces a perfect Septenary. ... Therein is concluded all the occult wisdom of things [whose] wisdom God hath made openly manifest to men," though he subsequently proposes mystical applications of that learning. The way to find the "true elixir" of the science of magic is through a list of enigmas. One such enigma holds that there are 7 cities, 7 metals, 7 days, 7 letters, 7 words, 7 seasons, 7 arts, and 7 little stones. Thus, this enigma concludes, "All things do quietly rest and prevail in this number."[121]

Despite his interest in number and his vague use of the term "Kabbalah," Paracelsus's passion for the exploration of experimental knowledge and its translation into mystical propositions led him far astray from his heroes, the Pythagoreans, and into controversies that eventually rendered him ineffectual, though his ideas would inspire a significant following. Some of his contemporaries in other countries, the alchemist and astrologer John Dee (1527–1608), for example, in England, did not stray so far from more traditional Pythagorean views that all mysteries could be explained by the divine science of mathematics that aimed, through the symbolic application of number, to unify the celestial and terrestrial worlds. Dee saw the possibilities of mathematics as infinite in their relation to geography and cosmography ("anthropography").[122] Such ideas were continued in the work of Thomas Browne (1605–1682), who professed his admiration for Pythagoras as he discussed the secret magic of numbers of "the leading philosopher" (Pythagoras) and his follower, Plato. Browne was as drawn to the concept of the infinity of the world-soul and the basic nature that unites all as exemplified by Plato's *Timaeus* as he was to Pythagorean concepts of morality.[123] By the end of the sixteenth century another Englishman, Edward Kelly (1555–1608), returned to the long-standing but not yet dead medieval interest in the homogeneous affinity of metals and the quest for the philosopher's magical stone that would transform inferior metals into gold. Quoting liberally from the *Turba philosophorum*, he laid out the details for this quest in a treatise dedicated to Rudolf II of Prague, an emperor with a personal interest in alchemy.[124]

Unlike his colleagues in Germany and England, Giambattista Della Porta's belief in the use of "divine" mathematics for understanding the relation of humankind to the universe, which was Pythagorean at heart, had a pronounced Kabbalistic twist inspired by the combined influence of Ficino, Pico, and Reuchlin. Della Porta's interpretation of Pythagoreanism was different from the eccentricities of the Germans Agrippa and Paracelsus in that it constituted a veritable encyclopedia of the occult. First published in 1558 and expanded in 1589, his *Magiae naturalis* (*Natural Magic*) is a compendium of occupations and processes (such as distillation, invisible writing, and making cosmetics) that can be improved by "magical" methods. In this work the author obliquely sketches a history of ancient sources traditionally believed to have been associated with the education and influence of Pythagoras: Zoroaster and the Magi of Persia, the Gymnosophists of India, Chaldeans, Egyptians, Druids, Celts, and the Kabbalists. Relying on classical history, Della Porta provides supportive citations from ancient authors, mostly Pythagoreans. This brew of historical legitimacy prepares the reader to learn about the various types of magic, of which he claims to prefer the "natural" type, which for him meant magic based on the observation of the presence of intrinsic opposites in nature. This magic, he explains, had been cherished by Pythagoras and his followers, and it required that its practitioners be trained philosophers with a good understanding of mathematics and the four elements.

Della Porta's description of the universe may seem bizarre to pragmatists of the twenty-first century, but his contemporaries, who were accustomed to thinking in terms of (Pythagorean) contrarieties, could probably understand the extraordinary descriptive catalogue that follows, in which hatred and love, wildness and gentleness, warmth and cold, and sympathy and antipathy between various forms of nature are juxtaposed. It is in his examples, however, that Della Porta shows that he is perhaps the most bizarre of his "magical" generation: Combats between elephants and dragons, and between cabbages and vines, and other such curiosities and wonders are described. Fantastic as is his catalogue, its methodology remains essentially Pythagorean: the reconciliation of opposites and the affinity of all things in the universe.[125]

FINDING HEAVEN: ON THE BRINK OF A NEW SCIENCE – FROM COPERNICUS TO KEPLER AND BEYOND

Not everyone was seduced by the potential of Pythagorean thought for recondite applications. Nor did everyone agree that the universe was a storehouse of bizarre curiosities that, deviating from the norm, required reconciliation. Nicholaus Copernicus was but one example of the many scholars who had little liking for superstition. Inspired by the venerable Pythagorean cosmology of the past, he attempted to adapt it by using new observational methods. While the first Pythagoreans of Antiquity (e.g., Philolaus and Empedocles) had believed there was fire in the center of the universe, later ones (e.g., Macrobius, who was not an astronomer) had suggested a spherical earth might be situated in the center of the universe encircled by seven music-making planetary spheres. In this ancient history, two things are clear: (1) Early Pythagoreans had strong interests in astronomy and cosmology; and (2) contrary to what some have suggested, there was no fixed Pythagorean doctrine on the place of the earth and certainly there was none claiming that the earth was "immovable" at the center of the universe (as the ancient astronomer Ptolemy, who was not a Pythagorean, had held). If anything, ancient Pythagoreans were proponents of the idea that the earth revolves around a central fire. Aristotle acknowledged this and regarded it as the prevailing Pythagorean belief in his time.[126]

It was therefore fitting that, when Copernicus first circulated his ideas in manuscript form, before their eventual posthumous publication in 1543 as six books in the *De revolutionibus orbium coelestium* (*The Revolutions of the Heavenly Spheres*), he should pay his respects to Pythagoreanism. His dedication notes the well-ordered scheme on which the organization of the cosmos is based. Frequently reflecting on the "harmony" of the universe, the body of his text proposes the substitution of the heliocentric system, according to which the earth is one of many planets that revolve around the sun, for the geocentric system, which held that a stationery earth was at the center of the universe.[127]

This proposal was not so astonishingly new as is often suggested.[128] Cardinal Cusanus, who as we saw earlier was a Pythagorean as well as a scholar of mathematics and astronomy, had discussed, in 1440 – a century before Copernicus – an earth that was not at the center of the universe and that was in constant movement, as a "noble" star, because of its circularity and sphericity.[129]

Copernicus makes it clear that, like that of Cusanus, his inspiration had a Pythagorean source:

> Some think that the earth remains at rest. But Philolaus the Pythagorean believes that, like the sun and moon, it revolves around the fire in an oblique circle. ... That the earth rotates, that it also travels with several motions, and that it is one of the heavenly bodies are said to have been the opinions of Philolaus the Pythagorean. He was no ordinary astronomer, inasmuch as Plato did not delay going to Italy for the sake of visiting him, as Plato's biographers report.[130]

Like his Pythagorean predecessors and contemporaries, Copernicus describes God as the "best and most systematic Artisan of all" who worked with "His hands" so that we are "drawn to the contemplation of the highest good" by his creation.[131] As though he knew Pythagoras's ancient reputation for "measuring heaven," Copernicus sweeps his reader, in the very beginning of his text, into this contemplation: "What indeed is more beautiful than heaven?"[132] Expressing his admiration for the harmony of the universe, he admits that he wondered whether he should publish his findings or should follow the example of the Pythagoreans who communicate mysteries only by word of mouth to the initiated.[133] In an earlier, preparatory, work written in 1514, the *Commentariolius* (*Brief Commentary*), he explained that he had aligned himself with the ancient Pythagoreans because they saw mobility rather than immobility in the earth. His pupil, George Joachim Reticus, who supervised the printing of the *De revolutionibus* as Copernicus lay dying, affirms his teacher's admiration of "the Pythagoreans" and asserts that Copernicus "followed" Plato and the Pythagoreans. Copernicus's Platonic sympathies were surely, he suggests, inspired by Ficino's translations of the Platonic corpus, as well as by Bessarion's major works.[134] Thus, it appears, Copernicus was deeply aware not only of his ancient Pythagorean predecessors but also of more modern ones. Reticus reports that Copernicus particularly admired their reflective and prudent conduct.

The ties of Copernicus to Pythagoreanism are tantalizing, especially when we take several unknowns into account. Modern scholarship has suggested that Copernicus must have been in touch with Giorgio Valla (who, as mentioned earlier, was a Pythagorean and proponent of geo-heliocentrism in the late fifteenth century), for similarities exist in their writings. Perhaps the young Copernicus had intended to meet Valla when he arranged to study at Padua (the closest university city to Venice) in 1501; however, when he arrived Valla had just died. It was, presumably, while Copernicus was at Padua that he obtained a copy of Valla's *De expetendis et fugiendis rebus*, which came out in that year and surely ignited his enthusiasm to study the work of his Greek predecessors in mathematics and cosmology, not to mention heliocentrism.[135] In the preceding year, he had gone to Rome, where he had been invited (at age twenty-seven) to give a lecture in mathematics.[136] We do not know what his subject was; nor do we know who had invited him or who was in his "large audience" there. Lastly, Copernicus himself tells us of his friendship with Paulus de Middelbourg, the Pythagorean mathematician–astronomer of Urbino, a friendship about which little is known.[137] Perhaps it was in Rome in 1500 that Copernicus and Paulus (who was there at the time under the auspices of Cardinal Giovanni della Rovere, the future Pope Julius II) met.[138]

Copernicus had direct links with other Pythagorean astronomers. One of these was Celio Calcagnini, whom Copernicus almost certainly knew personally in Ferrara, where he completed his studies in 1503. At that time Calcagnini was assembling a rich library there. Perhaps it was at Copernicus's invitation that they met again in Krakow in 1518 when Calcagnini visited that city. The visit from the Ferrarese astronomer must have aroused attention, for on that occasion he was awarded a title of Polish nobility.[139] Far removed from the world of magic and demons, Calcagnini and Copernicus had much in common insofar as their scholarly approaches are concerned, for both were interested in a cosmography that attempted to explain the movement of the earth. Early writings of Calcagnini's express the view that the earth rotates diurnally (daily) while, however, remaining in the center of the universe. Perhaps because they were composed before Copernicus's masterpiece was available in print, they cite the authority of Cusanus for corroboration.[140]

The encyclopedic approach of Calcagnini's major treatises demonstrates his wide reading. His works are dedicated to cataloguing the natural and celestial worlds. Calcagnini openly asserts his Pythagoreanism. Among the subjects dear to him are what he calls "harmonious calculation," as well as the divinity of number and that of plane and solid geometrical shapes, and the Pythagorean uses of music as therapy to cure illness.[141] Among his personal friends were the Pythagorean Fabio Calvo, Raphael's closest friend, whose vegetarianism he describes, and the most avid and famous of Reuchlin's many defenders, the probable Pythagorean, Erasmus.

Among astronomers in the next generation, Copernicus was to be very much admired by Galileo, who viewed him as a Pythagorean. This is important because it shows that whatever modern commentators may think about Copernicus's Pythagoreanism, in the sixteenth century, he was regarded as one.[142] Galileo was not alone. Among the many others who shared this view was the Spanish Augustinian Fray Diego Ortiz de Zúñiga (ac. late 1500s). In 1584 he explained that while God had made the universe, it was Copernicus, because he understood the ancient

Pythagorean concept that the earth moved by its own nature and disdained to follow the tenets of Ptolemaic astronomy, which could not explain the motion of the quinoctial points, who had discovered the motion of the planets.[143]

While Copernicus was certain of his findings, with due respect to his Pythagorean inspirators and friends, it is important to note that his views did not immediately transform all scientific opinion. Doubts about his views would linger in the minds of many later astronomers, such as Tycho Brahe of Denmark, who vacillated in accepting them, and, especially, Athanasius Kircher of Germany, who even a century later would reject them completely.[144]

Another of those who continued to believe in a stationary earth located in the center of the cosmos was the eminent mathematician and physician Girolamo Cardano. Although his literary works disagree with Copernicus, he shared with his great contemporary some notable Pythagorean leanings. Among these were an interest in numbers, which he used as a tool to define the matter and form of nature. Cardano also wrote a book on the immortality of the soul – the great "discovery" attributed to Pythagoras since Antiquity.[145] Cardano prided himself on his activity as an astrologer, an area in which he demonstrated his "cosmic" perspective. This can be seen in the variations he introduced, based on what he believed was his God-given gift of prophesy, to the time-honored medical prognosticational device, the Pythagorean Sphere.[146]

Shortly after Cardano's death in 1576, the brilliant and exuberant mathematical philosopher Giordano Bruno had begun to publish an important sequence of texts. In these Bruno, a Dominican turned Lutheran who was excommunicated by the Catholics as well as by the Calvinists and eventually burned at the stake, shows himself to be what he was: an eccentric original. To the extent that he can be associated with any body of concepts, he was closest to the Pythagoreans. This he demonstrated in his intense interest in geometry, which, under the influence of Ficino and Cusanus, concentrated on the triangle, pyramid, circle, and sphere.[147] His fascination with numbers and numerological systems and their relation to cosmography can be seen in many of his works. As well as being a believer in metempsychosis (transmigration of the soul), he was interested in contraries and opposites, which frequently took on the appearance of magical games in his work. His many writings paid special attention not only to magic but also to the Kabbalah and to the apparatus of the Hermetic corpus, which appears to have been a source of endless fascination for him.[148] What the modern scholar Arielle Saiber adroitly terms his "circumlocutions" could well have been a form of (Pythagorean) enigmatic communication.[149]

Not at all enigmatic about his Pythagoreanism was the Austrian Johannes Kepler. Given his background in theology and mathematics, it is, perhaps, not surprising that he should have had – as he certainly did – an appreciation for Pythagorean cosmology and geometry. What is surprising is the way in which he expressed it.[150] In his first book, the *Mysterium cosmographicum* (*The Secret of the Universe*), published in 1596 (which led him to become a serious astronomer establishing his reputation in that field), he refers repeatedly to his Pythagorean convictions. However, he had an agenda. His plan was to update what he regarded as fundamentally true but outdated doctrines. In outlining, in his preface, the cosmological "law" that he had discovered regarding the geometric relationship in the average distances of the planets from the sun, he explains his intention to prove that when God created the cosmos and arranged the order of the planets, he had in mind the five regular bodies discovered by Pythagoras and passed on to Plato:

> It is my intention to show in this little book that the most great and good Creator, in the creation of this moving universe and the arrangement of the heavens, looked to those five regular solids, which have been so celebrated from the time of Pythagoras and Plato down to our own, and that he fitted to the nature of those solids the number of the heavens, their proportions, and the law of their motions.[151]

While he suggests that Pythagoreans and Copernicans are compatible and closely tied, his main purpose, as described in his dedication, is to "modernize" Pythagorean cosmology, which, because it was two thousand years old, was in need of revision. Speaking of the Pythagoreans, he says:

> Two thousand years before: Because the doctrine of the five geometrical figures' being distributed among the bodies of the universe is traced back to Pythagoras, from whom Plato borrowed this part of his philosophy. … For they and I had the same five figures in mind, and the same universe. … I alluded to the sphere of the planetary system, constructed of the planetary spheres, and the five regular Pythagorean solids.[152]

Soon thereafter in another work, the *Harmonice mundi* (*Harmony of the World*), Kepler reaffirmed his original hypothesis and sought to carry it further. Composed in the late 1590s and planned as a sequel to his first book, the *Harmonice mundi* aimed to construct a rational proof, based on geometry, of the apparatus of cosmic harmony. This harmony, he declares, is identifiable with the divine intelligence of God. As such, it can be deduced from the dimensions of the cosmos and the corresponding movements of the planets. Essentially, he was seeking to replace the mysteriously audible music of the spheres that Cicero had described in ancient times with a rational geometrical explanation of the phenomenon of the consonances that make cosmic harmony work – in other words, to add more specific information to what the Pythagoreans had proposed in ancient times:

> Yet however ancient be the pattern of human melody … the causes of the intervals have remained unknown to men – so much so that

before Pythagoras they were not even sought; and after they have been sought for two thousand years, I shall be the first, unless I am mistaken, to reveal them with such accuracy.[153]

In this way did Kepler view his discovery, based on the mathematics of quantitative measurement, as a confirmation of the perpetual but inaudible concert (or music of the spheres) of the movements of the heavens. The idea, he argues, appears to be sublime and incredible because it is rational and geometric rather than audible. In closing, Kepler reaffirms the role of God who established the perfect harmonies first discovered by the Pythagoreans and, at long last, elucidated by himself: "Great is our Lord ... praise Him, heavenly harmonies, praise Him, judges of the harmonies which have been disclosed."[154] Enormously proud of himself, Kepler triumphantly declares that his newly discovered mathematically based harmonies prove what God had waited six thousand years for someone to discover.[155]

For Kepler, Pythagorean though he was, the symbolism of numbers was obsolete. Indeed, he argued against numerical symbolism and in favor of a new role for mathematics in his correspondence with his younger English contemporary, Robert Fludd, who, as mentioned earlier, continued to believe in the traditional Pythagorean number symbolism well into the seventeenth century.[156]

In chiding Galileo, his senior by seven years, for his reluctance to declare his attachment to Pythagoras (as mentioned in Chapter 3), Kepler surely understood that his great contemporary had broken a barrier and ushered in a new scientific era. Even so, in rhapsodizing in his first scientific work, the *Siderus Nuncius* (*Sidereal Messenger*), over what he could see with the newly discovered telescope, Galileo admits that for him, Pythagoreanism had never died:

> [I]f anyone wanted to resuscitate the old opinion of the Pythagoreans that the Moon is, as it were, another Earth, its brighter part would represent the land surface while its darker part would more appropriately represent the water surface. Indeed, for me there has never been any doubt that when the terrestrial globe, bathed in sunlight, is observed from a distance, the land surface will present itself brighter to the view and the water surface darker.[157]

In a long handwritten response to Galileo's work, Kepler recalls the importance of their Pythagorean and Platonic precedents, including Cusanus and Giordano Bruno, for his discovery (which constitutes our first description of the lunar surface).[158] In a later and more famous work, Galileo reminds his readers that Ptolemy had, in ancient times, propounded the theory of a stationary earth, and that it was the Pythagoreans who had been the earliest known proponents of the idea of a moving earth.[159] His biographer, Niccolo Gherardini, wrote that Galileo "praised Pythagoras above all others on account of his way of studying natural philosophy."[160]

To this generation also belonged Bernardino Baldi, the scholar of mathematics, who, it will be remembered, was the author of the longest and best-researched biography of Pythagoras since ancient times. Not only did he consider Pythagoras a great mathematician, he calls him the "prince of Italian philosophy." Thus did Baldi assert his Pythagoreanism. This is underlined by the fact that he came from Urbino and that he wrote two books on Vitruvius, as well as biographies of Archytas, Aristoxenus, Vitruvius, and Boethius – all famous Pythagoreans of Antiquity.[161]

By the sixteenth century's close Jewish Pythagoreanism was still alive and well, as can be seen in the works of Abraham ben Yagel (b. 1553). His *Gei Hizzayon* (*Valley of Vision*) documents his multiple interplicated interests in astronomy, medicine, astrology, prognostication, and number. In the emotionally charged atmosphere of the Counter-Reformation, Jews were beginning to suffer in unexpected ways and, for him, the combination of scientific and Kabbalistic pursuits found expression in the now age-old Pythagorean language: Affluence is evil and should be shunned, he argues, and the Pythagoreans were right to believe in the transmigration of souls because this is the "correct" tradition as it was received from Moses.[162]

Also, by the end of the century, the intellectual stimulus that had created interest in numbers, geometry, the Kabbalah, and Hermeticism devolved into a form that appealed to those with more limited literacy. Practitioners of magic and witches circulated charts purported to be helpful for daily use that described the magic of sixes in two groups of three, nine circles containing four names totalling 72, and so forth. In this sense the influence of Pythagoras and his Hermetic brethren, once the domain of the esoteric, was transformed into dubious social practices that invited censorship.[163]

Several forces worked together to give Pythagoreanism, which reached the height of its development in the sixteenth century, its distinctive character. One was the acceleration in central Italy and Milan of interest in cosmology. This fascination contemplated principles that, as the divine goal of mathematics, produced harmony. Harmony could be musical, as well as astronomical, arithmetical, and geometrical. Pacioli's interest in the transformation of geometrical forms, such as the five regular solids associated with Pythagoreanism and Platonism, into "perfect" forms that could be circumscribed and centralized within a sphere provides but one illustration. Important to Plato and Boethius before him, the triangle and threefold classifications occur frequently in his concepts. His pupil, friend, and accomplice, Leonardo da Vinci, carried these ideas further in his own search for divine harmony. Between the two of them, it became clear that ideas about harmony and the reconciliation of opposites could be translated not only into architecture but also into sculpture and painting, for they said as much. While Vitruvius and Alberti were behind this intellectual notion of translation into the visual arts, Leonardo recorded his Pythagorean sympathies in his writings on protecting animals and abstinence from flesh, as well as in his personal life, in which he disdained riches and showed concern for the poor.

Other Pythagorean forces were at work in Bologna, Rome, and Venice. The moral authority of Pythagoreanism was always important, and it set the tone for the high-minded discussions of intellectuals who sought the purity of a well-ordered universe as it did, at the more popular level, for those who wanted simply to put order in their lives. In Venice, Zorzi described the abstract purity of Pythagorean cosmology and its harmony of the spheres, a subject that would fascinate music theorists for the rest of the century. His Pythagoreanism was similar to the refinements of social harmony described by Castiglione, whose roots were in Urbino. Meanwhile, in Rome an intellectual and vivacious papal librarian, Tommaso Inghirami, discovered Cicero's long sought-after lost work that had famously incorporated the first description of the harmony of the spheres. As an avid follower of Cicero and as one who had Pythagorean interests, Tommaso was in a position to influence the papal court of Julius II.[164] A medical doctor and intellectual, Fabio Calvo was attentive to the medical traditions of Pythagoreanism while following a lifestyle that disdained riches and practicing vegetarianism. All those just mentioned had high regard for the authority of Vitruvius. Both Inghirami and Fabio were friends of Raphael.

Another strain of Pythagoreanism can be regarded as more esoteric because it attempted to attach Pythagoreanism to the Kabbalah, two doctrines that, it held, were intertwined, and to proclaim the "true" harmony of Christianity as the inheritor of both. Describing the circle as symbolic of perfect harmony and the marriage of the pyramid and the cube as symbolic of the universe, Reuchlin was especially interested in demonstrating that Pythagorean numerical symbolism had descended from the authority of Moses – an idea that, born in Antiquity, resurfaced with vigor in his work. Continuing along these lines, Cardinal Egidio da Viterbo sought to discover the perfect unity in the incorporation of all truths, including Kabbalistic, into Christianity. England, too, produced its own brand of Pythagoreans. Though they admired Pico and Ficino, English Pythagoreans of the sixteenth century exhibited a certain stodginess that distanced them from the vividness of contemporary continental discussions. In the Netherlands, however, Pythagoreanism had a real friend in Erasmus, who admired not only Pythagorean learning and moral culture but also Reuchlin.

At the same time, occultism and the various numerological approaches that might support it came to be rampantly fashionable. At one extreme was the continuation of medieval practices such as the use of Pythagorean Spheres, the *Turba philosophorum*, and black magic. These relied on opposing ideas of good and evil to suggest the avenues to life and death, discovering the philosopher's stone, or contacting demons. At the other extreme were mathematicians who thought the secrets of mathematics were the true key to unlocking the mysteries of nature. These tended to be practitioners of "natural" magic, surveying nature in terms of Pythagorean systems of number, measure, and harmony. They admired Pico and Ficino, and believed Boethius was "divine." They also studied geometry – especially circles, spheres, triangles, and pyramids – while, at the same time, dabbling in the occult. Few went to the extremes of Postel, who described harmonic relationships in an almost incomprehensible mathematical language. The peculiar Agrippa and his countryman, the blustery Paracelsus, sought to use experimental science to discover magic, which, because it relied on number, they regarded as a perfect science. They used Pythagorean methodology to study natural history and pharmacology, while they provided significant distractions from the new generation of astronomers who were intent on studying the celestial and planetary spheres through mathematics. The respect of these astronomers for Pythagoreanism dignified the concept of cosmic beauty by providing a vocabulary that was vastly different from that of the gems and minerals, flora and fauna, and other miraculous wonders of the fantastic world described by Agrippa, Paracelsus, and, especially, Della Porta.

This new generation of astronomers included Copernicus in Poland, Calcagnini in Ferrara, Kepler in Austria, and Galileo in northern Italy. Copernicus and Calcagnini acknowledged their spiritual affinity with Pythagoreanism and suggested their debt to its greatest fifteenth-century interpreter, Cardinal Cusanus. At the end of the sixteenth century and the beginning of the seventeenth, Kepler and Galileo both remembered well their Pythagorean roots. Each had discovered, in his own way, new ways to "find heaven." In invoking Pythagorean Antiquity in order to advance modernity, Kepler was doing with words what, as we shall see in the chapters that follow, avant-garde architects and artists of the Renaissance were doing without words.

Part Three:
Pythagoreanism in
Architecture and Art

SEVEN:

RENAISSANCE IMAGES OF

PYTHAGORAS

Though Renaissance texts have little, if anything, to say respecting Pythagoras's appearance, ancient written evidence was well known to their authors. These sources had described Pythagoras as a tall and handsome man given to meditation, bearded, and with long hair. Dressed in white, he was graceful in speech and gesture and had exquisitely accurate hearing and eyesight. He had, they agreed, a dignified bearing and a graceful and harmonious manner. According to one of these sources, Aelian, Pythagoras wore trousers – a sign of his Persian education. No ancient literary source describes him as wearing a turban or headdress. Whereas ancient Greek images of Pythagoras were consistent in showing a bearded, curly-haired, middle-aged man, seated or standing, Roman images of him tended to be more diversified. During the Middle Ages he was represented in many ways, ranging from a boy genius, to an industrious craftsman, to a stern bishop.[1] A late fourteenth-century image of him in the Dominican church of Santa Maria Novella at Florence showed a rigid, serious, monkish man with a high bald forehead and tight pursed lips.[2] Surely Renaissance artists knew various of these images from the past, perhaps even some that, believed to be him at the time, are lost to us today.

The first Renaissance images of Pythagoras are from Florence. They suggest a return to the Greek type – a figure dressed in classical robes, with long hair and a long beard. These appear in the relief decorations of the campanile, or bell tower, of Santa Maria del Fiore, the cathedral of Florence. Commissioned in 1437 to the then already eminent sculptor Luca della Robbia, a series of five hexagonally shaped panels present two images of Pythagoras.[3] Taking their place in a vast encyclopedic program that had been begun before Luca's time and would be completed by others afterward, these images are uninscribed. Though this has led to some confusion in the past, the probable identity of Pythagoras in both is clear.

In one of these panels, two well-dressed men wearing long robes and himations, or rectangular cloths draped over their left shoulders (an ancient Greek

1: Luca della Robbia, *Pythagoras Teaching Arithmetic to Plato*, Florence, Campanile (now in Museo del Opera del Duomo), 1437. Photo: Allan Foy

custom evidently known to the sculptor), stand facing each other (fig. 1). One holds a tablet, pointing to it while the other responds by gesticulating. Both wear turbans, certainly meant to emphasize their Greekness. Contemporaries do not identify them.[4] Giorgio Vasari, the first art historian, thought, a century after their completion, that they represented Plato and Aristotle.[5] Vasari was obviously guessing, mistakenly, for they do not behave in a way that would suggest this pair of famous philosophers from Antiquity; nor did a tradition for representing this particular pair together exist at the time (though it existed in Vasari's time). In the late nineteenth century, Julius von Schlosser suggested that they were Euclid and Pythagoras, who, deriving from the tradition of Martianus Capella, represented geometry and arithmetic.[6] However, this panel does not form part of a series of the Seven Liberal Arts. (Such a series is in fact located above on the campanile, together with the Seven Planets, Seven Virtues, and Seven Sacraments.) The figure to the left holds a tablet – not a persuasive Euclidian attribute. The figure to the right appears to be counting on his fingers in response to the teachings of his companion – not a convincing behavior for the wisest sage of Antiquity.

If only we could read what was originally inscribed on the tablet (now effaced), which is tilted so as to show its contents to the observer, we would probably have seen a *tetraktys*. This would explain why the figure to the left is almost surely Pythagoras, rather than Euclid. The pupil he instructs is very likely Plato. Pythagoras points to the tablet and the pupil responds with a perfectly appropriate gesture, counting numbers with his fingers. Pythagoras is taller than the pupil, and his face is clearly visible while that of the pupil is averted. Very likely, this panel refers to the discovery of arithmetic, for which Pythagoras was famous throughout the Middle Ages and which Plato, his most famous pupil, was reputed to have learned from him.

A second panel, showing a seated figure holding two hammers, certainly represents Pythagoras (fig. 2). Vasari identified it as Ptolemy inventing astrology, though its contents have no relation to astrology.[7] Schlosser thought that, because he holds hammers, this figure represented Tubalcain, the biblical inventor of instruments made of bronze and iron.[8] However, Tubalcain had already been represented in a previously executed series, dedicated to biblical figures, on the base of the campanile.[9] Though some accepted the suggestion that this solitary seated bearded man was Tubalcain, others, following Vasari, continued to maintain that he represented Ptolemy, or even "Astrology." However, in 1980 John Pope-Hennessy offered a completely different theory – that he is Pythagoras.[10]

Clearly, this is the case. A long medieval tradition stemming from the ancient writer Nicomachus linked Pythagoras with hammers, which, when striking an anvil, made different sounds according to the weight of the hammers, giving him the vocabulary to illustrate the intervals of musical scale that corresponded to the distances between the planets and the fixed stars.[11] Pythagoras set to work himself, examining the weights of hammers and listening to their impacts; thus did he discover harmony. Dressed in antique robes and a cap to protect his head, the seated sculptured figure listens carefully, with head cocked, to the sounds he is making with the hammers he holds, one in each hand. As the inventor of music, Pythagoras's face and beard are exactly the same as that of Pythagoras in the other panel, which shows him as the inventor of arithmetic, a role for which he was equally well known.

The double role allotted to Pythagoras on the campanile of the Cathedral of Florence in the 1430s clearly reflects the importance that was accorded him in the early years of the fifteenth century in that city under the influence of Petrarch and, more specifically, Coluccio Salutati and Leonardo Bruni. Salutati had described in great detail Pythagoras's invention of musical sequences and

2: Luca della Robbia, *Pythagoras Discovering Music*, Florence, Campanile, 1437. Photo: Alinari (Art Resource)

harmony. Thus were the struggles of Pythagoras to invent musical harmony fresh in the minds of Florentines in the 1430s. Both Salutati and Bruni had high praise for Pythagoras as the inventor of mathematics. As the most influential literary man of his time, Bruni maintained that Pythagoras's discovery of mathematics was of the greatest importance, and one that he shared with Plato, his most prominent pupil. Not only was Leonardo Bruni the Chancellor of Florence at the time, he had also just been appointed a member of the Twelve Good Men, an important executive council of the city. Thus Pythagoras as the inventor of mathematics instructing Plato, and Pythagoras the inventor of harmony would have been most timely subjects in 1437, the year of the commissioning of these panels to Luca della Robbia.

3: *Pythagoras Spitting out Mathematical Formulas*, colored drawing, New York, Pierpont Morgan Library, *MS.B.27*, fol. 31r. Photo: Pierpont Morgan Library

A very different Pythagoras appears in a previously unpublished image from a medical-astronomical handbook decorated in Germany during the third quarter of the fifteenth century (fig. 3).[12] This full-page colored drawing depicts a three-quarter length figure, inscribed "Pitagoras," as a mathematician. Dressed as a monk with a cowl covering his head and his right arm raised in benediction, he is spitting out mathematical formulas to which he points with his left hand. Divided into an upper group and lower group of three sections each, the assemblages of numbers correspond with the old medieval numerical arrangements seen in Pythagorean Spheres.[13] In these, as here, the upper range consists of numbers arranged in order and according to decads (1–10, 11–20, 20–30), thus numbers considered "lucky" for the particular occasion that required the drawing, while the lower range is characterized by disorder, thus numbers considered "unlucky" for the occasion. Two decorative scrolls here make this clear. One reads "Gelück gat uff" (or *Gelück geht auf*, Fortune goes up), and the other reads "Unglück gat unter" (or *Unglück geht unter*, Misfortune goes down).

This clear example of the association of Pythagoras with magic is completed and complemented by an inscription in the upper part of the folio, above the name "Pitagoras":

> Dear God, give us to drink and eat, so that we won't forget you. Your crown of thorns is our sorrow. The wound you received from a sword is our misery. Your rose-colored blood is our drink. Lord, all your words are our thoughts. Our Father/Hail Mary.[14]

This inscription, in association with the prognosticating Pythagoras, shows that even when demonstrating the uses of mathematics he continued to be well regarded by Christians (as he had been throughout the Middle Ages), who associated him not only with magic but also with holiness.[15]

Pythagoras's intimate association with Christianity is underlined by his presence – and by his status – in the Cathedral of Ulm, an important city of medieval Swabia and one still prosperous in late fifteenth-century Germany. Here the sculptor Jörg Syrlin the Elder was commissioned, in 1468, to execute a series of sculptural representations of apostles and martyrs, as well as of mythological, legendary, and historical figures, in a vast encyclopedic display that, completed in 1474, included eighty nine portraits. Most of these took the form of relief busts on the backs of the cathedral's choir stools. Four figures, however, were selected for three-dimensional representation marking the entrances and exits to the seats. One of these was Pythagoras (fig. 4). Despite his prominent setting in the heart of a religious structure, Pythagoras is hardly the severe monkish personality we met earlier, though his bearded face looks directly at the high altar.

At Ulm, Pythagoras is dressed in a contemporary costume richly carved in deep folds. He wears a soft plush "chapeau" over his thick curly locks. Given the rakish tilt of his hat we can even picture the Pythagoras that Porphyry and Iamblichus had described, who not only played and sang music but enjoyed dancing.[16] His half-open mouth and furrowed brow suggest that, while he plays with both hands, he is singing a sad or serious song with a slow beat. The accompanying inscription explains that Pythagoras was the inventor of music and that under his influence music could be used to cure social ills and keep evils from the soul:

> Pythagoras, the founder of music. By all possible means these things should be avoided and expelled: sluggishness from the body, ignorance from the mind, excessive craving from the community, strife from the home, discord and intemperance from all situations.[17]

4: Jörg Syrlin the Elder, *Pythagoras Singing*, Ulm, Cathedral, choir stalls, 1468–74. Photo: Bildarchiv Foto Marburg (Art Resource)

This clearly refers to a tradition still extant, first expressed by Quintilian in the first century (A.D.), which held that Pythagoras was able to heal the soul with music. According to Quintilian's account, by changing the frenetic beat of the music to which some unrestrained youths were listening to a slower one with longer phrases, Pythagoras discovered how to instill self-control in the youths and preserve the chastity of a woman.[18] Very likely, Johannes Reuchlin, growing up in the 1460s and 1470s in nearby Pforzheim, knew this image.

Not long after Pythagoras was memorialized at Ulm as the inventor of music, he appears as the inventor of arithmetic in the first printed Italian arithmetic text (fig. 5). Published in Florence in 1491, and again in 1492 and 1518, Filippo Calandri's beautifully printed *Aritmetica* is adorned with a woodcut frontispiece showing a full-page image of Pythagoras seated at a desk teaching two young pupils.[19] A title above reads: "Pictagoras arithmetrice introductor." Long-haired

5: *Pythagoras in His Study*, woodcut, from Filippo Calandri, *Aritmetica*, Florence, 1491. Photo: Pierpont Morgan Library, PML 408

and bearded (as Luca della Robbia's Pythagorases, perhaps his model), this famous teacher wears a professorial robe and a hat featuring a six-sided crown over a sixteen-sided brim – numbers that were favored by Pythagoreans. On the tablet he holds is inscribed "200/400," a reference to numbers derived from the decad (the all-important number of Pythagoreans, 10).

Over his desk is represented a geometrical symbol showing a circle containing a bisected triangle (perhaps suggesting the sides of a pyramid), an image that is represented as a problem toward the back of the book where the author discusses how to measure pyramids based on equilateral triangles inserted into circles. This geometrical image identifying Pythagoras is also used as a symbol in the portrait of Luca Pacioli (who was alive at this time) painted by Jacopo de'Barbari now in the Museo Capodimonte at Naples. In that portrait Pacioli, who as discussed earlier was surely a Pythagorean, points as he instructs to precisely this geometric symbol, inscribed on a tablet.[20] These circumstances lead us to conclude that as the fifteenth century came to an end, the teachings of Pythagoras were associated – in the minds of mathematicians – with the pyramid/triangle circumscribed by a circle. As we shall see later, at this moment this very idea was also preoccupying Pythagorean architects and artists in Italy.

At the same time that Calandri commemorated Pythagoras as the inventor of arithmetic, Pythagoras's role as the inventor of music theory was being celebrated by Gaffurio. His *Theorica musicae*, the first work on music theory to be printed in Italy, contains a four-part illustration that established the history of music theory as it was understood in the 1490s (fig. 6).[21] According to Gaffurio's text, it was the ancient biblical character Jubal who had discovered music when, long before the Flood, he had listened to the various sounds of hammers beating on a piece of iron.[22] Following along these lines, it was Pythagoras who made the prodigious discovery of the rules of harmony. Pythagoras built a monochord on which he was able to similarly reproduce the different sounds of tones by stretching strings and then tested this discovery on a variety of other instruments.[23]

The four scenes contained in this illustration depict these events. What Gaffurio does not tell us, however, is that he was precisely following Nicomachus's first-century (A.D.) description (well known to the Renaissance through its verbatim repetition by Iamblichus) of Pythagoras's discovery of the marvels of acoustical truth – except that Gaffurio substituted Jubal for Pythagoras.[24] In the first scene (*upper left*), Jubal (whose name, "IV-BAL," is inscribed above) is shown witnessing – exactly as Nicomachus had described Pythagoras – the harmonious blacksmith at work with his assistants. In beating a chunk of iron on an anvil they give off a combination of sounds as noted on each hammer – 4, 6, 8, 9, 12, 16. The second scene (*lower left*) shows Pythagoras (whose name is inscribed) with the instrument he built to replicate the sounds made by the hammers of different weights. Just as Nicomachus describes, the monochord is diagonally placed in the space. Its strings, of equal thickness and length, are strung from pegs from one side of the instrument to the other, where their ends terminate with different weights – labeled 4, 6, 8, 9, and 16 – attached to them. This suggests that the different pulling forces determine the different pitches that produce harmony. In striking two strings simultaneously, Pythagoras hears (as Nicomachus had described) the consonance produced by each pair, thus discovering the numerical laws of musical proportion. In the next two scenes, also inscribed with his name, Pythagoras is depicted doing exactly what Nicomachus said he did in order to confirm the validity of his discovery – extending the test to various other instruments, first to a series of bells (*upper right*) and then to a series of pipes (*lower right*), all labeled with the appropriate numbers. In the last scene, he is accompanied by Philolaus who helps him test flutes, an embellishment added by Gaffurio suggesting that the work of this first Pythagorean philosopher to

6: *Clockwise from upper left: Jubal Inventing Music, Pythagoras Inventing Harmony, Pythagoras Testing His Theory on a Monochord,* and *Pythagoras Testing His Theory on Flutes,* woodcut, from Franchino Gaffurio, *Theorica musicae,* 1492. Photo: Pierpont Morgan Library, PML 391

describe the sequences of the musical scale was known to him.[25] Thus do these four scenes demonstrate that Pythagoras was able, through various experiments, to discover that musical pitch had a numerical basis and that the intervals formed have a natural progression, or proportion, that produces different sounds.

An early sixteenth-century compendium of universal knowledge intended for young students and, as mentioned in Chapter 6, one of the first printed encyclopedias, Gregororius Reisch's *Margarita philosophica* contains sections on the Seven Liberal Arts, as well as on many other subjects useful for the education of students. In this work, which underwent numerous reprintings following its original publication in 1503, Pythagoras and Boethius are shown as "handmaids" of Lady Arithmetic (fig. 7).[26]

7: *Boethius and Pythagoras*, woodcut, from Gregorius Reisch, *Margarita philosophica*, 1504. Photo: Harvard University, Houghton Library

While the representation of the liberal arts as female figures was a familiar sight to late-medieval audiences,[27] the depiction of Boethius, a Pythagorean arithmetician well known to the medieval world, and Pythagoras as a pair is notable. Here they are represented (inscribed) as the best-known mathematicians from Antiquity – Pythagoras through legend and Boethius through surviving works (in particular, his *De institutione arithmetica*, a work still widely used and influential in the Renaissance).[28]

In this hand-colored woodcut of 1503, Boethius and Pythagoras share a study, each seated at a desk whose top is tilted forward to show the viewer what the author deemed was the most important aspect of their collaborative example. A suave, princely, and well-dressed Boethius counts with Arabic numerals, while his counterpart and ancestor, Pythagoras, wearing a high-buttoned jacket and

8: Raphael, *Pythagoras*, from *School of Athens*, Vatican, Stanza della Segnatura, 1510. Photo: Musei Vaticani, Archivio Fotografico

velvet slippers and a worried look on his face, counts with tokens on a layout that suggests an abacus. Although Reisch does not appear to know that it was Fibonacci in the thirteenth century (and not Boethius in the fifth) who replaced Roman numerals with Arabic numbers in the West, he clearly suggests his acquaintance with Fibonacci's work. (This is evoked by the oddity of two fractions in the upper corner of his desk, 1/2 and 2/3. If extended into a sequence they could imply 1/2, 2/3, 3/5, 5/8. … These component numbers [1, 2, 3, 5, 8] are elements of the "Fibonnaci series," whose fractions eventually converge into the "golden section.")[29] In conceptualizing Boethius's role in the history of mathematics as improving on what Pythagoras had originally taught, Reisch appears to be reminding his viewers of Pythagoras's celebrated status as the inventor of arithmetic.

It was during this time that Raphael, at work in the Stanza della Segnatura at the Vatican, painted his now famous image of Pythagoras (fig. 8). Completed in about 1510, the *School of Athens* shows Pythagoras in the lower left of the painting and, in a correspondingly opposite position, Euclid in the lower right. This placement suggests the different disciplines that constitute mathematics – arithmetic and geometry. Another opposition (which will be discussed later) is suggested in the contrast between Pythagoras and a man with short black hair and a black beard who confronts him by insistently pointing to a book. Pythagoras's reaction is one of isolation. He is focused on the act of writing in a book he holds in his lap. His psychological distance from the energetic young man tells us that he is absorbed in his thoughts, suggesting that the mystical side of him was most appealing to Raphael.

The tablet held before him by a youth not only suggests the subject of his contemplation but makes his identity unmistakable. On the tablet is represented the *tetraktys*, the universal symbol of Pythagoreanism. Above the *tetraktys* is a diagram showing the dependence of musical intervals on numerical ratios that, as described by Nicomachus (and later by Iamblichus), form the basis of harmony.[30] As though to make this indisputable, Raphael has numbered the intervals 6, 8, 9, and 12, just as they were described in Antiquity. The title above them reads (in Greek) "Tonal ratios," and the subtitles refer to the diapente, diatesseron, and diapason, the compass of musical intervals that produce harmony.[31] By placing the *tetraktys* and the diagram together, Raphael emphasizes that the four integers composing the *tetraktys* and the four composite musical proportions are related. Together they imply that the harmony of music symbolizes the principle of order in the universe, as the ancient Pythagorean, Philolaus, had first suggested.

In several other respects, Raphael shows his familiarity with ancient traditions respecting Pythagoras. Pythagoras is dressed in white. He is writing a book. His curly hair and curly beard are reminiscent of the earliest known ancient Greek representations of Pythagoras. Since we know Raphael sent his assistants to Greece to gather visual information,[32] it is tempting to postulate that a genuine ancient Greek image, or drawing from it, served as his model, rather than a Roman example.[33] On the other hand, the similarity of the face of Raphael's Pythagoras to the two of Luca della Robbia, which he would have known well from his years in Florence, suggests that Luca's campanile reliefs may have been his source. The remarkable similarity of the three also supports the hypothesis presented earlier respecting the identity of both images by Luca (which are uninscribed) as Pythagoras.

Very different from Raphael's Pythagoras, created for the Pope's library at the Vatican, is that created for the monumental vaulted library of King Philip II of Spain. Envisioned later in the century for his vast monastery-palace complex, El Escorial, this image is one of a series of frescoes devoted to representations of the Seven Liberal Arts in the palace library. Here Pythagoras takes his place as the founder of arithmetic, with Jubal (surely well known to Spanish literati through Gaffurio) as the founder of music, in a lunette in which the names of both are inscribed (fig. 9). Jubal is represented nude to suggest his ancient antediluvian status, while Pythagoras is clothed. Blowing on a pipe, Jubal offers an effective contrast with Pythagoras, who is depicted in deep thought while he does two

9: Pellegrino Tibaldi, *Jubal and Pythagoras as Inventors of Music and Arithmetic*, El Escorial, 1588. Photo: Author

things at once. With his right hand he counts, and with his left he holds a hammer in his lap (fig. 10).

Thus does Pythagoras make clear the intimate connection between arithmetic and music. Both were reported by Fray José de Sigüenza (the first director of this famous library that aimed to collect books from all over the world) as forming related aspects of mathematics, as opposed to geometry – which is represented elsewhere on the walls. Music was, Fray Sigüenza tells us, a derivative of arithmetic.[34]

The transparent aquamarine shirt in which Pythagoras is dressed reveals, for the first time ever, a well-built Pythagoras. It is matched by the trousers he wears, of the same color. These are complemented by an ample golden mantel that cascades in deep folds behind and around him. On his head he wears a red hat, while his feet are covered with stockings of a deep indigo color. His long white beard suggests the authority of late-Antique works that claimed that Pythagoras had lived to be a hundred years old.

The superhuman character of this image, due in equal parts to the physical splendor of the figure, the brilliance and bold variegation of its coloring, and the violation of the rationale of space that is only hinted at by the dark limitless background, emphasizes its abstraction. This image strongly suggests the influence of Michelangelo – especially of that artist's powerful *ignudi* (nude men), prophets and sibyls, and ancestors of Christ painted for the Sistine Ceiling in 1508–12.

10: Pellegrino Tibaldi, detail of Pythagoras from *Jubal and Pythagoras as Inventors of Music and Arithmetic*, El Escorial, 1588. Photo: Author

Surely the influence of Michelangelo's powerful images was still very much alive, two decades after his death, in the commissioning of these paintings to Pellegrino Tibaldi. A famous Italian painter and architect, Tibaldi was perhaps best known as one who could re-create Michelangelesque concepts, colors, and forms, to which his nickname, "Il Buonarroti reformato" ("Michelangelo reborn") testifies.[35] Tibaldi was an excellent choice to represent images related to the Seven Liberal Arts, which had traditionally been associated with Pythagoras (4, the quadrivium, + 3, the trivium, = 7, the most revered number by Pythagoreans), for he was apparently himself a Pythagorean.[36]

Michelangelo is the inspiration for yet another image of Pythagoras, one executed soon after that of the Escorial (fig. 11). An allegory, *Hercules Bearing the Globe,* painted in Rome for the Gallery of the Palazzo Farnese by Annibale

11: Annibale Carracci, *Hercules Bearing the Globe (with Pythagoras, and Euclid)*, Rome, Farnese Gallery, ca. 1595. Photo: Alinari (Art Resource)

Carracci (1560–1609) in about 1595, shows Hercules (who was believed to have learned the science of the heavens from Atlas) bending under the weight of the globe that he is supporting on his back, while to either side of him, Pythagoras and Euclid recline. Pythagoras holds aloft an astrolabe (an instrument used to calculate the positions of the celestial bodies), while Euclid composes a geometrical design on a tablet. The contrast between the two figures suggests that between arithmetic and geometry. Like Pythagoras, the hero-god Hercules was associated with philosophy as he is in this case, for the celestial sphere indicates that he is a seeker after wisdom.[37]

Here the figure of Pythagoras is borrowed from Michelangelo's figure of Day in the Tomb of Giuliano de'Medici in the Medici Chapel at Florence. The polish and giganticism of the marble sculpture are mimicked in the painted figure, which is represented in the nude except for a cloth cast over his legs. Contemporaneous with Galileo and Kepler, he is up to date not only stylistically but also iconographically. Because he lifts his curly-haired, bearded, head heavenward and directs the astrolabe toward the center of the fresco, the viewer is invited to remember that Pythagoras was the most famous and universally admired figure from Antiquity to have "measured the heavens."

In the early years of the Renaissance, a new image of Pythagoras was born. This Pythagoras was more like the ancient Greek type than had been his medieval predecessors. This suggests that an ancient image of him, unknown to us, may have inspired early Florentine artists. On the other hand, this new image may have been imagined from ancient literary sources, now increasingly well known. With long curly hair and a curly beard, Pythagoras is represented in the various roles for which he was known – as the inventor of arithmetic, the founder of music, a mystic who pondered the harmony of the spheres, and a therapist who induced social good and cured mental illness through song.

Renaissance images of Pythagoras are known throughout Europe in sculpture, drawings, woodcuts, and paintings. While some of these were small and formed an intimate part of documents such as manuscripts and books, others were on public view, and still others took their place as heroes in series of famous men adorning exemplary libraries.

These representations of Pythagoras appear to follow closely the views expounded about him by intellectual, civic, and religious leaders. Thus Pythagoras in early fifteenth-century Florentine art is the same Pythagoras adulated by Coluccio Salutati and Leonardo Bruni as the founder of mathematics and the discoverer of musical consonances, while Pythagoras of Raphael's *School of Athens* reflects the great cosmological harmonizer that Ficino and Pico had rediscovered. By the end of the Renaissance we see Pythagoras measuring the heavens, even as Galileo and Kepler were finding new ways to do just that in their own discoveries. Long after the Renaissance had been eclipsed by Baroque ideas, which embraced the scientific "revolution" of the seventeenth century, representations of Pythagoras in commissions to major artists did not cease. One example can be seen in a large canvas painting of 1662 by Salvator Rosa representing *Pythagoras Emerging from the Underworld*, or the "resurrection" of Pythagoras.[38]

EIGHT:

THE SEARCH FOR HARMONY IN ARCHITECTURE AND ART IN THE FIFTEENTH CENTURY

Fifteenth-century Florentines well knew Pythagoras's medieval reputation as the one who had discovered that all things were created by God according to proportion, measure, and number. They also knew that Petrarch had compared Pythagoras with Christ and equated Pythagoras's and Plato's heavenly order with that of Saint Peter and the Church.[1] The idea that a visual system proving that proportion resulted from the collaboration of number and form might, in its rational simplicity, reflect divine order was put forward in the early years of the fifteenth century by Filippo Brunelleschi (1377–1446), the first great architect of the Renaissance. The ideality of this order for religious structures was endorsed, if not suggested, by the prevailing Petrarchian mood in the Florence of Coluccio Salutati and Leonardo Bruni. Reinforcing this intellectual tradition was another one: the underlying occult philosophy of a world that believed that the universe was enlivened by obscure correspondences and sympathies. For both traditions, number and form were pregnant with hidden meanings. These meanings yearned to find an expression of the harmony of the universe that would confirm the perfection of divinity. As the rediscovery of classical knowledge opened new avenues of Pythagorean inspiration, the medieval concentration on verticality, dazzling color, and glittering east ends in churches came to be replaced by a new standard of perfection.

EARLY BEGINNINGS IN THE FLORENCE OF BRUNELLESCHI AND MICHELOZZO

Brunelleschi's new approach to constructing a visible world gave birth to the idea of articulating a building so that it could instantly be perceived as the invention of a single mind rather than the result of the struggles and agglomerations of a series

12: Florence, Pazzi Chapel, interior to vault (Brunelleschi). Photo: Allan Foy

of problem solvers. In this sense, the major innovation of this famous architect was the concept of architecture as the contemplation of measurement. For this mathematics was key. Together, number and geometry could bestow on buildings a new concept of unity.

Erected, for the most part, in the 1440s in Florence, Brunelleschi's buildings speak the language of whitewashed walls and gray stone frames.[2] Though geometrical contrasts have a long history, especially in Tuscany, where black and white marble had been used to decorate interiors and exteriors of religious buildings throughout medieval times, Brunelleschi did not have decoration in mind. His white walls and gray frames articulate the construction of the surfaces, as they define the organization of the spaces they enclose. One can see clearly the way in which the different parts of a building are fitted together (fig. 12). In this new visual world nothing is left to chance. Everything is rational and clear. Even the light is clear. Daylight illuminates the interiors, inviting the beholder to contemplate their geometry and clarity, undisturbed by frescoes, tapestries, or other embellishments. Far from creating immeasurable interiors in which translucent colors shimmer and vibrate mysteriously as in the world of Gothic architecture (which continued to prevail elsewhere), this clear light invited Florentine viewers to grasp immediately the depth, size, and articulation of each unit of space. The space itself was beauty. The light, which reveals this, was that of heaven – coming from above; it was the same clear light that, in Antiquity, had entered Pythagorean buildings.[3] Its power accompanied the reemergence of the long-standing tradition that Pythagoras studied the heavens, worshipped the sun, and taught that knowledge is symbolized by light.[4]

Brunelleschi's yearning to divide and measure building surfaces can be seen in his façades (e.g., the loggia of the Ospedale degli Innocenti); it can also be seen in his concept of the articulation of space, as in the sacristy and church of San Lorenzo, both of which he built for Cosimo de'Medici. The sacristy is modeled on the concept of a cube, over which a dome, suspended on pendentives (concave triangular supports) and bringing in the light of heaven through an oculus, appears to float (fig. 13). While this idea brings to mind Antique example, it also suggests the Pythagorean idea that Plato had put forward in the *Timaeus* – that the cube represents earth and the sphere heaven, implying that heaven is held aloft over earth. Coluccio Salutati, admirer of Pythagoras, had just written that the careful study of geometry leads the viewer to advance to the contemplation of God.[5] As the celestial realm floats over the earthly world, their conjunction is made plain by the new aesthetic of light. Twelve bull's-eye windows of clear glass are cut into the twelve cells formed by the twelve ribs that cut into the circle of the dome. Thus light is number. This number recalls Plato's division of an ideal town (a circle) into twelve equal parts joined at the center in the *Laws*, a work Pletho was promoting at this very time.[6] In the *Timaeus*, Plato had defined the cosmos as a ball made from twelve pieces. He also spoke of twelve world spheres beyond the rim of heaven, perhaps referring to the zodiac. Contemporary Florentines were familiar with Plato's praise for the triangle as the building block of the universe: its beauty lay in the fact that the sum of its sides was 12 (as Plutarch explained).[7]

Brunelleschi's project for the church of San Lorenzo repeats, in the crossing of nave and transept, the idea of a dome suspended over a cube. The cube, a square in plan, becomes a module that is implied in the progression from entrance to apse (fig. 14). Each of these implicit geometrical "squares," slightly elongated to fit the needs of a Latin cross plan while making the numbers work, equals four of the smaller "squares" articulated in the bays of the side aisles. The latter therefore appear to be its quadrants. The design of the ceiling confirms the architect's idea. It is divided into coffers forming large squares, each containing twenty-five (the numerical square of 5, 5 x 5) coffers. For Pythagoreans, the number

13: Florence, San Lorenzo, Sacristy, interior, to vault (Brunelleschi). Photo: Bildarchiv Foto Marburg (Art Resource)

5 was important as the only number that divides the decad and as the number of planets. It was also the first circular number, for both its square and its cube end in the same digit (5 x 5 = 25, 5 x 5 x 5 = 125), a Pythagorean concept that would be praised by Ficino.[8] This ceiling provides the first example of the use of figurate numbers (items that, in their numerical array, form a geometrical pattern, such as a square) in architecture – a practice that would be encouraged in the Pythagorean writings of Giorgio Valla later in the century.

Indeed, numbers appear to have been important in San Lorenzo. The six quadrangles of the nave intersect with the three of the transept. (According to Pythagorean arithmetical ideas, six, the first mathematically perfect number, incorporates the triad's perfection twice, thus symbolizing the perfection of the universe, while 3, which derives from Apollo's tripod and Pythagoras's worship

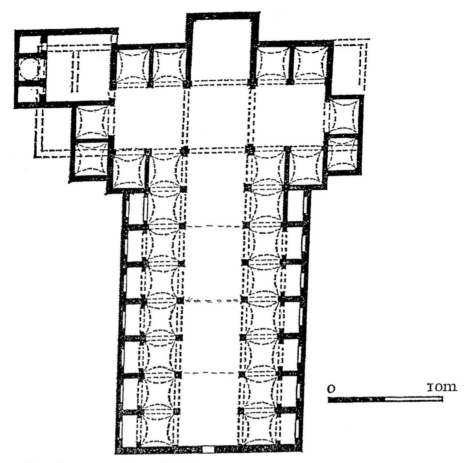

14: Plan of San Lorenzo (Brunelleschi) begun 1421. After Ludwig Heydenreich and Wolfgang Lotz, *Architecture in Italy, 1400–1600*, Harmondsworth, 1974, 9

of Apollo, is primary perfection because it has a beginning, middle, and end. Its corollary, the triad, inevitably leads, because it is a trinitarian symbol, to perfection. Celestial arithmetic held that this number symbolized divine unity for it could be divided only by itself, as exemplified by the division of the universe into three equal parts.)[9] These are complemented by sixteen arches supported by sixteen columns (16 is the square of 4, or the tetrad – the basic number of the Pythagorean *tetraktys* – multiplied by itself; it was believed by Pythagoreans to reflect the division of the "whole" heaven into sixteen regions), symmetrically divided to form eight bays (a numerical cube [2 x 2 x 2 = 8] that signifies equilibration, equality, and harmonious tuning) to either side of the nave.[10] An important precedent for the division of sixteen columns into two symmetrical groups of eight can be found in the façade columns of the celebrated Pantheon of Rome, a Pythagorean structure of Antiquity.[11]

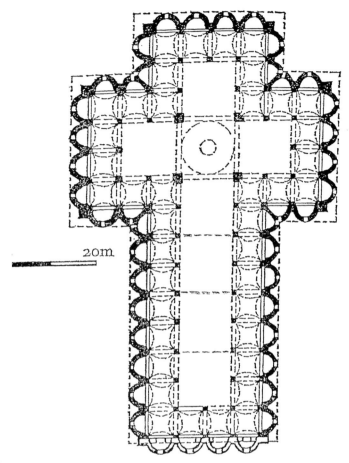

15: Plan of Santo Spirito (Brunelleschi), begun 1436. After Ludwig Heydenreich and Wolfgang Lotz, *Architecture in Italy, 1400–1600*, Harmondsworth, 1974, 9.

The importance of measurement and number to Brunelleschi is reinforced in his project for the church of Santo Spirito (fig. 15). Here also the crossing incorporates a geometrical cube, evoked by the square of the crossing, related to the side aisles in the same order and proportion. The numbers – 3, 6, 8, and 16 – are the same as at San Lorenzo. The major difference between the two structures lies in Brunelleschi's projection of the side aisle as a continuous unifying device in Santo Spirito. This provides an added 4 bays in the façade, 4 in the apse, and 4 ending each arm of the transept, totaling 16. As in San Lorenzo, each of the large square areas is surmounted by a coffered ceiling that demonstrates that the same figurate number, 25, makes up each large geometrical and numerical square (25 = 5 x 5). The duplication of this formula makes clear the importance of geometry and number for Brunelleschi.

The theme of white walls and gray frames and domes on pendentives appearing to float over cubes is continued in what is perhaps Brunelleschi's most

16: Florence, Pazzi Chapel, façade (Brunelleschi). Photo: Allan Foy

original creation, the Pazzi Chapel. Here Brunelleschi's composition is divided into three parts horizontally and laterally. A dome, again composed of twelve sections, rises over the central square suggesting a cubelike space echoing the cubelike shape of the whole (fig. 12). The façade contains four squares divided into four quadrants (or the tetrad multiplied by itself, a numerical square: 4 x 4 = 16), supported by six (a perfect number) free-standing columns arranged in two triads, or groups of three (fig. 16).

Sixteen is the number of outer sides originally planned by Brunelleschi for the oratory of Santa Maria degli Angeli (figs. 17 and 18).[12] Though never completed by him, this project received the high praise of his contemporary and biographer, Antonio Manetti, for its originality. Referring to it as a "temple," Manetti says it was designed to be an independent building. Perhaps because there was no tradition of free-standing octagonal ecclesiastical structures in Tuscany, this building, whose sixteen exterior sides were condensed to eight in its interior plan, seemed a marvel at the time.[13] This conflation of the cube (2 x 2 x 2 = 8), the square (4 x 4 = 16), and the circle suggests that, given the sixteen exterior sides, sixteen pilasters were originally planned for its exterior angles. Indeed, this experiment was paralleled in Brunelleschi's design for the lantern over the cupola of his famous dome for the Cathedral of Florence (fig. 19). There he was constrained by the preexisting octagonal shape of the dome's foundation to build what is essentially a free-standing round "temple" articulated by eight volutes and

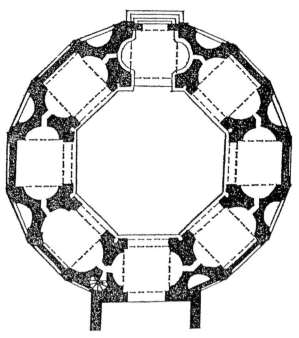

17: Plan of Santa Maria degli Angeli (Brunelleschi), begun 1437. From Ludwig Heydenreich and Wolfgang Lotz, *Architecture in Italy, 1400–1600*, Harmondsworth, 1974, 9.

18: Florence, Santa Maria degli Angeli as later completed (plan, Brunelleschi). Photo: Allan Foy

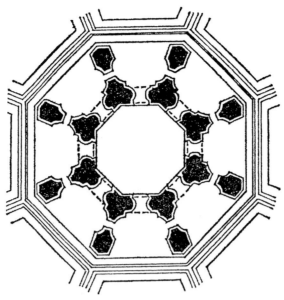

19: Plan of Cathedral of Florence Lantern (Brunelleschi). From Ludwig Heydenreich and Wolfgang Lotz, *Architecture in Italy, 1400–1600*, Harmondsworth, 1974, 9.

crowned at the top by a sphere. Its essential shape is, however, defined by eight double pilasters at each corner, suggesting they are, in fact, sixteen.

Thus does the number 16, which will have an important life later in the century, make its decisive debut in the Renaissance. This suggests Brunelleschi's acquaintance with Vitruvius's *De architectura*, known in manuscript form at least since the time of Petrarch. A Pythagorean, Vitruvius had praised this number, which, resulting from the addition of 6 and 10 – both "perfect" numbers in his view – was "most perfect" and ideal for temples.[14] He had also praised the triad and the number 6; and he had expressed his admiration for the cube as a Pythagorean device, as he had for the use of a module.[15] Brunelleschi's design for Santa Maria degli Angeli, based on the bisection of 8 to create 16, may have been adapted from a suggestion of Vitruvius.[16] Though Manetti does not specifically say that Brunelleschi read Vitruvius, he assures us that Brunelleschi read Latin. He also reports Brunelleschi's friendship with the mathematician-astronomer Paolo Toscanelli who may, as noted earlier in this book, have been a Pythagorean. In critiquing Brunelleschi's projects, most of which were not completed in his lifetime, Manetti repeatedly refers to Brunelleschi's love of proportion and measure. "He decided to rediscover ... the harmonious proportions of the ancients," Manetti rhapsodizes.[17] Those who completed Brunelleschi's buildings are decried by Manetti as scoundrels who did not understand the beauty of proportion and measurement "rediscovered" by the master.

Brunelleschi's interest in composing with arithmetic and geometric form reflects the interests of contemporary humanists: Coluccio Salutati's admiration for numbers of "mystical perfection," Leonardo Bruni's regard for measurement and mathematics, and Pletho's fascination for arithmetic and, especially, for the triad – worlds in which Pythagoras ranked highest – were all surely known to him. Nor could the resurgent popularity of Pythagoras's *Golden Verses* have escaped his notice. These stressed Pythagoras's respect for the sun and the search of the soul for knowledge, which was light.

That numerical structure appears to have been a well-known concept in early fifteenth-century Florence is also evident in the world of sculpture. The south doors of the prestigious Baptistery of Florence, completed in the 1330s by Andrea Pisano, has twenty-eight bronze panels; the north doors, completed in 1424 by Lorenzo Ghiberti (1378–1455), also has twenty-eight panels. The number 28 is one of the exemplary "perfect" numbers cited by Pythagorean writers of Antiquity whose works were already known in Florence.[18] Salutati cited it as an exemplary perfect number necessary to understanding sacred literature. Its significance is underlined by Bruni's advice that the Baptistery's east doors, the last to be commissioned, should also contain twenty-eight panels.[19] For an unknown reason, the famous east doors, executed by Ghiberti in the 1430s, at the same time as Luca della Robbia was portraying Pythagoras twice on the nearby campanile, contain ten scenes (fig. 20). The decad was, of course, the universal number of Pythagoreans and was also regarded by Pythagoreans of Antiquity as perfect because it formed the *tetraktys*, the geometric triangular symbol of the cosmos.[20] Perhaps it was chosen, in this case, because it was the number of laws God gave to Moses. Planned during the lifetime and under the influence of Coluccio Salutati, the doors of the Florentine Baptistery strongly reflect his insistence that the mysticism of numbers is necessary to teaching a clear understanding of sacred subjects. Without mastering this tradition, Salutati held, one could never attain a command of theology.[21]

Perhaps the most important innovator in Renaissance painting, Masaccio (1401–1428), a contemporary of Brunelleschi, also appears to have been acquainted with Pythagorean ideas as they were understood early in the century. Two of his most famous paintings, both completed in the 1420s, demonstrate most clearly his departure from medieval practice. In one, the *Tribute Money*, rather than lining up his figures in a row, he arranges them in a geometrical order demonstrating the theological significance of the circle, because Christ is in its center (fig. 21). Indeed, the use of the circle in this way is a first in the history of art. Instead of functioning centrifugally (directing its components outward into an expansive design, a practice known in late medieval times), it is directed centripetally. Thus are all the figures unified, integrated, and centralized. In the other painting, the *Trinity*, Masaccio demonstrates the theological significance of the triangle in the arrangement of its protagonists, because they form an equilateral triangle whose

20: Lorenzo Ghiberti, east doors of the Florentine Baptistery, 1430s. Photo: Alinari (Art Resource)

apex occurs in the head of Christ. The "inexpressible Trinity" is best imagined in geometrical terms of the triangle, Coluccio Salutati, Masaccio's contemporary, writes.[22] In addition, Masaccio chose a square ground plan for this work and adorned its architecture with an arrangement of seven (the number of divinity) bands of eight (the number of justice) coffers, suggesting the theme of divine justice.[23]

In all his paintings, Masaccio's representation of the human figure in a serious, unadorned, way challenges the Gothic view of human beings as fancy,

21: Masaccio, *Tribute Money*, Florence, Santa Maria del Carmine (Brancacci Chapel), ca. 1425.
Photo: Alinari (Art Resource)

gesticulating, and embellished. It permitted, for the first time, a deep naturalistic
modeling. He portrayed the human figure in a way that showed he was in touch
with contemporary humanist ideals such as Petrarch and Salutati's view of
Pythagoras as a model of humility, simplicity, and moral virtue. In the next decade,
the Chanceller of Florence Poggio Bracciolini would express his admiration for
Pythagoras's social responsibility, humility, and simplicity.[24] From Masaccio, Fra
Angelico and Domenico Veneziano learned the value of geometrical organization, pure light, and simplicity – values that were not shared by all other painters
of the time. Fra Filippo Lippi and Benozzo Gozzoli, for example, chose to cling
more closely to Gothic traditions of enrichment and linearism either because
they had little interest in contemporary science or because they wanted to please
their patrons, or both.

Brunelleschi's successor, Michelozzo di Bartolommeo (1396–1472), was also
imbued with Pythagorean ideas. His architectural language recalls Brunelleschi's
insistence on proportion and measure. This can be seen in the courtyard of his
most original building, the Palazzo Medici, completed in 1459 (fig. 22). Here the
array of classical columns supporting arches suggest the same "ratio" (proportional relationships) as those in Brunelleschi's works. However, it also indicates
a tighter numerical composition. Composed of 3 bays each, the 4 faces of the
courtyard are articulated by 3 stories – hence, the triple triad, 9, multiplied by 4
walls = 36, a perfect numerical (6 x 6) as well as geometrical square.[25] The perfect
square created at ground level becomes a perfect cube in space when viewed up
to the cornice on which the windows rest. The importance of the triad in this
design clearly suggests the significance that Pletho had recently attributed to the
Pythagorean triad in Plato's work. It will be remembered that Pletho held that the
triad, derived from Apollo's tripod, was sacred to Pythagoreans and indicated a

22: Florence, Palazzo Medici, interior courtyard (Michelozzo). Photo: Bildarchiv Foto Marburg (Art Resource)

foreknowledge of the Trinity and the three divisions of the universe. Triple triads were favored by Pletho in the organization of his own writings. His major work, it will be remembered, was organized into three books, to which were appended twenty-seven (a cubic number, the result of 3 x 3 x 3) hymns. Each hymn was composed of nine (the sum of 3 + 3 + 3) verses.[26]

Not only did the idea of the cube dominate the design of the palace courtyard it also dominated the design of the Palazzo Medici as a whole. As originally conceived, this palace had three (the triad) stories incorporating ten (the universe) bays on each of its visible façades (fig. 23). George Hersey shows that the ground floor of the Medici Palace was based on a cubical plan that supported the geometrical cube of the construction that was, in essence, an independent block.[27] He connects this with the fact that Vitruvius, in promoting Pythagorean cubic doctrines, claimed that Pythagoras had written books on the cube. Both Vitruvius and Nicomachus had explained that Pythagoras had favored the cube as shape and as number.[28] The division of palace façades into three stories (as opposed to the multiple and unequal stories of Gothic secular buildings) was to become standard "modern" language in the design of Renaissance palaces.

23: Florence, Palazzo Medici, exterior, fifteenth century (Michelozzo). Photo: From Ferdinando del Migliore, *Firenze città nobilissima* (1684) as in George L. Hersey, *Pythagorean Palaces*, Ithaca and London, 1976, 165.

Michelozzo's yen to experiment with round forms suggests his attraction to another Pythagorean idea, for it was commonly noted in ancient writings known to the Renaissance that Pythagoras's favorite shape was the circle and his favorite solid the sphere. When given the opportunity in 1444 to build a tribune for the church of Santissima Annunziata, Michelozzo took the unusual step of adding a round form to the preexisting rectangular one. That rotunda, his chief religious work, is in fact a nearly autonomous centralized building. Radiating from its center, Michelozzo planned seven chapels, suggesting the center of the universe surrounded by seven spheres.[29] The importance of the number 7, as the most "divine" of Pythagorean numbers, had been revived in contemporary Florence by Pletho. He claimed that number 7 paved the way to paradise and, as the music of the spheres, demonstrated the eternal harmony and concord of the universe.[30] Michelozzo had, perhaps, first experimented with the circular plan in the temple of the *Joseph Scene* of the east doors of the Florentine Baptistery designed during the 1430s when he was collaborating with the sculptor Lorenzo Ghiberti. Completely round and speaking a classical language, this temple accommodates figures inside and outside far more successfully than that of Solomon in another panel on the same set of doors, which, probably designed later by Ghiberti himself, is Gothic in character.[31] The idea of the round "temple," or church, that could be circumscribed by a circle was to be advocated by Alberti, an emerging

Pythagorean architect at the time. It would become an important preoccupation of the future.

PYTHAGOREAN CONCEPTS DEVELOP: ALBERTI IN FLORENCE AND HIS CONTEMPORARIES IN PIENZA AND URBINO

After Brunelleschi's death in 1446, his experimental focus on proportion, measure, number, clear light, the square, and the circle was raised to the level of theory by Alberti. Alberti demonstrated his debt to the inspiration of Brunelleschi in 1435, before he became an architect, in the dedication of his treatise on painting to the older master. His philosophical underpinnings in the work of Vitruvius are unambiguous. So also is his admission that he was a Pythagorean. This surely explains why, in 1462, a time when he was deeply engrossed in a variety of architectural projects, he took the trouble to copy the *Golden Verses* of Pythagoras as a Christmas gift to his nephews.[32]

Although Alberti's new theories may have been far easier to explicate in the 1450s, when he wrote his revolutionary treatise putting forward the importance of symmetry, proportion, and music, than in the 1460s, when he found himself engaged in the practicalities of construction, his buildings nonetheless demonstrate his Pythagoreanism. Their extant forms, largely uncompleted at the time of his death in 1472, make clear his intention to practice what he preached.

Alberti endeavored to eliminate the heterogeneous and irregular organization characteristic of medieval structures by unifying surface design and space through plane and solid geometry and the classical language of columns, pilasters, entablatures, pediments, arches, and vaults. The cube and the sphere were of special interest to him and constitute the major unifying devices he employed. Resulting from its unique unity, the cube's stability was based on its extended squareness. This meant that the four sides of the square were transposed into six surfaces, eight angles, and twelve edges of the geometrical cube, numbers that had come to signify the proportions of musical harmony. As the ancient Pythagorean Nicomachus had put it, "the cube is harmony," a proposition which agreed with Vitruvius.[33] Hersey points out the many ways in which Alberti raised the status of the cube to a divine one by intermixing its geometry (its physical shape) and its arithmetic (cube roots). He also shows that in terms of design, the square (the modular surface of the cube) was primary and that, even when imagining rectangles, Alberti had the square in mind (thus he speaks of "a square and a third," "a square and a half," etc.).[34] Parallel to Alberti's notion of cubic form and number was his admiration of the sphere, Pythagoras's favorite shape, which represented the universe and ideal celestial beauty.

In the Rucellai Palace Alberti clearly demonstrated the primacy of the cube (fig. 24).[35] The division of the façade into three stories accompanied by the division

24: Florence, Palazzo Rucellai (Alberti), begun 1460. Photo: Allan Foy

of each window of the upper stories into three parts underlines the importance of the triad as the universal symbol of unification. The progeny of the (geometrical) cube and the (numerical) triad can be seen in the number of bays originally planned (one of which remains unfinished). Here Alberti chose the first cube, 8 (2 x 2 x 2 = 8), which suggests harmony, or "even" evenness. A central vertical that traverses the structure from its base to the raking cornice of the roof allows for four bays to either side. In the 3 stories, these 4 bays form a triple tetrad to either side totaling 12 (3 stories x 4 bays = 12), the number of the edges of the cube. This was, as Martianus Capella had put it in Antiquity, the "tetrad measured by triplication."[36] In this way, Alberti demonstrated proportion and balance by using not only the cube itself as form but numbers associated with it (6, 8, and 12) that were also associated with musical theory and the creation of harmony. This *perfetta*

25: Rimini, Alberti's design for the Tempio Malatestiano, medal by Matteo dei Pasti, begun ca. 1459. Photo: Paris, Bibliothèque Nationale de France

harmonia corresponds with his own written recommendation that the adornment of a building be based on number.[37] Thus did the secular palace façade, divided vertically as well as horizontally, become a complete harmonic unit in which each part, as in music, played a role in the composition of the whole.

The Tempio Malatestiano at Rimini provided Alberti with the seemingly insurmountable problem of transforming a Gothic church into one imbued with modern ideas. He solved this problem by imagining a large hemisphere, a dome, resting on an imaginary cube below (figs. 25 and 26). The entire building was to have been adjusted to this plan, which was never fully executed. Actually constructed were seven (the number of divinity and the music of the spheres) arched vaults to either exterior side, elevated on a pedestal, detaching the building from its surroundings. In one of these the bones of Pletho, the favorite philosopher of its commissioner, Sigismundo Pandolfo Malatesta, were buried.[38] The

26: Rimini, Tempio Malatestiano (Alberti). Photo: Allan Foy

Pythagorean nature of the building as a whole is underlined by the dedication of one of its chapels to the seven planets and another to the Seven Liberal Arts. In this light, it should not be surprising that Sigismundo was reputed to have chosen the concept for the interior layout "from among the innermost secrets of philosophy" – good reason to select a Pythagorean architect.[39]

At Santa Maria Novella in Florence, Alberti faced a different problem. Here he was constrained to design a façade to disguise the enormous preexisting medieval church that disappeared behind it (fig. 27). Working only with a surface, he married number and plane geometry, thereby demonstrating Pythagorean unity, balance, and divinity. Unity is instantly apparent for the entire façade can be circumscribed by a perfect square that, in turn, can be circumscribed by a circle.[40] Unity is also evident in the symmetry of each side of the façade as well as in the fact that the façade can be imagined as a grand triangle in which one square, centralized over two, is itself surmounted by a triangular pediment.[41] Perhaps not incidentally the triangle (recalling Apollo's tripod and the basis of Plato's cosmos), which forms the apex of the church, contains not the crucified Christ or the Madonna after whom the church is named, but a gigantic image of the sun. This sun forms, together with two circular devices below, a third triangle. Balance is achieved in the placement of opposites, or geometric

27: Florence, Santa Maria Novella (Alberti). Photo: Allan Foy

contraries, as can be seen in the reverse curvature (or oppositional geometry) of the gigantic scrolls to either side that form an important part of the two-dimensional design.[42] Number, too, plays an essential role, suggesting its divine meaning. The marble panels of the lower part of the façade are articulated as two tetrads (thus 4 arches to either side, forming in their harmonious union the first cube, 8) and a set of four colossal columns that are in turn surmounted by four pilasters in the upper story. Between the pilasters, high above the pavement and forming the most visible part of the building, are represented celestial stars. Not surprisingly for a temple design à la Vitruvius, their number is sixteen, the "most perfect" number for a temple.

These indicate but a few of the many ways in which Alberti appears consciously to have used Pythagorean principles to compact and unify his designs. His belief in the symbolism and significance of number is articulated, as we have seen, in his writings.[43] His buildings suggest that, for him, a palace, being an earthly object, was a cube (the earth) and that "temples," or churches, were centered, if possible, on the idea that a sphere (the heavens) was suspended above the cube of the earth. Geometric metaphor, contraries, and number all contributed to the creation of his harmony. Through geometry and number Alberti constructed objective, concrete, tangible beauty that could be measured and interlocked in what he called *concinnitas* (the harmony of all parts fitted together), a concept he perhaps borrowed from Plato's *Timaeus*. Order and system are synonymous in the physical language of his buildings; they are based on the square, the circle, and the triangle. With its four equal sides, the square becomes, in solid form, the cube. The circle has eternal continuity, while the sides of a triangle mutually balance each other.

At this same time, Cardinal Bessarion was advocating Plato's mathematics as superior to all other studies and was seeking harmony in all aspects of scholarship, while another cardinal, Alberti's friend the mathematician Nicholas Cusanus, was writing that God used arithmetic (for number), geometry (for form), and music (for proportion) to create a world in which every element takes its place in the harmony created by its immutable relation to the whole.[44] God considered in advance, Cusanus explains, the sizes, placement, and motion of the stars and calculated their distances in such a way that their order was equal and perfect.[45] Such a statement brings to mind the careful organization of Alberti's sixteen stars at the summit of Santa Maria Novella. Among the many interests Alberti appears to have shared with his close friend, Toscanelli, was one in astronomy. Together they made measurements of the heavens, as Pythagoras was reputed to have done in Antiquity.[46]

Other architects who were likewise touched by the avant-garde aims of this generation included Bernardo Rossellino (1409–1464). The redesigning of Pienza, a small city in Tuscany, stands out among the numerous architectural projects with which Rossellino's name is associated. Of the four buildings that, arranged around a trapezoidal space, form the heart of this first planned city of the Renaissance to actually take shape, the most important will be considered here – the cathedral and the palace of the Piccolomini family.[47]

The cathedral is most unusual, both in its façade and in its plan (fig. 28). Its façade is articulated in three vertical divisions formed by three sets of pilasters that remarkably, even divide the triangular pediment above. Laterally, the façade is composed of a series of three bays in the lower range with another series of three bays above and crowned by three arches. This suggests a strong interest in the triple triad. A similar concern is evident in the interior planning. The interior space is divided into three aisles (including the central nave), all of equal height, a division that functions horizontally (toward the altar) and laterally (wall to wall). The nave is articulated by a set of three arches leading to the altar.

Threes also provide the theme of the central courtyard of the Piccolomini palace (fig. 29). Here every face consists in three arches, a division that is continued through all three levels, thus forming, at the heart of this secular building, a spatial cube and a numerical square ($3 \times 3 = 9 \times 4$ sides $= 36$ or 6×6). In terms of the exterior, the palace block assumes the shape of a cube, defined by eight (a numerical cube) bays on its east façade (fig. 30). This system is continued in the loggia, or "garden façade," to the rear of the building, which is composed of three levels, each

28: Pienza, Cathedral (Bernardo Rossellino), ca. 1460–62. Photo: Allan Foy

consisting in eight open bays. Even the pavement connecting the structures appears to follow this peculiar arithmo-geometrical systematization for, as it leads to the entrance of the cathedral, the number of its full rectangles is nine, laid out 3 x 3.

Though we may never know what intricate details Rossellino had in mind, his interest in using the triple triad as a unifying and harmonizing device for the cathedral is as clear as is his interest in thinking of the palace as a cube. Thus does each building, through its plan and façade treatment, and through its use of number to obtain proportion, form a harmonious ensemble of its own while enhancing the unity of the whole.

Rossellino's struggle to incorporate Pythagorean ideas in his search for new ways to create harmony suggests that his aim, like Alberti's, was to work out new aesthetic principles. Cusanus, whom Rossellino – as a collaborator with Alberti – surely

29: Pienza, Palazzo Piccolomini, courtyard (Bernardo Rossellino), ca. 1460–62. Photo: Allan Foy

knew personally, is more to the point: "Three is oneness, just as oneness is threeness." Praising the triad as beautiful beyond all numbers because it is perfection and unification, Cusanus referred to it, as we have seen, as "trine oneness." Through number, he explained, we can apprehend divine truths, including the triplicate structure of the universe, which can be thought of as nine unities circumscribable by a circle. This approach also reflects the current teachings of Bessarion, who, in praising the symbolism of number, indicated his respect for the use of enigma to express esoteric doctrines. Such considerations would have been meaningful to the commissioner of Pienza, Aeneas Sylvius Piccolomini (Pope Pius II), though perhaps not understood by all. Rossellino's choice of new humanist language to modernize the hometown of the new Pope, was most appropriate for, it will be remembered, Pius II was a great admirer of Pythagoras and Pythagorean ideas of harmony.[48]

30: Pienza, Palazzo Piccolomini, east façade (Bernardo Rossellino), ca. 1460–62. Photo: Allan Foy

As it developed from Michelozzo to Alberti and Rossellino, the Renaissance palace's embodiment of the cube came to be widely accepted. This can be seen in later Florentine palaces, such as the Palazzo Gondi and the more monumental Palazzo Strozzi, and was further developed in Rome and elsewhere, as Hersey has so incisively documented. The situation at Urbino, however, was different.

In Urbino the Palazzo Ducale – a project to which Federigo da Montefeltro devoted twenty years, leaving it incomplete at the time of his death in 1482 – bears the unique stamp of the Pythagoreanism that permeated that Duke's court. The second phase of the work (1468–72) on the "most beautiful palace of Italy, really a city in the form of a palace," as Castiglione described it, corresponds with the presence of the architect Luciano Laurana (ca. 1420–1479) in that city.[49] Laurana's major project there was the construction of the Grand Courtyard, a geometrically organized space that, speaking an Albertian language of vertical and horizontal classically ordered subdivisions, brings together the entire sprawling multileveled mountainous medieval structure into an ultramodern center remarkable for its unity and coherence (fig. 31).[50] Despite having to adapt to the surrounding structure, it is not a square, though it looks like a square and is treated like a square.[51] This is evident in the design of the pavement. The stone pavement is divided into eight equal sections, all congruent triangles, by marble "rays" that meet in a central octagon. Thus is its double reference to the first numerical cube clear. Federigo's Pythagoreanism is certainly suggested in the inscription on the

31: Urbino, Palazzo Ducale, Grand Courtyard (Luciano Laurana), ca. 1468–72. With modern added upper story. Photo: Alinari (Art Resource)

frieze above, which praises his justice, mercy, generosity, and piety. A Pythagorean counterpart of the Grand Courtyard exists in the unfinished loggia of a secondary courtyard of this palace, probably designed by Francesco di Giorgio (whose writings, it will be remembered, leaned heavily on Vitruvius). There the seven arched arcade system suggests the music of the spheres, bringing to mind Federigo's interests in astronomy and astrology.[52] Both courtyards were likely undertaken on the advice of Alberti, with whom Federigo had close contacts.[53]

The "twin" chapels, constructed after Laurana's departure in 1472 and possibly designed by the aspiring young painter-architect Donato Bramante (1443–1514) under the influence of his teacher Piero della Francesca, provide a clear example of Federigo's Pythagoreanism. This is evident in the fact that they were planned together as part of an ideological and physical triad that included the private study of Federigo directly above, where, in a somewhat triangular-shaped room, twenty-eight ancient writers – including Plato, Boethius, and other Pythagoreans – were portrayed in seven groups of four.[54] Not only is 28 the second mathematically perfect number, but it is also, as Michael Allen points out, the final hidden part of the most abstruse of all of Plato's mathematical speculations

32: Urbino, Palazzo Ducale, Cappella del Perdono (Bramante?), 1474–82. Photo: Allan Foy

about the universe according to Ficino, a contemporary and friend of Duke Federigo. From the point of view of one who made astrological observations (Federigo), it is perhaps significant that the arrangement of 7 x 4 reflects the number of the planets times the number of elements.[55] Accessible by a small private staircase, the twin chapels below suggest the reconciliation of opposites that refers to the universal unity contemplated by Pythagoreans. A Christian chapel, now known as the Cappella del Perdono (absolution), and a pagan chapel, now called the Tempietto delle Muse (the Muses), form, as will be seen, a single sanctuary divided into two balancing and equal parts conjoined by a common vestibule.

While the Cappella del Perdono has often been described as related to the work of Piero della Francesca, its organizational system has been ignored (fig. 32). The barrel vault overhead, made up of cherub heads (which could have been of any number and organization) discloses its Pythagorean inspiration: 7 transversal

33: Urbino, Palazzo Ducale, Tempietto delle Muse (Bramante?), 1474–82. Photo: Allan Foy

rows and 10 orthogonal rows, the two most divine numbers of Pythagorean arithmetic. The side walls are each divided into nine bays (the triple triad) articulated by decorative marble panels, each having three levels. The altar wall appropriately expresses the Trinitarian number in its own three panels, echoed by three divisions in the pavement. The Christian theme is explained by the continuous inscription on a frieze that unites the room. It begs the Holy Spirit for the remission of sins. The original altar decorations are unknown.

The Tempietto delle Muse is laid out in the same way as the Christian chapel, with the apse and altar in a parallel position (fig. 33). Although all the paintings originally decorating this chapel have been removed, its dedication to Apollo (the "divine father" of Pythagoras and the director of the music of the spheres) is apparent in the fact that a small barrel vault over the altar contains seven (Apollo's number) transversal coffers arranged in three (Apollo's tripod, the precursor of the Trinity) orthogonal rows.[56] The coffers of the main barrel vault again vaunt the number 7 in the number of transversal rosetted coffers and in the number of the orthogonal rosetted coffers (7 x 7), thus forming a figurate number (49) and a numerical square, as well as a geometrical square. The number of paintings originally covering the walls appears to have been ten, representing Apollo himself and the Muses.[57] The original intarsia door to the chapel, still in place, shows Apollo playing his seven-stringed lyre, together with Palla Athena, who was known to the Renaissance, through Cicero, as his mother.[58] An old description of the Tempietto by the Pythagorean mathematician Bernardino Baldi suggests that images of Apollo and Athena (now lost) originally adorned the altar.[59] Still intact, the frieze praises the Muses and the music of the lyre. Playing his music and engaging his accomplices, the nine Muses who sing in unison, Apollo, as the thematic center of this chapel in which he is represented three times, counterbalances the possible original theme of the Trinity next door.

The usual explanation that these chapels represent "Federigo's love of nature and humanity" appears rather banal in the face of a Pythagorean interpretation. Taking into account the esteem for number by Federigo and the mathematicians-astrologers of his court, the Pythagorean theme of this grouping becomes clear. Unity – or *harmonia* – is the result, as was well known among Pythagoreans since Antiquity, of reconciling opposites.[60] Looking at the remains of the apse of the Tempietto delle Muse, only an eagle remains above. Because Apollo and Athena are represented on the entrance doors, as they were on the altar, we may deduce some interesting conclusions. The eagle (usually ignored) probably signifies Zeus, the father of both Apollo and Athena, and also Federigo himself. This conflation had been bestowed on Federigo by none other than his esteemed correspondent Ficino (who was known to favor the idea of twin chapels).[61] The position of the eagle above Apollo and Athena makes it plain that a triad was involved, just as, most likely, on the Christian altar.[62] In this case Zeus would have balanced God, Apollo his son Christ, and Athena (goddess of wisdom and sometimes, like the Holy Spirit, represented as a bird) the Holy Spirit.[63] Their equipoise, concord, and reciprocity would thus have been expressed through enigmatic Pythagorean language. In this way the harmony is clear: The chapels are not two chapels, one Christian and one pagan, but are a unity made up of two balancing parts that symbolize the reconciliation of Christianity with classicism. This is confirmed by the frieze in the vestibule shared by the two chapels. "You see two sanctuaries joined by a small intervening space. One part is sacred to the Muses, the other part to God."[64]

Federigo's interest in number and the reconciliation of opposites are but two aspects of his larger interest in ancient cosmography and mathematics, an interest that he consummated by inviting *sapientes*, or wise men, who specialized in arithmetic and astrology, including Paulus de Middelbourg, to his court.

34: Piero della Francesca, *Flagellation*, Urbino, National Gallery of the Marches, ca. 1460–70. Photo: Alinari (Art Resource)

Among these was Ottaviano Ubaldini who, as will be seen later, has been linked to the Cappella del Perdono. Known as the "prince of astrologers," Ottaviano appears to be a major character in a painting by Piero della Francesca, a painter well known to the court of Urbino.[65]

The original purpose of this major work by Piero, the *Flagellation*, has remained a mystery (fig. 34). Dating from about 1460–70, and presently in the National Gallery of the Marches (the former palace of Federigo), it would appear that it has always been in Urbino. Years ago Kenneth Clark recognized three important characteristics of this painting: (1) its architectural style is dependent on Alberti, who Piero surely knew personally, (2) a module was used in its construction, and (3) its design is enigmatic and a complete expression of the "mystique" of measurement.[66] While art historians are generally in agreement on the first two of Clark's observations, they have been reluctant to consider the third. However, in 1953, Rudolf Wittkower and B. A. R. Carter collaborated in a brilliant analysis, discovering that the module with which Piero worked in laying out his design corresponds to one published by Pacioli in *De divina proportione* (a work, it will be remembered, in which Pacioli demonstrated his admiration for Pythagorean principles).[67] Though they concluded that this painting is "infused" with mathematical symbolism, they offered no explanation regarding its possible meaning.

They found, however, through an elaborate reconstruction of the plan and elevation of the architectural setting of the picture, that the pattern of squares in its marble pavement was not based on the planning module, but on the significance of the number 8, the first cube. Thus does the square become, as Piero demonstrated in his own writings, a cube.[68] Accordingly, each of the large horizontal squares of the pavement is subdivided as eight small squares wide and eight small squares deep, as Piero had demonstrated in his writings.[69] This means that 8 is a key number for, in constructing the geometrical divisions of the floor tiles, its result (8 x 8), 64, is a figurate number, as well as a square, a cube, and a circular cube. However, the pavement squares of the hall where Christ is being flagellated are different. Each consists in a pattern made up of an exploding eight-pointed star in the center, surround by eight dark, eight white, and eight dark (in that order) geometrical shapes.[70] Thus is the design of each of these squares based on 8 x 4, or 32, a number with significant cosmological implications because it describes mathematically the parts of a circle, or the points of the compass.[71] Therefore the entire painting, including its anteroom, side passage, and interior hall, is based on a floor pattern in which 8 prevails (as squares are transformed into cubes) not only as the dominant number, but as the only number. The only exception is the central square on which Christ stands, in which a circle – certainly symbolic of his divinity – is inscribed. This is not to mention the fact that the *dramatis personae* (the characters on stage) consist of eight figures.

The ceiling, too, uses a figurate number, as well as a square number, 49, demonstrated in the construction of its squares (7 x 7). By inserting a decorative band between its coffers, the artist was able to show a complete correspondence between the square coffers of the ceiling and the squares of the pavement.[72] This pictorial construction allows for the circle on which Christ stands, at the heart of this work, to be surrounded by squares. This suggests that Piero may have been preoccupied, as were Pythagoreans of Antiquity, with calculating the quadrature of the circle. Indeed, the problem of measuring the circle was well known to Nicholas Cusanus, who wrote a treatise on the subject in 1457 and who was, as Pacioli tells us, "venerated" at the court of Urbino.[73]

Taking into account the importance of Pythagoreanism at the court of Urbino and its close contacts with Alberti, Ficino, Cusanus, Paulus de Middelbourg, and others whom we have met, it is possible to offer an interpretation of the symbolism of this painting that though enigmatic to us would have been understood by the initiated in the time and place of its creation. Aside from its figural subject matter, the *Flagellation* appears to demonstrate the perfection of the cube below (8), which refers to the earth, and the divinity above (7), which refers to the heavens. This is not unlike the concept with which Brunelleschi and Alberti had struggled in order to lift the dome of heaven high up over the cube of the earth, an idea well known through Plato's *Timaeus*. Such a painting could well have formed the altar frontal, as Marilyn Aronberg Lavin suggests, in Federigo's

35: Luciano Laurana (?), *Ideal City*, Baltimore, Walters Art Museum, ca. 1475. Photo: Walters Art Museum, Baltimore

private chapel, the Cappella del Perdono, for its dimensions correspond. Christ's flagellation would thus have given visible meaning to the frieze that speaks of remission of sins.[74] In this case, the advice of Ottaviano Ubaldini, the bearded man who appears to be commemorated in this painting, would have been deeply intertwined with its construction for he would have known that eight-pointed stars constitute, as Lavin suggests, astrological signs for the planets.[75] After the death in 1482 of Federigo, who held dear both mathematics and astrology, this chapel was put under the patronage of Ottaviano, who was both court mathematician and astrologer. Its iconography – with the flagellated Christ attached to a column supporting a golden Apollo-like statue – would have been in keeping with the balance between Christianity and the sun god, Apollo, of the twin chapels.

Piero expressed his interest in the cube as an element of construction in other paintings. His design of Solomon's temple in the *Meeting of Solomon and the Queen of Sheba* at Arezzo is based on a central chamber that is a geometrical (spatial) cube reinforced, because it appears to have eight bays, by a numerical cube. His ideal church in an accompanying fresco, the *Proof of the True Cross*, is based on a triple triad not dissimilar to the tripartite organization of the then new cathedral at Pienza.[76]

Such ideality was also expressed in a series of paintings commonly known, because no one has yet discovered their author or purpose, as "*Ideal Cities.*" Exclusively architectural in subject matter, one of these, now in Baltimore's Walters Art Museum, shows two palaces, both of which appear to be cubes, framing a central space that itself suggests a cube, especially as it is defined by an octagon (8) and set within four columns (fig. 35). A triple triumphal arch lies in the center distance, flanked by two buildings, one of which is a church based on the shape of an octagon. Although this painting and the works like it are focused on studying perspective, the ideality of their settings is nonetheless clear. Though they have been attributed to many artists, these pictures have generally been

36: Cortona, Santa Maria delle Grazie al Calcinaio, interior view to dome (Francesco di Giorgio), 1485–88. Photo: Alinari (Art Resource)

associated with Piero or with Alberti or the chief architect of the Palazzo Ducale, Luciano Laurana.[77]

Contemplating Harmony at Cortona, Prato, Milan, and Rome

On a sloping meadow of olives and figs, Francesco di Giorgio designed the church of Santa Maria delle Grazie al Calcinaio in the late 1480s (fig. 36). By eliminating side aisles and depending on thick exterior walls to contain the thrust of the nave's barrel vault, the architect concentrated on the simple unity of three nave bays leading to a central square, the module of the entire church, which,

37: Cortona, Santa Maria delle Grazie al Calcinaio (Francesco di Giorgio), 1485–88. Photo: Shannon Pritchard

forming a cube, is surmounted by a dome in eight sections. The pairs of pilasters articulating each angle bring the total number of vertical (columnar) elements to 16, the perfect Vitruvian number for a "temple." The conformation of the scale of the church to that of a human figure (the legs = the nave, the chest = the transept, and the head = the apse or altar), a Vitruvian proportion, has been noted by scholars.[78] Francesco di Giorgio's efforts to obtain harmony can be noted in a view of this building from above, which reveals the architect's struggle to distribute the eight windows of the dome's lantern and drum in perfect proportion to the four arms of the church (cf. fig. 37 and front cover).

At the same time, two other architects were discovering other ways to achieve even more consolidated harmonious ecclesiastical structures. In the Tuscan city of Prato, Giuliano da Sangallo (1445–1516) built a church whose four arms are exactly equal in height and area and arranged around a central square whose cubic manifestation supports a dome that dominates a building that can be totally circumscribed by a circle (fig. 38).[79] Clear light pours in from the twelve windows of the dome of the unfinished Church of Santa Maria delle Carceri and the six windows of its lantern (both cosmological numbers). Its pavement, centered in a geometrical square, is articulated by thirty-six (a numerical square, 6 x 6 = 36) white marble rays radiating from the center. Though unfinished, this masterpiece in symmetry

38: Prato, Santa Maria delle Carceri (Giuliano da Sangallo), 1485. Photo: Allan Foy

provides the first example of a pure Greek cross plan (four arms of equal length that perfectly balance each other), as well as of regularity of form, harmony of proportion, and concentration on the center. Detached and visible from all sides, unified in exterior and interior design, dominated by a crowning dome based on the circle and sphere, this church initiates the example that Alberti had dreamed of: perfect centralized geometric form that creates perfect harmony.[80]

Meanwhile Bramante, who had left Urbino, where he knew Francesco di Giorgio, and gone to Milan – where he worked side by side with Leonardo da Vinci and surely also knew Pacioli, and Gaffurio – built there two religious structures centered on the geometry of number and form. The first was an innovative choir for the preexisting church of Santa Maria presso San Satiro. The tribune added by Bramante consists in three arms, each of which is defined by three

39: Milan, Santa Maria presso San Satiro, interior to altar (Bramante), 1490. Photo: Allan Foy

arches on each of its three sides (fig. 39). Thus each arm is defined by a triple triad and the total number of arches in the three arms is 27 (3 x 9 = 27), suggesting that the space is also a numerical cube (3 x 3 x 3 = 27). This calls to mind Nicholas Cusanus's description of the relation of three nines to the number 27 as one of absolute unity.[81] To underline his resolve, Bramante executed the central arm, which would not otherwise have permitted these divisions because of its shallowness (owing to a street behind the church), in paint.

For another preexisting church, that of Santa Maria delle Grazie, Bramante built an altar end addition that gives the impression of a free-standing centralized structure based on a central square – a temple worthy of Alberti's dreams. That square forms a perfect cube up to the feet of the pendentives that support a dome of the same height as the cube below (fig. 40). The dome is divided into sixteen parts inside, allowing the clear light of heaven to stream in from sixteen windows, while outside it forms a sixteen-sided polyhedron (fig. 41). Each of the sixteen sides is divided into two, forming an outer ring of thirty-two bays, the cosmological number that corresponds with the points of the compass. Each of the three apsidal protrusions is composed of ten sections, suggesting that the perfect temple to God is supported by a base reflecting the universality of the church. The visionary architecture first expressed by Bramante in Milan surely owes a great deal to the demonstrations of hypothetical centralized churches drawn on paper at the time by his friend Leonardo.[82]

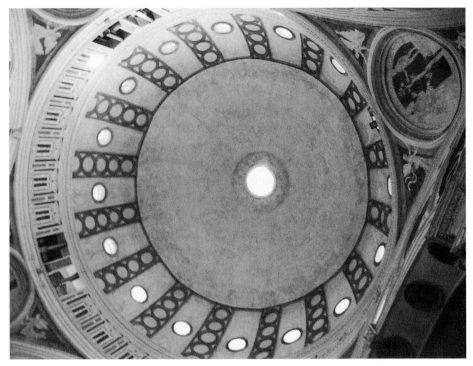

40: Milan, Santa Maria delle Grazie, interior view of dome (Bramante), 1492. Photo: Allan Foy

Meanwhile, in Rome, numbers were more important than geometry until Bramante's arrival in the early 1500s when both would come to have equal significance. After becoming pope in 1471, Sixtus IV began construction of the Sistine (or Sixtine) Chapel in about 1475, a time that, chronologically, corresponds with his decision to have the complete works of Philo of Alexandria, which demonstrated the interlocking of arithmetic and theology, translated from Greek into Latin.[83] The strong interest Sixtus showed in Philo is reflected not only in the fact that the pope was the dedicatee of this enormous translation project but also in the unusual plan that was devised for the construction of his private papal sanctuary.

Instead of being based on a cross plan, the Sistine Chapel presented a rectangle whose interior was (prior to the closing off of the far wall in the next century to accommodate Michelangelo's *Last Judgment*) composed of sixteen parts articulated by sixteen large frescoes separated by sixteen painted pilasters, eight to either side (fig. 42). The eight frescoes on the north side are devoted to the establishment of New Testament law by Christ, while the eight on the south are devoted to Moses and the old law. Their preoccupation with justice and the law is not surprising for in the Pythagorean view of number, not only is 8 a numerical cube (2 x 2 x 2 = 8) but, as the product of equals (2 x 4), 8 also symbolizes equality

41: Milan, Santa Maria delle Grazie, exterior (Bramante), 1492. Photo: Allan Foy

and justice.[84] Indeed, the inscriptions of the accompanying friezes testify to Sixtus's preoccupation with justice and the law in the choice of historical scenes. The total number of scenes (16) suggests that the interior was meant to have the aura of a temple. The number 16 also dominates the design of the pavement in the most sacred part of the chapel. Here a large square is represented. Tangential to its sides are circles, four on each side, each containing four subsidiary circles.[85]

An elegant marble choir screen, now considerably altered, formed the entrance to the most sacred part of the Sistine Chapel, which included the altar and the papal throne. Raised on a platform of three steps, this screen, divided into three parts – seven sculptured lower bays, seven gilded grilles above, and seven magnificent gilded candelabra at the top – must have formed an exalted introduction to the most sacred zone of the chapel.[86] Its seven great lights (changed in modern times to eight) majestically illuminated the interior. This suggests the

42: Rome, Sistine Chapel, original appearance ca. 1480s. Engraving from Ernst Steinmann, *Der Sixtinische Kapelle*, Munich, 1901–5, I(VIII).

influence of Philo, who had written that Moses introduced the concept of law because he understood the order of God, which – because order involves number – was dependent on the number 7. It also suggests a link to important biblical and Roman traditions. The seven-branched candelabrum that was made together with the Ark of the Covenant by the Israelites in the wilderness and used by Moses to illuminate the Tabernacle was, the Book of Exodus tells us, protected by a screen. The most precious object contained in the altar of the Tabernacle was the Ark of the Covenant inside which were the Tables of Law inscribed by God and given to Moses. The Ark of the Covenant, the Tables of the Law, and the seven-branched candelabrum were among the spoils brought to Rome from Jerusalem by the Emperor Titus in the first century A.D. Early medieval Roman tradition held that these precious Hebrew relics were buried in the high altar of the Lateran, the official church of the pope. Among Constantine's documented gifts to the Lateran were seven golden candelabra, each ten feet high, which were placed before the altar. In late-medieval times these candelabra still existed in the Pope's (official) church.[87] Thus does it appear that their inspiration was influential in illuminating the balance of old and new laws in the Pope's new (private) church.[88]

While not all pagan themes in fifteenth-century art are Pythagorean,[89] those that are were not always related to contemporary literary thought. Older ideas

43: *Pythagorean Sphere*, from *Astrological and Medical Compilation*, HM 64, fol. 15v. English, fifteenth century, Huntington Library (San Marino, Calif.). Photo: Huntington Library

tied to ancient views of Pythagoras as a worker of magic, an idea that had persisted throughout medieval times, continued to present themselves in a network of popular images. Some of these took the form of two-dimensional designs such as Pythagorean Spheres whose use continued throughout the century. An example can be seen in a folio from an English astrological and medical compilation that explains, in Latin and English, the use of Pythagoras's Sphere to help medical doctors to predict the outcome of illness (fig. 43).

The solar religion of ancient Pythagoreans, who worshipped Apollo and whose only known temple was an elaborate subterranean structure lit by a single shaft of sunlight, had survived through medieval times in Christian ecclesiastical architecture in the form of an east and bedazzled with translucent colored glass. In Renaissance Florence the imagery of the sun began to have a changed significance as the creation of God to provide clear light, which was knowledge that could be discovered by measurement.[90] Plato's Pythagorean teachings that the eternal Being who had begotten the universe lived in the spherical dome of the firmament, from where he regulated the planetary spheres and overlooked the cube of the earth below, appears to have inspired Brunelleschi. Perhaps through the influence of his astronomer-mathematician friend Toscanelli, Brunelleschi experimented with this concept in the central crossings of his churches where he placed a dome over a central cube. This suggests his familiarity with Nicomachus's assertion that "the cube is harmony."[91] Brunelleschi found classical language useful for illustrating number and proportion in his walls and spaces, and he valued clear glass as the vehicle for allowing its constitutive units to suggest the suprarational plan of God.[92] Michelozzo, his heir, led the way in the transformation of the irregular complicated Gothic fortified home into the three-story Italian palace, which, as an earthly dwelling, was inspired by the geometric representative of the earth, the cube.

All those who sought Pythagorean solutions to achieve a new language of modernity had one thing in common with Brunelleschi: a belief in simplicity as a virtue and in the avoidance of extravagance. The anonymous fifteenth-century art critic known to us as the Anonimo Magliabechiano noted this novel quality in describing Masaccio's work.[93] Alberti raised this concept to the level of theory, adding to it the idea that the circle (which Masaccio had introduced as a basis of composition) is the purest of all forms. In his practice, Alberti demonstrated his disdain for extravagance while showing his admiration for the balancing of opposites, the symbolic use of number, and the correspondence of all parts within an immutable whole. The visionary new ideas of Masaccio, Brunelleschi, Michelozzo, and Alberti were certainly connected with those of their contemporaries Coluccio Salutati, Leonardo Bruni, Toscanelli, Pletho, Bessarion, and Cusanus. In attaching themselves to the Pythagorean investigations of their humanist contemporaries, they became the first to define visual unity and harmony. Nurtured by Alberti, the modernization of art and architecture in Urbino followed similar principles. Meanwhile in Rome, where Philo had been rediscovered by the pope himself, a resurgence of interest in the symbolism of number occurred in the planning of the Sistine Chapel.

Just as Alberti died, leaving all his major works unfinished, Ficino began to describe metaphysical avenues to harmony. Inspired by Cusanus, he and his contemporaries Pico and Gaffurio sought to discover the hidden harmonies in the Pythagorean contemplation of the universe. Ficino argued that for Plato the divine sun is best seen in its own light, which spreads over the universe; its contemplation leads, he held, to the contemplation of God, the architect of the universe. Buildings, he suggested, could be models of the cosmos. He valued the role of number for expressing these ideas. For him the numbers 3 and 4 were extremely important (as they had been for Alberti in theory and practice); together they resulted in 7, the number of the planets and of Apollo, the god of the sun, who guides them with his music. God had put his altar in the sun. Intrinsic to Ficino's thinking was the symbolic significance of the squared number and the cubed number. God's monadic perfection was the sphere and the circle as well as the center.

Pico argued similarly, stressing the importance of concord because it obliterates all discord. The universe was a sphere and God is the circle and the sun, the only pure uncompounded unity. To fifteenth-century architects and artists, these inspirations appear to have been present, however difficult to achieve in practice. In Milan, Leonardo made drawings of just such perfectly centralized structures, while Bramante struggled to give them life. Gaffurio reiterated the ideas of Alberti, Ficino, and Pico. He argued that only through number and concord could true harmony be discovered. Meanwhile, Pacioli expressed the interests of his generation in expounding not only the mystical importance of number, a concept that fascinated his compatriot, colleague, and friend, Piero della Francesca. He also had great praise for the triangle, the basis of Plato's universe, which with its three equal sides formed the beginning, middle, and end of everything, and for its progeny, the four-sided pyramid that could be contained in the sphere. This idea would be basic to the achievement of "perfect" harmony by artists and architects of the High Renaissance.

NINE:

FINDING HARMONY: FORM AND MEANING IN ARCHITECTURE AND ART OF THE SIXTEENTH CENTURY

The early sixteenth century is the chronological home of the High Renaissance, a concept applied to the achievement of "perfect" harmony in the art and architecture of Italy – an accomplishment that spread to other countries that received its completed ideas in more or less fragmentary form. This chapter will attempt to highlight the places where these developments occurred and the artistic personalities who shaped them. We shall see that the modernity of the language these architects and artists proposed was centered on the teachings of contemporary humanists who were exponents of Pythagoreanism, and that this achievement was governed by geometric discipline that incorporated the significance of number. In this sense, these productions can be thought of as an art of ideas. Paradoxically perhaps, the new concepts of the High Renaissance were born well before the opening of the new century, in the visionary ideas of a pair of artists, both from Florence, Leonardo and Michelangelo.

PRELUDE: THE PYTHAGOREAN EXPERIMENTS OF LEONARDO, EARLY MICHELANGELO, AND YOUNG RAPHAEL

Although Leonardo never called himself a Pythagorean, his Pythagorean interests appear to have been formed early on in the Florence of Cusanus and Ficino, and then been reinforced when he went to the Milan of Gaffurio and Pacioli and associated with Bramante of Urbino. Although Cusanus had just died when Leonardo arrived in Florence in the early 1470s, the legacy of this erudite philosophizing mathematician was strong in central Italy. Leonardo demonstrates this in one of his early works that is based on the preeminence of the circle and its

44: Leonardo, *Benois Madonna*, St. Petersburg, State Hermitage Museum, ca. 1478–79. Photo: Courtesy State Hermitage Museum

counterpart, the sphere, the *Benois Madonna* (fig. 44). The spherical arrangement of the figures is instantly perceivable as the figures are engaged in a continuously circular movement, an arrangement that makes them harmoniously alive and, thus, modern in accordance with the principle recently laid down by Nicholas Cusanas concerning the integrity of the circle as perfect truth.

Painted in about 1478, this work marks the earliest presentation of two figures as a single, unified, whole. Their unity is the result of Leonardo's appreciation, for the first time in the history of painting, of the sphere as a unifying device for two figures. As opposed to the traditional side-by-side arrangements of the Madonna and Child of the past and continued in the present by his contemporaries (e.g., Filippo Lippi, Botticelli, Verrocchio, and Ghirlandaio), whose works demonstrated little interest in the application of Pythagorean ideas, Leonardo imposes the discipline of geometry on his composition. The circle, first introduced by Masaccio and now expanded into a three-dimensional sphere, allows the figures not only to be conjoined physically but also to move and turn in a continuous rotation away from the picture plane and back into it. Thus is the group bound together into a single moving unity from which, as in Alberti's architectural theory, nothing can be added and nothing subtracted without destroying the harmony of the entirety. Its organic wholeness, so different from the traditional additive conceptions still in use by Leonardo's fellow painters, allows for a continuous, inseparable, and harmonious relation between the two figures. In this synthetic relation the two are interlocked in an endless spiritual exchange reflecting the unity of their geometry. That the creation of a complete, self-sufficient, geometric unity was Leonardo's intent is confirmed by his numerous studies for this picture.[1]

Soon after he completed this painting, his desire to integrate inspired Leonardo to again study the governance of geometry, this time in the structuring of a larger painting. In the *Adoration of the Magi* of ca. 1481–82, his solution – which can be seen clearly as the painting was left unfinished – was different (fig. 45). Here Leonardo's geometric arrangement is expanded into multiple circles. These are articulated through the figures who form concentric circles around the Madonna. As Sydney Freedberg observes, the varying expressions of doubt, scrutiny, amazement, and devotion of each group correspond to the distance of its circle from the center, the Madonna.[2] As these waves break in upon her, the Madonna remains the calm centerpoint of the picture, the recipient of the increasingly intense emotions that encircle and close in on her.

The circle is not the only geometric form used by Leonardo in this painting. A triangle is introduced in the arrangement of the major figures that dominate the design: the Madonna, Child, and three Magi. First introduced by Masaccio, the triangular shape is used here as the basis of the composition. One triangle organizes the surface while another creates depth. The Madonna forms the all-important apex in the conflation of the surface triangle and its counterpart, the spatial triangle. In interlocking the triangles with the surrounding circles that attach to them from both sides, Leonardo achieves a masterful synthesis not only of two figures but of an entire humanity. The geometrical framework upon which the composition is built is utterly unified. Together these forms control, balance, and energize the entire design, allowing for a third principle, the reconciliation of opposites, to be their natural partner. Progressing in tandem from both sides, these balancing energies are webbed together in a knot at the apex of the triangle. The Madonna's head thereby becomes the dramatic and psychological center of a painting whose unified harmony is geometrically conceived and geometrically controlled.

Such geometric combinations, though never before applied to painting, were well known in the work of Plato, of whom Leonardo was very fond. In

45: Leonardo, *Adoration of the Magi*, Florence, Uffizi, ca. 1481–82. Photo: Alinari (Art Resource)

Plato's *Timaeus*, circles are the governing force of the universe whose spherical shape deprives the cosmos of its propensity to be disorderly and inharmonious, bestowing on it harmonious motion and making order out of disorder. Plato asserts that the sphere is the "best" form.[3] In analyzing the sphere of the cosmos, he deduces that it is made up of "beautiful" triangles that are essential to its geometric order.[4] This fabulous concept was rediscovered by Cusanus, who contemplated the cosmos as an infinite sphere, the corporeal world as round and constantly in motion, the triangle as symbolic of God's plan, and the balancing of opposites as the essential parts of the geometrical processes for achieving union. Ficino also held these concepts aloft, describing the circle as God himself giving life to the universe. Leonardo's preoccupation with these concepts is evident for even after his arrival in Milan in 1483 he continued, in painting the *Madonna of the Rocks*, to ponder – and with more intensive results – the unification of the

46: Leonardo, *Madonna of the Rocks*, Paris, Louvre, 1483–85. Photo: Réunion des Musées Nationaux (Art Resource)

circle, the triangle, and the sphere (fig. 46). Based on the triangle, the design rests on a circular base over which the continuous interchange of the figures above suggests their spherical union and, therefore, the idea of the pyramid. Composed of curves rather than straight lines, Leonardo's pyramid is not rigid and static, but active and dynamic. Though we do not know if he knew the ancient history of the geometrical-numerical concept of the pyramid, based on the tetrad and the *tetraktys*,[5] he surely knew the recent work of Nicholas of Cusa. Cusanus had stressed, as discussed earlier, that the perfection of the number 10 was illustrated by the pyramid; he had also suggested that God's harmony could be discovered in the relation between a triangle, a circle, and a sphere.[6] The concept of the pyramid and its relation to the sphere was a problem that fascinated Leonardo's collaborator and housemate in Milan, Pacioli.

It was while Leonardo was in Milan that he painted the now famous *Last Supper*, a fresco in which his tremendous respect for the ordering principles of number and proportion are clearly evident, as noted by the modern scholar Thomas Brachert, in the musical canon he devised. Not unlike that propounded by Alberti, the figures are deployed according to a spatial grid dependent on the ratios of 12:6:4:3.[7] This suggests that Leonardo was experimenting with Gaffurio's theories of musical harmony at the very time that the Pythagorean music theorist was a colleague of his at the court of Milan. The same numerical proportions, which symbolized the world and the universe, appear on the tablet that Raphael placed directly in front of Pythagoras in the *School of Athens* (fig. 8), painted a few years later in Rome.

Though his approach was less arduously intellectual, the young Michelangelo (Michelangelo Buonarotti, 1475–1564), too, explored Pythagorean ideas in his early work – at a time when he was close, through his association with Lorenzo de'Medici, to Ficino. In the *Madonna of the Steps*, a relief of his youth executed about 1490–92 (fig. 47), Michelangelo takes the Madonna and Child, the one completely immersed in the circular body movements of the other, and shows them resting on a cube – suggesting the cube of the earth. In this work, the future redemption that will be enabled through the miraculous child is hinted at by the otherwise mysterious five steps. While it has been recognized that their number must have been chosen by the artist for symbolic reasons, these have never been deciphered.[8] Plato had noted, in the *Timaeus*, the fifth regular solid (the dodecahedron) as the universe, a meaning endorsed by other ancient Pythagorean writers who pointed out that 5 was preferable to 10 for symbolizing the universe because inasmuch as 2 x 5 = 10, 5 (which is not divisible by any other number) gives life to the universe whereas 10, being based on a duality or equivalence of two times this number is therefore, on its own, general and ambivalent. The number 5, in addition, was known to Pythagoreans as representing light, since as a circular number its square (25) and its cube (125) both terminate in the same number (5).[9] In this context, the enigmatic nature of this subject becomes clear. The sleeping Christ is the light of the universe over the earth. The scene is intensively unified by the fact that Michelangelo gave it a self-enclosing frame of the same material, marble. Number, symbolism, unification – and enigma – were, as we know, favorite themes of Ficino in contemporary Florence.

A few years later, Michelangelo enlarged his search for the harmony inherent in combining two adult figures in the monumental Vatican *Pietà*, executed by him in 1499 (fig. 48). Here he sacrificed one kind of logic (that of the anguished emotion used in northern interpretations of this subject) and replaced it with another (where emotion is expressed through its geometrical containment). Accordingly, the dead Christ is splayed on the lap of the Madonna, forming with his lower limbs and upper torso the sides of a triangle that, given dimension by the voluminous draperies and bowed head of the Madonna, becomes a pyramid. Exactly as Piero della Francesca

47: Michelangelo, *Madonna of the Steps*, Florence, Casa Buonarotti, ca. 1490–92. Photo: Alinari (Art Resource)

and Pacioli had imagined and illustrated, and as Reuchlin would soon note, the base of the pyramid can be inscribed into a circle into which it fits perfectly. The center of the piece, if viewed from above as originally intended (and not as presently displayed), is the object of the Madonna's gaze: the broken lap of Christ.

While it may not seem that a figural sculpture and a small temple could share much in common, what is most significant about the new "modern" art that appeared in Rome at the turn of the century is the inspiration that drove both Michelangelo's *Pietà* and Bramante's Tempietto, which will be discussed in the next section. Both are essentially triangular structures amplified into pyramids and resting on circular bases.

Meanwhile, the young Raphael of Urbino, who had not yet arrived in Florence, demonstrated a different use of Pythagorean ideas in order to reach an

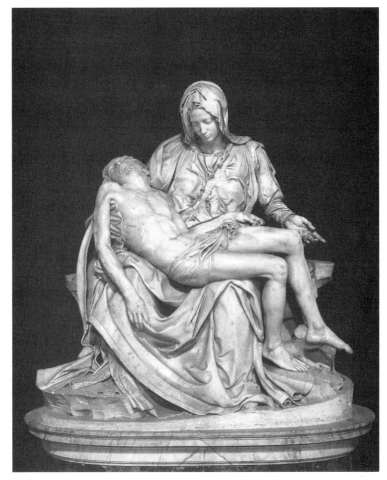

48: Michelangelo, *Pietà*, Vatican, St. Peter's, 1499. Photo: Alinari (Art Resource)

equally compelling, and modern, harmony of order. Not only is the *Three Graces*, which he painted ca. 1501–2, a composition made up of 3s and 6s (3 heads, 3 torsos, 3 balls, 6 legs, 6 arms), both "perfect" numbers in the Pythagorean vocabulary, but its figures are composed into a circle that is set into a perfect square (fig. 49). Its Pythagorean inspiration is underlined by the subject that originally formed its obverse side, the so-called *Dream of a Knight*, which clearly suggests, in its two different landscapes, one rocky and the other smooth, the choice of Hercules – a popular subject in Italy since Petrarch and Coluccio Salutati had explicated it as an example of the Pythagorean "Y," or the choice between good and evil.[10]

In his *Sposalizio*, or *Marriage of the Virgin*, painted in 1504 for a chapel in Perugia, Raphael independently conceived a pyramidal design of his own (fig. 50). Its base is lodged in three interlocked triangles (formed by the group of women

49: Raphael, *Three Graces*, Chantilly, Musée Condé, ca. 1501–2. Photo: Réunion des Musées Nationaux (Art Resource)

culminating in the Virgin, the group of men culminating in Joseph, and the foreground space culminating in the high priest) whose apexes meet in the center. This base is the foundation for a circular temple that rises pyramidally in the distance, crowning the space. Standing in detached purity, that building is articulated by sixteen columns, pilasters, volutes, and bays. Sixteen paths of pavement radiate to all parts of the composition, implying a grand circular setting for a grand circular temple. Thus even before he arrived in Florence Raphael (who was born in Urbino) was experimenting with the idea that idealized unity might be discovered by bolstering a circular design with a substructure of triangles. Though the result is somewhat complicated visually and he did not experiment with this scheme again, Raphael's struggle to achieve harmony is evident. The eight steps leading to the temple suggest, as ancient authorities well known to the Renaissance had

50: Raphael, *Marriage of the Virgin*, Milan, Brera Gallery, 1504. Photo: Ministero per i Beni e le Attività Culturali

stipulated, the essential "personality" of the number 8 as both foundation and embracer of all harmonies.[11] As a numerical cube (2 x 2 x 2 = 8), this number then forms the foundation in the painting for a numerical square (16 columns above, or 4 x 4). Both the steps and the columns of the temple are articulated by circles subsumed into the circularity of the surrounding space.

BRAMANTE AND THE PERFECT CHURCH

The interplication of the square and the circle was pondered by another son of Urbino, Bramante, when he arrived in Rome from Milan and built, in 1502, the previously mentioned Tempietto at San Pietro in Montorio. His project imagined

51: Rome, Tempietto at San Pietro in Montorio (Bramante), 1502. Photo: Bildarchiv Foto Marburg (Art Resource)

a large square structure within which was set an ambulatory zone in the form of a circle defined by sixteen columns and four exedrae (or recesses) connecting the circle to the square. Of his elaborate plan for this perfect "temple" (actually a martyrium or memorial chapel) only the nucleus was completed (fig. 51). Situated in the center of the colonnaded circular space, the small circular temple whose semispherical dome is supported by sixteen columns rests on steps that form four circles. The component numbers make clear their symbolic meaning (4 as the basic number of the Pythagorean *tetraktys* multiplied by itself = 16, the most perfect number and the ideal number of columns recommended by Vitruvius for temples). This perfect little temple illustrates the concept of complete cosmological unity that Ficino had described as based on the four circles of the universe and the four stages of the soul's search for God.[12] Its ideality can be seen further

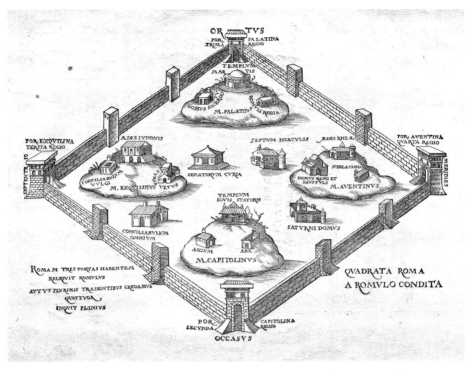

52: Fabio Calvo, view of ancient Rome, ca. 1510. Photo: From Calvo, *Antiqvae vrbis Romae cvm regionibvs simvlachrvm*, ed. Frobenivm and Episcopivm, Basel, 1558

in that it forms a spherical pyramid, in profile suggesting a triangle, set into a circle and placed in the center of a square. The interior axis from the entrance to the opposite point in the structure allows for eight columns to either side, thus fulfilling the "egalitarian" role of this number.

Bramante was not alone in applying Pythagorean solutions to architectural problems in early Cinquecento Rome. Not only did Fabio Calvo – described in Chapter 6 as a medical doctor and noted Pythagorean – make a personal translation of Vitruvius into Italian for his friend Raphael, he also illustrated it. These woodcut illustrations demonstrate his high regard for the governance of the square and the circle, the parameters into which he tried to fit his visions of ancient Rome (figs. 52 and 53). In the case of the square, it was divided into twelve equal parts; in that of the circle, sixteen.

That such basic ideas saturated Bramante's thinking in Rome can be seen in two other major projects that dominated his years in this city. In the first of these, the courtyard of Santa Maria della Pace, he built, despite the physical problems presented by the site, a square courtyard. Each of its four faces contained four bays (4 x 4 = 16) that articulated its space and fixed its height. These were central-ized by a pavement divided into eight (a numerical cube) congruent triangles.

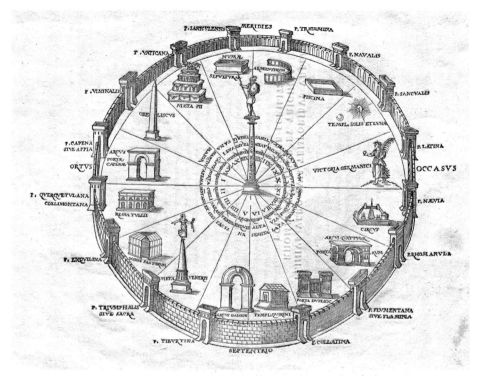

53: Fabio Calvo, view of ancient Rome, ca. 1510. Photo: From Calvo, *Antiqvae vrbis Romae cvm regionibvs simvlachrvm*, ed. Frobenivm and Episcopivm, Basel, 1558

Thus does the square space become a cube numerically and spatially. Bramante's masterpiece, however, was to be the new St. Peter's, which had only been begun at the time of his death in 1514 (fig. 54). Here the circular shape of the interior ambulatory space was adapted to the square shape of the whole, which, punctuated by four towers at the corners, framed a spherical dome that, with forty-eight columns, supported a lantern consisting of sixteen columns. Had it been built, the dome of this perfectly centralized building would have had a total of sixty-four columns.[13] The number 64, it will be remembered, was the great unifying number in Antiquity because it was the first that is both a square and a cube, and because it is a "circular" cube – that is, it ends with the same digit (4) as the number whose cube it is (64).[14] Even as the dome was to be built later by Michelangelo, this numerical essence was retained. Michelangelo's dome and its lantern are adorned with sixteen double engaged columns at each of its two levels, bringing the total to sixty-four columns. This is the case inside and out.[15]

Bramante's reputed ability to understand information that had been buried since Antiquity was surely inspired by the writings of both his predecessors and his contemporaries. Bessarion (whose house still existed in Rome) had left

54: Cristoforo Caradosso, medal commemorating the foundation of St. Peter's by Bramante, British Museum, 1506. Photo: British Museum

a powerful legacy that championed Pythagoras's use of enigma and number to express divine truths. Cusanus had pondered ways to demonstrate the close proportions between the circle and the square inscribed within each other, which he called the "squaring of the circle." Ficino had argued that four circles continuously revolve around a center that is God, himself a circle. Polydore Vergil had stressed that the fixed order that Pythagoras taught exemplified the harmony of heaven on earth, noting that the square was used not only in measuring but also in building. Gaffurio had recently maintained that true harmonic proportion could be found in the same definition of harmony that Alberti had proposed.[16] And Pacioli, still alive and still vastly influential, had demonstrated ways in which triangles, pyramids, squares, and circles could be inscribed within each other while at the same time respecting the symbolism of number. For Pacioli, a good

55: Montepulciano, San Biagio (Antonio da Sangallo the Elder), 1518–29. Photo: Allan Foy

architect was one who could apply Pythagorean ideas. Meanwhile, the "magic book" of Vitruvius had become, since its first printing in 1486, more influential than ever. Bramante's early experiences in Urbino and Milan had provided him with a strong background in the mathematics of structure, space, and proportion that inspired him to further develop new Pythagorean concepts of unity.[17] His reputation as the guiding light of modern architecture was enormously influential, during his life and after his death.

In the heart of Tuscany, at Montepulciano, Antonio da Sangallo the Elder (1455–1534), the brother of the architect who had designed the Carceri church at Prato, built the church of San Biagio (fig. 55 and frontispiece). The "tempio" of San Biagio, as it came to be known, shows the purity obtainable from the unifying powers of geometry and number. The dome of this centralized church is articulated with sixteen pilasters inside and out and raised over a central square that forms a perfect cube, for each side of the square is equal to the height of its piers.[18] The diameter of the dome is equal to the length of each side of the square below. Directly below the dome the pavement is composed of a triple circular motif with four rays leading to each of the supporting piers. Each pier supports a vault articulated by ten rosettes. Viewed as a whole, the vertical proportions are compatible in every way with the horizontal ones of this perfect pyramid that

56: Todi, Santa Maria delle Consolazione, begun 1508. Photo: George Tatge

can, in the magnificent isolation of its built-up geometrical forms, be fitted into an imaginary square – or circle.

Another example of geometric and numerical purity is the church of Santa Maria delle Consolazione at Todi, an ancient town in Umbria, not far from Rome (fig. 56). Its form, conceived in about 1508, invites us to remember Cusanus's idea that the Divine Mind manifests itself as the indivisible perfect unity in the circle, which, as the dome, represents the cosmos. In a dazzling display of geometric purity, the dome rests on a cube, or the sensible world below, unfolding into four apses. Thus are divergences merged into one. On the basis of number, Cusanus had explained, our intelligence can contemplate God's oneness as fourfold and manifested in a centralizing cube: "The number 4, which is an unfolding of oneness, contains the power of every number. For universal oneness is instantiated in the four onenesses that are configured in a fitting order."[19] This consolidation into a harmonious whole speaks a language parallel to that of the Pythagoras's *tetraktys*, he observed. Celebrating the number 16 in the number of its cells and ribs (fig. 57), the dome is illuminated by eight windows that correspond with the eight rays in the stone design of the floor below, thus emphasizing the cube of the whole. Each of the 4 apses consists in 7 divisions, totaling 28, a perfect number and the number of

57: Todi, Santa Maria delle Consolazione, begun 1508, interior view to dome. Photo: George Tatge

planets times the number of elements (7 x 4 = 28), as well as a number invested with hidden universal meaning.[20] The triangular, pyramidal, and spherical aspirations of this most perfect of all Pythagorean churches are thus flawlessly harmonized in interior and exterior, as Cusanus had suggested, allowing for God as unity and light to rule from above.[21] Ironically, its architect is not known to us with certainty;[22] it is known, however, that Todi was the place where Cusanus died.

HARMONIOUS UNITIES IN THE MATURATION OF LEONARDO, MICHELANGELO, RAPHAEL, AND FRA BARTOLOMEO

The motif of the triangle expanded into a pyramid that in turn is inscribed, or inscribable, within a circle, as just described, was the distinctly preferred method of harmonization in the work of those artists who were the creators of the new classic style of High Renaissance art. In eliminating the "facts" of landscape in his cartoon for the *Madonna and Child and St. Anne* (ca. 1500), Leonardo demonstrated that he could discover a more concentrated form of this unity (fig. 58). The elliptical nature of the pyramidal arrangement of figures invites the spectator's eye to enter the composition from the left and to witness the melting

58: Leonardo, *Burlington House Cartoon*, black chalk, London, National Gallery, ca. 1500. Photo: National Gallery of London

together of the figures in a form that is instantly perceived as single though it is modulated by a musical arabesque of internal shapes. Even more condensed in the final painting, the controlling geometry of the design is deprived of rigidity and enlivened by the dynamism of its spiritually mobile inhabitants (fig. 59). Its universality is emphasized by the optical extension of the setting, which, without physical references to distract the eye, suggests a world so unified that it is on the brink of dissolution. Thus both in its form and in the universality of its meaning, the composition becomes utterly modern as opposed to the work of many of Leonardo's contemporaries who were still painting additive compositions filled with laterally organized details.

Leonardo's structure provided a fresh avenue of inquiry for the youthful Raphael, newly arrived in Florence in 1504. While Raphael's *Bella Jardiniere* of

59: Leonardo, *Madonna and Child with St. Anne*, Paris, Louvre, 1501–6. Photo: Réunion des Musées Nationaux (Art Resource)

ca. 1506 posits a similar structure, his Canigiani *Holy Family* of the following year shows his experimental appropriation of this "tetraktian" concept in a different sort of universal setting where an idealized but subdued world is invented in the infinitely receding landscape (fig. 60).[23] This painting suggests that Raphael's extraordinary visual intelligence was constantly seeking new ways to modernize a given subject.

During these years, Michelangelo continued to experiment with the idea he had first presented in the Vatican *Pietà*. In his *Bruges Madonna* the Madonna's bowed head looks down, encompassing the entire composition.[24] Inscribed by her arms, which encircle the Christ child who clambers in her drapery rather than standing independently, the entirety of the triangular composition is expanded into a pyramidal form resting on a circle.

60: Raphael, *Canigiani Holy Family*, Munich, Alta Pinakothek, 1507. Photo: Bayerische Staatsgemäldesammlungen Fotoarchiv

Disdaining the propensities of many of his fellow sculptors to be additive in their figural arrangements, Michelangelo presents, in his *Pitti tondo* of about 1505–8 (fig. 61), a Madonna and Child resting on a cube that suggests more than the earth to be redeemed. Protruding from the format of the whole, the cube unifies the viewer's space with that of the relief. Seated sideways, the body of the Madonna deepens the space, transforming the dominant triangle into which the entire surface composition is compressed into a broad pyramid that extends well back from the surface. This pyramid is imagined within a circular setting that is echoed by the circle of the frame, suggesting that the entire composition has spherical properties. This sphericity is emphasized by the fact that the head of the Madonna protrudes from the confines of the circle; looking outward, it articulates the compact unity of form that is at once intensely foreshortened

61: Michelangelo, *Pitti tondo*, Florence, Bargello, ca. 1505–8. Photo: Alinari (Art Resource)

and deeply excavated. The Madonna's spiritual mobility thus transforms, in this work of Michelangelo's early Florentine years, a static geometry into a dynamic one comparable to the achievement of Raphael in an approximately contemporary painting, the *Alba Madonna*, executed shortly after his arrival in Rome from Florence.[25] Whereas the original frame of Raphael's *Alba Madonna* (which doubtless was circular) is lost, that Michelangelo considered his self-contained sculpture complete is evident by the fact that he fashioned his own frame for the *Pitti tondo*. A protruding lip defines the perimeter of the sculpture (indicating that it was not to be framed or set into something else). The idea that a work of sculpture might be self-framed suggests a new level of harmony: Nothing can be added or subtracted – not even a frame – without destroying the unity of the whole. This too is a tribute to its modernity.

62: Michelangelo, Sistine Ceiling, Vatican, Sistine Chapel, 1508–12. Photo: Musei Vaticani Archivio Fotografico

The iconographical organization of the Sistine Ceiling (1508–12) shows that Michelangelo relied in great part on Ovid's *Metamorphoses*, well known in his time as the "pagan" bible, for its general subject matter (fig. 62). Ovid's account of the Creation moves from the creation of the world out of chaos by a God who acts single-mindedly to God's punishment of the sins of humankind through a fabulous flood. Early on in his account, Ovid explains the primordial chaos of Nature, a rounded body of rolling elements unified into one, not unlike Michelangelo's conception of the first *Creation* scene. God separated land and water, and light from dark. Yet the earth was not complete, Ovid asserts, until man was molded out of clay mixed with the living fluid of God so that he, man created in the likeness of God and therefore different from the beasts of the earth, was godlike himself. Ovid's great hexameter poem portrays the race of humans who lived in these early days, which was an Age of Gold. In this time, peace and abundance reigned. The earth was innocent, and men subsisted on acorns from the regal oak tree. Because the shade of the oak made for an eternal spring with no harsh seasons and no need of shelter or covering, this race of humans was eternally youthful and had no need of clothing. Thus are explained the twenty magnificent youths who are deployed throughout the ceiling. Hardly innocent children or figures devoid of symbolic meaning as has been suggested, these magnificently imagined *ignudi* carry oak leaves and acorns (coincidentally the symbol of the papal commissioner of the ceiling, Julius II). Humankind's happy days before corruption are recalled toward the end of the *Metamorphoses* when Ovid makes a powerful argument for Pythagoreanism in having Pythagoras himself appear to recommend, in a long speech, that the foods of the earth's plants and trees be eaten as they had before humans had learned to defile their lips with the blood of animals.[26] While Michelangelo's sensitivity to Pythagorean ideas was no doubt stimulated by Ovid's strongly sympathetic description of Pythagoras, he surely also knew Ficino's recent recommendation, described in Chapter 5, that human beings should follow the example of ancient Pythagorean vegetarians, who, like their predecessors in the Golden Age before the Great Flood, did not eat animals.

Although the historian Edgar Wind has found other recondite references to Pythagoreanism (or "Neoplatonism") in the Sistine Ceiling,[27] some less abstruse examples might be found in the following: The rather odd numbers in the schema of the ceiling suggest that Michelangelo's decision to divide his surface into nine scenes rather than the eight to which the building's structure would have more easily lent itself implies his admiration for the divine number that suggests the Trinity for it contains the triple triad. That Philo, the famous Pythagorean of late Antiquity who had written extensively on Pythagorean number symbolism and was important for the planning of the Sistine Chapel, might also have served as a source for Michelangelo's ceiling is suggested by the true subject of the third historical scene. This scene quite clearly represents the *Sacrifice of Abel* rather than the *Sacrifice of Noah* (a seldom depicted subject that in any case would be out of historical order), as it is commonly, and mistakenly, called. Philo's important excursus on the sacrifice of Abel, in which a ram was offered rather than fowl, was widely known in the Renaissance.[28] It appears to be significant that the number of prophets and sibyls represented on the sloping sides of the ceiling deviates from their customary grouping in even pairs. Here are composed 7 prophets and 5 sibyls – numbers full of significance for Philo. Also significant was their total, 12. In discussing Plato's view that the globe was made of twelve parts, Ficino – a person well known to the young Michelangelo – had recently pointed out the cosmic significance of this number. Too, Ficino had suggested that the prophets observed the sacredness of this number in their writings.[29] A subject that remains to be studied is whether the arrangement of these figures suggests, in their iconography, a mutual balancing of opposites. Though, like Leonardo's, Michelangelo's Pythagoreanism has not been given sufficient attention in our time, it should be noted that in the later sixteenth century it was understood that the harmonies of Leonardo and Michelangelo were inspired by Pythagorean principles.[30]

One work of Michelangelo that has often been described by modern writers as "Platonic" and sometimes as "Pythagorean" is his *Last Judgment*.[31] Painted for the altar wall of the Sistine Chapel in the 1530s, this celebrated fresco is a powerful departure from earlier conceptions of this subject that were more theological in that the celestial, terrestrial, and infernal worlds were distinguished in compositions that were laterally organized. The great Michelangelo scholar Charles De Tolnay saw this design as fundamentally circular and dependent on what he termed a pagan astral theme in which Christ functioned as Apollo, taking his place at the center of an exalted cosmic universe far beyond the tangible world.[32] In this universe, the souls formed concentric circles around this dominating force, which De Tolnay saw as related to ancient Pythagorean ideas of the astral aspect of departed souls. Brilliantly, he connected Michelangelo's conceptual ideas for this great cosmic drama not only with Ficino, its probable inspirator, but also with the heliocentric ideas of Copernicus that would be published only three years after the completion of Michelangelo's masterpiece. This interpretation has recently been studied and essentially reaffirmed by Valerie Shrimplin, who proposes that Plato and Ficino were outstanding among those who were major characters in Renaissance attempts to explain the universe, providing a field of influence available not only to Michelangelo but also to the scientific-minded Copernicus and his predecessors.[33]

Perhaps the most intensely Pythagorean of all Renaissance works of art is the Stanza della Segnatura, painted by Raphael as the setting for the private library of Pope Julius II.[34] Through Raphael's ingenuity and genius, the irregular shape of the chamber was transformed into a cube whose six surfaces – ceiling, four walls, and pavement – declare a perfect geometrical unity. This unity is also iconographical not only in that 6 is the first truly perfect number but also in that each surface forms, together with its counterpart, a reconciliation of opposites that characterizes the entire space as it is brought to a stunning unity under the guidance of Apollo, who, as the sun, forms a centralized fictive oculus in the ceiling (fig. 63).[35] The ultimate monad, the oculus, was associated in ancient Rome, as contemporary humanists were well aware, with Apollo ("A-pollo" = without multiplicity, or, unity personified).[36] Surrounded by sixteen painted scenes (in four sets of four) studding the ceiling like planets, the oculus lends to the ceiling the semblance of a vault, or dome, resting (with its corner pendentives) on a cube – or, in Pythagorean-Platonic terms, of heaven resting on earth. The sixteen compartments that supervise the space from above thus evoke the aura of a temple. The "perfection" of the number 16 was certainly well known in Urbino (where Raphael grew up), as would soon be made clear by the famous Pythagorean mathematician of that city, Baldi, in his writings. The significance of the tetrad is reflected in the pavement below, which is devoted to the ancestry of Christianity. With its Kabbalistic designs arranged as a tetrad, the pavement suggests the contemporary revival among humanists in Rome of ancient ideas that

63: Raphael, Ceiling, Vatican, Stanza della Segnatura, 1508–9. Photo: Musei Vaticani Archivio Fotografico

claimed Pythagoras had been a student of Moses. They knew that this connection had inspired Pythagoras's monotheism and his admiration of the number 4, which, sacred to Hebrews as the number of letters in the Hebrew name of God, was imagined by Reuchlin and others at the time as the model for the Pythagorean *tetraktys*.[37]

The themes of the Stanza ceiling, as stated in its accompanying inscriptions, refer to Philosophy, Theology, Poetry and Music, and the Law, the four disciplines of human knowledge celebrated in this chamber. A central theme is the "knowledge of divine things," inscribed on the scroll held aloft by the figure of Theology. It will be remembered that this was a principal theme of both Ficino and Pico. Indirectly, the ceiling refers to the ancient Pythagorean writers who had first

64: Raphael, *School of Athens*, Vatican, Stanza della Segnatura, 1510. Photo: Musei Vaticani Archivio Fotografico

identified and discussed the quadrivium. The number of its disciplines (4) formed the basis of the *tetraktys* that is represented as an attribute of Pythagoras in the *School of Athens* (fig. 64).[38] In this fresco, whose true subject is the reconciliation of the philosophies of Plato and Aristotle, Pythagoras contemplates not only the *tetraktys* but also the musical concords that express, numerically, perfect idealized harmony, as the ancient Pythagorean Martianus Capella had described and as the modern Pythagoreans Alberti and Gaffurio had so clearly explained.[39]

Lost in his contemplation of these mystical numerical concepts, Pythagoras is unaware of the argument being presented by a man with short black hair and a black beard who stands in front of him, insistently pointing to his factual information – surely Anaximander, whose articulate naturalism provided a contrasting balance to the mysticism of Pythagoras, as Diogenes Laertius had noted in Antiquity and as Polydore Vergil, a Renaissance humanist from Urbino, had repeated. Both Pythagoras and Anaximander are on the side of Plato in the great balancing division of this painting, for Plato benefited from the ideas of both. Near Anaximander, whom he followed, but in isolation, for he was a "loner," is Heraclitus of Ephesus who rests his body on an enormous cube that surely suggests, in Pythagorean terms, the earth whose place in the cosmic order he struggled to understand. For Pythagoreans the cube signified not only the earth

65: Raphael, *Disputà*, Vatican, Stanza della Segnatura, 1509–10. Photo: Musei Vaticani Archivio Fotografico

(as Plato had suggested in the *Timaeus*) but also procreation, through the numerical cube (as Alberti had discussed).[40] Opposite Pythagoras on the other side of the painting, devoted to ideas associated with Aristotle, is Pythagoras's counterpart, Euclid, shown demonstrating a geometrical proof. Such a contrast derives quite clearly from the work of Martianus Capella, where Euclid was in charge of geometry and Pythagoras was in charge of arithmetic.[41] Together the two make up the unity (and harmony) of mathematics.

On the opposite wall, Raphael's tribute to theology, the *Disputa* (fig. 65), is represented as a church without walls whose altar points directly east, to the land of the rising sun declared by Vitruvius as the preferred direction for "temples" to face. The altar in the sun, seen here, had been imagined by both Ficino and Pico. The great trinitarian division of this fresco reflects the writings of both, who spoke extensively of the three worlds of the universe. We are invited into this scene by a blond young man to the left who strongly resembles Pico himself.[42] While the trinitarian theme is repeated in the painting devoted to *Jurisprudence* on the south wall, which represents civic law and canon law supervised by divine law, the painting of the *Parnassus* has a different Pythagorean theme (fig. 66).

Here Apollo forms the apex of a triangle. Inspired by ancient literature this surely refers to the meaning of Apollo's name as a single indivisible point. Also, as

66: Raphael, *Parnassus*, Vatican, Stanza della Segnatura, 1511. Photo: Musei Vaticani Archivio Fotografico

Ficino had recently suggested, as the most divine practitioner of poetry Apollo presides over the triangle (derived from his tripod). The triangle is completed by Sappho and Pindar, two poets of Antiquity who, in contrasting languages, devoted themselves to him and played his instrument, the lyre.[43] That these two ancient poets were early Pythagoreans was surely known to Tommaso Inghirami, the humanist who collaborated with Raphael in this chamber: Ficino had already linked Pindar with Pythagoras, and Lomazzo would soon link Sappho with Pythagoras.[44] This scene shows Apollo on Parnassus, as Martianus Capella had described him, rather than on Helicon.[45] Surrounded by the nine Muses, he plays his lyre with a bow, as had been described in remote Antiquity in the *Homeric Hymn to Delian Apollo* and as Pindar himself had described. The scene is a tribute to the civilizing attributes of Apollo, the god of Pythagoras, who brought the gifts of music and the arts to humankind.[46] Not only does Apollo's lyre have seven strings (referring to the day of his birth and to his divinity, as well as to the music of the spheres that he conducts); the laurel grove in which he has gathered his entourage consists of seven trees. In the Renaissance it was commonly known that Plato had the good fortune to be born on the seventh and to die on the seventh of the same month.[47] Surely not accidentally, this fresco abuts Plato's side of the *School of Athens*. Nor does it appear, in this light, to have been accidental that Raphael, whose closest friend and architectural adviser was the Pythagorean Fabio Calvo, chose as his burial place the most Pythagorean building of ancient Rome, the Pantheon.[48]

Though he was less inventive than his great contemporaries Leonardo, Michelangelo, and Raphael, the Florentine painter Fra Bartolomeo della Porta (1475–1517) experimented, particularly between 1509 and 1512, with Pythagorean ideas similar to those that had been put forward in their works. His 1509 painting *God the Father with Saints Mary Magdalene and Catherine of Siena* shows his struggle to obtain perfect harmony through the use of a triangular design with circular implications.[49] Two years later, in the *Marriage of St. Catherine*, the Fra was able to demonstrate a more suave and ambitious unity, now between the pyramid and the sphere – which appear to rotate together in space, interlocking the smooth grace of the earthly figures with that of the floating drapery-bearing angels above (fig. 67). Such paintings by Fra Bartolomeo, with their harmonious shapes, geometrical perfection, pure colors, and untroubled atmospheres were, however, followed by a tendency in his later works to disrupt this serene sense of harmony by the use of sharp, stabbing, lights and darks. This suggests that though he was imitating for a while the Pythagorean avenue to modernity, his intellectual depth was more modest than – or at least nor as consistent as – that of the great innovators.

VENICE AND THE DIVINITY OF PROPORTION

Not only were Pythagorean concepts of order such as those just discussed well known in central Italy and Lombardy, they were also important in the Veneto, where, as we have seen, Pythagorean theorists were active. In Venice the masterpiece of the famous Pythagorean scholar Giorgio Valla, published in 1501, had, it will be remembered, attracted the attention of artists, scientists, and scholars, including Leonardo and Copernicus. His work was followed, shortly after, by Francesco Zorzi's *De harmonia mundi* – a work extolling the divinity of number. Zorzi's advice is known to have been sought by contemporary architects. His influence is especially apparent in the church of San Francesco della Vigna, which, as Wittkower has shown, is based on the Pythagorean numbers 3, 9, and 27 that in combination demonstrate the divinity of God's cosmos.[50] Thus it would appear that Pythagorean ideas were well embedded in Venice and were known to artists in the early 1500s. In nearby Verona the Palazzo del Consiglio, a building whose proportions stand out from the heterogeneous designs of its neighbors, demonstrates the relationship between 8, the first cube, and its component sections of 4. Its inspiration has been attributed to Fra Giovanni Giocondo (1433–1515), an

67: Fra Bartolomeo, *Marriage of St. Catherine*, Paris, Louvre, 1511. Photo: Réunion des Musées Nationaux (Art Resource)

architect and the scholar responsible for the most magnificent edition of Vitruvius published during the Renaissance.[51]

These interests are clearly, and elegantly, reflected in a painting now known as the *Fête Champêtre*, planned by Giorgione (1477–1510) and completed by the young Titian in about 1510 (fig. 68). Here we can visualize the writings of Giorgio Valla, which centered on music and the cosmos. In his writings Giorgio had stressed that in nature all things are harmoniously related. The triangular composition of the three protagonists of this painting illustrates such a modern view of harmony. Visual evidence strongly suggests that the central character was originally meant to be Apollo. Ancient references to competitions between Apollo, who played the lyre, the stringed instrument that symbolized the purity of heavenly bliss and the order of the universe, and Marsyas, who played the flute,

68: Giorgione and Titian, *Fête Champêtre* (*Memorial to Giorgione*), Paris, Louvre, 1510. Photo: Réunion des Musées Nationaux (Art Resource)

which connoted the more carnal pleasures of the earth, were well known in the Renaissance. The person holding the instrument of heaven is a young man who wears a red hat and whose satin and velvet garments are richly colored with shining ivory and glowing cranberry and rose – the only bright colors in the entire painting. Indeed, the brilliance of his presence makes it clear that he is central to the painting. His incontestable importance is underlined by his placement, carefully calculated to be the focus of the painting. Equidistant from both sides as he is from top and bottom, Apollo, the greatest practitioner of poetry and music, can be imagined in his ancient role, forming the apex of the equilateral triangle that invites the viewer into the picture.[52] Though when the painting was taken over by Titian this figure was changed to become a portrait of Giorgione, who had just died, Titian reminds us that like Apollo (and like Pythagoras), Giorgione played the lyre.[53] Probably this picture was a memorial tribute to Giorgione.

The influence of Giorgio Valla on Giorgione can perhaps also be seen in the so-called *Three Philosophers*, a painting whose true subject is not yet clearly understood.[54] Here both the seated protagonist and the standing one to the far right each hold a pair of dividers (used for measuring distances). The latter displays a folio in which the sun is surrounded by an inscribed annulus containing the numbers 1 through 7 (surely referring to Apollo, as the sun god who leads the music of the seven planets). This appears to confirm the importance of numerical symbolism for the activities of this group, perhaps reflected by the actual sun seen rising in the distance, and suggests that they are measuring time astronomically, perhaps in relation to the geo-heliocentric theory that had been put forward a few years earlier in Venice by Giorgio Valla. Such speculations suggest strongly that the work of this recently deceased Venetian intellectual (for whom the number 7 was of great significance) was important for this painting and may, with further study, provide a precise explanation of the subject of this painting, perhaps the imagined calculations made by the three Magi.[55]

Although the great Venetian sixteenth-century architect Andrea Palladio (1508–1580) never declared himself a Pythagorean, his treatise on architecture expresses great admiration for Vitruvius and Alberti, indicating that he was deeply influenced by their concepts of harmony as based on the perfect union of geometry, number, and proportion. Though only four books had appeared by the time of his death in 1580, speculation suggests that his treatise, like theirs, was to have been divided into ten books.[56] While he considers the circle a perfect form for a "temple," he was constrained, in actual practice, to build longitudinal (or Latin cross-plan) churches. These show clearly lit interior spaces, proportionally divided into threes and fours. His masterpiece of domestic architecture, the Villa Rotonda at Vicenza, built in the 1560s, is a perfect example of the merging of the square and the circle in a centralized cube with four perfectly symmetrical façades defining each of the cardinal directions (fig. 69). It is an eloquent example of Cusanus's attempts to merge the two under the guise of the "squaring of the circle."[57] As in the "perfect churches," the dome rests on a cube. The building fits, from each of its four sides, into the format of a triangle while the whole forms a perfect pyramid. The ideal symmetry on which Palladio's country houses rely, and which they extend into nature from their epicenters, constitutes a study in relationships not dissimilar to those Kepler was inspired to undertake in the next decade when he sought to discover the harmonic ratios in the universe.

THE THEOLOGY OF ARITHMETIC IN SPAIN

While it appears that, despite the successes of the Italian architect Sebastiano Serlio in France,[58] Northern tastes and conditions were not as conducive to the imitation of building designs that had come to be admired in Italy, it is clear that the Spaniards strove to emulate if not surpass the new visual programs of their neighbor to the east. In this sense they had been prepared early on by followers of Sepulzio da Veroli (editor of the first printed edition of Vitruvius), who were esteemed in early sixteenth-century Salamanca. Vitruvius was well known

69:Vicenza,Villa Rotonda (Andrea Palladio), completed 1569. Photo: Bildarchiv Foto Marburg (Art Resource)

to Spanish architects through several editions as was also the work of Alberti.[59] While concepts of symmetry and order began to provide an "italianizing" accent to Spanish architecture as the century developed, it was in Granada that an astounding confrontation occurred.

Here, despite Emperor Charles V's indifference to (or even distrust of) "Italian" ideas, Pedro Machuca (ca. 1490–1550), the architect who Charles put in charge of building his grand palace on the Alhambra in 1528, was differently disposed.[60] Machuca's education had included long stays in early sixteenth-century Florence and Rome where, doubtless, he had come into contact with Pythagorean ideas of modernization. His design for Charles's noble residence centered on a circular courtyard incorporated within a square plan (echoing Vitruvius and Bramante) whose four sides were axially oriented to the cardinal points.

This courtyard, the hub of the entire structure, was designed with a double colonnade containing thirty-two free-standing columns (fig. 70). When doubled in height (as the square of the ground plan aspires to become a geometrical cube in space) the thirty-two columns become sixty-four (as discussed earlier, a universal symbol of the significance of the number 4, as well as of a square, a cube, and a circular cube). Machuca had, doubtless, admired this number in the circular interior of the Pantheon at Rome, which, in the sixteenth century still possessed its original complement of sixty-four pilasters.[61] His plan also invites us to think

70: Granada, Palace of Charles V, courtyard (Pedro Machuca), 1527–68. Photo: Bildarchiv Foto Marburg (Art Resource)

of Bramante's intention, precisely at the time of Machuca's stay in Rome, of setting the circular dome of St. Peter's within a square and articulating it with a double range totaling sixty-four columns.

In 1567, when Juan de Herrera (ca. 1530–1590) was put in charge of the already partially built Escorial (a complex of church, monastery, college, and palace) near Madrid, Pythagoreanism may not have been foremost in the list of tremendous responsibilities he inherited. However, it is clear that, not only in terms of its geometry, number, and proportion but also in those of its austerity of style, the finished product of Herrera betrays his own admiration of Pythagorean values – an interest corroborated by the contents of his personal library. His library (as that of his patron, King Philip II) was filled with Pythagorean and Platonic works. Surviving records testify to his active pursuit of works on harmonic proportions; his admiration for Vitruvius, Boethius, and Alberti; his eagerness to obtain Italian editions of various works; and the enthusiasm of his interests in the cube, the "secrets" of arithmetic, and the "philosophy" of Moses.[62]

Though the plan of El Escorial's complex had established its basic geometry as a large square (including the handle section of the grid) prior to Herrera's tenure, his view of the importance of geometric order was emphasized by the

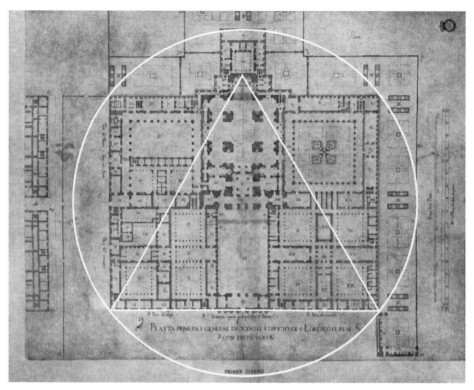

71: Madrid: El Escorial, plan (Juan de Toledo and Juan de Herrera), 1562–82. Photo: After René Taylor, "Architecture and Magic: Considerations on the Idea of the Escorial," in *Essays in the History of Architecture Presented to Rudolf Wittkower*, ed. Douglas Fraser, Howard Hibberd, and Milton J. Lewine, London (Phaidon), 1967, Pl. XI, fig. 25

clean lines and surfaces he gave to the entire yellow-gray granite construction. Its grand entrance, with its sixteen vertical elements, provides a temple-like epicenter in the extremely long façade. A composition of 3s and 4s, the entrance opens to four arcaded courts of the monastery on the right, balanced by the four of the college on the left. Beyond and directly on the central axis is the church – rectangular in original plan but transformed so as to form a perfectly centralized Greek cross plan. The apex of an equilateral triangle that can be inscribed in the circle that circumscribes the entire square of the structure, corresponds with, as the scholar René Taylor points out, the most hallowed part of the church (fig. 71). That this is not accidental is underlined by the representation of the Trinity in the fresco directly above. In this fresco, a large cube serves as the pedestal for Christ and God the father (fig. 72).[63] Resting on the spatial cube below, the dome is articulated by eight pairs of pilasters surmounted by ribs, totaling 16. Thus is it connected with the grand entrance to the complex over which it appears – on approach – to preside.

72: Luca Cambiaso, *Trinity*, detail of *Gloria*, El Escorial, church, 1580s. Photo: Madrid, Archivio Fotografico, Patrimonio Nacional

The Escorial provides a vivid illustration of the reconciliation of Christian civic ideals with Pythagorean lore. Enshrined in their geometrical forms the enigmatic numerical codes suggest sublime truths that would have been apparent to the initiated. Versed in the meaning of number, they could see cosmological implications in its planning and imagine its resemblance to the great Temple of King Solomon in Jerusalem. No wonder, then, that Herrera's assistant, Juan Battista Villalpando (1552–1608) designed, for King Philip, a reconstruction of Solomon's Temple. And little wonder that, like the Escorial, the temple took the form of a gigantic square. The forty-nine bays of each of its façades are, in themselves, numerical squares based on the divine number 7 ($7 \times 7 = 49$) that Philo had extolled as the most revered number of Pythagoreans. In forming a square, the four multiples of 49 suggest a numerical square (196, the square of 14, or $4 \times 49 = 196 = 14 \times 14$), as well as a geometrical square. Within the square of the whole the imaginary temple was divided into a triple triad composed of nine squares in three ranges of three. Villalpando's interest in the geometry of number is abundantly visible in his practical work, for example, in his plan for a church in

Málaga to which were attached two courtyards whose different dimensions and shapes each accommodated exactly the same number of columns (5) and bays (4) in every direction.[64]

Though scholars have suggested that Herrera's preference for simplification of form and reduction of ornament separated him from contemporary Italian currents of classicism, it is this very preference that links him with Pythagorean traditions. Pythagoras and his followers had always been associated with simplicity. Pythagoreans in the Renaissance (Bessarion, Ficino, and Pico, among others) abstained from luxury and lived their lives with only the barest of necessities, while Alberti advocated simplicity in architecture. Also noteworthy in this connection, the decoration of the library of El Escorial, which was organized into 2 parts, each divided into 3 sections, totaling 6 (the number of faces of a cube), was commissioned to the Italian artist Pellegrino Tibaldi, a Pythagorean.[65] This artist was thus the perfect choice for adorning the Escorial Library with frescoes that included a portrait of Pythagoras himself (figs. 9 and 10).

The parallelism between the spread of Pythagorean ideas in the late fifteenth and early sixteenth centuries and the development of a new "modernism" in the art and architecture of the sixteenth century is striking, especially in Italy. There the intellectual soil that had been fertilized earlier by Pletho and Bessarion, Greeks; Cusanus, a German; and Ficino and Pico, both Italians – all working in Italy – would flower in works such as those of Gaffurio and Francesco Zorzi that attempted to further define the harmony of the world and of the cosmos. This complex of fundamental ideas developed into an ethos for harmony and order that became the priority of avant-garde artists. Starting with Leonardo da Vinci, who clearly admired his predecessor Alberti, and continuing in the work of Bramante, Michelangelo, Raphael, and Giorgione, the aims of painters, architects, and sculptors came to be fused as the search for new ways to produce the ultimately harmonious work proceeded. Geometry, numbers, and proportion were used in combination by these artists to create a new modern style that was imitated by some (e.g., Fra Bartolomeo) and was ignored by others (e.g., Botticelli, Filippino Lippi, and Pinturicchio) content to please their patrons with enriched compositions based on designs that vaunted their virtuosity. This new style we now call High Renaissance, a style first defined by Heinrich Wölfflin.[66]

This new modern style paid particular attention not only to Plato and his major work, the *Timaeus*, which explained the ultimate beauty of Pythagorean cosmic order, but also to Vitruvius, who had pointed out practical ways to transfer these ideas into works of art. While Alberti, inspired by Vitruvius, was unable to build the buildings he dreamed of in his own time, the sixteenth century saw them realized as centralized geometric blocks based on a cube, which, surrounded by a pyramid, led to a unifying dome above. The same structural ideas were applied to painting and sculpture. Pythagorean ideas were to have an important development in Spain where architects such as Herrera and Villalpando attempted to interest their patrons in the modernity of simplicity based on pure geometric form. This was accompanied by an interest in Pythagorean painting, as can be seen in the work of an imported Italian Pythagorean artist at El Escorial.

A significant footnote to the order and magnitude of the High Renaissance achievement must, however, be added. The fascination for the magic of number and for magic itself, which had always been associated with Pythagoras, had never died. It constituted a parallel development that can be seen in the double influence of Ficino – at once philosopher of geometric symbolism and transcendental medical guide – on the sixteenth century. The rapid spread of his ideas, as well as those of Pico and Zorzi, can be seen in the frequency with which their works were reprinted in various languages throughout Europe.[67]

Surely the "explorations" of writers like Postel, Agrippa, Paracelsus, Bruno, and Della Porta, who were as fascinated with the pseudoscientific as with the scientific, were behind the program of the Studiolo of the melancholic and introverted Grand Duke Francesco I in the Palazzo Vecchio at Florence, executed in the 1570s by a number of painters under the direction of Giorgio Vasari. This program of paintings has recently been masterfully explicated by Joscelyn Godwin, who shows that the overall theme of this interior grottolike space is the magic of nature, demonstrated in the celebration of the numbers 4 and 8 whose symbolism unites the ancient past with the scientific present through alchemy and other practical experiments.[68] Exotic as it may seem to us, such a program constituted the other side of the Pythagorean coin for it too sought to define the cosmos and to discover universal knowledge in the pseudoscience of divinity.

TEN:

CONCLUSIONS: THE PRINCE OF PHILOSOPHERS AND THE BIRTH OF HARMONY AS AN AESTHETIC NOTION

Although Pythagoras may have been thought of as the "prince of philosophers" at the beginning of the Renaissance, he was not actually called that until the sixteenth century, first by Reuchlin, then by Baldi. Many (despite those who remained suspicious of esoteric knowledge as a dark art) in the Early Renaissance regarded him as an ancestral sage who, as a practitioner of the theology of arithmetic, understood number as it applied to the serious study of the cosmos. Perhaps his greatest relevance lay in his having been the teacher of Plato, whose *Timaeus* had long been regarded as his most Pythagorean work. As Greek influence penetrated Italy, Plato became increasingly important, to the point that both he and Pythagoras were considered to be predecessors of Christianity, prophets, and honorary Christians. As texts by Plato were rediscovered, disseminated, and interpreted, Plato was established as a great luminary of Antiquity. In the background, Pythagoras loomed in the public memory.

Renaissance enthusiasm for Pythagoras provided a compelling motivation for his devotees to study the various forms of intellectual and spiritual thought with which he was associated. Statesmen, philosophers, arithmeticians, geometricians, and theologians strove toward their common goal of explaining the harmony of the universe in a compelling way through rational interchange. Others, more eccentric, demonstrated their search for the same wisdom through avenues of secrecy and enigma. All found in his legacy the tools of order and morality.

Among intellectuals, the enlivening inspiration of Pythagoreanism spread primarily from Italy, where interest in ancient works was at first most intense, to the rest of Europe. Humanists were inspired to study the quadrivium – arithmetic, geometry, music, and astronomy – as a single, unified, agglomeration of ancient

Pythagorean-Platonic wisdom; for them it was an elixir that exuded evidence of the sacrosanct nature of the number 4, whose components, when added together, produced 10, the number that signified the universe. This lofty intellectual stimulus inspired them to interpret and explain the world about them in terms of number, especially the numbers of the decad, all of which formed aspects of one universal truth. Thus did they apply their fervor to finding meaning in all its component numbers. Most significantly, the triad vested the roots of Christianity with trinitarian concepts of ancient authority.[1] As humanists reading the works of ancient Pythagorean mathematicians came to understand that divine emanations could be attributed to the cubes and squares of these numbers, the triadic multiplication of the triad must have seemed compelling. Interest in numerical cubes and squares was accompanied by an interest in their geometrical counterparts. Thus did the mediation of mathematics serve as an important tool for understanding the cosmos. It showed the path to God, the master artisan and creator of harmony in the universe.

One could argue that, because everything has to have some number, the presence of a certain number of bays in a building does not make it Pythagorean. This is of course true, for in isolation such numbers would have no meaning. However, in the Renaissance it was in coordination with concepts of geometry and proportion that number served as an enabler in the pursuit of clearly measured unity and harmony. Certain numbers, such as 2, which signified opposition, and 11, 13, 14, 15, and 17, which have no meaning in Pythagorean thought, are not found in the works of those architects and artists who appear to have been intellectually connected to the struggles of their literary counterparts and predecessors to comprehend God's work in creating the cosmos. Though architects could have designed domes with fourteen slices, or temples with fourteen columns, they did not. Instead, the symbolic patterns they chose, where proportion was dependent on geometry and number, aimed to create a unity so perfect that it would reflect the cosmic order that had been defined in such ancient examples as the *Timaeus*.

For some, Pythagorean studies were vested with secret meanings, enigma, and hidden analogies that led to investigations in the occult sciences. This was true especially in the North, where, in differing ways, the Pythagorean ancestry of Antiquity was exploited in discussions that turned mainly on number mysticism (as in the case of the esoteric numerical significances of Postel), a resurgence of interest in the Kabbalah (as in the case of the "Jewish Pythagoreanism" of Reuchlin), and dark magic (as in the case of the numerical incantations of Agrippa and the magical explorations of Paracelsus). Yet in their collective esoteric wisdom they shared with humanists a devotion to the circle as the perfect figure. They regarded its cohorts the cube, the pyramid, and the sphere as having powers equal to those of numbers.

For many more, the authority of Pythagoras was unmysterious. They considered the *Golden Verses*, *Symbola*, and other rules of life believed to have been authored by Pythagoras himself to be guides to conduct – something like the Ten Commandments. Though Pythagorean moral codes differed in their details according to their individual interpreters, the latter held in common their inspiration from ancient sources. In general, the codes advocated ethical conduct, altruism, frugality, temperance, and abstinence of different forms – especially from meat. This lifestyle, it was believed, accorded with the example of Pythagoras and his most famous ancient followers, Plato, Plotinus, and Porphyry. It was useful in reducing the desires of the body that distracted the soul from its goal to achieve purity, and it was exemplified in the Renaissance particularly by Ficino, Leonardo, Fabio Calvo, and Giorgio Valla.

Taken together, these interplicated tentacles of Pythagoreanism led to a search for hidden concordances that inevitably led to unity and to the contemplation of the most perfect unity of all, God. Basic to this search were the Pythagorean values of order that gave meaning to the universe. Pythagorean thought was known throughout Europe during the Renaissance. It was synonymous with the search for harmony. Though those in the North were more prone to be interested in the Kabbalah, the occult sciences, and the language of magic and mystery, rational voices, such as that of Erasmus, were also heard there. Conversely, in Italy, where philosophical discussions based on mathematics preponderated, strong interest in the occult also existed, as exemplified by Egidio da Viterbo and Giovanni Della Porta. By the end of the Renaissance, a genuine pan-European interest in the "prince of philosophers" was powerfully reasserted by Kepler, a Northerner with ties to Italy, and Baldi, an Italian with ties to the North. For all these humanists probably the most important inspirators were the Greek Bessarion, the German Cusanus, and the Italians Ficino and Pico. From Cusanus to Kepler, leading mathematicians saw a harmonious and beautiful result in the integration of mathematics and theology. Harmony, which obliterates discord, could be achieved by discovering concord. Concord culminates in God, the architect of the universe, who reconciles all opposites.

This harmony could best be expressed in no more visual a way than in works of architecture and art. Intellectuals were well aware of this. Pacioli recommended that architects study Pythagoras; Lomazzo acknowledged that Pythagoras inspired painters; and Baldi said that Pythagoras was very fond of architecture. In France, Germany, and England few works betrayed a significant Pythagorean inspiration except in lingering Gothic architectural practice.[2] Medieval strains of Pythagoreanism also survived in the North through the sixteenth century in the use of prognostication devices such as Pythagorean Spheres.

In Italy, however, things were different. It was here that the new ideas were first transformed into the language of architecture and art. Architects and artists had visionary ideas that they developed, often with considerable struggle. Eventually, their efforts achieved a demonstrable integrity of pure geometrical form. The eye, the mind, and the spirit could all appreciate the beauty of measure;

the perfect forms it enabled could be used to express the tangibility of God. God was the circle, the sphere, the triangle, and the center; and the geometry of structure – far from being paganizing – proved it. The marriage of the triangle with the sphere, and the pyramid with the cube symbolized (as Reuchlin had described) the universe, over which God presided. In architecture this was seen in the dome held aloft over the cube-pyramid. In painting these forms were ingeniously merged.

The concept of the artist as intellectual is born in these times. The intellectual interests of artists were propelled by an educated élite, including those who "bet" on the new art. These included Cosimo de'Medici, Pope Pius II, Federigo da Montefeltro, Pope Sixtus IV, and Julius II, especially through Tommaso Inghirami. Perhaps ironically, its highest flowering corresponded with the departure of the Medici in late fifteenth- and early sixteenth-century Florence. In Spain a unique situation unfolded toward the end of the sixteenth century. Here, under the authority of King Philip II – particularly at the Escorial – developed, in the works of Herrera and Villalpando, a powerful interest in the interlocking of the purity of Pythagorean geometry with the mysticism of the occult. In contrast, some practitioners of the occult, such as Rudolf II of Prague, appear to have been more interested in collecting exotica than in demonstrating the passion for order that marked Pythagorean thought.

It was in Italy that works of art and architecture most prominently displayed mathematical interests that led to the creation of a new aesthetic. Gleaned by humanists in different ways from Antiquity, number and numerical squares and cubes, together with their geometric counterparts, came to be highly regarded by architects and artists. Among these, Brunelleschi and Alberti led the way to a development that would bloom magnificently in the sixteenth century, a century that invented an idealized architecture composed of mutually balanced parts harmoniously fused in an indissoluble organic synthesis. This unity proclaimed a cosmic kingdom with heaven above and earth below. The modern worldview proclaimed by this architecture replaced the medieval hierarchic cosmos with one based on unity. Those artists who imagined the High Renaissance style found that this new language enabled them to create new, idealized, harmonious works based on the marriage of geometry and number. These interests can be traced from Masaccio to Piero della Francesca to Leonardo, Michelangelo, and Raphael, the greatest innovators of the Renaissance. Their art was an art of ideas. Its most distinctive characteristic was the idealization of nature through the creation of a mode of order that transformed a subject into an object, one that exemplified an undefiled and unequivocal harmony. Thus did Pythagorean thinking lay behind the great geometric compositional structures of the Renaissance. But not everyone was a modernist in the sense that he could see and seize from the dissemination of Pythagorean ideas the potential for transforming the language of art. Most other artists remained traditional, and conservative, applying new ideas of surface realism or of numeric or geometric form in piecemeal ways by rule of thumb, making additive rather than synthetic art.

Essentially, then, the Renaissance was the site of a great rift between the avant-garde and the conservatives. Paradoxically, the avant-garde created their quintessential modernism through the study of ancient ideas that, thanks largely to the memory of Pythagoras, provided them with avenues to explore a new and exhilarating common goal: harmony. Inspired by ancient Pythagorean sources, these architects and artists reaffirmed what the natural philosophers, mathematicians, and theologians had agreed — that, being primary, divine, pure, and unchanging, harmony is the most beautiful thing.[3]

APPENDIX A:

PYTHAGOREAN WORKS IN SIX

RENAISSANCE LIBRARIES

The famous library of the Visconti family at Pavia (founded by Gian Galeazzo Visconti, who died in 1402, and developed by his son Filippo Maria, who died in 1447) was, in 1426, composed of 988 manuscripts of which classical texts were a significant number.[1] Readers eager to reinforce their knowledge or to discover new ideas could study Pythagoras and his doctrines by consulting Plato (whose *Timaeus*, as translated by Chalcidius, was held in three copies), Pompeius Trogus, Ovid (whose *Metamorphoses* existed in four manuscript editions), Vitruvius, Pliny the Elder, Julius Caesar, Aulus Gellius, Valerius Maximus (whose *Facta et dicta memorabilia* existed in six manuscript editions), Varro, Quintilian, Eusebius (including his *Cronica* and other works), Saint Augustine (whose *City of God* was held in seven copies), Saint Jerome, Clement of Alexandria (including his *Stromateius*), Cassiodorus (whose works were collected in five copies), Martianus Capella (whose *De nuptiis Philologiae et Mercurii* existed in four manuscripts), Boethius (whose *De musica* existed in a single copy while his *De arithmetica* was held in two), Dionysius the Areopagite, and Isidore of Seville (whose *Etymologiae* existed in five examples and various excerpts). Also prominent in this collection were the works of French medieval Platonists and the School of Chartres, including texts by William of Conches, Bernard Silvester, and Hugh of St. Victor. As well, works by Vincent of Beauvais, Arnaldo da Villanova, and Petrarch were numerous, as were works on alchemy – including the *Turba Philosophurum* (*Assembly of Philosophers*) – astrology, astronomy, and geometry. A second inventory of 1459 lists 824 volumes, including another copy of Plato's *Timaeus*, two more copies of Boethius's *De arithmetica*, and more texts by Cassiodorus. The last known inventory, made in 1469 (before the library was sacked and despoiled of its contents in 1499–1500 by the invading troops of Louis XII of France), lists 126 additional volumes, including a new copy of Valerius Maximus.

The library that Cardinal Giovanni Basilio Bessarion (1395–1472) bequeathed to the city of Venice four years before his death contained the texts of most of the authors mentioned in the Visconti library in addition to many more important sources of Pythagoriana. The number of Greek editions in Bessarion's library distinguished it as the richest Greek library in existence at the time.[2] This erudite prelate, who supervised the translating of Greek manuscripts into Latin for two popes (Eugenius IV and Nicholas V), and who himself almost became pope though he was a patriarch of the Orthodox Church, spent the greater part of his income on the purchase and copying of manuscripts.[3]

The first two of several inventories of this library, made in 1468 and 1474, reveal Cardinal Bessarion's particular devotion to Plato (whose *Timaeus* he held in five editions). In his collection were important new sources (for the Renaissance) on Pythagoras and his doctrines.[4] These included Herodotus, Isocrates, Nicomachus (whose *Introduction to Arithmetic* he held in nine examples and whose work on music, *Manual of Harmonics*, he held in two). Also among these were Philostratus's *Life of Apollonius of Tyre* (in three copies), Philo ("omnia opera"), Plutarch (whose *Moralia*, as well as other works, was in this collection), Plotinus ("omnia opera"), Diogenes Laertius's *Lives and Opinions of Eminent Philosophers* (in three copies), Proclus, Porphyry (numerous works, though not his *Life of Pythagoras*), Iamblichus (*De secta Pythagorae*, held in four copies – one a "liber novus, pulcher"), Macrobius's *Commentary on the Somnium Scipionis*, Simplicius, Apuleius, and Photius. In addition, Bessarion had collected manuscripts of late-medieval thinkers friendly to Pythagoras and his teachings, including those of Durandus (in several editions) and Walter Burley, as well as works on astronomy, geometry, the sphere, and various occult sciences like geomancy (a form of divination). Bessarion owned a *Theology of Arithmetic*, possibly that today associated with Iamblichus.[5] Of special interest are two works that were not in Pavia: Pythagoras's *Golden Verses* (of which he owned three copies, one of which was a "liber novus et pulcher") and a compilation of works attributed to Hermes Trismegistus. A manuscript now in Turin, which includes texts by Iamblichus and Hierocles, as well as one attributed to Pythagoras, was once owned by Bessarion, for it contains glosses by him.[6]

The great library of the popes, the Vatican Library, officially established by Sixtus IV (r. 1471–1484), contained – notwithstanding its vast holdings in theology, canon law, and medicine – many of the same volumes as the Visconti and Bessarion libraries.[7] Among these texts the names of Boethius, Dionysius the Areopagite, Saint Jerome, Saint Augustine, and Petrarch are encountered with greatest frequency. In addition, the aggregate of twenty-five hundred volumes listed in an inventory of 1475 included three codices of Macrobius's *Commentary on the Somnium Scipionis*, three each of Herodotus, Nicomachus, and Diogenes Laertius, and two of Theon of Smyrna's volume on Pythagorean numerology. Notably, the *Pimander* of Hermes Trismegistus, a work of enormous current popularity in Italy, was represented in the papal library.

Among the private libraries of the fifteenth century, that of Pico della Mirandola (1463–1494), an independent Florentine intellectual, merits consideration because of the fame and influence of its young founder. Known through an inventory of 1498, its contents (1,697 manuscripts and early printed books) reveal Pico's enthusiasm for Arabic and Hebrew texts, as well as for those in Latin and Greek.[8] Among the authors who described Pythagoras or commented on his ideas were virtually all those mentioned in the previous inventories. In addition, Pico possessed a copy of Ovid's *Letter from Sappho to Faon* and several commentaries on the Kabbalah. Two works by Pythagoras himself are listed in this inventory, one the *Golden Verses* (recently translated into Latin and printed in 1474 prior to being immediately reprinted in 1475 and again in 1493) and the other a volume, whose contents are unknown to us, entitled *Pithagoras sophista* (*The Wise Pythagoras*). Pico also owned works attributed to Orpheus, a shadowy figure, perhaps mythological, of the ancient world whom some in Antiquity had connected with Pythagoras. Significantly, Pico owned four copies of Vitruvius's *De architectura*, one of which was the first edition printed in Rome in 1486. He also owned the first edition of Diogenes Laertius, which, printed in Rome in 1474, was to be reprinted in 1475, 1483, and 1485. Notably, Pico owned three copies of Theon of Smyrna's text on Pythagorean mathematics. Indeed, by now all the major Antique sources on Pythagoras and his doctrines figured prominently, often in multiple copies, in the collections of Renaissance intellectuals.

An example of a German library formed in the late fifteenth century and early years of the sixteenth, that of the Christian legal scholar and friend of Hebraic studies Johannes Reuchlin (1455–1522), reveals that over the Alps scholars could indulge their interests in Pythagoras by consulting a similar reading list.[9] The many Greek works that Reuchlin owned, including two editions of Pythagoras's *Golden Verses*, were complemented by a plethora of Hebrew works on the Kabbalah, an esoteric Jewish tradition that incorporated a system of numerology similar to if not derived from that associated with Pythagoras himself.

That these "must haves" were also considered important elsewhere in Europe can be seen in the contents of the Escorial library, founded in mid-sixteenth-century Spain by Philip II.[10] Partial surviving inventories from 1579 and 1587 provide only a glimpse of its contents. All the names mentioned earlier were represented in this library. It was significant too that Iamblichus's *Life of Pythagoras* and Theon of Smyrna's *Arithmetic* were each present in four copies, while Nicomachus's *Introduction to Arithmetic* was present in three. The works of Philo, a major Pythagorean of Antiquity, must have been particularly valued here, for his collected works existed in five copies. In the Escorial Library, as well as in all the other libraries previously discussed, works on alchemy, astronomy, astrology, and harmonics, areas in which Pythagoras was considered an authority, were highly valued.

APPENDIX B:

ENGLISH TRANSLATION OF

FILIPPO BEROALDO'S *SYMBOLA*

PYTHAGORICA (1503)

Filippo Beroaldo Senior (1453–1505) was a prolific and highly respected humanist and philologist. (He is not to be confused with his cousin Filippo Beroaldo Junior, 1477–1518, a poet and papal librarian.) In this essay, published in Bologna in 1503, Filippo declares his profound admiration for Pythagoras, whom he considered to be, above all else, an arbiter of morals.

FILIPPO BEROALDO SENIOR, *THE SYMBOLS OF PYTHAGORAS*

TRANSLATED AND EDITED BY CAROLYN P. TUTTLE

The ancient Greek world distinguished between two types of philosophers, Ionian and Italian. They considered Thales of Miletus, the leader of the Ionian school, to be one of the seven most illustrious men whom they called "the wise." But Pythagoras of Samos, the founder of the Italian school, was held to be the most renowned of all ancient philosophers and the one who first gave us the name "philosopher." Leon, the ruler of Phlius, once asked Pythagoras what above all he professed and by what name he would call himself. In answer he said that he was a "lover of wisdom," because it seemed arrogant for one to call himself wise. From that time on, those who had formerly been called "wise men" were instead called "philosophers."

Pythagoras, using sacred resources of learning, developed a systematic, principled code of living which is wonderfully advantageous for human beings. Plato himself imitated Pythagoras in a great many instances, for Pythagoras' authority had become so outstanding that his followers took to answering questions of argument or proof simply by saying, "Pythagoras himself said so." The Pythagoreans learned by heart the precepts of their teacher, using memory in place of books.

His doctrines included two concepts, obscure to us but esteemed by some eminent writers on Pythagoras, called metempsychosis and palingenesis, or the transmigration of souls and their regeneration or rebirth. According to these doctrines, one could argue that if anyone is born, he or she may also be frequently reborn. But more pertinent to our present discussion of ethics were his doctrines concerning frugality and restraint. He urged abstinence from rich food and lavish, gourmet restaurants, with the result that the Pythagorean family, following his precepts, ate simple meals, without meat. Similarly, he taught his followers the importance of restraining the tongue "within the wall of the teeth," and of applying themselves to philosophy for long periods of silence. Once students were accepted into his "communion of friends," he formed a cohort of discipleship wherein all their resources were held and shared in common. This inseparable community became proverbial among Greeks and was later called cenobism.

Pythagoras was a man of very keen and wide-ranging talents. He observed the cosmos, studying the stars and calculating distances … He demonstrated the characteristics of a triangle, discovering them without benefit of artificial instrumentation. It is said that he so rejoiced in this invention that he offered greatest thanks and sacrifices to the gods. But I must omit countless other commendations of this famous man, in order to focus on my present theme and not burden the reader. We must restrict our attention to the "symbols" of Pythagoras, which are precious treasures of understanding. I offer this course of instruction not for amusement or trivial pursuit, but as a serious undertaking for those few who are willing to distance themselves from ordinary, profane concerns. I hope, however, to please as well as edify.

A symbol is a comparison, a combination that brings many relations or meanings into one. One ancient use of it was a token in the form of coins to pay for food or contribute to a dinner party. Both the comic poet Plautus and Terence described characters eating "according to the symbols" they had offered. On the other hand, a person who brought nothing as contribution to a dinner was referred to as *asymbolos* – what we would call a "mooch," one who expects a "free hand-out". … A second use for the word "symbol" was a ring worn by a religious figure, signifying their faith. … Thirdly, symbols were devised by Aristotle for Etymology, as a guide for proof of identity, as the flight or cries of birds were symbols for interpretation or divination of an oracle, augury, or prophecy. We can also find examples of such customary signs used in warfare, such as a signal given to soldiers to prevent trickery or deceit. … The god Lar was the symbol of Marius, Apollo the symbol of Sulla, Venus the symbol of Caesar. The palm of victory became a symbol for manliness and courage, the poppy for fertility, Adonis for enjoyment, Attis for youthful chastity, Satyrs for sexual power. Foam of the sea, which in Greek is *aphros*, was a symbol of birth, causing Venus to be called Aphrodite.

The symbols of Pythagoras are tokens or signs of his sacred doctrine of mysteries, within which ethical purposes and models are contained, just as precious treasures may be enclosed within small clay pots. To a certain extent these symbols of his clearly resemble laws or precepts, scanty in words but plentiful in meaning, like fruits whose skins are tough but which inside are juicy and succulent. Some of his symbols are ambiguous, others clear, but within them there is a certain universal rule, for they are all concerned with living life conscientiously, happily, and harmoniously. I have here selected a certain few which I believe to be the most profitable and wholesome for the life and conduct of human affairs. ...

Among the so-called Golden Sacred Symbols of Pythagoras, which are mystic and enigmatic, one stands out as preeminent and most worth remembering. Literally it says, *"Do not leap across a balance beam."* That is, don't overstep the bounds of justice or violate a state of equity. To any leader we must say, "If you want to hold the reins of power and stand atop the citadel, you must make and administer laws in such a way that all people will respect your rule. Do not upset the balance or golden mean. Do not exceed the bounds of justice. This 'golden rule' of equity was made for you as a goal or signpost to follow. Everything you say, do, or think must be referred to this standard." To any judiciary magistrate we must say, "If you sit in court with power over the life and property of human beings, weigh carefully your decisions with a balanced scale, treating each side fairly. Strive in every case to be like Bocchus of Egypt, an inspiration and model for unbiased judgments, honor and equity. ..." A judge should be a master of justice, inviolable and strict, incorrupt and inaccessible to flattery, mighty with the force and majesty of equity and truth.

Similarly, to any religious leader we must say, "If you put yourself in a position of sacred trust, and of godlike reverence, do not 'leap across the balance beam.' In every circumstance make sure that you are a leader who maintains justice and does not cause injustice, by any sort of treachery. For many conceal tyrannical injustice under their holy robes. Be constantly aware that the eye of justice is upon you, and pay attention to your own actions; look at them objectively, as if from some heavenly vantage point or observation tower in the sky. Examine all your thoughts and intentions from the point of view of justice." We remember the goddess of justice called Astraea, who hated the depravity and injustice of mortal affairs, and left the impious lands of earth for a place in the sky. ... Her story implies that no matter how we may yearn for justice, we cannot find it intact anywhere on earth. ...

Plutarch ingeniously compared justice to oil, which when stored in the body [as fat] may be injurious to health, but when administered externally [as lotion] may be beneficial. By his analogy justice may be of more benefit to the community when administered from the outside, by impartial leaders, than from within, by our own governors. But, as Ambrose has said, a fair man neglects his own advantage in order to secure equity for others. He holds what is common to all as his own, and what is his own as common to the whole community. Since the first duty of justice is to keep people from injuring one another and to grant the same law to all, then it follows that whoever is just is good and whoever is good is just.

We find in Menander's teachings and in Pollux's *Onomasticon* the Greek expression for "a just piece of land," which means that one should give back as much as one receives. Accordingly, to any banker or businessman we must say, "If you wish to be known as 'good security,' be sure you deliver as much as you take, or give as much as you gain, without fraud. Refrain from any kind of deceit or swindling, so that you will not deviate even 'a finger's breadth' from the balance or mean." The Greeks called Aristides "the Just" for his eminent standard of justice and considered that reputation for fair conduct and kindness to be the most prized possession, deserving more respect than that incurred by any other sort of triumph or distinction. I would certainly prefer it to that of Pompey "the Great," Sulla "the Fortunate," or Demetrius "the Stormer of Cities." In fact, we can define a worthy leader as one who wishes to be known as just and who acts with impartiality and integrity. When the great Agesilaus was asked which virtue of the two was more desirable, fortitude or fairness, he cleverly and wisely responded, "We would need no fortitude if we were all just."

The Greek author Stephanus claimed that the Pozzuolian people of Italy were named "Dicarchians" ("just leaders") for their reputation for justice. … How admirable it would be if our state and its citizens could deserve such a name for their just rule. The Greek word for justice combines the connotations of righteousness with comprehension or intelligence, signifying an understanding of the just. As Plato explains in his *Cratylus*, all mortals, and especially leaders, recognize that they are naturally constituted to be in a state of union with justice. Consequently they know whether or not they have "leaped across the balance beam" which Pythagoras established as his symbol.

Pythagoras united to this symbol a second, closely related one, equally relevant. This symbol warns that *the "crown" of cities should not be seized* or destroyed, meaning that the laws of societies must be protected and preserved. Pindar wisely said that law governs all things. Aristotle, the founder of the Peripatetic School, also counsels us to be obedient to law, as to God. But Plato, that supreme thinker whose voice is clearest and brightest in philosophy, remains the most ardent champion of law. He cries out, as if from a watchtower, to mortals who are heedless of truth. We can foresee annihilation for any state in which law does not command its magistrates but a magistrate commands the law, as if able to manipulate or overturn it at his own whim. On the other hand, welfare abides in a state in which law has dominion over rulers; on such a state the gods seem to bestow all their bounties.

I believe that law should be like a queen, enthroned on high, correcting faults that occur in the business of the state, rewarding virtue appropriately, leading people to live in the right way, and benefiting the whole state. Cicero used a maxim which I wish could be carved on the door of every judge's office, on the headboard of every administrator's bed, and on the opening page of every lawyer's brief – namely, that the laws incorporate the mind and spirit, purpose and will of the state. Just as our body cannot be of use without the mind, so the state cannot function without laws for its citizens. Laws are its brain, nerves, blood, and limbs.

As magistrates are ministers of the laws, and judges are interpreters of the laws, so we all are servants of the laws – in order that we may be free. Any citizen who is a friend of the state and desires the public welfare must understand that the state is sustained and safeguarded by the law, not by men. Such a citizen will honor the Pythagorean symbol telling us not to allow that "crown" of law to be seized, violated, or destroyed, for without law public life will collapse.

The Roman Cato taught that laws are the sinews of the state, vital to the health, safety, peace and prosperity of all. The Greeks believed that Ceres invented laws, therefore calling her "law-giving" (*Thesmophoria*), a name attached to her festival and sacred rites. That conception deserves remembrance and respect. Law was devised and propagated not so much by the ingenuity of men as by divine disposition. It follows that law is a sovereign that commands, prohibits, and judges, as ordained by God above. Greek compilers of the law, such as Draco and Solon, were highly esteemed, and guardians of the law were chosen from the most admired candidates. As Columella said, their duty was to praise and honor those who obeyed the law and to punish those who did not. Surely the most observant and faithful guardians of the law should be our rulers.

But the sad truth is that most of these "guardians" are instead counterfeits and hypocrites, who repeatedly violate their function by acting as if leaders were free from the law, unfettered by it, and as if their power took precedence over law. One example relates to the Roman emperor Antoninus Caracalla, who chose his wealthy stepmother Julia for an incestuous love, trampled the law underfoot, and married her. … Another example was Nero, who poisoned his brother Britannicus, ordering his death because he believed in ruling the law, not the law ruling him. … A third example is that of Cambyses, a king of the Persians, who desired to marry his sister and asked the royal judges whether any law permitted it. The judges cleverly responded that a certain law permitted a Persian king to do whatever he pleased. Thus they neither abrogated the law nor endangered themselves, but enabled Cambyses to have his own way. … No wonder such tyrants hold the law to be no more than a spider's web, for just as the web retains weaker animals and lets stronger ones through, so the lowly and poor are constricted by law, while the rich and powerful remain free.

We can see plenty of examples, in our times as well, of leaders who behave as if boiling water were frigid and construe laws to mean their opposites. But we believe in the importance of preserving Pythagoras' symbols which tell us not to leap across a balance or pluck the crown of law and justice. We must guard these laws tenaciously and live conscientiously, taking utmost care not to be guilty of lawbreaking. The Greeks had a name for the "lawless and unlawful," which they used for both unjust and villainous men.

A third symbol of Pythagoras is one on which the happiness of life rests: *the heart should not be consumed*, or as our popular expression goes, "Don't eat your heart out." Grief must be expelled from the spirit, though we all know how much of it there is in human affairs. What heart does not daily corrode as it feeds on grief? Who doesn't get depressed and exhausted by sorrow? Human beings, as Apuleius shrewdly defined them, are anxious of mind and heavy of body, their lives full of complaints. And as the saintly Ambrose said, our mortal life is "a den of thieves" (*Piraterium*). That word *Piraterium* expresses our daily life surrounded by evils that continually attack us in the form of deadly sorrows, troubles, or emotions. The plunderers that raid are the torments that pierce or the passions that rage, disturbing the entire life of man. Pliny described life as a factory of grief, forcing us to feed on our troubles almost as daily food. The philosopher Heraclitus is much admired for the fact that whenever he went forth in public, he wept tears for the plight of man, for it seemed to him that the whole human race was occupied in weeping. We often think that those in high office, clad in purple and thronged by attendants, are fortunate – the crowd calls them blessed. But their happiness is a mask, a gilded fixture, a counterfeit; for they, as much as any other, grieve and sigh; as often as any, they are weakened by depression and deformed by the wounds of sadness.

Historians used to marvel at the rumor of certain Ethiopians who neither grieved nor got angry nor were disturbed by any human emotion. These men were accordingly called *Apathes*, or "the passionless." Pliny reported certain strivers after wisdom who had hard, inflexible natures, devoid of human passions, who were called *Apathes*. But it seems quite unbelievable to me, pondering the human condition and nature of life, that humans can be found who do not frequently "eat their heart out," who do not taste grief and sorrow. A person who is not attended and encircled by care, misery, sickness, tears, suffering, as Plautus' miserable lover was, is indeed a *rara avis*.

Recently I was forced to "eat my heart out," filled with overwhelming sorrow at the death of Minus Roscius. No man was a greater friend or more beloved, congenial soul. About thirty years ago we both began literary studies and teaching duties under an eminent classical professor. A friendship took root, strengthened by the almost daily habit of reading together the works of Latin writers. Roscius had an ingenious wit and quick intelligence, eloquence of speech, and extraordinary skills in business and political affairs. He could be called a man of all hours or seasons. He was made head of the Senate, and his opinion was sought on all important matters. … Because of the faith and wisdom he inspired, Roscius was esteemed both at home and abroad for his agreeable nature, political astuteness, liberal education, and refined manners. … He and I were on intimate terms, at ease with one another, and were admired for our friendship.

But in fact, no happiness is long-lasting. Life seems to give us more of bitter than of sweet, like a mother whose ministrations often seem to contain more vinegar than honey. In myth we learn of two casks located in the house of Jove, one a repository of good fortunes, the other of misfortunes, and we can't help but notice how much more often the days and hours are supplied from the cask of evils. How fallacious and vain are our hopes, how frail and fleeting our time on earth. How often joy is turned to sorrow and celebration to regret. On the first of September Minus Roscius, full of optimism and high spirits, became the standard-bearer of justice and director of the Republic. Suddenly struck with a deadly disease, seized by a consuming fever, he returned home from the palace and within fifteen days died. That day, the fourth of October, to me is the most woeful day of my life, full of dark omens, because just eight years later on the same day I lost my mother. October 4th snatched from me my best and most tender support, as well as my greatest friend. A horrible anxiety and uncontrollable grief still burn in me whenever I think of Roscius and his last words to me: "Farewell, my Beroaldo, I leave you and am called to a greater tribunal."

The ancient sources say that the Roman Republic was debilitated by the death of Scipio Africanus and that the Senate was left an orphan by the death of Cato. I in turn would say that the death of Minus Roscius has deprived the Bolognan Republic of its best patron and robbed me of a jewel of a friend. He will always be mourned by me as much as any blood relation. In fact, a friend may be mourned more than a relative, because, as Cicero perceptively says, "Friendship surpasses blood-relationship, in that from kinship affection can be removed; from friendship it cannot." With kindness gone, the name of friendship is annulled, while that of kinship remains. As the old saying goes, true love knows no bounds. ...

His premature death made me temporarily forget the symbol of Pythagoras which warns us not to be obsessed with excessive grief and not to lose our heads or our reasoning power. Thankfully, even though I was consumed with grief, I had the sense to take refuge in the world of books, which when properly chosen can, in a wonderful way, renew the sorrowing soul and restore balance and health. Another consolation which helped a good deal was the little voice that began to speak within me, nudging me into a realization that in some ways it can be a blessing to die. After all, Roscius departed in good fortune, in fullest bloom, full of honor, favor and prosperity. ... He had achieved the most exalted rank of a private man. He died at age 52, at the turning-point to old age. He should have lived longer than this, but "You don't know what late evening may bring." You don't know how often men's fortunes are liable to change. In a long life, in which there is the most mire and toil, death snatches one not from good things but from bad. Death is the tribute which all mortals must pay, willingly or not. The precarious life given us must be accepted as a favor. A debtor has no just cause to demand what belongs to his creditor. But the dead can go on living in the hearts, conversation, and memory of those still alive.

These consolations restore and recall me from corroding grief and vain tears. I must submit to his death – what else can I do? Shall I torture and torment myself? What then shall I gain? I shall gain more if now, with my spirit composed and my mind tranquil, I entreat God to receive the departed spirit of Roscius into His home of eternal grace, where he may live happily in the company of the blessed. That celestial state is merited by anyone so highly regarded by his country. His whole life was a preparation for it. This testimonial, which is something like an inscription for his tombstone or a funeral lament, I dutifully offer with most loving memory, since there is nothing more we can do for the deceased.

If you, my reader, have enough freedom from other serious matters to attend to this, I ask that you read my essay through, harboring neither contempt nor lack of sympathy, and that you ponder whether anything in life is sweeter or more desirable than a friend, one with whom you may talk about anything just as freely and safely as with yourself, and one who equally rejoices with you in all good, happy times and warms you with consolation in adversities. Such a friend, I know, is not easily found, and once found, may be lost, causing great torment to your soul. The passing of Roscius was such a heavy loss to me that I feel compelled to express this eulogy in the hope that it may help perpetuate or even enhance his memory. When posterity names three or four most notable, long-standing pairs of friends, I hope the friendship of Minus Roscius and Philippo Beroaldo will be among them.

I have purposely digressed from my main theme, out of the sympathy of sincere love, and in order to refresh readers who may be growing weary. … But to return to our main focus, we are asking how to apply the symbol of Pythagoras that warns us not to eat our hearts out. Certainly our minds must be distracted from devouring cares. Life must be lived with a measure of good humor and light-heartedness, for the rejoicing spirit, as Solomon says, creates the bloom of youth, whereas a broken spirit dries up the bones. Clearly, sickness and sorrow are torture, consuming and utterly subduing the spirit. Chrysippus judged that grief or pain, of body or mind, is like a dissolution or breakdown of the whole person, since a person weakened by it grows thin or lethargic, aged or completely worn out. … Galen, the famous founder of medicine, perceived that we must abstain from anger, sadness, and especially anxiety, because these maladies disturb, dry up, exhaust, and kill our bodies. … Plato, in his *Menexenus*, warns that we must obey that old proverb "Nothing in excess," if we wish to live well and happily. For anyone obeying it, by doing nothing immoderate or extreme, will remain on an even keel, without too much joy or sadness. Such a person will rejoice less but also grieve less.

Democritus was nicknamed "the laugher" by the Greeks. He thought that tranquility of mind led to the greatest good. Since all people want to be free from undue public and private cares, they should strive to keep the tranquility of Democritus in their hearts and banish grief and sadness. In *Ecclesiastes* it is written, "I have praised joy, because there is no good thing for man under the sun except that he should eat and drink and be glad." So let us enjoy life, in cheerfulness and serenity, keeping our brow smooth, not wrinkled. Let us emulate Socrates, the father of moral philosophy, whose wife Xantippe maintained that she always saw him leave home and return with the same serene and tranquil face. He managed to preserve equanimity, despite great inequality of fortune. We too can have a positive outlook and spirit, if we cultivate and apply these teachings. In this way our mind will be nourished and healthy.

Certain studies are austere and heavy. With them our mind grows somber, even though they may be beneficial, like a bitter medicine. But the humane studies, the humanities and liberal arts, have an energizing power and sweetness that flows from their foundation in the Muses. They are the sun which clears away the clouds of the human spirit. They are like the Siren who soothes hearts with a song. They are that Nepenthes by which sadness is dispelled, cares are dulled, and good cheer is gained, and which ought to be furnished to all mortals. Literature can be the greatest pleasure when our circumstances are happy and the greatest comfort when we are beset with adversities. There is nothing sad that cannot be made less so by means of literature, and nothing happy that cannot be augmented by it. Let us use the consolation of reading and writing to wipe away the stains of sadness, brighten the brow, and purify the mind, like a sky clear and light, undisturbed by clouds.

There are other remedies for grief, including herbs and wine. One herb, called "helenium" because legend claimed it was born from the tears of Helen, can be added to a drink of wine to create merriment and abolish sadness. The same effect comes from the herb bugloss, whose name means mirth and good cheer, or from music, which can charm every living creature and calm the agitations of body and soul. ... All our days should include some tonic for dissipating cares and cheering the spirit ...

Let no one think, though, that I am condoning drunkenness. I don't advise anyone to overindulge and thus destroy the vigor of the mind. But it is advisable to pay due respect to Dionysus, who not only cures certain maladies but also heals sadness and drives care from the mind. Seneca maintained that a free man is characterized not by licentious behavior but by the way he liberates the mind and draws it away from care. ... Plato, as well, said temperance and even work may be enhanced by moderate drinking ... So let us use wine with reason and judgment, for the sake of pleasure as well as thirst, but adapting freely to abstinence, if need be.

Other remedies for grief and distress include the use of expert story-tellers or comedians. Baths, too, are both pleasurable and healthful, the name "bath" deriving from a Greek phrase meaning to strike at troubles, or cast out anxieties from the mind. By one or another method, then, we should follow the counsel of Pythagoras to drive distress from our minds. In conducting a life of good cheer we can make a serene countenance reflect our inner joy and tranquility. We can dispel the clouds of melancholy, mourning, and anxiety. True life depends on both a cheerful heart and a mind free from vexation.

A fourth symbol of Pythagoras says, "*One must not taste 'melanurus'*"– a fish with a black tail. Metaphorically we take this to mean that we should not closely associate with people of "black" or evil character, since habitual contact with evildoers may promote evil customs and behavior. It is an important precept, one that should be fixed in the heart for remembrance. It warns us to beware of commerce with the wicked. The two colors white and black are symbolic, the first of virtue or purity, the second of vice or corruption. ... The melanurus with its black tail is said to live among rocks. ... But our revered philosopher Pythagoras was not asking us to abstain from that kind of fish. Rather, he was teaching symbolically that we must guard against evil men stained with the blackness of crimes. There is a great tribe of them, including deceitful impostors, cheats, embezzlers, and others of malicious intent. And here I have to add what may seem surprising to you, that not few but many who are clothed in white are really the blackest of all. They pass time among us on friendly terms, ... publicly looking stern but in reality being dissolute, publicly walking modestly with heads bowed down but actually filled with arrogance and sinister design. By their white "clothing" you would consider them sincere and worthy of respect, but one can never trust appearances. For what street or town does not abound in debased or offensive people? Those clothed in black, as if for mourning, may have insidious minds that correspond to their black exterior. If so, they are the "melanuri" that Pythagoras' symbol warns us to guard against.

However, it is difficult to identify and avoid the "melanuri" of society, since their evil is often not perceptible. They disguise it with facial masks, with cloaks of words and the hypocrisy of false pretense. These wolves hide under the appearance of sheep. And as Plautus cleverly says, "Man is a wolf to other men, who do not recognize his true nature." It is not easy for any of us to judge another man, since human beings have such hidden desires and complex natures. Our brows, eyes, faces very often mask what is underneath, and our speech deceives even more often. Cicero once satirized man as having eyes, eyebrows, forehead, face, in short every outward part, that can delude and ensnare, beguile and mislead the unsuspecting. ... Man is a chameleon, for he changes color by altering his words, varying his plans, and transforming himself into diverse images, as he thinks expedient. ... Man is a variegated gem that remains the same through a kaleidoscope of varying colors, by his fluctuating, deceptive behavior which can so easily mask his true nature. The prophet Jeremiah asserted that the Ethiopian cannot change his skin, nor the leopard his spots. But man makes himself a skin-changer by willing himself to be fickle, mutable, slippery. ... Pythagoras' "melanuri" are prolific. Indeed, good men are rare, scarcely ever as many as the proverbial hundred gates of Thebes or the visible stars of a constellation in the sky.

We observe that even a person who takes great care not to be deceived, and who is constantly on guard, is often caught by the net of deception. Therefore, Pythagoras bids us to beware of tasting "melanuri" and to flee as far as possible from the presence of "black" or evil persons, so that we ourselves may not be tainted by their evil. Behavior and character are influenced by the company we keep. As Menander said, discoursing with the worst will corrupt and destroy good habits. Let us live in the manner of Laelius and Cato, who were able to bring out the best in good men. And whenever a "melanurus" appears before us, let us cry out, "This person is bad. Beware of him." Ennius once described a column of elephants as "a black army marching on the field," a description also used by Vergil in comparing the Trojans to ants. ... We too could use that same phrase to refer to the multitudes of mortals tarnished with the stain of vices, infected with evil habits, and continually trooping about us. The symbol of Pythagoras beneficially warns us to avoid even a taste of evil, for whoever does forbear and refrain from that taste will live both more freely and honorably.

A fifth symbol of Pythagoras asserts, "*Don't stir fire with a sword*" or add fuel to the fire. In other words, don't arouse the wrath of the mighty or provoke anyone in power whose mind is already fired with emotion, because to do so is clearly more hazardous that to attack a hornet's nest. Tiberius Caesar used to declare repeatedly that the tongue and mind ought to be free. Certainly in a free state there would be great advantages for citizens to be unrestrained in speech and thought. But in the presence of leaders one must act cautiously, so as not to "stir fire with a sword," that is, not to offend and provoke them to violent anger. Aristotle wisely warned Callisthenes that in the presence of the great Alexander he should speak either very rarely or very agreeably. Callisthenes clearly did not heed the advice, for he exasperated the king with untimely witticisms, whereupon the king had him tortured and killed for being too free of wit and tongue. Whatever one advocates to a person in power must be delivered with tact and discretion. ... The soul resides partly in the ears, especially in the ears of the more powerful, who hear according to whether the matter and manner are gratifying or grating, and who then grow cheerful or indignant.

Rulers crave adulation, but adulation borders closely on flattery, so we must make an important distinction between courtesy and flattery. One can be pleasing without being a sycophant, and courtesies should not be to one's own detriment and expense. ... Once some Athenians greeted Mark Antony as Dionysus and pledged their Minerva in marriage to him, if he would take her as his wife. Antony replied that he would accept, if a dowry was provided, and ordered from them one thousand talents for that purpose, causing their immoderate flattery to result in a heavy tax.

Another ancient example of the Pythagorean symbol occurred in the time of King Antigonus, who was blind in one eye. The Greek poet Theocritus "stirred fire with a sword," eliciting royal ire by abusive words, and suffered punishment for his biting wit. For when Theocritus spoke sarcastically to the Euterpean cook, saying, "You will serve me raw to Cyclops," he offended King Antigonus. Theocritus further slandered the culinary offerings of the cook and was beaten for his insults to the Euterpean, but still did not cease in his facetious abuse. Antigonus responded, "You will pay a penalty for this taunt and feel the want of your head," to which Theocritus retorted, "Because I continue, he has sent in murderers." He was then beaten on the head for his bold tongue.

We need to ensure, then, that a person in power not be exasperated by some little indiscreet word or deed which causes indignation. A slip of the tongue can bring evil or ruin upon ourselves, just as the northeast wind brings clouds, so we need to exercise foresight and prudence as we speak. … If we want our ruler to be kindly and merciful, we should behave toward him with courtesy and respect. Alexander said the clemency of leaders depends upon not only their own nature but also that of their subjects, since by accommodation to their will rulers are appeased, and by obstinacy they become cruel. What comes to mind here is the observation that certain philosophers are insolent, obstinate, and contemptuous of leaders and magistrates. They apparently think they are truly philosophizing if they are criticizing freely and boldly, as though philosophy were a license for speaking and living according to their own inclination. But such men should treat with respect the rulers through whom they are allowed to enjoy peaceful leisure. … There is commonly no great praise for rulers who simply make themselves pleasing to others. Furthermore, philosophers should know that men of top rank are very "long-armed" in their hold on power, and can command the life and death of mortals. If kings say to kill, they kill, or to exile, they exile. Therefore, let philosophers not be slanderers and revilers, I beg; let the snarling of cynics be far removed from public affairs. Many who make vicious, unrestrained criticisms get killed for it. The best treasure for man, Hesiod said, is the treasure of the tongue, but it must be held within the wall of the teeth. Aesop also taught that the tongue is both the best and worst thing for mortals. It is dangerous to give free rein to a poisonous tongue, a tongue malevolent as that of a serpent, agitating to and fro, and piercing the vital parts like a sharp sword. How few are those who would rather throw away a word than a friend! How few are those who check the sting of the tongue, the sharp-cutting word, the biting attack on others; in short, how few do not stir fire with a sword! We all could benefit by learning the Pythagorean rule of silence. …

Finally, if we are not able to be accommodating and satisfy others, we should at least strive not to injure them. What we have said about not exasperating rulers should apply to all people generally – we should neither speak nor do anything to arouse wrath, instigate rage, or inflame an excited mind. If you have a quarrelsome and peevish wife, as they say Xantippe was to Socrates, don't stir up a hornet's nest. If you have business to tackle with an irritable, pugnacious person, don't provoke him or her with abusive words. In short, wherever you are, be mindful of the Pythagorean symbol not to stir fire with a sword. For as Solomon said, "A soft answer turns away wrath; a harsh word arouses fury."

A sixth symbol of Pythagoras is "*Do not wear a tight ring.*" This signifies that liberty must be cultivated and people must not be bound by any chain of slavery. A great expert of law in a Plautus play says that we all live more cheerfully when free than as slaves. For example, Plautus' character points out that while "It's a pleasant business to beget children … to keep one's freedom is far more pleasant!" Cicero said that all servitude is miserable and unbearable. To both Romans and Greeks death was preferable to servitude. Once the royal commander Hydarnes promised the Spartans the sovereignty of Greece, if they surrendered themselves to the supreme Persian ruler. But the envoys responded, "O Hydarnes, your plan does not pertain equally to us and to you. The condition you urge on us is one you but not we are experienced in. For you, a slave, are certainly aware of freedom but not yet experienced in whether it is sweet or not. If freedom were well known to you, you would urge that we fight for it not with spears but with battle-axes." These ambassadors of Sparta both spoke and acted freely. When they came into the presence of the king, his royal attendants ordered them to prostrate themselves with that form of supplicating obeisance we call a salaam. They stubbornly refused, asserting that for them it was not customary to worship a man. In that way they demonstrated the value of liberty among men who consider servitude the greatest of all evils.

There is a similar case of Athenian reaction often praised by Greek writers. Fearing that the Spartans would make a treaty with the foreigners, the Athenians proclaimed that no amount of gold or territorial gain could seduce them into handing over Greece to servitude, subjecting her to barbarians. So long as the sun and morning star rose and set, they would never enter into an alliance with Xerxes. The same Athenians worshiped Zeus the Deliverer, just as if he had liberated them from the bonds of servitude to the Persians. To that Zeus illustrious Romans continued to pour out libations at the end of life, a tradition which the dying Seneca followed. The Stoic philosopher Thrasea, whose death was ordered by Nero, cut the veins of each arm, poured out his blood, besprinkling the soil, and said, "Let us dedicate it to Jupiter the Liberator." Plautus' slave is another example, for he brought about his own freedom, celebrating the sacred rites of liberty, compared to which nothing is more precious.

But as Horace rightly tells us, he alone who is wise will be called free. The free man does not obey any kind of absolute dominion, including bondage to his own desires, habits, and cupidity. … In reality it is rare to find anyone truly free and able to enjoy his liberty. Chiefs, leaders, rulers all have masters and are in a servitude of the most tyrannical kind. One is a slave to lust, others to greed, anger, ambition, glory, cruelty, or all. There are as many slaves of such faults that gnaw and tear us to pieces as there are slaves of other people. We must take utmost care that there is nothing enslaving us like the tight ring in the symbol of Pythagoras. Let us live unfettered, shaking off the yoke of bad habits and addictions. Roman priests of Jove had a rule not to wear a ring unless it was pierced and hollow, without a gem. We too should put on no "ring" that binds or subjects us to anything. …

A seventh symbol of Pythagoras is that *one should not keep swallows under his own roof*. This signifies that the garrulous and talkative should be hissed off the stage and turned out of doors. Such people are a deadly influence. Horace instructs us to guard ourselves against them, for they will ruin every occasion. A Greek expression says, "Throw a babbling, prattling man out of your house." Let your intimate acquaintance be a person who understands and practices reserve in conversation. Nature gave mortals two ears but one mouth, evidently so that we should listen and hear more and talk less. Pythagoras, repudiating loquacity at all times, required his disciples to keep silence before he would teach them anything, silence being for him the preeminent beginning of wisdom. His students had to learn how to meditate, and anyone too talkative had to keep silence for five years. To follow Pythagoras' teachings we must also guard against fellowship with idle talkers, babblers, and chatterboxes, the ones whose mouths gush with worthless words, who talk profusely and carelessly, like jackdaws, with a great force of inane sounds without knowledge or judgment. These are the swallows whose chattering must be driven off, not kept under your roof. They talk not only too much but also falsely. If you throw them out or shun them, you will live more wisely and safely. It is said that those who listen are more pleasing to others than those who speak. Trogus maintained that you can distinguish in a split second whether or not a person is loquacious by looking at the size of his or her ears!

An eighth symbol of Pythagoras is "*Don't sit on a bushel*," a bushel representing a day's ration of grain. Pythagoras thereby warns us that we must think about tomorrow and take care for the future. Cicero rebukes the uncouth who continually live from hand to mouth, those who live only for the present hour or who "eat and drink as if tomorrow they will die." Such profligates defend themselves by citing, for example, a verse of Vergil's that one who takes care for the morrow will perish anyway, or one of Horace's that we should stop worrying about tomorrow and count as gain whatever Fortune deals us. Seneca, too, charged that he who depends upon tomorrow squanders today and the life it offers. Such a view is reflected on the tomb carving of Sardanapalus, which bears these words: "Eat, drink, be merry, and since you know that you are mortal, fill your soul with present delights, for after death there is no pleasure." There is even that Evangelist's sentiment, "Take therefore no thought for the morrow. … Sufficient unto the day is the evil thereof." That passage, like the others, is often used by gluttons who distort its intent to fit their viewpoint.

Instead, we can interpret this idea in coordination with Pythagoras' wiser conception. Diogenes was nicknamed an "*ephemeron*," implying "sustenance for the day," because he could live contentedly in one day with scanty and easily procured provisions. In fact, the Greeks made a famous proverb about him called "life in a wine tub." His example of thrift leads to Pythagoras' teaching to shake off sloth and torpor, and to imitate the ants, who, mindful of winter, gather provisions in the summer, and deposit them in a storehouse. As the noble Vergil says, "They carry their booty through the grass on a narrow path, some pushing the load of grain with might and main with their backs, others bringing up the rear and punishing stragglers, so the whole path swarms with their work." Good gods, how much zeal there is in such creatures; how prodigiously they work and run about! If we consider the burdens ants bear in comparison with their bodies, we have to admit that no men, proportionately, can surpass them. Wise old Solomon tells us to observe and imitate the ants, saying, "Go to the ant, O thou sluggard, and contemplate her ways ... who ... provides her food in the summer and gathers throughout the harvest what she will eat," while you, lazy one, sleep. ... "Poverty will come upon you like a vagabond, and deprivation like an armed man." We can easily find such sayings in Plautus: "A man who is lazy is worthless beyond measure, and beyond measure do I hate that sort. ... To be alert and active befits a man who wants to accomplish his goals in good season. ... He who sleeps at any time he wants will rest without gain and with misfortune. ... When you are young and have strength unimpaired, then it is fit to give your attention to anything you need." Therefore, let us live vigorously and industriously while we have the strength; let us live our youth "on the sea," so that in old age we may rest "in port" in idleness and leisure, if we want. If we comply with the symbol of Pythagoras, we will not "sit upon our bushel," not live for the day alone, nor be called "creatures of a day." But by the example of the little ant, gathering into the storehouse, we shall prepare for the future and ensure that poverty not steal upon us unforeseen. It is shameful for a sensible man to say, "I should have thought about it."

Finally, a ninth symbol of Pythagoras instructs us to *abstain from beans*. Scholars have various opinions as to why Pythagoras came to that judgment. Cicero thought that Pythagoras prohibited eating beans because they produce a great amount of gas, which destroys peace of mind. Pliny's version was that beans dull the faculty of critical perception and cause loss of sleep. Others have claimed that the souls of the dead are in beans, so those souls must be appeased, as some beggars plead even today in festivals of the dead. Varro, for example, reported that a priest would not eat them, whereas now that notion is regarded as spurious or silly. Horace, in his usual sly way, wrote that beans were "brothers" to Pythagoras, because he abstained from beans just as he would keep away from kinsmen. Another satirist speaking of Pythagoras argued that since not every legume is unpleasant to the stomach or bowels, one should not treat beans with contempt. He cited the episode of Pythagoras refusing to enter and trample upon a field of beans, even though that act resulted in his being killed by hostile persecutors.

Some commentators who are more accurate and skilled in pondering the secret teachings of Pythagoras interpret the symbolism to mean a prohibition on wanton behavior. They say that the Greek word for beans also means testicles. In truth, beans are similar in shape to genitals and especially to the penis, a similarity which Greek writers also recorded. When Pythagoras said to abstain from beans, he wished us to restrain from sexual intercourse, so that we might live chastely and be morally pure. Once, on being asked when intercourse should be engaged in, he answered, "When you wish to be made weaker and more debilitated than you are." There is a verse by Empedocles which reportedly refers to this interpretation: "Ah, wretches, take your hands away from my wretched bean!"

However, I believe sexual relations are not altogether forbidden to us, for such total abstinence would be more ruinous than overindulgence. Just as excessive sexual practice may weaken the body, too little of it may disturb the body. If sex is practiced moderately, it is not pernicious. In fact, almost nothing is more beneficial to good health than occasional sexual engagement. Galen, the great medical authority, reported that he knew men of virtue and moral purity who were so depressed by voluntary abstinence from sex that their appetite, digestion, and good health were affected. We also recall the example of Diogenes the Cynic, who was most restrained in passions by his practice of philosophy, but who used copulation as if it were a sort of purgative medicine, for health, not pleasure. … Nature dictates that excretions of the genitals need to pass out just as those of the intestines do. Seneca argued that sensual desire and expression happen unavoidably, while Aristotle and Pliny both stressed that love-making heals the enslaving gloom of the mind, the ache of the loins, and the dullness of the eyes.

We repeat that this final symbol of Pythagoras must be open to varied interpretations. Plutarch, that much-learned man and prolific writer, thought that it meant we should abstain from the management of public affairs. His argument was that from ancient times (even the iron age) the right of suffrage was carried on by means of beans. Men voted in favor of something with white beans or against it with black beans. Pythagoras' injunction can mean that we should not undertake service to the state, because that business is too troublesome and hazardous. Plutarch gave the example of Demosthenes, that pinnacle of oratory and eloquence, who ended up dissuading young men from going into politics. Demosthenes posed the scenario of two paths laid out for mortals from the beginning of life. One path led to state affairs, the other to ruin and death. If men knew the inevitable consequences for those in charge of political affairs – namely, animosities, false accusations, envy, jealousy, rivalry, hostility, and anxiety, – they would readily prefer the path that leads to certain death. Demosthenes' opinion resulted from his long experience in political life. Having been whirled about endlessly in the state affairs of Athens, and having seen at close hand what evils were there, he well knew what injuries and troubles are in store for those intending to manage the state.

Though basically in disagreement with regard to this matter, two schools of philosophers, the Epicureans and Stoics, almost came to be in agreement, each tending by a different path to the same end. Epicurus said, "A judicious man does not enter upon the service of the state, unless it interferes with him." Zeno said, "A wise man does the service of the state, unless it shackles or obstructs him." Both sects seek a certain measure of freedom or repose, one (the Epicurean) by means of a way of life, the other (the Stoic) out of just cause or necessity. I hear both sides and understand the opposing arguments. On the Stoic side, we see that a person is born to defend and protect others. It is natural to want to participate in and even manage public affairs. Since we all seek praise and honor, how can we earn greater respect than from such leadership? And because life demands action, why not engage in one of the greatest actions, namely service to the state? One clear requirement for human beings is to be good to others, if possible to many, if not, to a few. … Therefore we ask how we can best be good to others. But is it not conceivable that the best way (as the Epicureans held) may actually be to sever oneself from the troubles of management and to exile oneself into leisure?

There are two kinds of commonwealth. One is the greater, higher, communal order of being, within which both gods and men are contained. The other is the lesser, particular polity to which the condition of birth assigns us. We can see examples of differing relationships to these two commonwealths in the case of certain men, whether Roman or Athenian or Bolognan. Some give their attention to both the greater and the lesser common weal. They devote themselves to higher, universal wisdom, yet also carry on practical affairs of state or business. Others attend to the lesser order, as do senators, government officials, and civil servants. Still others serve primarily the greater order, as do philosophers and the most zealous of students. I believe we ought to give more serious attention to the greater common weal, which can better be done in leisure than in business, in free time than employment. In this higher order we can be of service to a wider community more freely, extensively, and favorably than in the lesser, practical order of local business. An educated person seeks to help the most universal community, having regard for not only those living but also his descendants and posterity.

Furthermore, I ask you which commonwealth would a wise Athenian citizen serve? The one in which Socrates was condemned? The one in which Themistocles and Aristides were shamefully maltreated with exile? Would a wise citizen serve a state whose leaders were raised on the cross through inhuman cruelty? Or the one which banished Scipio? … Rome ought to have been indebted especially to him, both for its safety and power, and ought to have rewarded his services well. But probably no state can be relied upon to tolerate for very long a wise man. … A man who follows the advice of Pythagoras to abstain from "beans," that is, from service to public affairs, may likely say, "What the people approve I do not know. What I do know is not approved by the people, and therefore I shrink from ruling the state." Pythagoras entrusted to his students the ultimate wisdom that the state should be ruled by the learned, the mature, wise, and excellent. For he saw in the state so much turbulence that he was unwilling to take the helm unless he could keep control and avoid the "rocks" of danger and evil. On account of those rocks there were many who frankly refused the purple stripe of senatorial office. Though they could see the splendor of the senatorial life, the privileges and rank, they knew their present life was calm and quiet, removed from the hurricanes of jealousies and whirlwinds of state affairs. So they chose rather to follow true happiness and walk in tranquility.

Cicero judged that the fortunate are those who, free from ambition and the zealous struggle for power, are at leisure and peace. Some of these have chosen to devote themselves to literature, which I find the greatest blessing. But some have chosen to live on the land, being delighted with rustic pleasures and the compensations of country life. If we weigh the matter thoughtfully, we realize that nothing is more fruitful than farming, nothing more worthy of a free man. Many famous writers have eagerly written in praise of such a life. … But I think Columella did it best. He accurately laid out the whole subject of life on the land, just as a superior painter portrays an entire likeness, or a sculptor expresses in every part the distinctive characteristics of an image. We should especially honor, then, his seminal description of agriculture and continually peruse his useful and delightful books. …

I hope my readers feel enlightened and stimulated by this discussion of Pythagoras. … I have embellished this essay with plenty of seasoning, for the delight and nourishment of my readers. In the manner of the ancients, we always hope to serve our guests both substance and sweets.

Just as this essay began with the symbols of Pythagoras, so must it end with his teachings – teachings which I think should be preserved in our conversations and hearts. Whoever experiences them for himself will appreciate them, for we have described ones especially pertinent for our lives, namely to avoid laziness, ignorance, the craving for luxury, discord in our homes and communities, and excess in all our conduct. These few teachings contain the whole model for living. We ought to learn them by heart, keep them firmly in mind, and observe them in our behavior. We need to believe in them as if they were an oracle of divine will sent down from heaven, as many esteemed authors have proclaimed. What representative, after all, would God be able to find more worthy than Pythagoras, through whom to write down precepts for the human race? He is so renowned for wisdom that his very name, Pythagoras the Greek, is consigned to posterity as a symbol for truth just like Apollo the Pythian. We must keep his sacred teachings and symbols perpetually in our hearts and minds, if we aspire to live honestly and happily, short of harm and censure; if, in effect, we wish that the little skiff of our life may stay securely and calmly in the port of well-being.

As for the rest, I pray to the best and greatest God that he may extend my life long enough for me to publish these commentaries, annotations, and resources both moral and sacred. My principal goal is to be of use to the learned and of service to posterity. For it is by writing, reading, and pondering that we are proven to have lived well. I have spoken.

NOTES

INTRODUCTION

1 See Christiane L. Joost-Gaugier, *Measuring Heaven: Pythagoras and His Influence on Thought and Art in Antiquity and the Middle Ages*, Ithaca and London, 2006.

2 Manuele Crisolora arrived in Venice from Constantinople in about 1394 in search of help in the struggle against the Turks; two years later he returned from his homeland to live in Florence as a teacher of Greek. The Florentine humanists Roberto Rossi and Giacomo Angeli da Scarperia expressed a desire to learn Greek, and within a few years Giacomo Angeli voyaged to Constantinople in search of Greek codices. On these years and the enthusiasm for Crysoloras in the intellectual world of Florence, see Leonardo Bruni, *Commentarius rerum suo tempore gestarum*, ed. G. B. Di Pierro, *Rerum italicarum scriptores*, n.s. 193, Bologna, 1926, 341–42; Remigio Sabbadini, *Le scoperti dei codici latini e greci ne'secoli XIV e XV* (1905), ed. Eugenio Garin, Florence, 1967, I, 43–50; Roberto Weiss, "Gli inizi dello studio del greco a Firenze," in idem, *Medieval and Humanist Greek: Collected Essays*, Padua, 1977, 227–54; and James Hankins, *Plato in the Italian Renaissance*, Leiden, New York, Copenhagen, and Cologne, 1991, I, 29–30.

3 See François Lenormant, *La Grande Grèce, Paysages et Histoire*, Paris, 1881; Franz Cumont, *Recherches sur le Symbolisme Funéraire des Romains*, Paris, 1942; Cornelia J. de Vogel, *Pythagoras and Early Pythagoreanism*, Assen, 1966; S. K. Heninger, Jr., *Touches of Sweet Harmony: Pythagorean Cosmology and Renaissance Poetics*, San Marino (Calif.), 1974; idem, *The Cosmographical Glass: Renaissance Diagrams of the Universe*, San Marino (Calif.), 1977; Michael J. B. Allen, *Nuptial Arithmetic: Marsilio Ficino's Commentary on the Fatal Number in Book VIII of Plato's Republic*, Berkeley, Los Angeles, and London, 1994; idem, *Synoptic Art*, Florence, 1998; Christopher S. Celenza, "Pythagoras in the Renaissance: The Case of Marsilio Ficino," *Renaissance Quarterly*, LII (3), 1999, 667–711; idem, *Piety and Pythagoras in Renaissance Florence*, Leiden,

2001; Rudolf Wittkower, *Architectural Principles in the Age of Humanism* (1940), 2nd ed., London, 1952; André Chastel, *L'Art et Humanisme a Florence au Temps de Laurent le Magnifique*, Paris, 1959; George L. Hersey, *Pythagorean Palaces: Magic and Architecture in the Italian Renaissance*, Ithaca and London, 1976; J. V. Field, *Piero della Francesca: A Mathematician's Art*, New Haven and London, 2005; and Eileen Reeves, *Painting the Heavens: Art and Science in the Age of Galileo*, Princeton, 1997.

4 See, e.g., Brian P. Copenhaver, *Iamblichus, Synesius and the Chaldaean Oracles in Marsilio Ficino's De vita libri tres*, Binghamton (N.Y.), 1987; idem, *Natural Magic, Hermetism, and Occultism in Early Modern Science*, Cambridge, 1990; idem, *Magic and the Dignity of Man: De-Kanting Pico's Oration*, Florence, 2002; Allen G. Debus, *Man and Nature in the Renaissance*, Cambridge, 1978; Hankins, *Plato in the Italian Renaissance*; idem, *Chrysoloras and the Greek Studies of Leonardo Bruni*, Naples, 2002; idem, *Humanism and Platonism in the Italian Renaissance*, Rome, 2003–4 (2 vols.); Marsilio Ficino, *The Platonic Theology of Marsilio Ficino*, ed. James Hankins and William Bowen, trans. Michael J. B. Allen and John Warden, Cambridge (Mass.), 2001–6 (6 vols.); John Monfasani, "Platonic Paganism in the Fifteenth Century," in *Reconsidering the Renaissance*, ed. Mario A. Di Cesare, Binghamton, (N.Y.), 1992, 45–61; idem, *Byzantine Scholars in Renaissance Italy: Cardinal Bessarion and Other Émigrés*, Aldershot and Burlington, 1995; idem, *Greeks and Latins in Renaissance Italy*, Aldershot and Burlington, 2004; Pier Daniele Napolitani and Pierre Souffrin, eds., *Medieval and Classical Traditions and the Renaissance of Physico-Mathematical Sciences in the 16th Century*, Turnhout, 2001; Paul Lawrence Rose, *The Italian Renaissance of Mathematics*, Geneva, 1975; and Wayne Shumaker, *The Occult Sciences in the Renaissance*, Berkeley, Los Angeles, and London, 1972.

5 Vitruvius Pollio, *De architectura*, V, proem 3. (See Vitruvius, *Ten Books on Architecture*, ed. Ingrid D. Rowland, Rome, 2003.) Vitruvius wrote in the first century B.C.

6   For a lucid discussion of this subject, see F. M. Cornford, "Mysticism and Science in the Pythagorean Tradition," *Classical Quarterly*, XVII, 1923 (part 2), 1–12.

7   Vitruvius Pollio, *De architectura*, IX.vi. This theorem had previously been published by Euclid (*Elements*, I.xlvii), though Euclid did not attribute it to Pythagoras.

8   Regarding reports of the persecution of Pythagoras and his followers, see Diogenes Laertius, *Lives of Eminent Philosophers*, VIII.40. Lucian of Samosata mocked Pythagoras's golden thigh and had Pythagoras admit he no longer possessed it (*Dialogues of the Dead*, 415).

9   On this, see esp. Martianus Capella, *De nuptiis Mercurii et Philologiae* (known in English as *The Marriage of Philology and Mercury*, ed. William Harris Stahl, New York, 1977), a work that served as the foundation for explaining the Seven Liberal Arts in the Middle Ages, when it was widely used as a schoolbook. (See esp. ibid., secs. 11 and 924, which describe Apollo as the inventor of the lyre and of harmony and as the master of Parnassus.) See also Plutarch, *On Music*. 1135, where Apollo is cited as the inventor of music. On the popularity of Martianus's fantasy, in which Apollo reigns, see William Harris Stahl, *Martianus Capella and the Seven Liberal Arts*, New York, 1971. On the Muses, see esp. Iamblichus of Chalcis, *De vita Pythagorica liber*, ed. Ludwig Deubner (1937), rev. ed. Ulrich Klein, Stuttgart, 1975 (hereinafter *Vita Pythagorica*), 9; see also the English translation of Gillian Clark, in idem, *On the Pythagorean Way of Life*, Liverpool, 1989 (esp. at 18).

10 The importance of ancient Greek commentators on Pythagorean mathematics is discussed in Wilbur Richard Knorr, *Textual Studies in Ancient and Medieval Geometry*, Boston, Basel, and Berlin, 1989, esp. 4–9.

11 On the Druids and their Pythagoreanism, see Joost-Gaugier, *Measuring Heaven*, chs. 112–16.

12 This is from Thierry of Chartres's *Heptateuchon* (*Seven Books*), a work of the twelfth century; the only surviving manuscript was destroyed in a bombardment of Chartres in 1941. On it, see Édouard Jeauneau, *L'Âge d'or des Écoles de Chartres*, Chartres, 1995, 65–71 and 80. See also Martianus Capella, *The Marriage of Philology and Mercury*, passim.

13 On the philosophical cosmology of Pythagoras as interpreted in the *Timaeus*, see P. F. M. Fontaine, *The Light and the Dark: A Cultural History of Dualism*, Amsterdam, 1986, I, esp. 21–31.

14 On the protests of Albertus Magnus respecting this doctrine, see Lynn Thorndike, *A History of Magic and Experimental Science*, II, New York, 1929, 566.

15 See, e.g., the anonymous manuscript entitled *Prenostica Pitagorice*, in Oxford (*Digby.46*).

16 Though some medieval writers suggested that ecclesiastical structures faced east because they looked toward Jerusalem, the tradition that Pythagoras respected the sun (Apollo) is much older. This is reflected in ancient Pythagorean maxims that insist on respect for the rising sun, as well as in the fact that ancient Pythagorean places of worship appear to have been oriented toward the east (on this, see Joost-Gaugier, *Measuring Heaven*, chs. 9 and 12).

17 The notion of a numerically derived musical scale constructed entirely by adding and subtracting octaves (2:1), fifths (3:2), and fourths (4:3) to and from one another increasingly gave way to a scale with the next-smaller interval of the major third tuned so as to produce this pleasing harmony. Expressed numerically, this was understood as the "Pythagorean third."

18 In contradistinction, number 12 ($1 + 2 + 3 + 4 + 6 = 16$) is not perfect, for the sum of its divisors is different from 12, as is also the case for 16 ($1 + 2 + 4 + 8 = 15$).

ONE: PROLOGUE

1   On the medieval knowledge of Plato, see James Hankins, "Plato in the Middle Ages," in *Dictionary of the Middle Ages*, New York, 1987, IX, 694–704.

2   An example of this can be seen in the correspondence between Poggio Bracciolini and Nicolo Nicoli, two of the most active early humanists engaged in the search for texts that had been lost for centuries and were known only through mentions or quotations by other authors. Such a collection of letters expressing the zeal for literary discovery is published in Phyllis W. G. Gordan, *Two Renaissance Book Hunters: The Letters of Poggius Bracciolini to Nicolaus de Niccolis*, New York, 1974.

3   See Deno J. Geanakoplos, *Greek Scholars in Venice: Studies in the Dissemination of Greek Learning from Byzantium to Western Europe*, Cambridge (Mass.), 1962, 279ff. See also Giuseppe Cammelli, *I dotti Bizantini e le origini dell'umanesimo*, Florence, 1941–54 (4 vols.); and James Hankins, "Lo studio del greco in Occidente fra medioevo ed età moderna," *I Greci: Storia, cultura, arte, società*, ed. Salvatore Settis, Turin, III, 2001, 1245–62.

4   On this conference, first convened in Ferrara and moved to Florence, with Pope Eugenius IV presiding, see esp. Joseph Gill, *The Council of Florence*, New York, 1982; also see Luca D'Ascia, "Bessarione al Concilio di Firenze," in *Bessarione e l'umanesimo*, cat., ed. Gianfranco Fiaccadori, Naples, 1994, 67–79.

5   There is a vast literature on the Greek diaspora in the West. See, e.g., Geanakoplos, *Greek Scholars in Venice*.

6   The words of Michael Apostolis, a Byzantine copyist and manuscript collector, are recorded from a discourse of the 1450s in Geanakoplos, *Greek Scholars in Venice*, 109 (trans. Geanakopolos).

7   See, e.g., important early printed editions of Vitruvius in *L. Victrvvii Pollionis De architectura*, ed. Io. Svlpitivs, Rome, 1486; *L. Vitrvvii Pollionis ad Caesarem agvstvm De architectura*, Venice, 1497; and *L. Vitruuii Pollionis*

De architectura libri decem, ed. Fra Giocondo, Venice, 1511. For Cicero, see, e.g., *In M. T. Ciceronis de somnio Scipionis*, ed. Petri Olivarii, Basel, 1538. Examples of Martianus Capella can be found in *Martiani Capelle de nuptijs Philologie & Mercurij libri duo*, ed. Henricvm de Sancto Vrso, Vicenza, 1499; *Martiai Capellae De nvptiis Philologiae et Mercvrii Liberi dvo*, ed. Dionysiu Berthocum, Modena, 1500; and *M. Capella Martiani Minei Capella Carthaginensis De nuptijs Philologiae & Septem artibus liberalibus libri novem*, ed. Haeredes Simonis Vincentij, Lvgdvni, 1539. Important editions of Boethius included *Arithmetica Boetij*, ed. Erhardum Ratdolt, Augsburg, 1488; *Epitome in libros arithmeticos* and *Elementa musica*, ed. Jacobi Fabri Stapulensis, Paris, 1510; *Diviseverini Boetii Arithmetica*, ed. Simonem Colinaeum, Paris, 1521; *Iacobi Fabri Stapulensis in Arithmetica Boëthi epitome …* , ed. Henrichvm Petri, Basel, 1553; and *Anitii Manlii Severini Boethi philosophorvm et theologorvm principis opera omnia*, ed. Henricvs Petrina, Basel, 1570. A luxurious French manuscript edition of Pompeius Trogus appeared as late as 1500 in *Justinus, epitome in Trogi Pompeii historias* (Cambridge, Mass., *Houghton MS. typ. 123*).

8   For a partial list of fifteenth-century translations of Ovid's *Metamorphoses*, see R. R. Bolgar, *The Classical Heritage and Its Beneficiaries* (1954), Cambridge, 1977, 530–33.

9   A manuscript of Philo's works was brought to Florence in 1425, perhaps by the humanist Aurispa; within two years another was brought there by another humanist, Filelfo. (On these and later manuscripts of Philo, see Bolgar, *Classical Heritage*, 482.) On Domninus of Larissa, a Syrian fifth-century mathematician known for gorging himself with pork in order to prevent disease, and his appearance in fifteenth-century manuscripts, see Domninos de Larissa, *Le Manuel d'Introduction Arithmétique du Philosophe Domninos de Larissa*, ed. Paul Tannery, in *Mémoires Scientifiques: Sciences Exactes dans l'Antiquité*, Paris and Toulouse, 1915, III, 255–85. Respecting the body of theological-philosophical texts known collectively as the *Hermetica* (comprising primarily the Greek *Corpus Hermeticum* and the Latin *Asclepius*), which were probably composed in the first century A.D., see Copenhaver, *Hermetica: The Greek Corpus Hermeticum and the Latin Asclepius …* , Cambridge, 1992. The full text of the *Mysteries of Egypt* attributed to Iamblichus can be found in *Jamblique: Les Mystères d'Égypte*, ed. Édouard des Places, Paris, 2003. The *Mysteries of Egypt* have an extensive publishing record during the Renaissance. Respecting the history of editions of Hermetic manuscripts, the earliest of which dates from the eleventh century (Brussels, Koninklijke Bibliotheek 10054–10056) and the *Mysteries of Egypt*, see Joost R. Ritman, ed., *Bibliotheka Philosophica Hermetica Hermes Trismegistus Pater Philosophorum*, Amsterdam, 1990. Regarding the introduction of a Greek manuscript of the *Corpus Hermeticum* to Florence in 1460,

see Shumaker, *Occult Sciences in the Renaissance*, 201–2.

10   An excellent study of literary life in the late fourteenth and early fifteenth centuries is provided in Elisabeth Pellegrin, *Bibliothèques Retrouvées: Manuscrits, Bibliothèques et Bibliophiles du Moyen Âge et de la Renaissance*, Paris, 1988.

11   Numerous editions were published well into the sixteenth century throughout Europe, e.g., *Aureorum carminvm Pythagore versio*, ed. Prigenti Calvarini, Paris, 1539; *Avrea dicta Pythagorae*, ed. M. Georgium Prechtium Rotenpurgensem, Vienna, 1558; and *Carmina aurea*, ed. Michaelis Neandri, Leipzig, 1559.

TWO: THE EMERGENCE OF "SAINT" PYTHAGORAS IN THE EARLY RENAISSANCE

1   Coluccio Salutati, *De laboribus Hercules*, ed. Berthold L. Ullman, Zurich, 1951, II, 182, 189, and 572. On Coluccio Salutati's importance for Florence and his seminal influence on his successors in the world of Florentine historical literature, see esp. the collection of works presented in Stefano Ugo Baldassarri and Arielle Saiber, *Images of Quattrocento Florence*, New Haven and London, 2000. The two paths suggested by the letter "Y" were first discussed by the Pythagorean Parmenides of Elea in the sixth century B.C. and repeated many times thereafter, including by Saint Jerome.

2   Salutati, *De laboribus Hercules*, 25–27, 32, and 48.

3   Salutati, *De laboribus Hercules*, 172 and 259. Salutati also discusses the relationship between Pythagoras and his teacher Pherecydes (Coluccio Salutati, *De fato et fortuna* [ca. 1396–1400], III.4.54–55, ed. Concetta Bianca, Florence, 1985, 137).

4   Salutati, *De laboribus Hercules*, 120.

5   The words of fellow humanist Poggio Bracciolini are quoted (and trans.) in *The Humanism of Leonardo Bruni: Selected Texts*, ed. Gordon Griffiths, James Hankins, and David Thompson, Binghamton (N.Y.), 1987, 44 (hereinafter Griffiths et al.).

6   Bruni's translations from the Greek are summarized in James Hankins, "Leonardo Bruni," in *Encyclopedia of the Renaissance*, New York, 1999, I, 302–3.

7   Leonardo Bruni, *Dialogi ad Petrum Histrum (Dialogues Dedicated to Pier Paolo Vergerio)* (1405–6), ed. Garin, rep. in Griffiths et al., *Humanism of Leonardo Bruni*, 70. Much information about Bruni is provided by his contemporary, the celebrated Florentine bookseller Vespasiano da Bisticci (*The Vespasiano Memoirs: Lives of Illustrious Men of the XVth Century*, trans. William George and Emily Waters (1926), ed. Renaissance Society of America, Toronto, 1997, hereinafter cited as *Lives*, 358–69). The most complete modern biography of Bruni is that of Francesco Paolo Luiso, *Studi su l'epistolario di Leonardo Bruni*, ed. Lucia Gualdo Rosa, Rome, 1980.

8   Bruni, *De studiis et literis*, or *On the Study of Literature*, 1424, in Griffiths et al., *Humanism of Leonardo Bruni*, 247.

9   Bruni, *Letter to Lauro Quirini*, in Griffiths et al., *Humanism of Leonardo Bruni*, 295 (trans. Griffiths et al.).

10   The research spirit and zest of Poggio for communication about antique texts and ruins are revealed in his prolific correspondence. See Gordan, *Two Renaissance Book Hunters*. See also the vita of him in Vespasiano da Bisticci, *Lives*, 351–58.

11   The passage quoted is from *De nobilitate*, in Poggios Bracciolini, *Opera omnia*, ed. Riccardo Fubini, Turin, 1964, I, 66. On Pythagoras as an arbiter of social responsibility, see a letter by Poggio concerning the study of literature, whose full text is published in William Harrison Woodward, *Vittorino da Feltre and Other Humanist Educators*, Cambridge, 1963, 129.

12   See Pier Paolo Vergerio, in two letters dating from 1399 and 1400, in Vergerio, *Epistolario*, ed. Leonardo Smith, Rome, 1934, 405 and 424–25.

13   Trans. Carolyn Tuttle, from a letter Valla wrote at Gaeta in 1437 (*Laurentii Valle epistole*, ed. Ottavio Besomi and Mariangela Regoliosi, Padua, 1984, 164).

14   See esp. the preface of Valla's *Dialecticarum disputationum* in *Laurentius Valla Opera omnia*, ed. Eugenio Garin, Turin, 1962, I, 643–44; and the proemio to *De rebus a Ferdinando gestis*, in ibid., II, 5.

15   Trans. Carolyn Tuttle from Francesco Filelfo, *Epistula de opinionibus philosophorum* … , in Hankins, *Plato in the Italian Renaissance*, II, 515–23.

16   Filelfo, *Epistula de opinionibus philosophorum*, passim.

17   For the full text of this Latin work, whose relevant parts are summarized here, see Diana Robin, *Filelfo in Milan*, Princeton, 1991, esp. 226–42.

18   Cyriaco of Ancona, *Diary II*, in *Cyriac of Ancona, Later Travels*, ed. and trans. Edward W. Bodnar with Clive Foss, Cambridge (Mass.), 2003, 125.

19   Cyriaco of Ancona, *Letter 30*, in *Cyriac of Ancona*, 219.

20   Flavio Biondo, *Roma trionfante, tradotta per hora per Lucio Fauno di latino in buona lingua* (1482), Venice, 1548, 16–17.

21   This building is the subject of ch. 10 in Joost-Gaugier, *Measuring Heaven*.

22   Pliny the Elder, *Historia naturalibus*, II.vi.

23   Antonio Averlino Filarete, *Treatise on Architecture*, XIX, ed. and trans. John R. Spencer, New Haven and London, 1965, I, 260 and 266.

24   Marcus Fabius Quintilianus (Quintilian), *Institutio oratoria*, ed. Adriano Pennacini, Turin, 2001, I.x.32.

25   Aeneas Sylvius Piccolomini, *The Education of Boys*, in *Humanist Educational Treatises*, ed. and trans. Craig W. Kallendorf, Cambridge (Mass.) and London, 2002.

26   Pletho's alleged neopaganism is discussed by Monfasani in "Platonic Paganism in the Fifteenth Century," 45–46.

27   On Pletho's philosophical and political influence, see François Masai, *Pléthon et le Platonisme de Mistra*, Paris, 1956; and Christopher M. Woodhouse, *George Gemistos Plethon: The Last of the Hellenes*, Oxford, 1986.

28   George Gemistus Pletho, *Treatise on Law*, in Jacques-Paul Migne, *Patrologia Graeca, cursus completus* (hereinafter *Patrologia Graeca*), Paris, 1866, CLX, 958–74. The full surviving text is published in an annotated Greek and French edition in *Pléthon. Traité des Lois*, ed. Charles Alexandre, trans. A. Pellissier, Paris, 1858. It should be noted that this work, originally very large, survives only in fragments. See also an English translation in Woodhouse, *Plethon*, 322–56.

29   These views are expressed esp. in Books I and III of *Treatise on Law*.

30   Pletho, *Contra Scholarii defensionem Aristotelis* (*Reply to Scholarius*) in Migne, *Patrologia Graeca*, CLX, 979–1020, for full text. See also as quoted in Masai, *Pléthon et le Platonisme de Mistra*, 136; and Polymnia Athanassiadi, "Psellos and Plethon on the Chaldean Oracles," in *Byzantine Philosophy and Its Ancient Sources*, ed. Katerina Ierodoakonou, Oxford, 2002, esp. 248–61. Cf. Pletho, *Magica Zoroastri oracvla Plethonis Commentariis enarrata*, ed. Iacobo Marthano, Paris, 1539, passim.

31   George Gemistus Pletho, *De differentis* (1540), passim, esp. 26, 37, and 42 (see English translation in Woodhouse, *Pletho*, 191–214).

32   Woodhouse, *Pletho*, 221.

33   The comments of George Scholarius are quoted in Hankins, *Plato in the Italian Renaissance*, II, 437.

34   Woodhouse, *Pletho*, 158–70.

35   Cardinal Bessarion, *Adversus calumniatorem Platonis*, ed. Conradus Sweynheym and Arnoldus Pannartz, Rome, 1468 (no pp.). The passages discussed here are from Book I of this text. On this work, see esp. Henri Vast, *Le Cardinal Bessarion*, Paris, 1878, passim.

36   This letter was described by Diogenes Laertius as discussed in Chapter 1. Iamblichus quoted it in its entirety in *Vita Pythagorica*, 17.

37   An important biography of Nicholas Cusanus was written shortly after his death by another mathematician; see Bernardino Baldi, "Nicolò di Cusa," in *Le vite de' matematici* (1589), ed. Elio Nenci, Milan, 1998, 255–71. These quotes are from *De docta ignorantia* (*On Learned Ignorance*), an early masterwork by Cusanus, completed in 1440, that explored the quest to know God and understand divinity. Translation from Nicholas Cusanus, *Nicholas of Cusa on Learned Ignorance*, ed. and trans. Jasper Hopkins, Minneapolis, 1981, 56 and 58).

38   Cusanus frequently refers to the authority of Pythagoras on number and numerical symbology in *De docta ignorantia*. The quoted passage is by Hopkins in *Nicholas Cusa*, 59. See other passages on the significance of Pythagoras for number in other works by Cusanus, e.g., *De la caccia de la sapienza* (*The Hunt for Wisdom*), in *Toward a New Council of Florence, On the Peace of Faith, and Other Works by Nicholas of Cusa*, ed. William Wertz, Jr., Washington D.C., 1993.

39 Leon Battista Alberti, *Leonis Baptiste Alberti De re aedificatoria*, Florence, 1485, VIII.xvii and IX.v. For an English translation, see idem, *On the Art of Building in Ten Books*, trans. Joseph Rykwert, Neil Leach, and Robert Tavernor, Cambridge (Mass.), 1988, 241, and, for quoted passage, 305.

40 Alberti, *Momus*, III.58–59 (see new ed., ed. Virginia Brown and Sarah Knight, Cambridge [Mass.] and London, 2003, 257–59).

41 Cristoforo Landino, *Prolusione Dantesca*, I.6, in Roberto Cardini, *La critica del Landino*, Florence, 1973, 238; *Praefatio in Tusculanis*, in Cristoforo Landino, *Scritti critici e teorici*, ed. Roberto Cardini, Rome, 1974, I, 13; idem, *Orazione … quando cominciò a leggere le comedia di Dante*, in Cardini, *Scritti critici*, 46; idem, *Apologia nella quale si difende Dante e Florenzia da' falsi calunniatori*, in Cardini, *Scritti critici*, 143; idem, *Commento Dantesco*, in Cardini *Scritti critici*, II, 304; and idem, *Disputationum camaldulensium*, I, preface (Landino, *Disputationes camaldulenses*, ed. Peter Lohe, Florence, 1980, 60–61).

42 Marsilio Ficino, *De laudibus philosophiae* (ca. 1455), as quoted in Hankins, *Plato in the Italian Renaissance*, 460–61, n. 4. For the full text of most of Ficino's prolific writings, see Marsilio Ficino, *Opera omnia*, ed. Henrico Petrina, Basel, 1561–76 (rep. ed. Paul Oskar Kristeller, Turin, 1959, 2 vols.); also idem, *Svpplementvm Ficinianvm: Marsilii Ficini Florentini Opvscvla inedita et dispersa*, ed. Paul Oskar Kristeller, Florence, 1937, 2 vols.

43 This work survives in two fourteenth-century Greek manuscripts. The one known to Ficino (Hermes Trismegistus, *Poimandres*, now in the Biblioteca Medici at San Lorenzo in Florence) appeared in Florence in 1460 when a monk, who had acquired it in Macedonia, brought it to Cosimo de'Medici. The other is in Paris (same author and title, *Bib. Nat. Par. Graecus 1220*). On these, see Ritman, *Bibliotheka Philosophica Hermetica*, 50–53; on the background of the Florentine manuscript, see Shumaker, *Occult Sciences in the Renaissance*, 201.

44 For Ficino's translation into Latin, see *Liber de potestate et sapientia Dei tradvctus a Marsilio Ficino [in Poimandrem]*, *BAV.Cod.Vat.Lat.1009*, fol. 2r. On this, see the comments of Copenhaver, *Hermetica*, xlvii–xlvii.

45 Marsilio Ficino, *Commentary on Plato's Philebus*, XVII and XXVI (see *Marsilio Ficino: The Philebus Commentary*, ed. Michael J. B. Allen, Tempe [Ariz.], 2000, 180 and 246).

46 Ficino, *Theologia Platonica*, V.i, VI.i, and IX.i. (For two modern editions of this work, see *Marsile Ficin Théologie Platonicienne de l'Immortalité des Ames*, ed. Raymond Marcel, Paris, 1964, 3 vols.; and *Platonic Theology* ed. Hankins and Bowen, 6 vols.).

47 Ficino, *Theologia Platonica*, XIII and XI.v.

48 Ficino, *Theologia Platonica*, XII.i.

49 Diogenes Laertius, *Lives of Eminent Philosophers*, VIII.41. In this passage, Diogenes Laertius does not refer to ten years, though in another (cf. ibid., VIII.14)

he says that Pythagoras spent 207 years in Hades before returning to life.

50 Marsilio Ficino, *Theologia Platonica*, IV.i. Respecting the adventures of the soul and its Antique literary background in the works of Porphyry, Iamblichus, and Plotinus (all authors well known to Ficino), see esp. Franz V. Cumont, *Lux Perpetua*, Paris, 1949, esp. 372–80.

51 Ficino, *Theologia Platonica*, XIII.ii, XIII.ii, XIII.iv, XIV.viii, and XV.iii. Cf. also Diogenes Laertius, *Lives of Eminent Philosophers*, I.10.109; Porphyry, *Life of Pythagoras* (in *Porphyrii philosophi Platonici opuscula tria*, ed. Augustus Nauck, Leipzig, 1860), 29–30; Iamblichus, *Vita Pythagorica*, 27 and 28; and Macrobius, *Commentary on the Dream of Scipio*, trans. William Harris Stahl, New York, 1952, II.ii.

52 Ficino, *Theologia Platonica*, XV.vii, XVII.iv, and XVII.viii.

53 This controversy was primarily centered on the publication of *De immortalitate*, a work claiming that the human soul was mortal rather than immortal, by the Italian philosopher Pietro Pomponazzi. Because the immortality of the soul had, by this time, already been accepted as doctrine, Pomponazzi and his works (which attempted to follow Aristotle literally and which ridiculed Pythagoras for believing in transmigration of souls) was denounced throughout Italy.

54 Ficino collected the letters he wrote to others, organized them, wrote prefatory titles to them, and published them in twelve books that were first printed in Venice in 1495 and subsequently reprinted in Florence, Nuremburg, and Basel. For a translation of these into English, see *The Letters of Marsilio Ficino*, ed. Paul Oskar Kristeller, trans. Dept. of the School of Economic Science, London, 1975 (6 vols.) Unless otherwise noted in the case of quotes, the following paragraphs refer to these volumes, hereinafter, *Letters*.

55 Ficino, *Letters*, I, no. 109.

56 Ficino, *Letters*, I, no. 109.

57 Ficino, *Letters*, II, no. 12, and V, no. 48.

58 See, e.g., *Letters*, VI, no. 18.

59 Ficino, *Libro di Marsilio Ficino Fiorentineo della Christiana religione*, ed. Lorenzo Fiorentini and Seragno Fiorentini, Pisa, 1484, chs. 2 and 26 (no pp.). Ficino notes, in a general way, his sources: Aristobulus, Numenius, Ambrose, Eusebius, and Origen. This work, first published in 1482, appeared again in 1500.

60 See Arthur M. Lesley, Jr., *The Song of Solomon's Ascents by Yohanan Alemanno*, Ann Arbor, 1976, 10–12.

61 Planned for the opening of the convention on this subject that Pico called in Rome, the Oration was never actually delivered because of papal interference; but it was published posthumously in 1496.

62 Pico della Mirandola, *De hominis dignitate*, in *Opera omnia*, Basel, 1557, 320–21.

63 Pico della Mirandola, *De hominis dignitate*, 326–28.

64 Pico della Mirandola, *De hominis dignitate*, esp. 330–31. For translation, see idem, *On the Dignity of*

Man, On Being and the One, Heptaplus, ed. and trans. Charles Glenn Wallis, Paul J. W. Miller, and Douglas Carmichael, Indianapolis (1940), 1965, 32.

65 For the original text, see Pico della Mirandola, *Conclusiones sive Theses DCCCC*, ed. Bohdan Kieszkowski, Geneva, 1973. Two recent editions of this work are accompanied by particularly useful commentaries and notes. See idem, *Conclusiones nongentae*, ed. Albano Biondi, Florence, 1995 (Italian); and idem, *Syncretism in the West: Pico's 900 Theses (1486)*, ed. S. A. Farmer, Tempe (Ariz.), 1998 (English).

66 See the Farmer edition cited in n. 65, 335–37. Cf. Brian Copenhaver ("L'Occulto in Pico," in *Giovanni Pico della Mirandola: Convegno internazionale …*, ed. Gian Carlo Garfagnini, Florence, 1997, 234–35), who explains its likely Kabbalistic interpretation.

67 See the last part of the *Conclusiones* at III.25 and XI.10.

68 See Pico della Mirandola, *Heptaplus*, in *Opera omnia*, 1 and 37; also idem, *Disputationum in astrologiam (Dispute Against Astrology)*, in ibid. at 414 and 730. The latter work was published with important commentary as *Disputationum adversus astrologos*, ed. Eugenio Garin, Florence, 1943, I, 47; and II, 529–31. On fifteenth-century astrology, see esp. Garin, *Astrology in the Renaissance* (1976), trans. Carolyn Jackson and June Allen, London, 1983.

69 Pico, *Epistole*, in *Opera omnia*, 353.

70 Angelo Poliziano, *Silvae (Ambra)*, lines 535–57. See the edition of this work by Francesco Bausi (Florence, 1996), together with commentaries on these lines at 152 and 154; also *Angelo Poliziano Silvae*, ed. Charles Fantazzi, Cambridge (Mass.), 2004. See also *Praefatio in expositione Homeri* in *Angeli Politiani Opera, qvae qvidem extite … *, Basel, 1553, 484 and 485. See also idem, *Collectanea in enarrationem fastorum (1481)* in idem, *Commento inedito ai Fasti di Ovidio*, ed. Francesco Lo Monaco, Florence, 1991, esp. 9 and 240.

71 Poliziano, *Collectanea in enarrationem fastorum … *, esp. 17, 48, 62, and 236.

72 Constantinus Lascaris, *De scriptoribus Graecis patria calabaris* in *Constantini Lascaris Epistola ad Joannem Gatum …* (in Migne, *Patrologiae Graeca*, CLXI, 1866, 923–25; also 925–28).

73 On the life of Constantinus Lascaris, who was appointed to teach in Messina by Cardinal Bessarion, see the introduction of J. J. Fraenkel to Lascaris, *Greek Grammar (1476)*, trans. C. M. Breuning-Williamson, Amsterdam, 1966, 3–21.

74 Polydore Vergil, *De inventoribus rerum (On Discovery)*. See a recent edition of this work in idem, *On Discovery*, ed. and trans. Brian Copenhaver, Cambridge (Mass.), 2002, esp. the following passages: I.I.3, I.III.1, I.IX.2, I.XVI.2–3, I.XVII.3 and 7, I.XVIII.3, I.XIX.2, II.I.6, III.V.1, III.XIV.3, and III.XVII.11. The last passage is quoted from the translation of Copenhaver.

75 See, e.g., Philippi Calandri, *Aritmetica*, ed. Lorenzo de Morgiani and Giovanni Thedesco da Maganza, Florence, 1491. This volume, republished in 1492 and

1518, was the first printed Italian arithmetic with illustrations accompanying problems. The frontispiece shows a woodcut of Pythagoras titled "Pictagoras arithmetrice introductor."

76 Lancinus Curtius (d. 1511), "Poem," 50–56. For full text see Franchino Gaffurio, *The Theory of Music*, ed. Claude V. Palisca, ed. and trans. Walter K. Kreyszig, New Haven and London, 1993, 189–95.

77 Respecting Ockeghem of Flanders, see Howard Mayer Brown, *Music in the Renaissance*, Englewood Cliffs (N.J.), 1976, 80–81. For the music and text (a signed work of the composer) of Busnoys, entitled *In Hydraulis*, see *Antoine Busnoys Collected Works*, ed. Richard Taruskin, New York, 1990, parts II and III, 151–65 and 74–80, respectively.

78 Franchino Gaffurius (hereinafter Gaffurio), *Theoricum opus musice discipline*, Milan, 1492, I.1.250, 258; 2.37, 41, 54; 3.30, 61; and 8.34 (see *Theoricum opus musice discipline*, ed. Cesarino Ruini, Bologna, 1996 for a facsimile ed. of this work). For an English edition see idem, *The Theory of Music*.

79 Completed in 1500, this work was known in several manuscript editions prior to its publication in 1518. The first of many printed editions was *De harmonia musicorum instrumentorum opus*, published in Milan in 1518. See Franchino Gaffurio, *De harmonia musicorum instrumentorum opus*, ed. Clement A. Miller, Stuttgart, 1979. The quotation is from I.5 of this work (trans. Miller).

80 Gaffurio, *De harmonia musicorum instrumentorum opus* (trans. Miller), I.5.

81 Gaffurio, *De harmonia musicorum instrumentorum opus* (trans. Miller), II.39.

82 Gaffurio, *Theoricum opus musice discipline*, I.8.

83 Francesco Patrizi, *Compendiosa epitome commentariorum Francisci Patritii senensis episcopi*, ed. Hiérosme de Marnef, Paris, 1577, 28, 30, and 32; idem, *De regno et regis institutione*, Paris, 1519, 7, 97–98, 174, and 253.

84 Giovanni Garzoni da Bologna, *Laus medicinae* (or *Oratio in laudem medicine*), as quoted in Pearl Kibre, *Studies in Medieval Science: Alchemy, Astrology, Mathematics and Medicine*, London 1984, XIX.504–XIX.514 (at XIX.513).

85 This subject is discussed in Joost-Gaugier, *Measuring Heaven*, esp. chs. 7 and 11 (with bibliography). The origin of this design can be traced at least to late-Antique ivories (Roger Billoret, "Circonscription de Lorraine," *Gallia*, XXVIII, 1970, 308 and fig. 41); on their later manifestations, see Thorndike, *History of Magic and Experimental Science*, esp. vols. II and III, passim.

86 In a typical *Turba*, the assembly convened by the Master, Pythagoras, includes many eminent ancient authorities, such as Anaximander, Plato, and Socrates, who issue pronouncements and divulge recipes. See, e.g., *Turba philosophorum*, ed. Julius Ruska (1931), rep. Berlin, 1970.

87 See, e.g., a fifteenth-century manuscript of the *Turba philosophorum* in *Paris. Bib. Nat. MS. Fr. 19978*, which

contains as well other alchemical works. See also a
late fifteenth-century compendium of alchemy compiled by Arnaldus Lishout De Bruxella (d. ca. 1492)
in Bethlehem, Pa. (*Lehigh Univ. Ms. No. 1*). This work
comprises more than three hundred recipes and diagrams and specifically mentions "Pichtagoras" as a
master of magic (fol. 163v). Cf., generally, *Catalogue of
Alchemical MSS*, in *Osiris*, VI, Bruges, 1939 (ed. George
Sarton and Alexander Pogo).

88 Early editions of the collection of Hermetic texts
(*Corpus Hermeticum*) and their introduction and dis-
semination in Italy are discussed in Shumaker, *Occult
Sciences in the Renaissance*, esp. 53–54 and 200–202. On
this subject, see also Thorndike, *History of Magic and
Experimental Sciences*, III, passim.

89 See Iamblichus, *Les Mystères d'Égypte*, 39–41.

90 This work, which circulated in manuscript form, was
published by Alfredo Perifano, in *Documents oubliés sur
l'Alchimie, la Kabbale et Guillaume Postel* (hon. François
Secret), ed. Sylvain Matton, Geneva, 2001, 81–102, esp.
91.

91 See, e.g., Anon., *Sumari und ausszug von dem furnemes-
ten ...* , Washington, D.C., *Cath. Univ. of America MS.
129*, German, late fifteenth century, fol. lv: "so hat
auch Pythagoras seinen jungern verpotten was er sy
in den schuel von hochen khunsten wurd lerrnen,
das sy das nicht unter des gemain volckh pringen."

92 See a poem (1476) by Frate Migir quoted in Arturo
Graf, *Roma nella memoria e nelle immaginazioni del
medio evo* (1923), Bologna, 1987, 510. This refers to
Pythagoras as one of several "grandes estrologos."

93 See esp. Pietro Pomponazzi, *De imortalitate*, VIII (and
comments of Randall in *The Renaissance Philosophy
of Man*, ed. Ernst Cassirer, Paul Oskar Kristeller, and
John H. Randall, Jr., Chicago, 1948, 257–79 and
307–9).

94 Bruni, *Letter to Lauro Quirini*, in Griffiths et al.,
Humanism of Leonardo Bruni, 295.

95 These concepts, most prominent in the late Antique
works of Macrobius and Cassiodorus, and cited in
that of Christodorus of Thebes, are discussed in
Joost-Gaugier, *Measuring Heaven*, esp. ch. 4.

THREE: THE APOTHEOSIS OF PYTHAGORAS IN
THE SIXTEENTH CENTURY

1 On this see John F. D'Amico, *Renaissance Humanism in
Papal Rome*, Baltimore and London, 1983, 115–17.

2 Since the work of Arnaldo Della Torre (*Storia
dell'accademia Platonica di Firenze*, Florence, 1902),
many have assumed that Cosimo de'Medici founded
the Platonic Academy in Florence, which, under the
direction of Ficino, was subsequently supported by
Lorenzo. In a pair of studies, now reprinted, Hankins
has recently demonstrated that no "academy" existed
in Florence at this time and, as well, that Ficino's
teachings were on a variety of subjects in addition to

Plato and took place in a variety of sites. See "Cosimo
de'Medici and the 'Platonic Academy'" (1990) and
"The Myth of the Platonic Academy of Florence,"
(1991) in *Humanism and Platonism in the Italian
Renaissance*, Rome, 2004, II, 187–218 and 219–73,
respectively.

3 D'Amico, *Renaissance Humanism in Papal Rome*, 3–35.

4 See the discussion of D'Amico on classical humanism
in Rome, esp. *Renaissance Humanism in Papal Rome*,
152–60.

5 This parallel is discussed by John D'Amico, in
Renaissance Humanism in Papal Rome.

6 Luca Pacioli, *Luca Paciuolo summa de arithmetica
geometria proportioni et proportionalita*, ed. Paganino
de Paganini, Venice, 1494 (hereinafter *Summa arithmetica*). First published in Venice in 1494, this work
was published again in another edition in Toscolano
in 1523. The original 1494 edition is the one used
here. However, it must be noted that its foliation
(or pagination) contains many irregularities that are
due in part to the fact that the folios (or pages) were
separated and mistakenly inserted in different places
before they were rebound. Thus the folio numbers
cited in the notes that follow do not reflect a consistent order.

7 Luca Pacioli, *De divina proportione*, ed. A. Paganius
Paganinus, Venice, 1509. Respecting this work, the
annotated edition of Winterberg (hereinafter cited
as *Divina proportione*), is particularly useful. See idem,
Divina proportione (1509), ed. Constantin Winterberg,
Vienna, 1896.

8 Pacioli, *Divina proportione*, chs. II (39) and XLXI (95).

9 Giovanni Nanni (Annius da Viterbo), *Berosus sacerdotis
caldaici*, ed. J. Steelsius, Antwerp, 1545, 204. Pythagoras's
authorship of a work on politics is claimed by
Diogenes Laertius (*Lives of Eminent Philosophers*,
VIII.5) who adds that it was extant in his time.

10 Filippo Beroaldo Senior (not to be confused with
his cousin, Filippo Beroaldo Junior, also a humanist),
Symbola Pythagorae a Philippo Beroaldo moraliter explicata,
Bologna, 1503.

11 Beroaldo, *Symbola Pythagorae ...* ; see translation of
Carolyn Tuttle in Appendix B.

12 Beroaldo, *Symbola Pythagorae ...* ; trans. Tuttle in
Appendix B.

13 On Beroaldo's life, see the biography by Jean du
Pins, his sometime colleague in Paris, published in
the year of Beroaldo's death, *Divae Catherinae Senensis
simvl et clarissimi viri Philippi Beroaldi bononiensis vita
per Ioannem Pinvm gallvm tolosanvm*, Bologna, 1505.
See also the modern biography by Myron Gilmore in
"Beroaldo, Filippo, senior," in *Dizionario biografico degli
italiani*, Rome, 1967, IX, 382–84.

14 Filippo Beroaldo Senior, *De felicitate opusculum* (1495)
in *Foelicité humaine*, ed. Caluy de la Fontaine, Paris,
1543, XLI; and *Declamatio an orator sit philosopho &
medico anteponendus* (*Declamation on Whether an Orator
Should Be Preferred to a Philosopher and a Physician*)

in *Philippi Beroaldi Libellus Quo Septem Saptientium Sententia*, ed. Leone Argento, Paris, 1505, n.p.

15 One such work by Pietro del Monte is *De veritate unius legis et falsitate sectarum*, published in Milan in 1509. On this, see Marie Madeleine Fontaine, "Les Attaques de Pietro del Monte Contre l'Alchimie dans le *De Veritate Unius Legis* de 1509," in Matton, *Documents*, 103–29, esp. 104 and n. 6.

16 We know little about this poet, although he appears to have been known to Renaissance writers. For the citation, see Raffaele Maffei, *Commentaria Urbana*, Rome, 1506, 254r and v. (This vita is in the third section, "Philologia.") See also Angelo Poliziano, *Letters*, ed. Shane Butler, Cambridge (Mass.) and London, 2006, III.XII.

17 Two important studies on Lefèvre d'Étaples are those of Guy Bedouelle and Franco Giacone, *Lefèvre d'Étaples et ses disciples: Épistres et Évangiles pour les cinquante et deux dimanches de l'an*, Leiden, 1976; and Eugene F. Rice, Jr., ed., *The Prefatory Epistles of Jacques Lefèvre d'Étaples and Related Texts*, New York, 1972. For the epistles, dated 1496, 1499, and 1510, see Rice, *Prefatory Epistles of Lefèvre d'Étaples*, xii–xv, 30–31, 34, 61–63, and 225–26. These preface his *Arithmetica decem libris demonstrata*, *Musica libris demonstrata quattuor*, *Corpus Dionysiacum*, and *Commentary on De trinitate* (of Richard of St. Victor).

18 The seminal work on Clichtove is Jean-Pierre Massaut, *Josse Clichtove, L'Umanisme et la Réforme du Clergé*, Paris, 1968 (2 vols.). The statement by Clichtove is from his Epistle 34 published in Rice, *The Prefatory Epistles of Jacques Lefèvre d'Étaples*, 108–10.

19 For an early biography of Reuchlin, see Paolo Giovio, *Elogia virorum illustrium*, Basel, 1577, 217.

20 Johannes Reuchlin, *Recommendation on Whether to Confiscate, Destroy and Burn all Jewish Books* (1510, as unpublished letter to the Archbishop of Mainz), ed. and trans. Peter Wortsman, New York, 2000, esp. 58–60. For the earliest publication of Reuchlin's works, see Petrus Galatinus, *Opus de arcanis catholicae veritatis*, Basel, 1561.

21 Book I opens with "Italica philosophia beatissime Leo Decime religionis christiane Pontifex Maxime à Pythagora eius nominis parente primo." See Johannes Reuchlin, *Iohannis Revchlin, De arte Cabalistica libri tres*, Tübingen, 1517, beg. Bk. I.

22 Reuchlin, *De arte Cabalistica*, esp. 37–39.

23 For the words of Reuchlin ("renascentem Pythagoram"), see Reuchlin, *De arte Cabalistica libri tres*, loc. cit. For the text of this work in English, see Reuchlin, *On the Art of the Kabbalah, De arte Cabalistica* (hereinafter *De arte Cabalistica*), Latin and English texts trans. M. Goodman and S. Goodman, with intro. Moshe Idel, Lincoln (Neb.) and London, 1993. Unless otherwise indicated, future notes will refer to the Idel edition.

24 Reuchlin, *De arte Cabalistica*, 247 (trans. Goodman and Goodman).

25 Reuchlin, *De arte Cabalistica*, 233 (trans. Goodman and Goodman).

26 Reuchlin, *De arte Cabalistica*, 127 (trans. Goodman and Goodman).

27 Clement of Alexandria (in *Stromateius* I.xxii) summarizes for early Christians the Mosaic background of Plato by referring to the authority of these antique writers. On Pythagoras as the prince of philosophers, see Reuchlin, *De arte Cabalistica*, 167.

28 Reuchlin, *De arte Cabalistica*, Bk. II, passim.

29 Reuchlin, *De arte Cabalistica*, 201 (trans. Goodman and Goodman).

30 Reuchlin, *De arte Cabalistica*, 173–79 and 217.

31 Reuchlin, *De arte Cabalistica*, op. cit., 129 (trans. Goodman and Goodman).

32 Reuchlin, *De arte Cabalistica*, 185 and 227, respectively (trans. Goodman and Goodman).

33 Desiderius Erasmus, *Collected Works of Erasmus* (letters), ed. R. A. B. Mynors, Toronto, Buffalo, and London, 1989, IX, 14–15.

34 Erasmus, *Apotheosis capnionis/seu de incomparabili heroe iohanne Reuchlino in divorum numerum relato* (*Assumption into Heaven of Johannes Reuchlin Incomparable Hero of Wisdom*). This brief work, originally published in 1522, may be found in idem, *L'apoteosi di Giovanni Reuchlin*, ed. Giulio Vallese, Naples, 3rd ed., 1964. In this dialogue Erasmus expresses his admiration for Reuchlin by having him escorted to heaven by the father of The Church and great Christian scholar, Saint Jerome (ibid., esp. 249–52). Still fundamental to Reuchlin studies is the biography of Ludwig Geiger (*Johann Reuchlin sein Leben und seine Werke*, Leipzig, 1871, rep. 1964). For a complete list of works published by Reuchlin, see Josef Benzing, *Bibliographie der Schriften Johannes Reuchlins im 15. und 16. Jahrhundert*, Vienna, 1955. On the relation between Reuchlin and Erasmus, see Roland H. Bainton, *Erasmus of Christendom*, New York, 1969, 151–55.

35 Letter from Ulrich von Hutten dated 5 June 1519, in Vallese, *L'apoteosi di Giovanni Reuchlin*, VIII, 399.

36 Cornelius Agrippa von Nettesheim (hereinafter Agrippa), *Declamation on the Nobility and Preeminence of the Female Sex* (1532), ed. Albert Rabil, Jr., Chicago and London, 1996, 81.

37 See esp. Pliny the Elder, *Historia naturalis*, XXIV.99–102, and XXX, passim, and Bishop Hippolytus, *Philosophumena*, VI, preface; I.2, and IV.43–44.

38 Agrippa, *De occulta philosophia libri tres*, Antwerp, 1531, I.2. For a modern edition of this text see that edited by V. Perrone Compagni, Leiden, 1992. For an English edition see idem, *Three Books of Occult Philosophy*, ed. Donald Tyson, St. Paul (Minn.), 1993. To the three books a fourth, believed to be by the same author, was added. For the classic French edition of the four books, see idem, *La philosophie occulte* (1910), trans. A. Levasseur, 2nd ed., Paris, 1968 (4 vols.).

39 Agrippa, *De incertitudine at vanitate scientiarum et artium*, Antwerp, 1526, XV. For the full original text, see

Agrippa, *Opera*, ed. Richard H. Popkin, Hildesheim, 1970, II. Widely read, this work was also published in sixteenth-century England (1569 and 1575). It is reprinted in *Of the Vanitie and Vncertaintie of Artes and Sciences*, ed. Catherine M. Dunn, Northridge (Calif.), 1974, 62. Pythagorean Spheres are discussed (with bibliography) in Joost-Gaugier, *Measuring Heaven*, ch. 11. For an overview of this subject see the seminal work of Thorndike, in *History of Magic and Experimental Science*, I, esp. 672–91.

40 Paracelsus, introductory prefatory letter to *Aurora philosophorum* (1577), in *Avr. Philip. Theoph. Paracelsi. … Opera omnia*, I, Geneva, 1662 (trans. Carolyn Tuttle). On this see, Shumaker, *Occult Sciences in the Renaissance*, 182–83.

41 For an English translation, including some of his comments on Pythagoras, see Paracelsus, *Paracelsus His Aurora, & Treasure of the Philosophers as also the Water-Stone of the Wise Men. …*, ed. J. H. Oxon, London, 1659, *Aurora … :* II (6), V (13), and *Water-Stone …*, 83. On the literature of magic and alchemy in the Renaissance, see especially Thorndike, *History of Magic and Experimental Science*, IV and V, passim. See also Eugenio Garin, "Magia e astrologia nella cultura del Rinascimento," in *Magia e civiltà*, ed. Ernesto de Martino, Milan, 1976, 15–33; idem, *Astrology in the Renaissance*; and idem, *La magia naturale nel Rinascimento*, ed. Paolo Rossi, Turin, 1989; also Frances A. Yates, *Giordano Bruno and the Hermetic Tradition*, Chicago, 1964.

42 Giovanni Francesco Pico della Mirandola, *In examen vanitatis christianae disciplinae*, in Giovanni Pico della Mirandola, *Opera omnia Ioannis Pici Mirandvlae concordiaeque comitis …*, II, esp. at 729–32.

43 Giovanni Francesco Pico, in *In examen vanitatis christianae disciplinae*, esp. 730–31.

44 Baldassare Castiglione, *Il cortegiano*, ed. Aldus Manutius, Venice, 1528, II.14 and III.1, respectively. For an English translation, see idem, *The Book of the Courtier*, trans. Charles S. Singleton, New York, 1959, 106 and 201, respectively. Pythagoras's view of music as divine was widely reported in ancient literature (see, e.g., Cicero's *In somnium Scipionis*), and Plutarch was the first to report his method of measurement (in a fragment from a lost life of Hercules now in *Moralia*, ed. F. H. Sandbach, in *Plutarch*, ed. F. C. Babbitt, Cambridge [Mass.] and London, 1969, XV, 81).

45 Lodovico Ariosto's *Orlando Furioso* was first published in Ferrara (ed. Giovanni Mazzocci) in 1516. For an edition in English, based on the Ferrara edition, see idem, *Orlando Furioso*, trans. W. S. Rose, ed. Stewart Baker and Bartlett Giamatti, Indianapolis, 1968. Probably a pupil of Pythagoras's in Magna Grecia, Archytas of Tarentum was a highly regarded statesman of Tarentum in the early fourth century B.C. when Plato visited southern Italy; they corresponded, and it is thought they knew each other personally. On his significance, see W. K. C. Guthrie, *A History of Greek Philosophy*, I: *The Earlier Presocratics and the Pythagoreans*, Cambridge, 1962, 333–40.

46 Francesco Giorgio (Zorzi), *Francisci Georgii … De harmonia mvndi totivs cantica tria* (hereinafter *De harmonia mundi*), ed. Bernardini de Vitalibus, Venice, 1525. On the publication of this work and its enormous subsequent popularity, especially in France, see Cesare Vasoli, "Hermetism in Venice. From Francesco Giorgio Veneto to Agostino Steuco," in *Magia, alchimia, scienza dal '400 al '700*, ed. Carlos Gilly and Cis van Heertum, Florence, 2002, I, 50–51 (hereinafter Gilly and van Heertum).

47 See, e.g., Pseudo-Iamblichus, *The Theology of Arithmetic*, trans. Robin Waterfield, Grand Rapids, 1988, 101–4. On this author and this work, see n. 5 to Appendix A.

48 Giorgio, *De harmonia mundi*, proem (n.p.) and I.iii.

49 Giorgio, *De harmonia mundi*, I.v (trans. Carolyn Tuttle).

50 Regarding this book, see Giorgio, *L'Elegante poema*, ed. Jean-François Maillard, Milan, 1991, 33.

51 Egidio da Viterbo (Giles of Viterbo), *Scechina e libellus de litteris hebraicis*, ed. François Secret, Rome, 1959, I, 35 and 71. Both these works were previously unpublished. The *Libellus de litteris hebraicis*, a short text, was dedicated to Giulio de' Medici in 1517, while the *Scechina*, a longer work that treats the Kabbalah and studies numbers, letters, and divine names, was dedicated to Charles V some years later. These works came to be known through the eulogy published by Petrus Galatinus in *De arcanis catholicae veritatis*, Basel, 1550, 22; Galatinus characterized the *Scechina* as erudite and full of fundamental divine knowledge.

52 Reuchlin, *De arte Cabalistica*, 167 and 233.

53 This tradition in the visual arts of the Middle Ages is discussed in Joost-Gaugier, *Measuring Heaven*, ch. 11.

54 On this, see esp. Joseph Bloch, *Venetian Printers of Hebrew Books*, New York, 1932; and François Secret, *Les Kabbalistes chrétiens de la Renaissance*, Paris, 1964, 126ff.

55 Erasmus, *Antibarbarorum liber* (1520), in *Collected Works of Erasmus*, ed. Craig R. Thompson, XXIII, Toronto, Buffalo, London, 1978, trans. Margaret Phillips, 68–69.

56 Erasmus, *De duplici copia verborum ac rerum commentarii* (*Foundations of the Abundant Style*, 1512), in *Collected Works of Erasmus*, ed. Thompson, XXIV, Toronto, Buffalo, and London, 1978, trans. Betty Knott, 610.

57 Erasmus, *Moriae encomium* (1511), LB IV 434b, in *Collected Works of Erasmus*, ed. A. H. T. Levi, XXVII, Toronto, Buffalo, and London, 1986, trans. Betty Radice, 108.

58 Erasmus, *Lingua* (1525), in *Collected Works of Erasmus*, ed. E. Fantham and E. Rummel, XXIX, Toronto, Buffalo, and London, 1989, trans. Elaine Fantham from ded., 257.

59 Erasmus, *Dialogus Ciceronianus* (*The Ciceronian*, 1528), in *Collected Works of Erasmus*, ed. Levi, XXVIII, trans. Betty Knott, 350.

60 Erasmus, *Oratio de virtute amplectenda* (*Dialogue on Embracing Virtue*, 1528), in *Collected Works of Erasmus*, ed. Fantham and Rummel, 6; idem, *Letter to Guillaume*

de Croy, May 1519, in *Collected Works of Erasmus*, ed. R. A. B. Mynors and D. F. S. Thomson, VI, Toronto, Buffalo, and London, 1982; idem, *Declamatio in laudem artis medicae* (*Oration in Praise of the Art of Medicine*, 1518), in *Collected Works of Erasmus*, ed. Fantham and Rummel, 42; idem, *In nucem Ovidii* (*On Ovid's Nut Tree*, 1524), 166 (trans. passage by Fantham); and idem, *Lingua*, in *Collected Works of Erasmus*, ed. Fantham and Rummel, 286 and 322.

61 Erasmus, *Enchiridion militis christiani* (*A Manual for a Christian Soldier*, 1518), in *Collected Works of Erasmus*, ed. John W. O'Malley, LXVI, trans. Charles Fantazzi, Toronto, Buffalo, London, 1988, 69, 87, and 90.

62 Erasmus, *Letter to Hendrik van Bergen*, 1496; *Letter to François Deloynes*, 1517; *Letter to Jean de Nève*, 1514; and *Letter to Christopher Urswick*, 1506; published (in order of citation) in *Collected Works of Erasmus*, ed. Mynors and Thomson, I (103), IV (251), III (3), and II (116).

63 See quoted passage in *Collected Works of Erasmus*, ed. Mynors and Thomson, VI (56–57).

64 Erasmus, *Letter to Adrian VI*, 1522; and Herman Lethmaet, *Letter to Erasmus*, 1522, both in *Collected Works of Erasmus*, ed. Mynors and Thomson, XI, 155–56 and 196, respectively.

65 Erasmus, *Letter to Henry VIII*, 1523, and *Letter to Krysztof Szydlowiecki*, 1525, in *Collected Works of Erasmus*, ed. Mynors and Thomson, X, 65, and XI, 216, respectively.

66 See Ioannes Lodovicus Vives, *De anima et vita* (1538), rep. ed. Mario Sancipriano, Turin, 1959, esp. 171 and 199.

67 Celio Calcagnini, from a letter addressed to Andrea Minotto and a passage about *Pythagoras musicis modulis furiosum adolescentem pacavit* in *Caelii Calcagnini Ferrariensis Protonotarii Apostolici, Opera aliquot* (hereinafter *Opera aliquot*), Basel, 1544, 70–71 and 330, respectively.

68 "Pythagorae rerum abditarum pretium & excellens indicatura femur aureum fecit." This, under the subtitle "Pythagorae cur aureum foemur tribuatur Pythagorae praeceptor," is from *Epistolicarum questionum* in Calcagnini, *Opera aliquot*, 42.

69 On this recurrent theme in Calcagnini's work, see, e.g., idem, *Amatoriae Magiae compendium*, in Calcagnini, *Opera aliquot*, 497.

70 "Pythagoras Samius artem auxit, & celebrem reddidit." Girolamo Cardano, *Encomivm geometriae recitatvm anno 1535*, in *Hieronymi Cardani Mediolanensis medici De subtilitate libri XXI* …, Basel, 1554, 442.

71 Nicholaus Copernicus, *De revolutionibus orbium celestium*, ed. Johannes Petreius, Nuremberg, 1543. Though work on this text may have begun as early as 1512, it was not until 1542 that Copernicus composed his dedication to Pope Paul III. The work was published almost posthumously. As Copernicus lay dying, a copy of the first edition of this work, which would see so many future editions, was put in his hands. On the trajectory of this work from its earliest moments

of inspiration to its final publication, see Edward Rosen, in Copernicus, *Three Copernican Treatises: The Commentariolus of Copernicus, the Letter Against Werner, the Narration prima*, ed. Edward Rosen (1939), 3rd ed., New York, 1971, esp. 344–405.

72 Guillaume Postel, *Petit Traité de la Signification ultime des Cinq Corps Réguliers*, esp. secs. 15 and 19/20. This work, previously known only in manuscript form, was published by Jean-Pierre Brach, in Matton, *Documents Oubliés*, 223–44.

73 Vitruvius, *Dieci libri dell'architettvra di M. Vitrvvio tradotti & commentati da Monsig. Daniel Barbaro Patriarca d'Aquileia* … (1556), Venice, 1629, esp. 15 and 349. On this, see also Pierre Caye, "Commentaire sur *De Architectura* de Vitruve par Mgr. Daniele Barbaro," in *Le Savoir de Palladio*, Klincksieck, 1995, 93 and 193.

74 See Giovanni Paolo Lomazzo, *Libro de sogni: Secondo Ragionamento* (1563), in Lomazzo, *Scritti sulle arti*, ed. Roberto P. Ciardi, Florence, 1973, I, 24–41.

75 Lomazzo, *Libro de sogni: Quarto Ragionamento*, in idem, *Scritti sulle arti*, I, 67–68.

76 Lomazzo, *Libro de sogni: Settimo Ragionamento*, in idem, *Scritti sulle arti*, I, 169. Cf. Agrippa *De incertitudine et vanitate* …, ch. XLII.

77 See the description of the stucco relief over the altar of the Pythagorean Basilica at Portal Maguire of the first century A.D. (and bibliography) in Joost-Gaugier, *Measuring Heaven*, ch. 9.

78 Joost-Gaugier, *Measuring Heaven*, 205–7.

79 Lomazzo, *Trattato dell'arte de la pittura* (1584), in idem, *Scritti sulle arti*, II, 179, 224, 231, 304, 376, and 543.

80 Lomazzo, *Idea del tempio della pittura* (1590), ed. Robert Klein, Florence, 1974, I, 67, 310, 319, and 325.

81 Lomazzo, *Della forma delle muse* … (1591), in idem, *Scritti sulle arti*, 606, 620, 629, and 631 (for original passage as follows: "[Q]gusto Apollo non è alto chef Duo some, ill quake fu ditto dale grin Pitagora universal.") Cf. idem, *Della forma delle muse*, ed. Alessandra Ruffino, Trent, 2002, 79: "Or, questo Apollo non è altro che Dio sommo, il quale fu detto dal gran Pittagora universale."

82 Gregorio Comanini, *The Figino or On the Purpose of Painting*, ed. and trans. Ann Doyle-Anderson and Giancarlo Maiorino, Toronto, 2001, esp. 101–3.

83 Giordano Bruno, *La cena delle ceneri* (1584), Dialogues I and V. For an English edition, see *The Ash Wednesday Supper*, ed. and trans. Stanley L. Jaki, Mouton, The Hague, and Paris, 1975, 52, 66, and 148.

84 Giordano Bruno, *De la cause, principio, et uno* (1584), passim, esp. Dialogue II (see in *The Infinite in Giordano Bruno, with a Translation of His Dialogue Concerning the Cause, Principle, and One*, trans. Sidney T. Greenberg, New York, 1950); and idem, *De l'infinito universo e mondi* of the same year (see Dorothea W. Singer, *Giordano Bruno: His Life and Thought with an Annotated Translation of On the Infinite Universe and Worlds*, trans. Dorothea W. Singer, New York, 1968), passim. See also Giordano Bruno, *Cabala del cavallo Pegaseo con*

l'aggiunta dell'asino cillenico, descritta dal Nolano (1585). This work (*Cabal of the Cheval Pegasus*) is composed of three dialogues followed by an appended dialogue in which the Pythagorean speaker is an ape who discusses with an ass who represents Pegasus. See *Giordano Bruno Oeuvres Complèts: VI. Cabale du Cheval Pégaséen*, ed. Giovanni Aquilecchia, Paris, 1993. On Bruno's interest in magic, see Yates, *Giordano Bruno and the Hermetic Tradition*, esp. 257–74.

85 The poem, handwritten in 1587 and translated here by Arielle Saiber, is published in "Fra Giordano Bruno's Catholic Passion," *Supplementvm Festivvm: Studies in Honor of Paul Oskar Kristeller*, ed. James Hankins, John Monfasani, and Frederick Purnell, Jr., Binghamton (N.Y.), 1987, 560.

    Salomon et Pythagoras
    Quid est quo est?
    Ipsum quod fuit.
    Quid est quod fuit?
    Ipsum quod est.
    Nihil sub sole novum.
    Salus!

On it, see Saverio Ricci, *Giordano Bruno nell'Europa del Cinqecento*, Rome, 2000, 404–5.

86 Bernardino Baldi, *Vita di Pitagora* (1588), published in its entirety by Enrico Narducci, in *Bullettino di bibliographia e di storia delle scienze, matematiche e fisiche*, XX, 1897, 197–308.

87 Although he does not say so, Baldi is probably referring to Aristoxenus, Plutarch, and Clement of Alexandria, all antique authors who had suggested that Pythagoras was born in Tuscany.

88 "Pitagora fosse inferior à Dio, ma superiore a gli altri huomini." Baldi, *Vita di Pitagora*, 297.

89 See n. 88.

90 Johannes Kepler, *Letter to Galileo*, dated 16 March 1598, trans. in *The Portable Renaissance Reader*, ed. James B. Ross and Mary M. McLaughlin (1953), New York, 1968, 599. On Galileo's mathematization of physical science, see T. R. Girill, "Galileo and Platonistic Methodology," *Journal of the History of Ideas*, XXXI, 1970, esp. 501–15. On the observational methodology of Kepler, see Marie Boas, *The Scientific Renaissance, 1450–1630*, New York, 1962, esp. 287–312. On the relationship of Galileo to Copernicus and Pythagoras, see Reeves, *Painting the Heavens*, esp. 63, 163, and 240.

91 Kepler, *Mysterium cosmographicum di stella nova* (1596, 2nd ed. 1621). See full text in *Johannes Kepler Gesammelte Werke*, ed. Max Caspar, Munich, 1938, I, XIII (trans. mine). On his admiration of Cusanus, see Field, *Piero della Francesca*, 270.

92 Kepler, *Mysterium cosmographicum* ... , opening salutation and original dedication, at 2.

93 Kepler, *Mysterium cosmographicum* ... , XIII.

94 Giovanni Battistia Della Porta, *Magiae naturalis libri viginti*, Rouen, 1650, esp. I, passim. On this work, first

published in 1589, see esp. Schumaker, *Occult Sciences in the Renaissance*, 109–57.

95 Thorndike, *History of Magic and Experimental Science*, II, 227–28.

96 On the Cambridge Platonists, see Schumaker, *Occult Sciences in the Renaissance*, 245–46.

97 On the disagreements between Clichtove and Erasmus and their refusal to acknowledge each other personally, see Massaut, *Josse Clichtore*, I, 11–12.

98 On Pythagoras and Moses as authorities in such alchemical texts as the *Turba Philosophorum* and the *Phoenix*, see, e.g., Thorndike, *History of Magic and Experimental Science*, III, 637.

99 On the popularity of this book, see Carmen de Fez, *La estructura barroca de "El siglo pitagórico,"* Madrid, 1978.

100 The three works described here are Pseudo-Averroës, *Averroeana: Being a Transcript of Several Letters from Averroes ... to Metrodorus ... also several letters from Pythagoras to the King of India together with his reception at the Indian Court*, London, 1695, 80–97; Thomas Tryon, *Pythagoras and his Mystick Philosophy revived, or the Mystery of Dreams Unfolded*, London, 1691, passim; and Antonio Cocchi, *Régime de Pythagore*, Paris, 1762, esp. intro.

101 Lenormant, *La Grande Grèce*.

FOUR: THE PYTHAGOREAN TRADITION IN THE EARLY FIFTEENTH CENTURY

1 Plato's use of mathematical symbolism is analyzed in Robert S. Brumbaugh, *Plato's Mathematical Imagination*, Bloomington (Ind.), 1954.

2 An excellent discussion of the philosophical cosmology of Pythagoreanism is contained in P. F. M. Fontaine, *The Light and the Dark*, I, 20–35.

3 See, e.g., Petrarch, *De vita solitaria* (1346), I.4.2 and II.9.4. Petrarch knew that Cicero, too, was interested in the choice between virtue and vice. On this, see the discussion of Theodor E. Mommsen, "Petrarch and the Story of Hercules" (1953), rep. in *Medieval and Renaissance Studies*, ed. Eugene F. Rice, Jr., Ithaca, 1959, 175–96.

4 Salutati, *De laboribus Hercules*, 11; 182, 189, and 572.

5 Coluccio Salutati, *Linus Colucius Salutatus to His Venerable Father in Christ, Brother John Dominici of the Order of Preachers*, rep. and trans. in Ephraim Emerton, *Humanism and Tyranny: Studies in the Italian Trecento*, Cambridge (Mass.), 1925, 364–65.

6 Salutati, *Linus Colucius Salutatus* ... , 355 (trans. Emerton).

7 Pier Paolo Vergerio, *Petri Pauli Vergerii ad ubertinum de carraria De ingenuis moribus et liberalibus adulescentiae studiis liber*, 70; Leonardo Bruni, *Dialogi ad Petrum Histrum*, ed. Garin, rep. in Griffiths et al., *Humanism of Leonardo Bruni* (quoted text at 70); Guarino da Verona, *Baptista Guarinus ad Maffeum Gambaram Brixianum*

adulescentem generosum discipulum suum, de ordine docendi et studendi, 31; and Aeneas Sylvius Piccolomini, *De liberorum educatione*, 21, 35, 92, 96, and 97. The Vergerio, Guarino, and Piccolomini texts are reprinted in Craig Kallendorf, ed., *Humanist Educational Treatises*, Cambridge (Mass.) and London, 2002, 2–91, 260–310, and 126–259, respectively. For a recent critical edition of Bruni's dialogue, see *Dialogi ad Petrum Paulum Histrum*, ed. Stefano Ugo Baldassarri, Florence, 1994.

8   Pletho, *Contra Scholarii defensionem Aristotelis*, VII; and idem, *De differentiis*, XX-c. Both are published in Migne, *Patrologia Graeca*, CLX, 979–1020 and 889–934, respectively. On these works, see Woodhouse, *Plethon*, passim, esp. 205 and 285.

9   Pletho, *Commentary on the Chaldean Oracles*, passim. This *Commentary* occurs in two similar texts entitled *Magica Zoroastri oracvla, Plethonis commentariis enarrata*, Paris, 1539, and *Oracula magica Zoroastris cum scholiis Plethonis*, ed. Joannes Opsopäus, Paris, 1599, 16–51. Related to it is Pletho's brief note, untitled but known as *Explanation of Obscure Passages*, in Migne, *Patrologia Graeca*, CLX, 973–74. Regarding these, and a *Commentary* that Pletho wrote on the *Oracles*, see the valuable discussion in Woodhouse, *Plethon*, 54–59.

10   This subject is discussed by Edgar Wind, in "Pagan Vestiges of the Trinity," in idem, *Pagan Mysteries in the Renaissance* (1958), rev. ed., New York, 1968, 241–55.

11   See Plato's description of the subdivisions of the world's soul in *Timaeus*, 35–36. See also Baldi, who explains that Pythagoreans regarded the number 27 as mystical because it was achieved by multiplying the first linear number, 3, by itself and the result, 9, by itself again, thus arriving at 27, the first "cubical" number (*Vita di Pitagora* 231).

12   Pletho, *Treatise on Law*, XI and Appendix.

13   Pletho, *Contra Scholarii defensionem Aristotelis*, IV.10–5.14. See this work in Migne, *Patrologia Graeca*, CLX, 979–1020.

14   Pletho, *Treatise on Law*, appendix, as translated by Woodhouse in *Plethon*, at 356.

15   See, e.g., Pletho, *Contra Scholarii defensionem Aristotelis*, in Migne, *Patrologia Graeca*, CLX, 1013a.

16   On Pletho's text listing Pythagorean tenets, see Woodhouse, *Plethon*, 221. His personal manuscripts are discussed in Aubry Diller, "The Autographs of Georgius Gemistus Pletho," *Scriptorium*, X, 1956, 27–41.

17   This occurs in his *Contra Scholarii defensionem Aristotelis*. On this, see Hankins, *Plato in the Italian Renaissance*, II, 436–37, and John Monfasani, "L'insegnamento universitario e la cultura bizantina in Italia nel Quattrocento," in *Sapere e/è potere. Discipline, dispute e professioni nell'università medievale e moderna: Atti del 4 convegno*, I, ed. Luisa Avellini, Bologna, 1990, 58.

18   An illustrated manuscript on the construction of artificial (painted) space envisaged through the concept of the visual pyramid is attributed to Paolo Toscanelli (Florence, *Bib. Riccardiana 2110*). A transcription of its text is available in idem, *Della prospettiva*, ed. Alessandro

Parronchi, Milan, 1991. The claim that Toscanelli was a vegetarian occurs in Ross King, *Brunelleschi's Dome*, New York, 2000, 148. Cf. a Toscanelli family tax return that notes that in 1469–72 Toscanelli had a farm that was dedicated to agriculture and livestock. In conjunction with this farm, he had a tannery. These facts suggest that he raised animals for slaughter. Given the failure of his farming enterprise, he declared bankruptcy and bought a copper mine near Montecatini. Eventually, since he could not better his economic situation, he returned to the profession of medicine. See the *Catasto della famiglia Toscanelli*, in Florence, *Arch. di Stato, Catasto, 17*, as reproduced in *Firenze e la scoperta dell'America*, exh. cat., ed. Sebastiano Gentile, Florence, 1992, 136–38.

19   With the exception of the work mentioned in n. 18, no certain literary documents by Toscanelli survive. However, he is known to us through a variety of quotes and descriptions by the many contemporaries who knew and respected him. Of fundamental importance for Toscanelli studies is Gustavo Uzielli, *La vita e i tempi di Paolo dal Pozzo Toscanelli*, in *Raccolta di documenti e studi*, Part V, vol. I, Rome, 1848. Documents concerning Toscanelli are collected in *Firenze e la scoperta dell'America* (exh. cat.), 120–56. See also the late sixteenth-century biography of him ("Paolo Fiorentino") in Bernardino Baldi, *Le vite de' matematici* (1589), ed. Elio Nenci, Milan, 1998, 291–95.

20   The portrait of Toscanelli by Vasari is in the Sala di Cosimo il Vecchio of the Palazzo Vecchio in Florence. It serves as the frontispiece to Uzielli, *La vita e i tempi di Toscanelli*.

21   According to his first biographer, Bessarion (who, the biographer says, was born in 1395 rather than in 1403 as later scholars have suggested) studied with Pletho in his youth before coming to Italy. Aloysii Bandini, *De vita et rebus gestis Bessarionis*, in Migne, *Patrologia Graeca*, CLXI (iii–xcviii), vi. See also the biography of Bessarion contained in his funeral oration delivered by Nicolo Firmani (*Nicolai Episcopi Firmani, Oratio in funere Bessarionis*), in Ludwig Mohler, *Kardinal Bessarion als Theologe, Humanist und Staatsmann* (1923–42), rep. Aalen, 1967, III (404–14), 406. On the influence of Pletho on others, see Hankins, *Plato in the Italian Renaissance*, II, 436–40.

22   In his *Panegyricus in laudem amplissimi patris D. Bessarionis*, Bartolommeo Platina, a Roman intellectual and papal librarian, praises Bessarion for his levelheadedness. Bessarion observed things that could be approved of or disapproved of in every school of thought: "He passes over no sect of philosophers without making an observation about what each one said that could be approved of or disapproved of. Just as he criticizes the excessive piety of the Pythagoreans" (Migne, *Patrologia Graeca*, CLXI, cxiii).

23   For the text of Bessarion's letter to Pletho's sons, see Migne, *Patrologia Graeca*, CLXI, 695–98. Concerning this letter, cf. the views of Masai (*Pléthon et le Platonisme*

de Mistra, 307) and Edgar Wind, "Bessarion's Letter on Palingenesis," in *Pagan Mysteries in the Renaissance*, 256–58.

24 On the rapport between Bessarion and Pletho, see Mohler, *Kardinal Bessarion*, I, 335–45.

25 See Bessarion, *Oratio dogmatica sive de unione quam Graece … Latinam*, in Migne, *Patrologia Graeca*, CLXI, 543–614. Also see idem, *Orazione dogmatica sull'unione dei Greci e dei Latini*, ed. Gianfrancesco Lusini, Naples, 2001. On this discourse, see also Vast, *Le Cardinal Bessarion*, esp. 88–94. See also, generally, Jacquilyne E. Martin, "Cardinal Bessarion, Mystical Theology and Spiritual Union between East and West" (diss. University of Manitoba), Winnipeg, 2000.

26 This goal is evident in the major works of Bessarion, including *De natura et arte*, *De Sacramento Eucharistae*, *Ad Graecos Epistola*, and *De verbis consecrationis et transsubstantiatione*. The first two are published in Mohler, *Kardinal Bessarion*, III, 91–147 and 2–68; the latter in Migne, *Patrologia Graeca*, CLXI, 449–89 and 489–94. For a letter written by Pius II to Mahomet II, which, in a similar spirit, seeks reconciliation between the Muslim world and Christianity, see Pio II (Aeneas Sylvius Piccolomini), *Lettera a Maometto II (Epistola ad Mahumetem)*, ed. Giuseppe Toffanin, Naples, 1953, 3–8. See also Joost R. Ritman, "Bessarion and the Influence of Hermes Trismegistus," and Marino Zorzi, "Hermes Trismegistus in the Venetian Libraries," both in Gilly and van Heertum, *Magia alchima, scienza*, I, 17–22 and 126–34, respectively. For a group of specialized articles respecting Bessarion and his contemporaries, see Monfasani, *Byzantine Scholars in Renaissance Italy*.

27 See the discussion of Maurice de Gandillac, *La Philosophie de Nicolas de Cues*, Paris, 1941, esp. 38–56.

28 On this, see Zorzi, "Hermes Trismegistus in the Venetian Libraries," passim.

29 Bessarion, *Adversus calumniatorem Platonis*, 1468. Most of the information discussed here is contained in Book I.

30 This contrast is discussed (with bibliography) in Christiane L. Joost-Gaugier, "Plato and Aristotle and Their Retinue: Meaning in Raphael's *School of Athens*," *Gazette des Beaux-Arts*, CXXXVII, 2001, 149–64.

31 This statement is quoted by Vast in *Le Cardinal Bessarion*, at 154. On this alleged statement by Valla, see John Monfasani, "Bessarion, Valla, Agricola, and Erasmus," *Rinascimento*, ser. 2, XXIII, 1988, 319–20.

32 On Bessarion's lifestyle, as known through documents, correspondence, and various literary works, see esp. the biography of Bandini (*De vita et rebus gestis Bessarionis*); the funeral oration of Firmani (*Oratio in Funere Bessarionis*) who described him as "wise, ingenious, and divine"; and the panegyric in praise of him by Bartolommeo Platina (*Panegyricus in laudem amplissimi patris D. Bessarionis*). On this subject, see also the discussion of Vast, *Le Cardinal Bessarion*, at 155–57.

33 On the friendship between the young Cusanus and Toscanelli, see Field, *Piero della Francesca*, 269.

34 On the history and composition of this work, see the introduction by Paul E. Sigmund, in Nicholas Cusanus, *The Catholic Concordance*, ed. Sigmund, Cambridge, 1991.

35 Nicholas Cusanus, *De concordantia catholica*, in *The Catholic Concordance*, passim.

36 Nicholas Cusanus, *De docta ignorantia*.

37 Diogenes Laertius, *Life of Pythagoras*, in *Lives of Eminent Philosophers*, VIII.24–25; see also Pseudo-Iamblichus, *The Theology of Arithmetic*, 35–40.

38 Cf. Nicholas Cusanus, *De docta ignorantia*, I.7 and Pseudo-Iamblichus, *The Theology of Arithmetic*, 42–43 (quoted passage trans. Waterfield).

39 Nicholas Cusanus, *De docta ignorantia*, I.12.

40 Pseudo-Iamblichus, *The Theology of Arithmetic*, 49–53 (quoted passage trans. Waterfield at 51).

41 Nicholas Cusanus, *De docta ignorantia*, I.7, 10, and 12 (quoted passage trans. Hopkins, *Nicholas of Cusa on Learned Ignorance*, at 57–58). See also idem, *De staticis experimentis*, in *Nicholas of Cusa on Wisdom and Knowledge*, ed. Jasper Hopkins, Minneapolis, 1996, 322–23.

42 Nicholas Cusanus, *De docta ignorantia*, I.11 and I.1.

43 Nicholas Cusanus, *De docta ignorantia*, II.13. On this concept, see the discussions of Pierre Duhem, in *Medieval Cosmology: Theories of Infinity, Place, Time …*, ed. Rogier Ariew, Chicago, 1985, II, 505–10; idem, *Système du Monde: Histoires des doctrines cosmologiques de Platon à Copernic* (1914), Paris, 1954–59, X; and Alexandre Koyré, *From the Closed World to the Infinite Universe*, Baltimore, 1957, esp. 5–19. On Nicholas's mathematics, see also F. Edward Cranz, *Nicholas of Cusa and the Renaissance*, Aldershot (U.K.) and Brookfield (Vt.), 2000, esp. 66ff. and 92–95.

44 Nicholas Cusanus, *De docta ignorantia*, esp. I.15.

45 Nicholas Cusanus, *De docta ignorantia*, I.11.

46 Nicholas Cusanus, *Idiota de mente*, VI.88, in idem, *Nicholas of Cusa on Wisdom and Knowledge* (trans. Hopkins at 211).

47 Nicholas Cusanus, *Idiota de mente*, VI.89 (trans. Hopkins at 213).

48 Nicholas Cusanus, *De pace fidei*, 4, 20, and 21. See in idem, *Nicholas of Cusa on Interreligious Harmony (De pace fidei)*, ed. James E. Biechler and H. L. Bond, Lewiston (N.Y.), 1990. Nicholas's conciliatory attitude, similar to that of Bessarion, is considered in Masai, *Pléthon et le Platonisme de Mistra*, 312, n. 1. On the meaning of Apollo's name see, e.g., Plato, *Cratylus*, 404E–406C; Plutarch, *The E at Delphi*, 393C and 394A; idem, *Isis and Osiris*, 354F and 381F; and Plotinus, *Fifth Ennead*, V.6.

49 Pythagoras's coining of the word "philosophy," and its meaning, are frequently discussed in antique literature. See, e.g., Cicero, *Tusculanae disputationes*, V.8–10.

50 Nicholas Cusanus, *De ludo globi*, II. See in idem, *De ludo globi*, ed. Pauline M. Watts, New York, 1986, CLXII–CLXIII and CLXVI.

51 On the fire at the center of the universe, see the fragment quoted in Jonathan Barnes, *Early Greek*

Philosophy, London, 1987, 220. On the number 10, see, e.g., Pseudo-Iamblichus, quoting Speusippus (the nephew of Plato), in *The Theology of Arithmetic*, 112–13.

52 Nicholas Cusanus, *De ludo globi*, II. See in idem, *De ludo globi*, CLXVIIIv.

53 Nicholas Cusanus, *De la caccia de la sapienza*, 479–520.

54 Casanus's body was buried in San Pietro in Vincoli, in Rome, while his heart was buried in the chapel of the hospital he built at Cues in Germany. See Bernardino Baldi, quoting from previous biographers, in his vita, "Nicolò di Cusa," in Baldi, *Le vite de' matematici*.

55 On Regiomontanus, see the vita by Baldi in *Le vite de' matematici*, 272–90.

56 For Regiomontanus's praise of Pythagoras (in about 1464), see his *Oratio introductoria in omnes scientias mathematicas*, in *Joannis Regiomontani opera collectanea …*, ed. Felix Schmeidler, Osnabrück, 1949, 43–53. The work on triangles is entitled *De triangulis omnimodis*. See the modern translation of this work in idem, *Regiomontanus on Triangles*, trans. Barnabas Hughes, Madison (Wis.), 1967.

57 On Regiomontanus and on his work and associations, see Rose, *The Italian Renaissance of Mathematics*, esp. 90–117; and Antonio Rigo, "Gli interessi astronomici del cardinal Bessarione," in *Bessarione e l'umanesimo*, ed. Granfranc Fiaccadori, Naples, 1994, 109–13.

58 First described by Nicomachus (see idem, *The Manual of Harmonics*, ed. Flora R. Levin, Grand Rapids, 1994) in the first century A.D., the story of the invention of musical relationships and proportions by Pythagoras is repeated throughout medieval times, well into the fourteenth century, as, e.g., in the work of Peter of Abano. On this, see Nancy Siraisi, *Arts and Sciences at Padua: The Studium of Padua before 1350*, Toronto, 1973, 98–99.

59 Alberti, *Intercenales: Convelata*, passim. See in idem, *Dinner Pieces*, ed. David Marsh, Binghamton (N.Y.), 1987, 154–58.

60 There is an ample literature on Alberti's relation to Vitruvius. See, e.g., the summary presented by Joseph Rykwert in the introduction to Alberti, *On the Art of Building in Ten Books*, ix–x, and in the bibliography he provides.

61 Cf. Vitruvius, *De architectura* (for the first printing of this work, previously known in manuscript form, see *L. Victrvvii Pollionis De architectura*); and Theon of Smyrna, *Expositio rerum mathematicarum ad legendum Platonem*, ed. Eduard Hiller, Leipzig, 1878; Anatolius of Laodicea, *On the Decad* (described in Eusebius of Caesarea, *Ecclesiastical History*, VII.xxii.5–23); Iamblichus, *Description of Pythagoras and Early Pythagoreanism in Ten Volumes* (now lost); Pseudo-Iamblichus, *The Theology of Arithmetic*, and Boethius, *De institutione arithmetica*.

62 See, e.g., Iamblichus, *Vita Pythagorica*, 4, 6, 12, and 15.

63 Alberti, *De re aedificatura*, VIII.17.

64 Alberti, *De re aedificatura*, IX.i. For the phraseology, see the translation of Rykwert, *On the Art of Building*, at 291.

65 This building, which was discovered in 1917 beneath the railroad tracks leading from the Termini in Rome to Naples, has been published numerous times and is described in Joost-Gaugier, *Measuring Heaven*, ch. 9.

66 Alberti, *De re aedificatoria*, IX, v–vi. For translation of passage, see Rykwert, *On the Art of Building*, 304.

67 Alberti, *De re aedificatoria*, IX.v (trans. Rykwert, *On the Art of Building*, 305).

68 Alberti, *De re aedificatoria*, IX.v–viii.

69 On Pythagoras's discovery of harmony, see esp. Nicomachus, *Manual of Harmonics*, esp. IX. This work was well known in the fifteenth century as the number of manuscripts of this text testify. (See Domninos de Larissa, *Le Manuel d'Introduction Arithmétique du Philosophe Domninos de Larissa*, in Tannery, *Mémoirs Scientifiques*, 255–85.) In general, Nichomachus's works enjoyed a great popularity throughout medieval and Renaissance times.

70 See also Alberti, *Della pittura* (*On Painting*); and idem, *De scultura* (*On Sculpture*). Both these works considered the application of geometry (e.g., the "visual pyramid") to the visual arts in order to obtain perfect coordination of the parts of a given composition; both were composed prior to *De re aedificatoria*.

71 This work by Philo, translated by Lilio Tifernate (*Librum de vita Moysi*), is contained in *Vat. Lat. 182*. On its influence for the Sistine walls, see Leopold D. Ettlinger, *The Sistine Chapel before Michelangelo*, Oxford, 1965, passim.

72 Cusanus's views on the integrity of the circle were especially strong. These are discussed by Pierre Duhem, in *To Save the Phenomena: An Essay on the Idea of Physical Theory* (1960), trans. E. Doland and C. Maschler, Chicago and London, 1969, esp. 57–58.

73 Iamblichus, *Vita Pythagorica*, 3 and 5 (trans. Clark).

FIVE: THE STRENGTHENING AND DEEPENING OF PYTHAGOREANISM IN THE LATER FIFTEENTH CENTURY

1 Ficino, *Letters*, op. cit., II, no. 12; and V, no. 48. An important demonstration of Ficino's Pythagoreanism was made from the philosophical point of view by Celenza in "Pythagoras in the Renaissance: The Case of Marsilio Ficino," passim. For documents relating to Ficino's Pythagoreanism see *Marsilio Ficino e il ritorno di Platone*, ed. Sebastiano Gentile, Sandra Niccoli, and Paolo Viti (exh. cat.), Florence, 1984.

2 See the preface of Kristeller to Ficino, *Letters* (at 17).

3 Ficino, *Letters*, V, no. 27 (trans. from the latter by Members of Department of School of Economic Science, London, hereinafter Language Members).

4 Ficino, *Letters*, I, nos. 7 and 13.

5   Ficino, *Letters*, I, nos. 4–5, 21, and 109; IV, no. 33; V, nos. 12, 21, 27, and 48; and VII, Proem (trans. Language Members).

6   Ficino, *Letters*, II, no. 11; and V, no. 20 (trans. of the latter by Language Members).

7   Ficino, Letters, I, no. 21. For the ancient works, see Ficino, *Ex Porphyrio De abstinentia animalium, Spevsippi Platonis discipvli liber de Platonis definitionibus, Pythagorae philosophi avrea verba,* and *Symbola Pythagorae philosophi.* These can be found in Ficino, *Opera omnia*, II.2, 1932–79.

8   See Shumaker's discussion (accompanied by quoted passages) of Ficino's introduction to the fourteen *libelli,* which he translated in Shumaker, *Occult Sciences in the Renaissance*, 202–3.

9   See, e.g., Ficino, *Letters*, V, no. 21.

10 Ficino, *Letters*, I, no. 47; II, no. 34; III, no. 42; and IV, nos. 11 and 25 (trans. of the latter by Language Members). See also VII, nos. 7–8.

11 This subject is frequently discussed in his letters. See, e.g., Ficino, *Letters*, V.21.

12 See Ficino, *Letters*, III, no. 19, and V, no. 21.

13 See, e.g., Ficino, *Letters*, II, no. 43, VI, no. 2, and VII, no. 39 (trans. Language Members).

14 Ficino, *Letters*, e.g., I. nos. 20 and 108 (trans. Language Members).

15 Ficino, *Letters*, II, no. 42 (trans. Language Members).

16 See Ficino, *Letters*, VI, no. 22 and I, no. 20 (trans. Language Members).

17 Giovanni Corsi's *vita* of Ficino is in *Florence, Bib. Naz. Magl. IX*, 123. For an English translation (by Language Members), see idem, *Life of Marsilio Ficino*, in Ficino, *Letters*, III, 133–48.

18 See *Vita Ficini* (*Florence, Bib. Naz. Palat. 488*), possibly by Pietro Caponsacchi, in the fundamental work on Ficino by Raymond Marcel, *Marsile Ficin*, Paris, 1958, 690–730.

19 Ficino, *De vita* (editio princeps as *Liber de vita*, printer Antonius Mischominus, Florence, 1489), esp. II.vi, III.i, III.iii, III.xv, III.ii, III.xxi–xxii, and III.xxvi.

20 Ficino, *De vita*, III.xxi, and III, passim.

21 Ficino, *De vita*, proem to Bk. III (trans. in English edition as idem, *Three Books on Life*, trans. Carol V. Kaske and John R. Clark, Binghamton [N.Y.], 1989, at 239).

22 Ficino, *De vita*, I.vii, and III.xiv (trans. Kaske and Clark at 313). See also the discussion of this concept in Shumaker, *Occult Sciences in the Renaissance*, 131.

23 Ficino, *De vita*, III, 9–10 and 22.

24 The original text of this work is in *Florence, Bib. Ricc. 581*.

25 See Ficino's *Commentarium Marsilii Ficini Florentini in Convivium Platonis* in the Latin and French text edited by Marcel, *Commentaire sur le Banquet de Platon*, Paris, 1956.

26 Wind, "The Medal of Pico della Mirandola," in idem, *Pagan Mysteries in the Renaissance*, 36–53.

27 See e.g., the discussion in Ficino's *Commentary on the Timaeus*, 20–32. On this subject, see William R. Bowen,

"Ficino's Analysis of Musical *Harmonia*," in *Ficino and Renaissance Neoplatonism*, ed. Konrad Eisenbichler and Olga Z. Pugliese, Toronto, 1986, 17–27.

28 Ficino, *Iamblichi De secta pythagorica*, as reproduced in idem, *Svpplementvm Ficinianvm*, II, 98–100.

29 See, respectively, *Pythagorae symbola* and *Aurea praecepta Pythagorae*, both in Oxford, *Bod. Lib. 163* (*Marsili Ficini Florentini versiones variae quae sequnt* XV cent.). See also Oxford University, Bodleian Library, *Catalogi Codicum Manuscriptorum bibliothecae Bodleianae*, III, Oxford, 1854, 182; and a reprint of the former in Ficino, *Svpplementvm Ficinianvm*, 100–103.

30 Reuchlin's reference to Plotinus as "the distinguished Pythagorean" is in *De arte Cabalistica*, 205.

31 The immensity of interest among fifteenth-century scholars for the mysteries of Egypt, perhaps brought about by the diffusion of Plutarch's *Isis and Osiris*, is the subject of a modest but important work by Patrizia Castelli, *I geroglifici e il mito dell'Egitto nel Rinascimento*, Florence, 1979. For an excellent analysis of Ficino's linking of Platonism with Mosaic and Christian doctrine, see Paul Oskar Kristeller, *The Philosophy of Marsilio Ficino* (1938), trans. Virginia Conant, New York, 1943, esp. 24–29.

32 On this subject, see esp. Michael J. B. Allen, "Marsilio Ficino's Interpretation of Plato's Timaeus and Its Myth of the Demiurge," in *Svpplementvm festivvm: Studies in Honor of Paul Oskar Kristeller*, ed. James Hankins, John Monfasani, and Frederick Purnell, Jr., Binghamton, N.Y., 1987, 338–441, esp. 428–29.

33 Ficino, *Theologia Platonica*, passim. The relation of Ficino's text to the influence of Pletho and its influence in the Platonic "Academy" of Florence are discussed in Bohdar Kieszkowski, *Studi sul platonismo del Rinascimento in Italia*, Florence, 1936, esp. 24–125.

34 Ficino, *Theologia Platonica*, V.i.

35 See, e.g., Diogenes Laertius, *Lives of Eminent philosophers*, VIII.35.

36 Ficino, *Theologia Platonica*, XVII.xiii. (See with commentary in edition of Marcel at III.154.) See also Ficino, *Commentary on Plato's Symposium*, II.1, in *Commentaire sur le Banquet de Platon*, ed. Marcel, 145. The idea of Apollo as the apex of a triangle was suggested by Hierocles of Alexandria in the fifth century A.D. (*Hieroclis philosophi commentarius in aurea Pythagoreorum carmina*, ed. Joannes Curterio, London, 1654, 47), an idea that persisted in later versions of the *Golden Verses* attributed to Pythagoras. Hierocles said that Apollo was the top, or number 1, in the *tetraktys*.

37 On these concepts, see esp. Ficino, *Theologia Platonica*, passim. For Plutarch's description of the "beautiful" triangle, which, because it demonstrates $3^2 + 4^2 = 5^2$, or the Pythagorean theorem, see *De Iside et Osiride*, 56. On this, see also Allen, *Nuptial Arithmetic*, 36–40 and 97–101.

38 See, e.g., Plato's *Timaeus* in which the details of Plato's construction of the universe are couched

in complicated numerical terms. On the place of Pythagorean thinking in Ficino's view of Plato, see esp. Celenza, "Pythagoras in the Renaissance: The Case of Masilio Ficino." On Ficino's interest in number, see esp. Allen, *Nuptial Arithmetic*, passim.

39 See, e.g., Ficino, *Theologia Platonica*, II.ii–iv, II.i, IV.i, VI.i, and IX.i.

40 Ficino, *Theologia Platonica*, II.xi. See also Ficino's *Commentary on the Timaeus*, as quoted in Allen, "Marsilio Ficino's Interpretation of Plato's *Timaeus*," in *Svpplementvm Festivvm*, 427.

41 Regarding Ficino's veneration of the sun and his recognition of its connection with Pythagoras, see Celenza, "Pythagoras in the Renaissance: The Case of Morsilio Ficino," 688–89.

42 Ficino, *In librum de sole*, proem, in idem, *Opera omnia*, I.2, 963.

43 Ficino's *Commentary on the Timaeus*, trans. Allen, in idem, "Marsilio Ficino's Interpretation of Plato's *Timaeus*," in *Supplementum Festivvm*, 424.

44 Allen describes Ficino's lyre recitals, in which he intoned Platonic hymns to the sun, in *The Platonism of Marsilio Ficino*, Berkeley, Los Angeles, London, 1984, 60. On the so-called Platonic Academy, see Ch. 3, n. 2. Lorenzo's poem is published (in English trans.) in Paul Shorey, *Platonism Ancient and Modern*, Berkeley, 1938, 111–12.

45 This is the suggestion of Clement Salaman, in *The Letters of Marsilio Ficino*, VI, xx.

46 Pico della Mirandola, *De hominis dignitate*, 314, 317, 322, and 327. (Never delivered owing to papal objections, the oration was published posthumously.)

47 Pico della Mirandola, *De hominis dignitate*, 318–19.

48 Pico della Mirandola, *De hominis dignitate*, 315.

49 Pico della Mirandola, *De hominis dignitate*, 319–20.

50 Pico della Mirandola, *De hominis dignitate*, 322–23. See also idem, *Heptaplus*, 30.

51 Pico della Mirandola, *De hominis dignitate*, 326–27.

52 Pico della Mirandola, *De hominis dignitate*, 319–21 and 326–28.

53 Pico della Mirandola, *De hominis dignitate*, 330–31.

54 Pico della Mirandola, *Conclusiones*, passim.

55 This statement is Pico's fifth "conclusion" on the Orphic Hymns and is the translation of Farmer (*Syncretism in the West*), at 507.

56 See the discussion of Shumaker on this point in *Occult Sciences in the Renaissance*, 16.

57 See Pico's 55 "conclusions" on Proclus in Pico della Mirandola, *Conclusiones sive Theses DCCCC*, 44; and, his "conclusions" on the Kabbalah, no. 55, in ibid. at 63 (trans. by Farmer in Pico della Mirandola, *Syncretism in the West*, 543).

58 On this, see the the introduction of Farmer to Pico della Mirandola, *Syncretism in the West*, esp. 30–34.

59 Pico della Mirandola, *Syncretism in the West*, 32 (trans. Farmer).

60 This statement is taken from Pico's seventh "conclusion" on the Orphic Hymns and is the trans. of Farmer (Pico della Mirandola, *Syncretism in the West*), at 507.

61 On the influence of Jewish writings and mysticism on Pico, see esp. Joseph L. Blau, *The Christian Interpretation of the Cabala in the Renaissance*, New York, 1944, esp. 5–37; François Secret, "Pico della Mirandola e gli inizi della cabala cristiana," *Convivium*, N.S.I, 1957, 31–47; idem, *Les Kabbalistes chrétiens de la Renaissance*, passim; idem, "Nouvelles Precisions sur Flavius Mithraidates Maitre de Pic de la Mirandole et Traducteur de Commentaires de Kabbale," in *L'opera e il pensiero di Giovanni Pico della Mirandola ...* (Conveg. Int.), ed. Ist. Naz. di studi sul Rinascimento, Florence, II, 1965, 169–89; Gershom Scholem, *On the Kabbalah and Its Symbolism* (1965), trans. R. Manheim, New York, 1988, esp. 59–63; G. Dell'Acqua and L. Münster, "I rapporti di Giovanni Pico della Mirandola con alcuni filosofi ebrei," in *L'opera e il pensiero di Giovanni Pico della Mirandola*, II, 149–69; and Chaim Wirszubski, *Pico della Mirandola's Encounter with Jewish Mysticism*, Cambridge (Mass.), 1989, passim.

62 Pico della Mirandola, *Heptaplus*, First Proem, 6–8.

63 See, e.g., Pseudo-Iamblichus, *The Theology of Arithmetic*, 87–100.

64 Pico della Mirandola, *Heptaplus*, 5 and 10. Varro (who was reported by Pliny to have had a Pythagorean burial) wrote the *Hebdomades*, a work (now lost) in which the number 7 played a dominating role throughout; similarly, the twelfth-century *Heptateuchon* of Thierry of Chartres (certainly a Platonic if not a Pythagorean) was divided into seven books organized under the aegis of the Virgin Mary as patroness of the Seven Liberal Arts that embodied all wisdom.

65 Pico della Mirandola, *Heptaplus*, 18–24 (trans. Wallis, Miller, and Carmichael, at 107).

66 Pico della Mirandola, *Heptaplus*, 2–4 (trans. Wallis, Miller, and Carmichael, at 68–69).

67 Pico della Mirandola, *Heptaplus*, 4–8, 18, 29, 38, 51, and 55.

68 Pico della Mirandola, *De ente et uno opus*, IX, in idem, *Opera omnia*, 241–310 (trans. Wallis, Miller, and Carmichael, at 60).

69 Pico della Mirandola, *A Platonik Discourse upon Love*, passim, in *Poems*, ed. Thomas Stanley, London, 1651, 215–43. See also *Kommentar zu einem Lied der Liebe* (Ital/Ger), ed. Thorsten Bürklin, Hamburg, 2001.

70 For Pico's letter to Marsilio Ficino, see Pico della Mirandola, *Opera omnia*, 367–68 (trans. Carolyn Tuttle).

71 Pico della Mirandola, *Opera omnia* (trans. Language Members, in Ficino, *Letters*, VII, no. 91).

72 Giovanni Francesco Pico, *Giovanni Pico della Mirandola: His Life by His Nephew ...* (1510?), trans. Sir Thomas More, ed. J. M. Rigg, London, 1890, passim.

73 On Alamanno Rinuccini, see Vito R. Giustiniani, *Alamanno Rinuccini, 1426–1499*, Cologne, 1963. His famous plea for Florentine liberty (against Medici tyranny), *De libertate*, is published in *Humanism and*

Liberty: Writings on Freedom from Fifteenth Century Florence, ed. and trans. Renée Neu Watkins, Columbia (S.C.), 1978, 186–224. Alamanno's translation of Philostratus's work from Greek into Latin, dated 1488, survives in a sixteenth-century manuscript in the Vatican, *Vat.Lat.5732* (fols. 1–158).

74   Poliziano, *Silvae, Ambra*, lines 556–60; idem, *Oratio in expositione Homeri* (in idem, *Omnia opera*, printed Aldus Manutius, Venice, 1502, no ff. nos.); and *Panepistemon* (in *Omnia opera*, no ff. nos.) See also idem, *Ennarrationes in Fastos Ovidii*, I, in idem, *Commento inedito ai Fasti di Ovidio*, 62 and 186–87.

75   Poliziano, *Commento inedito all'epistola ovidiana di Saffo a Faone*, ed. Elisabetta Lazzeri, Florence, 1971. Cf. Ficino's reference to the words of Sappho in *Marsilio Ficino's Commentary on Plato's Symposium*, ed. Sears R. Jayne, Columbia (Mo.), 1944, 196. Respecting Sappho's possible early Pythagoreanism (she was still alive when Pythagoras was believed to have visited Lesbos), see Joost-Gauger, *Measuring Heaven*, 80–83.

76   See esp. Jerôme Carcopino, "Encore la Basilique de la 'Porta Maggiore,'" *Revue Archéologique*, XVIII (1923), 1–23. For a full bibliography on this subject, see Joost-Gauger, *Measuring Heaven*, ch. 9.

77   See the account of Federigo's literary tastes and library in Vespasiano da Bisticci, *Vite di uomini illustri* in Eng. ed. (*Lives*, op. cit.) 83–114. An inventory of the contents of the library made by its librarian, Agapitus, before 1487 is preserved in a manuscript in the Vatican, *BAV.Urb.Lat.167*. For a partial inventory of the library by century's end, see Cesare Guasti, "La biblioteca di Urbino," *Giornale storico degli archivi toscani*, n.s., XV, 1862, 133–47, and XVI, 1862, 127–47.

78   There is abundant evidence testifying to the friendship between Alberti and Duke Federigo, including letters, notices, and deluxe copies of Alberti's works in the library at Urbino. On these, see Maria Grazia Pernis, *Le Platonisme de Marsile Ficin et la Cour d'Urbin*, ed. François Roudaut, Paris, 1997, 27–31 (and notes).

79   Pernis, *Le Paltonisme de Marsile Ficin et la Cour d'urbin*, 31–62.

80   On Federigo's library, see Vespasiano da Bisticci, *Lives*, 83–114, and the discussion and further bibliography in Pernis, *Le Paltonisme de Marsile Ficin et la Cour d'urbin*, 45–62.

81   Patrizia Castelli, "Matematici e astrologi tedeschi alla 'corte' dei Montefeltro," *Die Kunst und das Studium der Natur vom 14. zum 16. Jahrhundert*, Weinheim, 1987, 238–39.

82   The translation, from a manuscript dated 1473 and copied later, is dedicated to Federigo with the words: "Ad illustrem Principem Federicum Feretranum Urbini Comitem Alamanni Rinuccini in Libros Philostrati de vita Apollonii Thyanei in Latinum conversos … ." (*BAV.Vat.Lat.9344*). On this, see Giorgio Radetti, "Un'aggiunta alla biblioteca di Pierleone Leoni da Spoleto," *Rinascimento*, ser. 2, V, 1965, 87–101.

83   The full inscription reads: "Federigo, Duke of Urbino and standardbearer of the enduring Holy Roman Church and commender of the Italian confederation, built this house from its foundations for his glory and for his descendants. He fought in war many times, six times carried the standards, eight times utterly destroyed the enemy; a victor in every battle, he increased his dominion. His justice, mercy, generosity, and piety in peacetime equaled and adorned his victories." Pasquale Rotondi, *Il Palazzo Ducale di Urbino*, Urbino, 1950–51, I, 434 (trans. author).

84   Concetta Bianca, "L'accademia del Bessarione tra Roma e Urbino," *Federico di Montefeltro: La cultura* (convegno 1982), ed. Giorgio C. Baiardi, Giorgio Chittolini, and Piero Floriani, Rome, 1986, 61–79, esp. 74–75.

85   Vespasiano da Bisticci, *Lives*, 100 and 104 (trans. passage by W. G. Waters and E. Waters in ibid.); and Baldi, "Pavolo di Middelburgo," in *Le vite de'matematici*, 355–97. See also Castelli, "Matematici e astrologi … ," passim.

86   On the tradition of mathematics at the court of Urbino, see Rose, *The Italian Renaissance of Mathematics*, 54ff., 204–5, and passim.

87   Baldi, "Pavolo di Middelburgo," 355–97.

88   Giovanni Santi, *La vita e le gesta di Federico di Montefeltro duca d'Urbino* (ca. 1482), ed. Luigi M. Tocci, Vatican City, 1985, II, LVII, 48–63.

89   See, e.g., a letter of 1492 from Ficino to Paulo. Not printed in the English edition of the *Letters*; for this letter see Ficino, *Opera omnia*, I.2, 944.

90   See, e.g., Paulus de Middelbourg, *Prognostica, ad viginti annos duratura*, Antwerp, 1484. Later, as bishop of Fossombrone, Paulus wrote a treatise in 1513 on the computation of holy days (e.g., Easter), a work that survives in manuscript form in the Vatican Library (*BAV.Vat.Lat.3684*). A study fundamental for work on Paulus is that of D. J. Struik, "Paulus van Middelbourg," *Mededeelingen van het Nederlandsch Historisch Instituut te Rome*, V, 1925, 79–118.

91   It is clear that Paulus was well known to Giovanni della Rovere before he assumed the Pontificate as Julius II, for as early as 1491 Paulus dedicated a manuscript to the then Cardinal della Rovere. Given his personal ties with the Pope and the fact that his friends from Urbino were at the court of Julius, it may be assumed that Paulus frequented the Vatican court before his appointment was made official in 1512. See Demetrio Marzi, *La questione della riforma del calendario nel Quinto Concilio Lateranese* (1512–17), in *Pubblicazioni del R. Istituto di Studi Superiori pratici e di perfezionamento in Firenze*, 1896, 39–72; also Baldi, "Pavolo di Middelburgo," *Le vite de' matematici*, 355–97, esp. 371ff.; and D'Amico, *Renaissance Humanism in Popal Rome*, 36.

92   Giovanni Gaye, ed., *Carteggio inedito d'artisti dei secoli XIV, XV, XVI*, Florence, 1849, I, 214. The document is dated 10 June 1468.

93   Laurana's origins and training are discussed in Ludwig H. Heydenreich and Wolfgang Lotz, *Architecture in Italy, 1400–1600* (trans. Mary Hottinger, Harmondsworth, 1974, 343–44). Respecting his work on the ducal palace at Urbino, see Werner Lutz, *Luciano Laurana und der Herzogspalast von Urbino*, Weimar, 1995. Rotondi speculates that the architectural planning of the Cappella del Perdono and the Temple of the Muses (the "twin chapels") was undertaken by Laurana; their decoration was completed by the young Bramante (*Il Palazzo Ducale di Urbino*, I, 85–92).

94   Vitruvius, *Il "Vitruvio Magliabechiano" di Francesco di Giorgio Martini*, ed. Gustina Scaglia, Florence, 1985.

95   Vitruvius, *De architectura*, III.i.8.

96   See Francesco di Giorgio Martini, *Trattato di architettura*, in Massimo Mussini, *Francesco di Giorgio e Vitruvio: Le traduzioni del "De architectura"…* , Florence, 2003 (2 vols.). This is usually regarded as the second "version" of the more technical first "version." For the complete treatises of Francesco, see idem, *Trattati di architettura, ingegneria e arte militare*, ed. Corrado Maltese, Milan, 1967 (2 vols.). On Francesco's Pythagoreanism, see the pioneering study of Hersey, *Pythagorean Palaces*, esp. 40–44, and passim.

97   Vitruvius, *De architectura*, ed. Sulpizio da Veroli, Rome, 1486. On this, see Lily B. Campbell, "The First Edition of Vitruvius," *Modern Philology*, XXIX, 1931, esp. 107–10; Francesco Pellati, "Giovanni Sulpicio da Veroli primo editore di Vitruvio," *Atti, secondo congresso Nazionale di Studi romani*, III, Rome, 1931, 382–86; and L. Marcucci, "Giovanni Sulpicio e la prima edizione del De architettura di Vitruvio," *Studi e documenti di architettura*, VIII, 1978, 193–95.

98   On this see note 97. Also, for documentation of Sulpizio's visit to Urbino and the full text of the epigram, see Rotondi, *Il Palazzo Ducale di Urbino*, I, 420.

99   Giovanni Santi, *La vita e le gesta di Montefeltro*, II, LVII, 48–63.

100   On the mathematical treatises of Piero della Francesca, see Margaret Daly Davis, *Piero della Francesca's Mathematical Treatises*, Ravenna, 1977; idem, "Piero's Treatises: The Mathematics of Form," in *Cambridge Companion to Piero della Francesca*, ed. Jeryldene M. Wood, Cambridge, 2002, 134–51; Field, "Piero della Franesca's Mathematics," in ibid., 152–70; and esp. idem, *Piero della Francesca*.

101   This work is known through an original manuscript recently recognized as Piero's in Florence (*Bib. Laur. Ashburnham. 359*). On this first of Piero della Francesca's treatises, see S. A. Jayawardene, "The 'Trattato d'Abaco' of Piero della Francesca," in *Cultural Aspects of the Italian Renaissance: Essays in Honour of Paul Oskar Kristeller*, ed. Cecil H. Clough, Manchester and New York, 1976, 229–43. See also Davis, "Piero's Treatises," op. cit., 137.

102   Piero's *De prospective pingendi* survives in a manuscript in Parma (*MS. Parmensis 1576*). See idem, *De la perspective en peinture*, ed. Hubert Damish, trans. Jean-Pierre Le Goff, Paris, 1998; and idem, *De prospectiva pingendi*, ed. Giustina Nicco-Fasola, Florence, 2005. The cited topics are from the opening lines of Bk. I and Bk. II, passim. References to Vitruvius are in Bk. III.

103   On the five regular polyhedra, which were described by Euclid, see J. V. Field, "Rediscovering the Archimedean Polyhedra: Piero della Francesca, Luca Pacioli, Leonardo da Vinci," in *Archive for History of the Exact Sciences*, L (3/4), 1997, esp. 244–53.

104   Piero's *Libellus de quinque corporibus regularibus* survives only in a single Latin copy (*BAV. Vat. Urb. Lat. 632*) though it was printed in Italian by Pacioli some years later in his *Divina proportione*. See *Libellus de quinque corporibus regularibus*, no ed., Florence, 1995 (3 vols.).

105   This is discussed by Davis, *Piero della Francesca's Mathematical Treatises*, 18–19 and 44–45.

106   Piero's *Trattato d'abaco* was published by Pacioli in 1494 in his *Summa arithmetica*, while Piero's *Libellus de quinque corporibus regularibus* was printed in its entirety, in Italian translation, by Pacioli in 1509 in his *Divina proportione*.

107   Polydore Vergil, *On Discovery*, I.xvi.

108   Those works which are not today dispersed are mostly in the Pio da Carpi library and the Biblioteca Estense at Modena. For an inventory of the library of Giorgio Valla, see Johan Ludwig Heiberg, "Beiträge zur Geschichte Georg Valla's und seiner Bibliothek," *Beihefte zum Centralblatt für Bibliothekswesen*, XVI, 1896, 353–482. See also Rose, *The Italian Renaissance of Mathematics*, 46–47.

109   Regarding Leonardo's acquaintance with Giorgio Valla, see the comprehensive analysis of Leonardo's sources by Edmondo Solmi, in *Le fonti dei manoscritti di Leonardo da Vinci* (*Giornale Storico della Letteratura Italiana*, supp/s. 10–11), 1908, 1–344, esp. 275–76; also Eugenio Garin, "Il problema delle fonti di Leonardo," *La cultura filosofica del Rinascimento italiano*, Florence, 1961, esp. 391–92. On that with Copernicus, see Rose, *The Italian Renaissance of Mathematics*, 48–49.

110   According to this theory, the sun was the center of some planetary orbits, i.e., those of Mercury and Venus. As these planets moved around the sun, the sun in turn revolved in an orbit around the earth. Hence this theory was geocentric respecting the seven planets while it was heliocentric respecting two of them. (While Pythagoreans had, historically, held that there was a "fire" in the center of the universe, around which the planets revolved, it was never quite clear that this was the sun, though the inference that it was seems fair.) Giorgio describes this theory in the first chapter of the third book devoted to astronomy in the *De expetendis …* (see n. 112). On this, see Grant McColley, "George Valla: An Unnoted Advocate of the Geo-Heliocentric Theory," *Isis*, XXXIII, 1941, 312–14. On similarities in the writings of Giorgio Valla and Copernicus, see Ludwik A. Birkenmajer, *Stromata Copernicana*, Krakow, 1924, esp. 154–67.

111 See esp. Giorgio Valla's letter to Jacopo Antiquario (a friend and supporter of Ficino's and Pico's) of 1489–90, printed in Heiberg, "Beiträge zur Geschichte Georg Valla's … ," 54–61; cf. a letter from Filelfo to Giorgio Valla in ibid., 97. On the probable Pythagoreanism of Jacopo Antiquario, a letter to him from Ficino praises his love of Platonism and his efforts to reinstitute the "golden days" of Greek philosophy in Italy (Ficino, *Letters*, VI, no. 40).

112 Giorgio Valla, *Georgii Vallae Placentini viri clarissimi De expetendis, et fvgiendis rebvs opvs* … , ed. Aldus Romano, Venice, 1501 (hereinafter *De expetendis* … . For the few important discussions of this work, see Heiberg, "Beiträge zur Geschichte Georg Valla's … ," idem, "Philologische Studien zu griechischen Mahemathikern," *Jahrbücher für classische Philologie*, supp. XII, 1881, esp. 377–99; Gianna Gardenal, "Giorgio Valla e le scienze esatte," *Giorgio Valla tra scienza e sapienza*, ed. Vittore Branca, Florence, 1981, esp. 12–19; and Rose, *The Italian Renaissance of Mathematics*, 46–49.

113 On this, see Rose, *The Italian Renaissance of Mathematics*, 48.

114 Giorgio Valla, *De expetendis* … , Bks. I–III, esp. III, x–xx.

115 In addition to his own original writings, Maximus Planudes (ca. 1260–ca. 1330) translated a number of Latin texts into Greek for the Byzantine world. Among these were Cicero (*In somnium Scipionis*) and Macrobius (*Commentary on the Somnium Scipionis*), as well as works by Ovid and Boethius, all of which were central to Pythagoreanism. For his original works, see Migne, *Patrologia Graeca*, CXLVII, and respecting his enormous influence as one of the few Greeks who made Latin works available to the Greek world, John E. Sandys, *History of Classical Scholarship* (1906), rep. New York, 1958, I, 257 and 427–28.

116 Giorgio Valla, *De expetendis* … , passim. See, e.g., III.x–xx.

117 So says the ancient author Nicomachus of Gerasa, *Introduction to Arithmetic*, I.I.I. (This work was published in the edition of Martin Luther D'Ooge, New York, 1926, 3–180.)

118 Giorgio Valla, *Cleonidae Harmonicum interprete Georgio Valla Placentino*, Venice, 1497.

119 Giorgio Valla, *Cleonidae Harmonicum*, proem (trans. Carolyn Tuttle).

120 See the text and commentary in P. L. Rose, "Bartolomeo Zamberti's Funeral Oration for the Humanist Encyclopaedist Giorgio Valla," *Cultural Aspects of the Italian Renaissance: Essays in Honour of Paul Oskar Kristeller*, ed. Cecil H. Clough, Manchester and New York, 1976, 299–310.

121 Constantinus Lascaris's *Ne aurea Pythagorae* is contained in *De octo partibus orationes* (published in 1503 by Aldus Manutius in Venice and again in 1510, 1512, 1515, 1533, 1540, and 1543).

122 Giovanni Cademosto, *Georgii Vallae vita per Johannem Petrum Cademustum Laudensem eius adoptivum filium*, printed in Heiberg, "Beiträge zur Geschichte Georg Valla's … ," 3–6.

123 See, e.g., the ten manuscript editions of Nicomachus's *Arithmetica* listed by Bolgar, in *Classical Heritage*, 481; also, e.g., *Martiani Capelle De nuptijs Philologie & Merurij libri duo*, ed. Henricvm de Sancto Vrso, Vicenza, 1499; *Arithmeticas Boetij*, ed. Erhardum Ratdolt, Venice, 1488; and *Arithmetica geometria et musica Boetii*, Venice, 1492.

124 The *Arithmetica thoma brauardini* by Thomas Bradwardine, who was archbishop of Canterbury in the fourteenth century, is known in editions of 1495, 1496, 1498, and 1500, for example, while the arithmetic text of Jordanus was also published well into the sixteenth century. The opening page of Bradwardine's text credits Pythagoras as the first to treat number in this (his) way (see Bradwardine, *Arithmethica Thome bravardini*, Paris, 1495, no pp.). Jordanus Nemorarius, from Paderborn, was a thirteenth-century contemporary of Leonardo of Pisa. See Jordanus, *De elementis arithmitice artis: A Medieval Treatise on Number Theory*, ed. H. L. L. Busard, Stuttgart, 1991. On this type of book, see David E. Smith, *Rara Arithmetica*, Boston and London, 1908, intro. and passim.

125 Filippo Calandri, *Calandri Philippi Aritmetica* (1491). This work was reprinted in 1492 and again in 1518.

126 On fifteenth-century astrology, see Garin, *Astrology in the Renaissance*.

127 Ptolemy's *Tetrabiblos* (2nd century A.D.) described the basic doctrines of astrology in his time.

128 Iamblichus, *Vita Pythagorica*, e.g., 28 and 29.

129 Lorenzo Bonincontri, *De vi ac potestate mentis humane* … , printed in Patrizia L. Ruffo, "Lorenzo Bonincontri e alcuni suoi scritti ignorati," *Rinascimento*, 2nd ser., V, 1965, 184. On him, see Thorndike, *History of Magic and Experimental Science*, IV, 405–12 and 455.

130 Regarding Pythagorean tuning in Spain and the efforts of Ramis de Pareja to stay within its framework, see Gustave Reese, *Music in the Renaissance* (1954), New York, 1959, 586–87.

131 On the diffusion of Pythagorean ideas about harmony and the music of the spheres in the sixteenth century, see Heninger, *Touches of Sweet Harmony*, passim.

132 Gaffurio, *De harmonia musicorum*, I.5 (trans. Miller, 46).

133 Gaffurio, *De harmonia musicorum*, passim.

134 For Bryennius's text, see Manuel Bryennius, *The Harmonics of Manuel Bryennius*, ed. Goverdus H. Jonker, Groningen, 1970. Gaffurio commissioned Gian Francesco Burana of Verona to accomplish this translation (preserved in Lodi, *Bib. Comm. Cod. XXVIII A8*, fols. 3–118).

135 Pseudo-Iamblichus, *The Theology of Arithmetic*, 65–74.

136 Gaffurio, *De harmonia musicorum*, passim, passage from IV.14 (trans. Miller, 203).

137 Gaffurio, *De harmonia musicorum*, esp. I.1–2; and idem, *Theoricum musice*, I.1.236–39; I.3.1–31; and I.4.6–12.

138 Niger of Cremona, *Hendecasyllabic poem*, in Gaffurio, *De harmonia musicorum*, ed. Miller, 26.

139 Gaffurio, *De harmonia musicorum*, ch. 12, esp. at 199–200 (with accompanying woodcut illustration). On this subject see Wind, "Gaffurius on the Harmony

140 For the original printed edition, see Platina, *De honesta volvptate*, ptr. Ulrich Han, Rome, 1475.

141 Diogenes Laertius, *Lives at Eminent Philosophers*, VIII.9.

142 Platina, proem. The library of Leonardo da Vinci will be discussed (with bibliography) in Chapter 6.

143 The bust of Plato, allegedly discovered in the debris of the Athenian Academy, was brought to Florence where it was revered. On this, see Niccolò Valori, *La Vie de Laurent de Médicis … traduite du Latin …* (1492), Paris, 1761, 63; Fr. Pacifico Burlamacchi, *Vita di Frate Girolamo Savonarola*, Lucca, 1761, 78; and Della Torre, *Storia dell' Accademia Platonica di Firenze*, 640.

144 See, e.g., Iamblichus, *Vita Pythagorica*, 28.

SIX: THE MATURATION AND VICISSITUDES OF PYTHAGOREANISM IN THE SIXTEENTH CENTURY

1 The admiration of Paulus de Middelbourg for Pacioli is noted by Baldi, in his biography of the latter. See "Fra' Luca dal Borgo S. Sepolcro," in Baldi, *Le vite de' matematici*, 343.

2 Luca Pacioli, *Summa arithmetica*, Bk. I, ch. I (fols. 2r–4r).

3 Pacioli, *Summa arithmetica*, unnumbered fol. in Bk. I.

4 While we may never know if, as suggested in the cultural anthropological study of Karl Menninger (*Number Words and Number Symbols: A Cultural History of Numbers* [1934], trans. Paul Broneer, Cambridge [Mass.], 1969), such concepts derived from the ten fingers of the hand, it would appear, given the consistence and orderliness of Pacioli's Pythagorean-mathematical interests that, like his admired predecessors Vitruvius and Alberti, he considered the number 10 to be a kind of perfect number. On the special significance of the decad for Pythagoreans, see Heninger, *Touches of Sweet Harmony*, esp. 84–85.

5 See, e.g., Boethius, *Arithmetica geometria et musica Boetii/ De institutione arithmetica*, Venice, 1492, VI-1, fol. 160v. The earliest example of a printed edition of this work was the *Arithmetica* by him printed in Augsburg in 1488. On the *mensula Pythagorae*, see George Sarton, *A History of Science*, Cambridge (Mass.), I, 1952, 208.

6 Pacioli, *Summa arithmetica*, fol. 72v.

7 On the symbolism of numbers see Pacioli, *Summa arithmetica*, fols. 2r–18v.

8 Pacioli, *Summa arithmetica*, fols. 143r and v.

9 Pacioli, *Summa arithmetica*, fols. 68r–74r.

10 The probability that Leonardo da Pisa (or Fibonacci), who relied on Nicomachus, was a Pythagorean is discussed in Joost-Gaugier, *Measuring Heaven*, ch. 7.

11 Pacioli testifies to his association with Leonardo, an association that is corroborated in Leonardo's notebooks. See, e.g., Pacioli, *Divina proportione*, ch. I. On their relationship see Field, *Piero della Francesca*, 6–7.

12 Pacioli, *Divina proportione*, title page.

13 On this, see the discussion in Field, "Rediscovering the Archimedean Polyhedra," esp. 254–61.

14 See, e.g., Pacioli, *Divina proportione*, ch. XXX, title.

15 Pacioli, *Divina proportione*, ch. LIV.

16 On this, see Bruno Nardi, "La scuola di Rialto e l'umanesimo veneziano," in *Umanesimo europeo e umanesimo veneziano*, ed. Vittore Branca, Florence, 1963, 115.

17 The text of this lecture (or "sermon") is printed in Nardi, "La scoula di Rialto," 114–16, n. 46.

18 Nardi, "La scoula di Rialto," 117.

19 Nardi, "La scoula di Rialto," proems in chs. I–III.

20 Leonardo's study of the "Pythagorean theorem" is contained in *London, Victoria and Albert Museum Codex Forster* 1, C.4v. His various manuscripts refer to a number of books, as well as to two libraries in Florence (the libraries of San Marco and of Santo Spirito). Partial lists of the books he owned are known from a book list, apparently from Leonardo's hand, now in Madrid. This lists a total of 116 books on such varied subjects as anatomy, surgery, grammar, astrology, medicine, and religion. Among the more "Pythagorean" sourcebooks he owned were works by authors such as Giorgio Valla, Saint Augustine, Saint Isidore of Seville, Walter Burley, Ovid, and Diogenes Laertius, in addition to Alberti, Francesco di Giorgio, and Pacioli. Of particular interest is a work he owned on the squaring of the circle (author unknown, but a subject traditionally regarded as a Pythagorean problem), and two books (authors unknown) from Urbino. His love of animals is reflected in the fact that he owned a number of books on animals. On these, see Ladislao Reti, "The Two Unpublished Manuscripts of Leonardo da Vinci in the Biblioteca Nacional of Madrid (I and II)," *Burlington Magazine*, CX, 1968, 10–22 and 81–89; Leonardo da Vinci, *The Madrid Codices*, ed. Ladislao Reti, New York, 1974, III, 92–107 (hereinafter Reti, The Madrid Codices). See also Garin, "Il problema delle fonti del pensiero di Leonardo," 388–401; Leonardo da Vinci, *The Notebooks of Leonardo da Vinci* (1938), ed. Edward MacCurdy, London, 1977, II, 507–8 (hereinafter MacCurdy, Notebooks of Leonardo); and Carlo Pedretti's *Commentary* to Leonardo da Vinci, *The Literary Works of Leonardo da Vinci, Compiled and Edited by Jean Paul Richter* (hereinafter Pedretti, *Commentary*), London, 1977, II, 35.

21 This passage is quoted by Solmi, *Le fonti dei manoscritti di Leonardo da Vinci*, 231–34.

22 Leonardo da Vinci, in MacCurdy, *Notebooks of Leonardo*, I, 250 (trans. MacCurdy).

23 Giorgio Vasari, *Le vite de' più eccellenti pittori scultori ed architettori*, ed. Gaetano Milanesi, Florence, 1906, IV, 18 and 28–29. For a testament to Leonardo's lyre playing by a contemporary, see Anonimo Fiorentino,

Il Codice Magliabechiano, ed. Karl Frey, Berlin, 1892 (rep. Franborough [U.K.], 1969), 110.

24   On their relation, see Giovanni Battista de Toni, "Leonardo da Vinci e Luca Paciolo," *Atti del Reale Istituto Veneto di Scienze, Lettere ed Arti*, LXV, 1905, 1145–49.

25   MacCurdy, *Notebooks of Leonardo,* II, 507.

26   Solmi, *Le fonti dei manoscritti di Leonardo da Vinci*, 104.

27   Pacioli arrived in Milan in 1496, whereas the date of the dedication of *De divina proportione* to the Duke of Milan is the ninth of February 1498 (Pacioli, *De divina proportione*, second fol.).

28   See Vitruvius, *De architectura,* IX, 13–14. This is discussed by Claire Farago in Leonardo da Vinci, *Leonardo da Vinci's Paragone*, ed. Claire Farago, Leiden and New York, 1992, 86, n. 152, also at 309 (hereinafter Farago, *Paragone*).

29   See esp. the discussion of Farago in *Paragone*, esp. 83–86.

30   On Vitruvius as an important source for Leonardo, see, e.g., Gabriella Ferri Piccaluga, "Leonardo, Pico e l'ambiente Ebraico," in *Leonardo e Pico* (Atti del Convegno di Mirandola, 2003), ed. Fabio Frosini, Florence, 2005, esp. 40. See also Farago, *Paragone*, 85–88.

31   Regarding Leonardo's annotations of Francesco di Giorgio's manuscript, see Pedretti, *Commentary*, 123. Regarding the friendship between the two, see the important discussion of Farago in *Paragone*, 86–87.

32   See Solmi, *Le fonti dei manoscritti di Leonardo da Vinci*, 297–301. This work, however, was not listed in the (incomplete) list of books he owned as published by Reti in 1968 and 1974.

33   Among Leonardo's books were two by Alberti, the *De re aedificatoria*, and a "volume on mathematics," surely the *Ludis rerum mathematicarum* (see Reti, "The Two Unpublished … ," and idem, *The Madrid Codices*).

34   See passage quoted in Solmi, *Le fonti dei manoscritti di Leonardo da Vinci,* esp. at 39–40.

35   See Solmi, *Le fonti dei manoscritti di Leonardo da Vinci*, 40–41.

36   Leonardo da Vinci, *Leonardo on Painting: An Anthology of Writings by Leonardo da Vinci*, ed. Martin Kemp, New Haven and London, 1989, 14–16 (hereinafter Kemp, *Leonardo on Painting*).

37   Quoted passage is translation of Kemp in *Leonardo on Painting*, 119.

38   Leonardo da Vinci, *The Literary Works of Leonardo da Vinci* (1883), ed. Jean Paul Richter, New York, 1970, II, 27 (hereinafter Richter, *Literary Works of Leonardo*).

39   See Reti, *The Madrid Codices*, 92. While Leonardo's general notation may have referred to a different work by Giorgio Valla (*Cleonidae Harmonicum*), this, based on what he has to say in the text of his notes, is unlikely.

40   See Reti, "The Two Unpublished … ," and idem, *The Madrid Codices*, and Pedretti, *Commentary*, at 356 and 372.

41   On Leonardo's philosophy, see Stéphane Toussaint, "Leonardo filosofo dei contrari," in *Leonardo e Pico*, ed. Frosini, 13–37.

42   Richter, *Literary Works of Leonardo*, I, 385–86 (trans. Richter).

43   See, e.g., Richter, *Literary Works of Leonardo,* I, 140 and II, 231.

44   MacCurdy, *Notebooks of Leonardo*, II, 408.

45   On this subject, see especially Meyer Schapiro, "Leonardo and Freud: An Art Historical Study," *Journal of the History of Ideas*, XVII, 1956, esp. 173–75; Leo Steinberg, "Leonardo's *Last Supper*," *Art Quarterly*, XXXVI, 1973, 297–410; and Bradley I. Collins, *Leonardo, Psychoanalysis, and Art History*, Evanston (Ill.), 1997, 68–69, 132–33, and, for further bibliography on this subject, 218–19. Schapiro assails Freud's selective approach that claimed that Leonardo's vegetarianism and his freeing of caged birds constituted evidence of his sadistic tendencies; Schapiro, to his credit, suggests that Leonardo might have been influenced by reading works by Porphyry (a Pythagorean of Antiquity). Steinberg, on the other hand, suggests that the apostles, present at the Last Supper, exhibited their shock at the concept of drinking the blood and eating the flesh of Christ. In discussing the extensive bibliography on this subject, Collins appears to accept Leonardo's vegetarianism as an established fact.

46   MacCurdy, *Notebooks of Leonardo*, II, 446 (trans. MacCurdy).

47   MacCurdy, *Notebooks of Leonardo*, II, 447 (trans. MacCurdy).

48   MacCurdy, *Notebooks of Leonardo* II, 447 (trans. MacCurdy).

49   MacCurdy, *Notebooks of Leonardo*, II, 453 (trans. MacCurdy).

50   MacCurdy, *Notebooks of Leonardo,* II, 453 (trans. MacCurdy).

51   MacCurdy, *Notebooks of Leonardo*, II, 454 (trans. MacCurdy).

52   MacCurdy, *Notebooks of Leonardo,* II, 454 (trans. MacCurdy).

53   MacCurdy, *Notebooks of Leonardo,,* II, 455 (trans. MacCurdy).

54   MacCurdy, *Notebooks of Leonardo*, II, 466 (trans. MacCurdy).

55   MacCurdy, *Notebooks of Leonardo*, II, 470 and 473 (trans. MacCurdy).

56   MacCurdy, *Notebooks of Leonardo*, II, 457 (trans. MacCurdy).

57   MacCurdy, *Notebooks of Leonardo*, II, 481.

58   Richter, *Literary Works of Leonardo*, II, 246 (trans. Richter).

59   Richter, *Literary Works of Leonardo*, II, 251 and 298 (trans. Richter).

60 Richter, *Literary Works of Leonardo*, II, 302 (trans. Richter).

61 See fragments of Leonardo's writings in Richter, *Literary Works of Leonardo*, II, 245 and 263–65 (trans. Richter).

62 Richter, *Literary Works of Leonardo*, II, 269 (trans. Richter).

63 See, e.g., Richter, *Literary Works of Leonardo*, II, 327, 106, 247, and I, 389, respectively.

64 The earliest known description of Pythagoras is that of Xenophanes. Subsequent discussions on the subject ranged from those of Empedocles and Aristoxenus to those of Porphyry and Iamblichus, in works well known in the Renaissance. Regarding this history, see Joost-Gaugier, *Measuring Heaven*, passim.

65 See the original text of the will (together with its English translation) in John William Brown, *The Life of Leonardo da Vinci*, London, 1828, 217–28.

66 Reisch, *Margarita philosophica* (1503). For his discussions on number, see esp. Bk. IV, Tractatus I of this work. On Reisch and his encyclopedia (which was reprinted in 1504, 1535, and 1599), see Smith, 82–85.

67 Johannes Martinus Blasius, *Liber arithmetice practice astrologis …* , Paris, 1513 (rep. Cambridge, 1960).

68 Baldassare Castiglione, *Il cortegiano*, passim.

69 See the concluding pages of Beroaldo, *Symbola Pythagorae* (trans. Carolyn Tuttle from Appendix B to this volume).

70 This is discussed by John W. O'Malley, *Praise and Blame in Renaissance Rome*, Durham (N.C.), 1979, 132–33.

71 More information, and bibliography, on Tommaso Inghirami is provided in chs. 2 and 12 of Christiane L. Joost-Gaugier, *Raphael's Stanza della Segnatura: Meaning and Invention*, Cambridge, 2002.

72 Respecting the find of ancient texts, including the Cicero text, in a monastery at Bobbio in 1494, see the discussion, with bibliography, in Joost-Gaugier, *Raphael's Stanza della Segnatura*, 25–26.

73 Cicero points this out in the preface to his commentary on Plato's *Timaeus*: *M. Tvlli Ciceronis Timaeus*, ed. Franciscvs Pini, Milan, 1965. In a letter (idem, *Epistulae ad familiares*, ed. D. R. Shackelton Bailey, Cambridge, 1977, II, no. 225) to Nigidius, Cicero tells him he is the most learned and virtuous of all men and the best of all his personal friends.

74 On this subject, see the discussion of Tommaso as a stand-in for the portrait of Epicurus in Raphael's *School of Athens* in Joost-Gaugier, *Raphael's Stanza della Segnatura*, 101–3.

75 Fabio Calvo's Latin edition, published in Rome in 1525, was accompanied by a Greek edition published by Manuzio in Venice in 1526. For a biography and bibliography on this medical doctor/mathematician/antiquarian see Fabio Calvo, *Vitruvio e Raffaello, Il De architectura di Vitruvio nella traduzione inedita di Fabio Calvo Ravennate*, ed. Vincenzo Fontana and Paolo Morachiello, Rome, 1975, 45–56; and R. Gualdo, "Fabio Calvo, Marco," *Dizionario biografico degli italiani*, Rome, 1993, XLIII, 723–27. Respecting the inserted note, see P. N. Pagliara, "La Roma antica di Fabio Calvo," in *Psicon*, III, 1976, 8/9, 66.

76 The first letter, by a Maddalena Tagliapietra, is quoted by Rodolfo Lanciani, in *The Golden Days of the Renaissance in Rome*, London, 1906, 252; the second, a letter from a contemporary (but younger) scientist, Celio Calcagnini, to the mathematician Jacob Ziegler, appears in Calcagnini, *Opera aliquot*, 100–101.

77 The original, annotated by Raphael, is in the Staatsbibliothek at Munich (*Cod. Ital. 37*). The last sentence of the volume confirms the circumstances of its creation: "Fine del libro di Victruvio architecto, tradoctodi latino in lingua e sermone, proprio e volgare da M[e]s[ser] Fabio Calvo ravenate, in Roma in casa I Raphaello." Respecting this work see Calvo, *Vitruvio e Raffaello*. On Raphael's loving care of Fabio, see Calcagnini's letter to Ziegler cited in note 76.

78 See, e.g., Porphyry, *Life of Pythagoras*, 33.

79 Francesco Giorgio (Zorzi), *Francesco Georgii veneti minoritanae familiae de Harmonia mvndi totivs cantica tria*, ptr. Bernardino de Vitalibus, Venice, 1525.

80 The history of translations and reprints of this work is discussed by Vasoli in "Hermetism in Venice," 31–69, esp. at 51–52.

81 The ancient pedigree of the association of number 3 with perfection and the triangle can be seen, e.g., in Pseudo-Iamblichus's fourth-century (A.D.) *Theology of Arithmetic* (49–53). See also Aristotle's earlier report on the significance of this number for Pythagoreans in *De caelo*, II, 284b.

82 Giorgio, *Harmonia mvndi*, proem and Bk. I, passim.

83 Giorgio, *Harmonia mvndi*, Bk. II, esp. ch. 35.

84 Giorgio, *Harmonia mvndi*, Bk. III, passim.

85 On "secret harmonies" and "alchemical music," see Joscelyn Godwin, *Harmonies of Heaven and Earth*, Rochester (Vt.), 1987, esp. 63–85.

86 To be noted are the following works: Gioseffo Zarlino, *Le istitutioni harmoniche* (1558); Vincenzo Galilei, *Dialogo della musica antica et della moderna* of 1581; Francesco Patrizi, *Della nuova geometria … Libri XV*, of 1587; idem, *Nova de universis philosophia …* of 1591; and Francisco Salinas, *Francisci Salinae Bvrgensis … De musica libri septem* (1577), Salamanca, 1592. For more on these and other musical theorists of the sixteenth century, see Joscelyn Godwin, *Harmony of the Spheres*, Rochester (Vt.), 1993; *Musique et Humanisme à la Renaissance*, ed. Robert Aulotte, Paris, 1993 (which contains several valuable articles); Gary Tomlinson, *Music in Renaissance Magic*, Chicago, 1993, 90–98; and H. M. Brown, *Music in the Renaissance*. On Patrizi, who was surely a Pythagorean, see Anna Laura Puliafito, "Searching for a New Physics: Metaphysics … in Francesco Patrizi da Cherso," in Gilly and van Heertum, *Magia, alchima scienza*, II, 255–66. See also Salinas, *Siete libros sobre la música*, ed. Ismael Fernández de la Cuesta, Madrid, 1983 (for Salinas's reference to Nicomachus, Boethius, and the Byzantine

Pythagorean Manuel Bryennius, see 26). The great Spanish poet Fray Luis de León paid tribute to the Pythagoreanism of Salinas in a poem dedicated to him that describes music as balm for the purification of the soul and cosmic music as the ultimate divine harmony. Referring to Salinas's quest for harmony through concordant numbers he calls him "the glory of Apollo's sacred choir." (See the poem in Fray Luis de León, *The Unknown Light: The Poems of Fray Luis de León*, ed. and trans. Willis Barnstone, Albany, 1979, 44–47.)

87 See these letters in (Reuchlin), *Illvstrivm virorvm epistolae hebraicae, graecae et latinae ad Ioannam Reuchlin Phorcensem …* , Stuttgart, 1519, 346v, 354r, 375v–376r, and 449v–450r; for the letter from Erasmus, see Erasmus, *Collected Works of Erasmus*, IV, 85.

88 Reuchlin, *De arte Cabalistica*, 39 (trans. Goodmans).

89 On this see, e.g., Reuchlin, *De arte Cabalistica*, 151.

90 See Reuchlin, *De arte Cabalistica,* 111, 115, 157, and 195 (trans. Goodmans).

91 See Reuchlin, *De arte Cabalistica*, 167, 209, 217, 221, 227, and passim.

92 See Erasmus, *Collected Works of Erasmus*, VI, 399.

93 This quote, from 1512, is from Karl Gillert, *Der Briefwechsel des Conradus Mutianus*, Halle, 1890, I, 303–4 (trans. Ulrich Weisstein, in Eckhard Bernstein, *German Humanism*, Boston, 1983, 91).

94 On this see Bernstein, *German Humanism*, 87.

95 A complete edition of this work, first "published" by Petrus Galatinus in the form of a eulogy in 1550, is available in Egidio da Viterbo, *Scechina e libellus de litteris hebraicis*, 2 vols.

96 The dedication is published in Secret, "Le Symbolisme de la Kabbale Chretienne dans la 'Scechina' de Egidio da Viterbo," in *Archivio di Filosofia*, II–III, 1958, 152–53. For discussion of the papal tiara, see John W. O'Malley, *Giles of Viterbo on Church and Reform*, Leiden, 1968, 79–80.

97 On the relation of Pseudo-Dionysius to the history of Pythagoreanism, see Joost-Gaugier, *Measuring Heaven*, 118–19.

98 See Colet's *Treatise on the Sacraments of the Church, Two Treatises on the Hierarchies of Dionysius*, and *Letters to Radulphus on the Mosaic Account of the Creation*, ed. and trans. J. H. Lupton, first published in 1867, 1869, and 1876 respectively, all reprinted (under Latin titles, no ed.) in Ridgewood (N.J.), 1966. Quoted passage is from Lupton's 1876 introduction, xxvi.

99 A good overview of the relation of Hermeticism to the developing Puritanism in England is in Shumaker, *Occult Sciences in the Renaissance*, esp. 238–39. On Robert Fludd's Pythagoreanism, see Heninger, *Touches of Sweet Harmony*, op. cit., passim.

100 Erasmus, *Enchiridion militis christiani*, LB-V 29E, op. cit., 69.

101 Erasmus, *De contemptu mundi (On Disdaining the World)*, LB-V 1254B, in *Collected Works of Erasmus*, LXVI, trans. Erika Rummel, ed. O'Malley, 160.

102 Geofroy Tory, *Champ Fleury ou L'art et Science de la Proportion des Lettres* (1529), ed. G. Cohen, Paris, 1931, rep. Geneva 1973.

103 See Lefèvre d'Étaples, *Jacobi Fabri Stapulensis elementa musicalia*, and idem, *Jacobi Fabri Stapulensis Epitome in duos libros Arithmeticos divi Severum Boetij*, published together in Paris, 1496, and reprinted, ed. Henrichvm Petri, in Basel, 1553. See also Hermes Trismegistus, *Pimander. Sapientia et potestate dei*, ed. Lefèvre d'Étaples, Paris, 1505.

104 One example is Symphorien Champier, *Liber de quadruplici vita. Theologia Asclepij hermetis*, Lyon, 1507. Though Lefèvre claimed to be opposed to the occult sciences, he showed his fascination with them in several works on medicine and prognostication, which he published in the following decade.

105 Josse Clichtove, *De mystica numerorum significatione opusculum*, ptr. Henricum Stephanum, Paris, 1513.

106 For the first letter (Epistle 34) see Rice, *The Prefatory Epistles of Jacques Lefèvre d'Étaples*, 108–9; for the second (Epistle 11), ibid., 34 (trans. Carolyn Tuttle). On the views and writings of Clichtove (which included works on death and hymns), see esp. Massaut, *Josse Clichtore* (2 vols.).

107 Among the latter were an interpretation of the Candelabre of Moses (1548), translations of texts based on the Zohar and Torah, and the Sefer Ietsirah (1552). For a full bibliography, see Secret, *Bibliographie des Manuscrits de Guillaume Postel*, Geneva, 1970, 108ff.

108 Guillaume Postel, *De vniuersitate liber, in qvo astronomiae doctrinaeue coelestis …* , Paris, 1563, fol. 3r.

109 On this theme, see Postel, *Quatuor librorum de orbis terrae concordio primus*, Paris, 1543; and idem, *De la republique des Turcs et là où l'occasion s'offrira …* , Poitiers, 1560.

110 On this, see William J. Bouwsma, *Concordia mundi: The Career and Thought of Guillaume Postel (1510–1581)*, Cambridge (Mass.), 1957, esp. 48–50.

111 Postel, *Des Admirables Secrets des Nombres Platoniciens* (1549), ed. Jean-Pierre Brach (Latin-French text), Paris, 2001, 33–37.

112 Postel, *Des Admirable Secrets …* , passim.

113 Oronce Fine, *Les canons & docvmens tresamples, touchant lusaige & practique des comuns almanachz …* , ptr. Simon de Colines, Paris, 1543 (no pp.); and idem, *De arithmetica practica libri quatuor*, ptr. Simon de Colinaei, Paris, 1542, passim. Fols. 40–41 of the latter display a table of proportion not unlike those of Boethius. His admiration for Boethius is evident in that he edited Reisch's *Margarita Philosophica* for a Paris printer. His *De quadratura circuli, tandem inventa …* was published in Paris in 1544. On Pythagorean traditions of the squaring of the circle, see Joost-Gaugier, *Measuring Heaven*, 174 and 313.

114 Agrippa, *De occulta philosophia*, passim; and Bk. IV in idem, *La philosophie occulte ou la magie*. On Agrippa's thought, see Charles G. Nauert, Jr., *Agrippa and the*

Crisis of Renaissance Thought, Urbana, 1965. For general background, see Raphael Patai, *The Jewish Alchemists*, Princeton, 1994.

115 Agrippa, *La philosophie occulte ou la magie*, passim.

116 See Agrippa, *De incertitude et vanitate ...* , opening of sec. 16.

117 Michael Neander (1529–1581), *Lapidis indago totius philisophiae et magiae naturalis*, Matheiss Passinger von Iniching's collection of medical texts and recipes (no title), both published in the sixteenth century, and Gómez Pereira's *Antoniana margarita*, published in 1554.

118 Paracelsus, *Sieben Defensiones: Antwort auf etliche Verunglimpfungen ... un Labyrinthus medicorum*, Basel, 1538, pref. and sec. 1. For the complete works of Paracelsus, see idem, *Sämtliche Werke*, ed. Bernhard Aschner, Jena, 1922–28 (4 vols.).

119 Paracelsus, *Aurora philosophorum*, passim.

120 On this, see Allen G. Debus, *The English Paracelsians*, New York, 1965, 25–28.

121 Paracelsus, *Aurora philosophorum*, in trans. and ed. of J. H. Oxon, 11; and idem, *The Water-Stone of the Wise Men*, in ibid., 122 (trans. Oxon).

122 On the contemporaries of Paracelsus, including John Dee, see the incisive study of Allen G. Debus, "Mathematics and Nature in the Chemical Texts of the Renaissance," *AMBIX: Journal of the Society for the Study of Alchemy and Early Chemistry*, XV, 1968, 1–28. See also Heninger, *Touches of Sweet Harmony*, passim, esp. 260–66.

123 See e.g. *Religio mundi* (esp. secs. 12 and 32) and *Enquiries into Vulgar and Common Errors* (i.4 and iv.12) in Thomas Browne, *The Works of Sir Thomas Browne*, ed. Geoffrey Keynes, Chicago, 1964, in vols. I and II, respectively.

124 See Edward Kelly, *The Alchemical Writings of Edward Kelly* (1676), London, 1893. Despite his interests in alchemy, Rudolf II (1552–1612) does not appear to have had a particular interest in Pythagoras. On him, see R. J. W. Evans, *Rudolf II and His World*, Oxford, 1973; and Hans Holzer, *The Alchemist: The Secret Magical Life of Rudolf von Habsburg*, New York, 1974.

125 Giambattista Della Porta, *Io.Bapt.Portae Neapolitani Magiae natvralis libri XX*, Naples, 1589. An excellent source on Della Porta's significance for the history of magic is Shumaker, *Occult Sciences in the Renaissance*, 109–20.

126 Regarding the revolution of the earth around a central fire in the thought of Philolaus, see the discussion of Thomas Heath, in *Aristarchus of Samos ... A History of Greek Astronomy to Aristarchus*, Oxford, 1913, 97. Aristotle's description is in *De caelo*, I.268a and II.284b–290b.

127 Copernicus and universal harmony is the subject of *Copernic 1473–1973, Centre de synthese*, in Palais de la Découverte, exh. cat., Paris, 1973 (see esp. the paper by P. L. Rose, "Universal Harmony in Regiomontanus and Copernicus," 35–43).

128 On the significance of the accomplishment of Copernicus regarding the diurnal movement of the earth, see Duhem, *Medieval Cosmology*, II, esp. 505–7.

129 Nicholas Cusanus, *De docta ignorantia*, II.11.57, and 12.156.

130 Nicholaus Copernicus, *Six Books on the Revolutions of the Heavenly Spheres* (trans. of Nuremberg, 1543 orig. ed.), ed. Jerzy Dobrzycki, trans. Edward Rosen, Baltimore, 1978, from preface and ch. 5, trans. Rosen, 5 and 12.

131 Copernicus, *Six Books*, pref. and intro. (trans. Rosen, 4 and 7).

132 Copernicus, *Six Books*, Intro. (trans. Rosen, 7).

133 Copernicus, *Six Books* pref.

134 Copernicus, *The Commentariolus*, assumption 7; see English ed. in Copernicus, *Three Copernican Treatises*, 58–59; and George Joachim Reticus, *Narratio prima*, in ibid., 147. Copernicus's Platonic readings are discussed by Rose in *The Italian Renaissance of Mathematics*, 129–30.

135 Birkenmajer, *Stromata Copernicana*, esp. 154–67 and Rose, *The Italian Renaissance of Mathematics*, 118–19 and 127.

136 Copernicus himself supposedly described this event to his pupil, Reticus who, writing in 1540, described it (*Three Copernican Treatises*, 111). On this, see Rosen's "Biography of Copernicus," at the end of ibid. (326).

137 At the end of his preface to *De revolutionibus*, he expresses gratitude to Paulus for his encouragement. Respecting this friendship, see Baldi, "Vita di Niccolò Copernico," in *Le vite de' matematici*, 405–8, who points out that they first met in 1499 when Copernicus was in Bologna and Paulus in Urbino and subsequently corresponded regularly; also Birkenmajer, *Stromata Copernica*, 169–92. Cf. P. L. Rose, "Copernicus and Urbino," in *Isis*, LXV, 1974, 387–89.

138 For a document that refers to Paulus's presence in Rome as early as 1491, see Pernis, *Le Platonisme de Marsile Ficin et la Cour d'urbin*, 40.

139 A. Lazzari, "Un enciclopedico del secolo XVI – Celio Calcagnini," *Atti e memorie della Deputazione ferrarese di storia patria*, XXX, 1936, 160. On Calcagnini as a mathematician and for his possible relation to Copernicus, see Rose, *The Italian Renaissance of Mathematics*, 123. Respecting similarities in the interests and work of Copernicus and Calcagnini, see Birkenmajer, *Stromata Copernica*, 169–92.

140 Calcagnini, *Quod coelum stet et terra moveatur commentatio* (1519), in idem, *Opera aliquot*, 387–95. Calcagnini's research interests are described by D'Ascia, in *Erasmo e l'umanesimo romano*, Florence, 1987, 153–59.

141 Calcagnini, *Opera aliquot*, esp. fols. 70, 71, 236, 244, 250, and 330.

142 For discussion of numerous instances when Galileo linked Copernican astronomy with Pythagoreanism, see Reeves, *Painting the Heavens*, 63 and 240.

143 For quotations from the manuscript work of Diego de Zúñiga, see Juan Verner, "Copernicus in Spain," in *Colloquia Copernicana: The Reception of Copernicus'*

Heliocentric Theory, ed. Jerzy Dobrzycki, Dordrecht and Boston, 1972, 171–93, esp. 175–76 (hereinafter *Colloquia Copernicana*). See also Reeves, *Painting the Heavens*, 185–86.

144   On the significance of the heliocentric debate for the literary world of the Renaissance, see Heninger, *Touches of Sweet Harmony*, 122–23. The waverings of Tycho Brahe concerning Copernican astronomy are described in Kristian Peder Moesgaard, "Copernican Influence on Tycho Brahe," in *Colloquia Copernicana*, 31–57.

145   Girolamo Cardano, *Artis magnae sive de regulis algebraicis* (or *Ars magna*), published in Nuremberg in 1545, a mathematical text that, written in ten books, pays tribute to such Pythagoreans as Plato and Pacioli; idem, *De subtilitate*, Basel, 1554, in which he describes the world of nature in terms of number; and his autobiography, the *De vita propria liber*, Lyon, 1557, esp. ch. 54, where he congratulates himself for his "further" discoveries concerning number and proportion. His *Liber de immortalitate animorum* was published in Lyon in 1545.

146   Cardano, *De vita propria liber*, ch. 2: "I was endowed with a stuttering tongue and … gifted with a kind of intense and instinctive desire to prophesy." (Idem, *The Book of My Life*, trans. Jean Stoner [1930], New York, 1962, 5.)

147   On this subject, see esp. the incisive comments of Arielle Saiber in *Giordano Bruno and the Geometry of Language*, Aldershot (U.K.) and Burlington (Vt.), 2005, passim.

148   For Bruno's interest in number, see esp. Bruno's Latin poem, *De monade, numero et figura*, Frankfurt, 1591 (where he speculates on the numbers 1 to 10); his *De la causa, principio et uno* (1584) discusses, with somewhat Platonic-Copernican concepts, the relation of God to the cosmos; regarding his interest in contraries and opposites, ibid., esp. III,350; and (re: the magic of alchemy vs. the predictability of pedantry) the play *Il candelaio* (1582), passim. In this work he styled himself "an academician of no academy" (ibid., I.ii). His belief in transmigration of the soul, and of human and animal souls, is illustrated in *Cabala del cavallo Pegaseo*, and in *Asino cillenico* (both 1585). On the relation of his tumultuous life to his interest in Kabbalah and Hermeticism, see esp. Yates, *Giordano Bruno and the Hermetric Tradition*.

149   Saiber, *Giordano Bruno and the Geometry of Language*, 117–41.

150   For the complete works of Kepler, see *Johannes Kepler Gesammelte Werke*, ed. Max Caspar, Munich, 1938, 14 vols. A lucid explanation of the basic tenets of Kepler is contained in Boas, *The Scientific Renaissance*, esp. 287–312.

151   Johannes Kepler, *Mysterium cosmographicum*, original preface to the reader: trans. A. M. Duncan, in Kepler, *Mysterium cosmographicum/The Secret of the Universe*, New York, 1981. On this, see also the preface to this translation by I. Bernard Cohen, 7–10; and Robert Lawlor, *Sacred Geometry*, New York, 1982, 106.

152   Kepler, *Mysterium cosmographicum*, original dedication (trans. Duncan).

153   Kepler, *Harmonice mundi*, end of Bk. V (trans. E. J. Aiton, A. M. Duncan, and J. V. Field, in Kepler, *The Harmony of the World*, Philadelphia, 1997, 130).

154   Kepler, *Harmonice mundi*, end of Bk.V.

155   Kepler, *Harmonice mundi*, Bk.V, pref.

156   The Fludd-Kepler "controversy" is discussed by Yates in *Giordano Bruno the Hermetric Tradition*, 439–442.

157   Galileo Galilei, *Siderevs nvntivs, magna … spectacula pandens … quae a Galeleo Galeleo … sun observata in lunae facie*, Venice, 1610, 9. Trans. from idem, *Sidereus nuncius or the Sidereal Messenger*, trans. and ed. Albert van Helden, Chicago, 1989, 43.

158   See Kepler's enthusiastic response contained in a letter entitled, *Joannis Kepleri … Dissertatio in nuncium sidereum*, Florence, 1610 (in Galileo, *Le opere di Galileo Galilei* [1846], rep. ed. Antonio Favaro, Bologna, 1890, III), esp. at 106–7.

159   Galileo, *Dialogo … sopra i due massimi sistemi del mondo tolemaico, e copernicano, …* , Florence, ed. Gio. Batista Landini, 1632, giorn. 2 (in English as *Galileo on the World Systems*, ed. and trans. Maurice A. Finocchiaro, Berkeley, 1997; see passage at 172). It was this work that occasioned the famous trial of Galileo, which, as Finocchiaro discusses (ibid., 3) was not an issue between religion and science, since many clerics supported Galileo while many scientists were against him, but one between conservative and progressive thinkers.

160   [M]a sopra ogni'altro lodava Pitagora per il modo di filosofare." Niccolò Gherardini, *Vita di Galileo*, in Galileo, *Le opere …* , XIX, 645 (trans. mine).

161   Baldi, *Vita di Pitagora* (1588). Regarding the two texts on Vitruvius, see ibid., 17, n. 15. The *vite* are published in Enrico Narducci, *Vite inedite di matematici italiani scritte da Bernardino Baldi*, Rome, 1887.

162   Abraham ben Hananiah Yagel, *A Valley of Vision: The Heavenly Journey*, trans. and ed. David B. Ruderman, Philadelphia, 1990, passim.

163   On this, see Federico Barbierato, "Magical Literature and the Venice Inquisition from the Sixteenth to the Eighteenth Centuries," in *Magia, alchimia, scienza dal '400 al '700*, ed. Gilly and van Heertum, Florence, 2002, I, 159–75.

164   On Cicero and his closeness to Pythagoreanism of his time, see Joost-Gaugier, *Measuring Heaven*, 27–29 and 97–100.

SEVEN: RENAISSANCE IMAGES OF PYTHAGORAS

1   For ancient literary descriptions and representations of Pythagoras in Greek and Roman Antiquity see Joost-Gaugier, *Measuring Heaven*, passim.

2   Joost-Gaugier, *Measuring Heaven*, 200 and figs. 34–35.

3   The history of the construction and the program of the decoration of the campanile of Sta. Maria del Fiore are described in great detail by Julius von Schlosser in "Giusto's Fresken in Padua und die Vorläufer der Stanza della Segnatura," *Jahrbuch der Kunsthistorischen Sammlungen des Allerhöchsten Kaiserhauses*, XVII, 1896, 13–100.

4   See, e.g., the Anonimo Fiorentino or Anonimo Magliabechiano (probably Antonio Manetti) who, writing in about 1501, only refers in a general way to Luca's work for the cathedral. *Il Codice Magliabechiano*, 80 and 308–13.

5   Vasari, *Le vite …* , II, 169.

6   Schlosser, "Giusto's Fresken … ," 73.

7   Vasari, *Le vite …* , II, 169.

8   Schlosser, "Giusto's Fresken … ," 73.

9   On the lower row are represented Adam, Eve, Jabal, Jubal, Tubalkain, and Noah, all figures from the Book of Genesis. On these, see Schlosser, "Giusto's Fresken … ," 71–73.

10 Cf. Leo Planiscig, *Luca della Robbia*, Florence, 1948, fig. 31, and John Pope-Hennessy, *Luca della Robbia*, Oxford, 1980, 31 and fig. 33.

11 For the first report of this incident, by Nicomachus in the first century (A.D.), see Nicomachus, *The Manual of Harmonics*, ch. 6 (82–85). This tradition was passed on to medieval audiences by Iamblichus, Macrobius, Fulgentius, Boethius, Isidore of Seville, and many others.

12 New York, Pierpont Morgan Library Manuscript *MS. B27*, fol. 31. The work, untitled, can be dated about 1450–75.

13 Regarding these prognostication devices, see Ch. 2. For a fuller treatment of this subject and a selection of medieval examples see Joost-Gaugier, *Measuring Heaven*, 209–15.

14 Trans. Helga Delisle. The original appears to read: "Herre Gott, gib uns Trinken und Essen; dass wir Dein nimmer vergessen. Dein Dornenkron ist unser Leid. Dein Speerstick ist unser Leid. Dein rosenfarben Blut ist unser Tranke. Herre, alle Deine Worde seien unser bedanken. Pater Noster/Ave Maria."

15 In Antiquity, the *tetraktys* was called "holy" by Theon of Smyrna and others; early Christians, such as Clement of Alexandria, regarded Pythagoras as a guide to holy life; as late as the fifteenth century, Pico della Mirandola refers to the "holy" teachings of Pythagoras, which were, he says, bequeathed to Christians (see Ch. 5).

16 Porphyry, *Life of Pythagoras*, 32; and Iamblichus, *Vita Pythagorica*, 25.

17 Trans. Carolyn Tuttle. The original reads: "Pittagoras musicae inventor. Fuganda sunt omnibus modis et abscindenda languor a corpore, imperitia ab anima, aventere luxuria a civitate, seditio a domo, discordia et a cunctis rebus intemperantia."

18 Marcus Fabius Quintilianus (Quintilian), *Institutiones oratoriae*, I.x.32. This story was frequently repeated in the works of later authors, such as Porphyry (*Life of Pythagoras*, 30–33); and Iamblichus (*Vita Pythagorica*, 25, 31, and 32).

19 Calandri, *Aritmetica*. On this work, see Smith, *Rara arithmetica*, 46–49. Calandri also authored a somewhat earlier manuscript entitled *Trattato di aritmetica* (Florence, Bib.Ricc.Cod. 2669). The topics covered by this text include multiplication and division tables and illustrated problems that for the most part focus on money, suggesting that this text was oriented toward commercial arithmetic.

20 For this portrait, see Stanley Morison, *Fra Luca de Pacioli*, New York, 1933, frontispiece; Enrico Giusti and Carlo Maccagni, eds., *Lvca Pacioli*, Florence, 1994, 63, or Fenella K. C. Smith, "Pacioli, Luca," *Encyclopedia of the Renaissance*, New York, 1999, IV, 358. A different portrait with the same symbol can be found in Giusti and Maccagni, *Lvca Pacioli*, 65.

21 The woodcut illustration is found in Gaffurio, *Theorica musicae*, at the end of Book I. This work was first published in Milan in 1492. (Its pages are not all numbered.)

22 Jubal is mentioned by Gaffurio in *Theorica musicae*, I.i.1, 36–37, and V.i.4. While Jubal is mentioned in Genesis 4:21 as a descendant of Cain, who was the ancestor of those who play the harp and the pipe, little note was taken of this except by the late-Antique writer Josephus (*Jewish Antiquities*, I.64). This in turn had inspired Johannes Gallicus, a teacher of music at Mantua and author of a work entitled *Ritus canendi* (ca. 1460), to make the startling statement that the observations of the blacksmith's hammers were those of Jubal rather than Pythagoras. (Johannes Gallicus, *Ritus canendi*, ed. Albert Seay, Colorado Springs, 1981, 20 [I.10.15]). Thus it came to the attention of Gaffurio. On this otherwise little-known biblical character, who would become more familiar as a result of Gaffurio's work, see Walter Blankenburg, "Jubal," *Die Musik in Geschichte*, ed. Friedrich Blume, Basel, London, and New York, 1958, VII, 222–23.

23 Gaffurio, *Theorica musicae*, I.ii.252–58; I.iii.37–50; I.viii.1–3 and 34; and passim.

24 Nicomachus, *The Manual of Harmonics*, Bk. VI. Cf. Iamblichus, *Vita Pythagorica*, 26.

25 Gaffurio, *Theorica musicae*, I.iii.30–31. Philolaus's major work, *On the World*, where this description occurs, was known through a significant extract preserved by the late-Antique writer Ioannis Stobaeus (*Anthologium*, I.xxi.7–8). An English translation is available in Barnes, 217–18.

26 Reisch, *Margarita philosphica*. Aside from the original 1503 edition, a second edition was printed in 1504 followed by later editions in 1508, 1512, 1515, 1517, 1523, 1535, 1583, and (in Italian translation) 1594, 1599, and 1600. For details of these editions, see Smith, *Rara arithmetica*, 82–84.

27 This is demonstrated in a series of related articles by Paolo D'Ancona: "Le rappresentazione allegoriche

delle arti liberali nel Medio Evo e nel Rinascimento," *L'Arte*, V, 1902, 137–55, 211–29, 269–89, and 370–85.

28 The work of Boethius was well known as the basic text in mathematics through the Middle Ages and well into the Renaissance; after the invention of printing, it was frequently reprinted. In addition, it inspired Renaissance mathematicians (e.g., Lefèvre d'Étaples and Clichetove) to write commentaries on it as well as imitative texts.

29 On the place of Leonardo da Pisa (also known as Fibonacci) in mathematical tradition see Joseph Gies and Frances Gies, *Leonard of Pisa and the New Mathematics of the Middle Ages*, New York, 1969. Regarding the Fibonacci series, so-named in 1877, see H. E. Huntley, *The Divine Proportion*, New York, 1970, esp. 46–57.

30 See Nicomachus, *Introduction to Arithmetic*, II.26 and 29.

31 The word that is the title, transcribed from the Greek, would be "epogdoos."

32 Vasari, *Le vite* …, IV, 361.

33 Greek and Roman portraits of Pythagoras are compared in Joost-Gaugier, *Measuring Heaven*, ch. 8.

34 According to Sigüenza, all the liberal arts are descendants of philosophy. On music, which he associates with arithmetic, see Fray José de Sigüenza, *La fundación del Monasterio de El Escorial*, ed. Antonio Fernandez Alba, Madrid, 1986, esp. 285–91.

35 Tibaldi was engaged in painting the vault of the Escorial library from 1588 to 1595. Respecting this commission, see George Kubler, *The Building of the Escorial*, Princeton, 1982, esp. 96–97 (with citations to documents), and Giuliano Briganti, *Il Manierismo e Pellegrino Tibaldi*, Rome, 1945. Regarding Tibaldi's nickname, see Kubler, *The Building of the Escorials*, 97, n. 64. See also Briganti, *Il Manierismo e Pellegrino Tibaldi*, 90ff., for a discussion of the reasons why Tibaldi's style, being so closely imitative of Michelangelo's, was out of step with current developments in Mannerism, or late Renaissance art, of his time.

36 This deduction is made on the basis of the praise he puts forward for Pythagoras and Pythagoreanism, as well as Vitruvius, in his treatise on architecture, which will be mentioned later in this book (Pellegrino Tibaldi, *L'Architettura*, crit. ed., Giorgio Panizza, Milan, 1990, passim).

37 On Annibale's masterpiece, see esp. John Rupert Martin, *The Farnese Gallery*, Princeton, 1965, esp. 27–28. On Atlas and the symbolism of the globe, see Erwin Panofsky, "Introductory: II," *Studies in Iconology*, New York, 1939, 20, n. 10. Heinrich Bodmer ("Die Fresken des Annibale Carracci im Camerino des Palazzo Farnese in Rom," *Pantheon*, XIX, 1937, 147) calls this figure Pythagoras. Martin (*The Farnese Gallery*, esp. 27–28) disagrees, suggesting that he might be Ptolemy. However, in my view, a contrast between Ptolemy and Euclid would be meaningless (as can be learned from Raphael's *School of Athens* where they are represented in conjunction with each other), while a contrast between arithmetic and geometry is both meaningful and traditional (as can also be seen in Raphael's painting, where Pythagoras and Euclid are represented on opposite sides of the fresco – which perhaps served as a precedent).

38 This painting, bought by Antonio Ruffo of Messina shortly after its creation, is now in the Kimbell Art Museum in Fort Worth. This event in the life of Pythagoras is described by Diogenes Laertius.

EIGHT: THE SEARCH FOR HARMONY IN ARCHITECTURE AND ART IN THE FIFTEENTH CENTURY

1 On this see Joost-Gaugier, *Measuring Heaven*, op. cit., 74–75.

2 For a solid study of Brunelleschi's buildings, with ample photographs, the reader is referred to Howard Saalman, *Filippo Brunelleschi – The Buildings*, London, 1993.

3 On the use of the oculus, or opening (to allow light to enter from above), in Pythagorean buildings of Antiquity, see Joost-Gaugier, *Measuring Heaven*, chs. 9 and 10.

4 Aside from his worship of Apollo (the god of light) the association of Pythagoras with light is confirmed by numerous Antique testimonials. See, e.g., Porphyry, *Life of Pythagoras*, 10, 38, and 40–41; also an anonymous ancient *Vita* of Pythagoras, perhaps based in part on a lost work by Aristotle, preserved by Photius, a ninth-century erudite (*Bibliothèque*, ed. René Henry, Paris, 1967, VII, no. 249, 13).

5 Salutati, letter to Brother John Dominici, in *Linus Colucius Salutatus* … (trans. Emerton), 365.

6 Plato, *Laws*, V.745be. On this, see Robert Klein, *Form and Meaning* (1970), trans. Madeline Jay and Leon Wieseltier, New York, 1979, 92.

7 Plutarch, *De Iside et Osiride*, 373F–374A(56). On the importance of this number for Plato, see Allen, *Nuptial Arithmetic*, 37, and 71–72. See also Bartel L. van der Waerden, *Science Awakening: The Birth of Astronomy*, trans. Arnold Dresden, Leiden, 1975, esp. 287.

8 On this circular number in the thought of Ficino, see Allen, *Nuptial Arithmetic*, 51, 62–63, 66–68, 72–74, 80, 103, and 131.

9 Many ancient Pythagorean writers testify to these concepts, e.g., Plutarch (*On the E at Delphi*, 385D), Iamblichus, (*Vita Pythagorica*, 28), Porphyry (*Life of Pythagoras*, 16 and 51), and the anonymous *Vita of Pythagoras* preserved by Photius (as cited in n. 4), 19. Discussion of the symbolism of numbers 3 and 6 can also by found, e.g., in the work of Nicomachus and Anatolius, as well as in other ancient sources known in medieval and Renaissance times (see, e.g., Pseudo-Iamblichus, *The Theology of Arithmetic*, esp. 75–85). On this subject, see Edgar Wind, "Pagan Vestiges of the Trinity," 241–55.

10 An example of the belief that heaven is divided into sixteen regions can be found in Martianus Capella, *The Marriage of Philology and Mercury*, VII.45. As discussed previously in this text, Vitruvius's praise for the number 16 was well noted in the Renaissance, e.g., by Francesco di Giorgio. The number 16 also had a long life as a magical number in medieval geomantic manuscripts (see, e.g., Joost-Gaugier, *Measuring Heaven*, 130). On the symbolism of number 8, see Pseudo-Iamblichus, *The Theology of Arithmetic*, 100–104.

11 Respecting Pythagoreanism and numerical articulation of the Pantheon see Joost-Gaugier, *Measuring Heaven*, ch. 10.

12 Ludwig Heydenreich (in Heydenreich and Lotz, *Architecture in Italy*, 20) notes that this rotunda is based on the ancient temple of Minerva Medica in Rome. For a thorough history of Sta. Maria degli Angeli and documents associated with it, see Divo Savelli, *La Rotonda del Brunelleschi: Storia e documenti*, Florence, 1992. See also Saalman, *Brunelleschi*, 381–409.

13 See Manetti's description of "el tempio per se medesimo" (a temple by itself) in *The Life of Brunelleschi*, trans. Catherine Enggass, ed. Howard Saalman, University Park (Pa.) and London, 1970, 173–74. Though it should be noted that free-standing round churches are known in earlier medieval architecture, e.g., at Brescia, Bergamo, and Mantua, these structures were not articulated with "sides." The only octagonal structures known were baptisteries.

14 Vitruvius, *De architectura*, III.i.8–9. Long before him, Speusippus, the nephew of Plato and also a Pythagorean, had insisted on the perfection of the number 6 and, especially, the number 10. (See Speusippus fragments preserved by Iamblichus in *Greek Mathematical Works*, ed. and trans. Ivor Thomas, 1951, I, 75–81.)

15 Vitruvius, *De architectura*, I.i.16, V.iv.3, III.i.6–9, V.intro.4, VIII.intro.1–4, and I.ii.4.

16 Vitruvius, *De architectura*, I.vi.13.

17 "[L]e loro proporzioni musichalj" (Manetti, *Life of Brunelleschi*, 329).

18 This number, 28, is a mathematically perfect number. According to the Pythagorean Nicomachus (*Introduction to Arithmetic*, II.xvi), such a number is equal to the sum of all its factors (divisors) ($28 = 14 + 7 + 4 + 2 + 1$).

19 Nicomachus, e.g., in his most famous Pythagorean work, had praised the perfection of 28 because its factors (1, 2, 4, 7, and 14) when added together make 28. Another reason he cites for its perfection is that $1 + 2 + 4 = 7$ times the last factor, $4 = 28$ (*Introduction to Arithmetic*, I.xvi). See Salutati's discussion of the sacramental meaning of this number in his letter to Brother John Dominici, published in Emerton, esp. 364–65. Leonardo Bruni's recommendation, in a letter, is discussed in Richard Krautheimer, *Lorenzo Ghiberti*, Princeton, 1970, I, 164.

20 Many ancient Pythagoreans had written on the perfection of the number 10, not only Nicomachus and Theon of Smyrna but also Pseudo-Iamblichus (see, e.g., his *Theology of Arithmetic*, 109–15), who, in another work preserved extracts from the now lost works of Speussipus, a famous Pythagorean of Antiquity (see n. 14), and Anatolius, Nicomachus's teacher. All praised 10 as a perfect number symbolized by the triangle.

21 Salutati, letter to Brother John Dominici, in *Linus Colucius Salutatus ...* (trans. Emerton), 363–65.

22 Salutati, *Linus Colucius Salutatus ...* (trans. Emerton), 363–65.

23 This fresco, designed for Sta. Maria Novella and still *in situ*, was studied in H. W. Janson, "Ground Plan and Elevation in Masaccio's Trinity Fresco," *Essays in the History of Art Presented to Rudolf Wittkower*, ed. Douglas Fraser, Howard Hibbard and Milton J. Lewine, London, 1967, esp. 83–88. Janson recognized that the composition was based on Pythagorean harmonious numbers.

24 This view of Masaccio is shared by Luciano Berti in *Masaccio*, University Park (Pa.) and London, 1967, 20.

25 It should be noted that the perfect square of 36 is not manifested as 6 x 6 here, but as 4 x 9. Four is a perfect square (2 x 2), while 9 is also a perfect square (3 x 3).

26 For more on Pletho's *Treatise on Law*, see Ch. 4.

27 Hersey, *Pythagorean Palaces*, 164–69, and fig. 5-2 for an early sixteenth-century engraving of the original structure. It should be noted that the building was subsequently expanded and changed.

28 Vitruvius, *De architectura*, V, intro., and Nicomachus, *Introduction to Arithmetic*, II.xvii.

29 On the history of this commission, see esp. Beverly Louise Brown, "The Patronage and Building History of the Tribuna of SS Annunziata in Florence," in *Mitteilungen des Kunsthistorischen Institutes in Florenz*, XXV, 1981, 59–146, esp. 68 (for the original plan). See also Eugenio M. Casalini, *Michelozzo di Bartolommeo e l'Annunziata di Firenze*, Florence, 1995.

30 Regarding Pletho's regard for this number, see Ch. 4.

31 The temple in the *Joseph Scene* has an indeterminate number of bays, perhaps 20. Respecting Michelozzo's presence in Ghiberti's workshop in the late 1430s, see Krautheimer, I, 6 and 87. It should be noted that Krautheimer speculates that Michelozzo's expertise was as a bronze chaser rather than as a designer. However, his position as a collaborator rather than an assistant may have allowed him to contribute to this design, which is otherwise unequaled in other works by Ghiberti himself.

32 Florence, *Bib. Naz. Cod. II. IV. 38*, fols. 151–52. See also "Sentenze Pitagoriche," in Alberti, *Opere volgare*, ed. Cecil Grayson, II, Bari, 1966, 299–300.

33 Although these proportions were suggested early on in Antiquity by Archytas and Philolaus, both Pythagoreans, it was Nicomachus who published this information in his first-century *Introduction to*

Arithmetic (II.29), maintaining that the cube therefore signified the most perfect proportion.

34   See Hersey, *Pythagorean Palaces*, esp. 28–31.

35   On the construction of the Palazzo Rucellai, see Brenda Preyer, "The Rucellai Palace," in *Giovanni Rucellai ed il suo Zibaldone*, ed. Alessandro Perosa, London, 1981, II, 156–225.

36   Martianus Capella, *The Marriage of Philology and Mercury*, VII.750.

37   Alberti, *De re aedificatoria*, VI.6 and VI.13.

38   The inscription on Pletho's tomb confirms that Pletho was his favorite philosopher. On this, see Woodhouse, *Plethon*, 374. The tombs placed in the arched vaults of the Tempio Malatesta are described (including their inscriptions) in Charles Yriarte, *Un Condottiere au XVe Siècle: Rimini*, Paris, 1882, 253–74.

39   Fundamental works on this building include Corrado Ricci's *Il Tempio Malatestiano* (1925), Rimini, 1974 (with full bibliography of earlier works), and Paolo Portoghesi, *Il Tempio Malatestiano*, Florence, 1965. The quoted passage is from the *De re militari* of Valturius, the mercenary general of Sigismundo Pandolfo Malatesta, the lord of Rimini and commissioner of the building (formerly, San Francesco), which he renamed after himself. On this, see Stanko Kokole, "'Cognitio formarum' and Agostino di Duccio's Reliefs for the Chapel of the Planets in the Tempio Malatestiano," in *Quattrocento Adriatico*, ed. Charles Dempsey, Bologna, 1996, 177–206 (trans. Kokole).

40   The geometry of this façade is analyzed in detail by Wittkower, 39–41. On the façade, see the study of Marcello Scalzo, "La facciata Albertiana di Santa Maria Novella a Firenze," in *Leon Battista Alberti architettura e cultura*, ed. Accademia Nazionale Virgiliana, Florence, 1999, 265–83.

41   See Wittkower, *Architectural Principles* … , esp. 40.

42   On this subject, see the interesting speculations of Tim Anstey in "Theology and Geometry in the Façade of S. Maria Novella," *Albertiana*, VI, Florence, 2003, 27–49.

43   On this subject, see further Joan Gadol, *Leon Battista Alberti, Universal Man of the Early Renaissance*, Chicago, 1969, 108–15.

44   On Alberti's relations with Nicholas Cusanus, see Girolamo Mancini, *Vita di Leon Battista Alberti* (1911), 2nd ed., Rome, 1971, 375; and Gadol, *Alberti*, 196–97.

45   Nicholas Cusanus, *De docta ignorantia*, 175–78, in *Nicholas of Cusa on Learned Ignorance*, trans. Hopkins, 122.

46   This is reported in a letter of 1464 by the German mathematician Regiomontanus. See Mancini, *Vita di Alberti*, 375–76 for text. See also Gadol, *Alberti*, 195–96.

47   For a plan of Pienza, see Heydenreich and Lotz, *Architecture in Italy*, 44. On Rossellino's project, see the detailed study of Jan Pieper: *Pienza: Il progetto di una visione umanistica del mondo*, Stuttgart, 2000; also Charles R. Mack, *Pienza*, Ithaca and London, 1987.

48   See the discussion of the Pythagoreanism of Pius II, Bessarion, and Nicholas Cusanus in Ch. 4. The latter's descriptions of the universe as number and proportion occur, for the most part, in *De docta ignorantia* and *De coniecturis*.

49   Castiglione, *Il cortegiano*, I.2. On this palace, see the monumental work of Pasquale Rotondi, *Il Palazzo Ducale di Urbino* (2 vols.)

50   See Rotondi, *Il Palazzo Ducale di Urbino*; Lutz, *Laurana und der Herzogspalast von Urbino* (which discusses the documents placing Laurana, who was reputedly fond of geometrical problems, in Urbino 1465–72); and the recent work of Janez Höfler, *Der Palazzo Ducale in Urbino unter den Montefeltro*, Regensburg, 2004. Of special significance for this subject is the original and perceptive work of Pernis (*Le Platonisme de Marsile Ficin et la Cour d'Urbin*), which studies the Pythagoreanism of Federigo.

51   Being a good Pythagorean, the sixteenth-century mathematician Bernardino Baldi (see Chs. 2 and 6), counted the arches in the Grand Courtyard. He notes there were two sequences of 5 and two of 6 arches, "de forma non quadrata, ma che tiene del lungo." Baldi wrote about the history of mathematics; his interest in Pythagorean subjects is clear for not only did he edit an edition of Vitruvius, he also wrote several commentaries on this ancient Pythagorean architect. He also translated a work by Heron of Alexandria and wrote biographies of ancient Pythagoreans such as Archytas, Nigidius Figulus, and Boethius, and last but not least, the most important, and by far the longest, biography of Pythagoras of Renaissance times. It may or may not be relevant that Baldi's biography of Federigo (who appears to have been a Pythagorean and had something of a Pythagorean burial) is composed of ten books organized into three volumes. For his work describing the palazzo of Urbino, see Baldi, *Memorie concernenti la città di Urbino*, Rome, 1724 (esp. 49 respecting the courtyard).

52   On the Cortile del Pasquino, see Rotondi, *Il Palazzo Ducale di Urbino*, I, 296–310.

53   In a letter of 1475 Federigo states "Nihil fruit familiarus neque amantius amicitia qua Batista et ego eramus coniuncti" (*Lettere di stato e d'arte di Federico da Montefeltro*, ed. Paolo Alatri, Rome, 1949, 102).

54   In the Renaissance, Moses was, of course, believed to have been the teacher of Pythagoras; Cicero was a probable Pythagorean, while Saint Augustine, Petrarch, Dante, and Bessarion (and probably also Vittorino da Feltre, Federigo's own teacher, whose school stressed frugal living, caring for others, and the quadrivium), were, at the very least, admirers of Pythagoras. On the studiolo in general, see Luciano Cheles, *The Studiolo of Urbino*, Wiesbaden, 1986.

55 On Ficino's appreciation of the number 28, see Allen, *Nuptial Arithmetic*, 71–79. The number of portraits originally comprising Federigo's studiolo is studied in Cheles, *Studiolo of Urbino*.

56 Many of the paintings once contained in this *tempietto* are now in the Galleria Corsini at Florence, where they are attributed to Giovanni Santi (Raphael's father) and assistants. Apollo's "priceless tripods" were first described in the ancient Greek work, the *Homeric Hymn to Pythian Apollo*, 441–44.

57 Most of these panels, today in the Corsini Gallery in Florence, survive.

58 Cicero, *De natura deorum*, III.xxii.55 and 59. For the association of Apollo and his half sister Athena, see the *Homeric Hymn to Pythian Apollo*, 476–80 and 531.

59 For Baldi's unfortunately vague description of the Cappella delle Muse, see *Memorie ... , 57*.

60 Speaking of the value of ancient knowledge, Federigo had great praise for both arithmetic and geometry, which enabled modern architects to use their ingenuity, something, he says, he much appreciated (see document of 1468 in Gaye, *Carteggio inedito ... *, I, Florence, 1849, 214). On the mathematicians in his court, see Castelli, "Matematici e astrologi ... ," 237–51. The theme of the reconciliation of opposites was first propounded by Philolaus, who was thought to have been a Pythagorean. On this, see Joost-Gaugier, *Measuring Heaven*, 84.

61 In one (undated) letter to his friend Federigo, Ficino exclaims that Jupiter (Zeus), with the help of Athena, bestowed him the crown of kingship on Federigo, giving him the sovereignty described by "divine" Plato. In another he says that Zeus, together with Athena, created Federico to rule the earth. Ficino, *Letters*, VI, nos. 22–23. On Ficino's partiality to twin chapels, see Pernis, *Le Platonisme de Marsile Ficino et la Cour d'Urbin*, 173.

62 Such substitutions are discussed by Wind ("Pagan Vestiges of the Trinity," 252).

63 Homer, e.g., describes Athena (Minerva) as a bird in *The Odyssey*, 3, 371–72.

64 BINDA VIDES PARVO DISCRIMINE IUNCTA SACELLA ALTERA PARS MUSIS ALTERA SACRA DEO EST.

65 On these links, see Pernis, *Le Platonisme de Marsile Ficin et la Cour d'Urbin*, esp. 178.

66 Kenneth Clark, *Piero della Francesca* (1951), London and New York, 1969, 33–36.

67 Rudolf Wittkower and B. A. R. Carter, "The Perspective of Piero della Francesca's 'Flagellation,'" *Journal of the Warburg and Courtauld Institutes*, XVI, 1953, 292–302. Cf. the further work of Field in *Piero della Francesca*, 174–81.

68 Piero's interest in the cube is evident in his *Libellus de quinque corporibus regularibus* but also in his *De prospectiva pingendi*. On this interest, see Field, *Piero della Francesca*, 183 and 187–88. On the translation of the square into the cube see Piero, *De prospectiva pingendi* (end of Bk. I and the beg. of Bk. II).

69 Piero, *De prospectiva pingendi*, I.13–14. On this see Field, *Piero della Francesca*, 177–79.

70 These are reconstructed in Wittkower and Carter, "Piero della Francesca's 'Flagellation,' " pl. 44.

71 The basic cosmological number is 4 (N, S, E, W); breaking 4 produces 8 directions (N, NE, E, SE, S, SW, W, NW), breaking 8 produces 16 (N, NNE, NE, ENE, E, ESE, SE, SSE, S, etc.), and breaking 16 produces 32 (N, N by E, NNE, NE by N, NE, NE by E, ENE, etc.), the number of points, quarter points, and degrees to the compass. The compass, known as *bossola*, traditionally used for navigation, was probably introduced into Europe by the Arabs in medieval times. Alberti's interest in dividing the circle is apparent in his works *Ludi matematici* and *Descriptio urbis Romae*, both well known at this time.

72 See the superimposition of Wittkower and Carter, "Piero della Francesca's 'Flagellation,'" pl. 45 and 298.

73 On this, see Wittkower and Carter, "Piero della Francesca's 'Flagellation,'" 302.

74 This was suggested by Marilyn Aronberg Lavin, *Piero della Francesca: The Flagellation*, New York, 1972, esp. 80–86.

75 Lavin, *Piero della Francesca*, 80. Cf. the different suggestion of Carlo Bertelli in *Piero della Francesca* (1991), trans. Edward Farrelly, New Haven and London, 1992, 115–26; and the comments of Carlo Ginzburg in *Indagini su Piero*, Turin, 1981, 58–59 (who suggests that the bearded man is Bessarion, in which case my comments still hold).

76 Illustrations of these may be found in any general source on Piero's works, e.g., Bertelli, *Piero della Francesca*, 7:3–4.

77 Regarding these attributions, see Philip Jacks, "The Renaissance *Prospettiva*," *Cambridge Companion to Piero della Francesca*, ed. Jeryldene M. Wood, Cambridge, 2002, 115–33. Cf. Carlo Ragghianti, who attributes them to a Florentine master in *Filippo Brunelleschi*, Florence, 1977, 369–72.

78 This observation, noted by Henry Millon, is discussed together with drawings by Francesco di Giorgio, in Pietro Matracchi's magnificent monograph, *La Chiesa di Santa Maria delle Grazie al Calcinaio*, Cortona, 1991, at 59.

79 On Giuliano da Sangallo and other buildings he designed (including the façade of SS. Annunziata in Florence, for which he designed a loggia of seven bays, and the Palazzo Gondi [also in Florence], whose façade consists in seven bays) an old but good source is Gustave Clausse, *Les San Gallo*, Paris, 1900. On Santa Maria delle Carceri, see the recent work (and excellent photographs), *Santa Maria delle Carceri a Prato*, ed. Anna Benvenuti, Florence, 2005.

80 On this concept, see Wolfgang Lotz, "Notes on the Centralized Church of the Renaissance," *Studies in Renaissance Architecture*, Cambridge (Mass.), 1977, 66–74. See also Amedeo Belluzzi, "Templi Albertiani

a pianta centrale," in *Leon Battista Alberti: Architettura e cultura*, ed. Acc. Naz. Virgiliana, Florence, 1999, 317–29.

81   Nicholas Cusanus, *De coniecturis*, I.13.

82   On the importance of Leonardo's drawings of central-ized churches see Wittkower, *Architectural Principles ...*, 16–19.

83   The translator was Lilio Tifernate. On this enor-mous project and its import, see Ettlinger, *The Sistine Chapel before Michelangelo*, esp. 116–17. On Philo's Pythagoreanism, see Joost-Gaugier, *Measuring Heaven*, esp. 102–3 and 125–26.

84   Regarding number 8 as symbolizing justice, see Macrobius, *Commentary on the Dream of Scipio*, V.15, and Pseudo-Iamblichus, *Theology of Arithmetic*, 102.

85   For a plan of the pavement, see Ernst Steinmann, *Die Sixtinische Kapelle*, Munich, 1901–5, I (plates), VIII.

86   The original choir screen is illustrated and described by Steinmann, in I (text), 170–75. Respecting its con-nection to Exodus, see Joost-Gaugier, "Michelangelo's *Ignudi* and the Sistine Chapel as a Symbol of Law and Justice," *Artibus et Historiae*, XXXIV, 19–43.

87   Probably influenced by pilgrims who had been to Rome, such examples are known in German medi-eval churches. See, e.g., a stained-glass representation of the seven-branched candelabrum in the Cathedral of Mulhausen (*Speculum humanae salvationis*, ed. Jean Miélot, 1448, rep. by Jules Lutz and Pierre Perdrizet, Leipzig, 1907, pl. 104).

88   See article cited in n. 86 for references.

89   One example of a work full of pagan ideas and devices that contains no elements that can be regarded as Pythagorean is the *Hypnerotomachia Poliphili*, an illus-trated book of ca. 1499. While its extravagance and enriched descriptive details betray its author's fasci-nation with Antiquity, the excesses and fantasies of its many threads suggest that it was a kind of imagi-nary collection of thoughts and images not in any way related to Pythagorean systems of order. See Francesco Colonna, *Hypnerotomachia Poliphili*, trans. Joscelyn Godwin, London, 1999.

90   Plato, *Timaeus*, 39b–c.

91   Nicomachus, *Introduction to Arithmetic*, II.xxix.

92   On the relation of the solar concerns of ancient Pythagoreans to architectural concepts, see Louis Hautecoeur, *Mystique et Architecture: Symbolisme du Cercle et de la Coupole*, Paris, 1954; on the optical refine-ments of Brunelleschi's architecture, see Wittkower, "Brunelleschi and 'Proportion in Perspective,'" *Journal of the Warburg and Courtauld Institutes*, XVI, 1953, esp. 288–89.

93   The anonymous fifteenth-century commentator on Florentine art known as the Anonimo Fiorentino, or the Anonimo Magliabechiano (whose comments about his contemporary artists are very brief), particu-larly notes Masaccio's unusual attention to nature and simplicity, *Il Codice Magliabechiano*, 81.

NINE: FINDING HARMONY

1   On these drawings, see the discussion of Clark, in *Leonardo da Vinci*, Cambridge, 1952, 18–22.

2   Sydney J. Freedberg, *Painting of the High Renaissance in Rome and Florence*, Cambridge (Mass.), 1961, 5–7.

3   Plato, *Timaeus*, 42c.

4   Plato, *Timaeus*, 54a.

5   See, e.g., Pseudo-Iamblichus, *The Theology of Arithmetic*, on the tetrad and on the decad. This author of late Antiquity connects the pyramid with the sphere and says that people in his time were "astounded" by the discovery of Pythagoras.

6   On the latter, see, e.g., Cusanus, *On Learned Ignorance*, I.13.

7   This aspect of Leonardo's interest in a Pythagorean harmonic "world formula" is described in a bril-liant essay by Thomas Brachert: "A Musical Canon of Proportion in Leonardo da Vinci's *Last Supper*," *Art Bulletin*, LIII (4), 1971, 461–66. Brachert laments that Leonardo's interest in Platonic notions has not been given due attention by modern scholars.

8   See Charles De Tolnay, *Michelangelo*, trans. Gaynor Woodhouse, Princeton, 1975, 189.

9   See Plato, *Timaeus*, 55c and, e.g., Anatolius as quoted by Pseudo-Iamblichus in *The Theology of Arithmetic*, 65–74.

10   Raphael's *Dream of a Knight* is no. 213, in the National Gallery at London and widely reproduced, e.g., in Jurg Meyer zur Capellen, *Raphael*, I, Landshut, 2001.

11   These qualities had been discussed by Anatolius and, it was believed, Iamblichus. See, e.g., Pseudo-Iamblichus, *The Theology of Arithmetic*, 101–4.

12   The Pythagorean nature of this concept has been explored in greater detail than is possible here in Claudio Tiberi, "Misure e contemporaneità di disegno del chiostro di S. Maria della Pace e del Tempietto," in Com. Naz. per le celebrazioni Bramantesche, *Studi Bramanteschi*, Rome, 1974, 437–82. For an example of sixteenth-century architects' reconstructions of Bramante's project, see Book III of Sebastiano Serlio's architectural treatise (*L'Architettura*, ed. Francesco P. Fiore, I, Milan, 2001, XXXIX–XLIIII). For Ficino's four circles of the universe and stages of the soul's search for God, see his *Commentary on Plato's Symposium* in Marcel, *Commentaire ...*, II, 12r–v; and III, 12v.

13   Respecting these buildings see Arnaldo Bruschi, *Bramante* (1969), trans. and intro. Peter Murray, London, 1977, 71–85 and 145–62. Bramante's design was clari-fied in a set of drawings by Sebastiano Serlio in 1540. See the views in Christof Thoenes, "Renaissance St. Peter's," in *St. Peter's in the Vatican*, ed. William Tronzo, Cambridge and New York, 2005, 79. A study for the cupola of St. Peter's attributed to Bramante exists in a drawing now in the Uffizi (Uffizi no. 7945Ar).

14   This is exemplified in the interior pilasters of Hadrian's Pantheon, which originally numbered sixty-four. On the Pythagoreanism of the Pantheon, see Joost-Gaugier,

Measuring Heaven, ch. 10. Bramante's drawing for the cupola of St. Peter's, showing two ranges of sixteen columns is today in the Uffizi (7945Ar). For a reproduction see Francesco Paolo Fiore and Manfredo Tafuri, eds., *Francesco di Giorgio architetto*, Milan, 1993, 56.

15 For photographs, see, e.g., James Lee Milne, *Saint Peter's*, Boston, 1967, illustrations at 117 and 150.

16 Respecting the reputation of Bramante, see Serlio, *L'Architettura*. See also Nicholas Cusanus, *De staticis experimentis*, 194; Ficino's *Commentary on Plato's Symposium*, IV, and *Platonic Theology*, passim (e.g., IV.ii.9); Polydore Vergil, *On Discovery*, I (ix) and III (xiv); and Gaffurio, *De harmonia musicorum*, 8 (cf. Alberti's *De re aedificatoria*, IX.6, where Alberti's definition of a musical/harmonic division agrees with the future one by Gaffurio).

17 Concerning this subject, see Castelli, "Matematici e astrologi … ."

18 For a history of this church, see Emo Barucci, *Il Tempio di San Biagio* (1979), Montepulciano, 2002.

19 These concepts are articulated repeatedly in *De docta ignorantia* and *De coniecturis*. For quoted passage, see *De coniecturis*, I.3 (trans. Hopkins, in *The Complete Philosophical and Theological Treatises of Nicholas of Cusa*, I, Minneapolis, 2001, 168). See also de Gandillac, "Neoplatonism and Christian Thought in the Fifteenth Century: Nicholas of Cusa and Marsilio Ficino," in *Neoplatonism and Christian Thought*, ed. Dominic J. O'Meara, Albany, 1982, 143–68.

20 On 28 as the final hidden part of Plato's fatal number see Allen, *Nuptial Arithmetic*, 5 and 79.

21 Cusanus, *On Learned Ignorance*, I.13 and II.13.

22 The building's design, attributed to Cola da Caprarole, is discussed by Wittkower, in *Architectural Principles…*, 17–18. On Bramante's importance for this building, see esp. Umberto Nofrini, *Il Tempio del Bramante a Todi*, intro. Arnaldo Bruschi, Todi, 1970.

23 For reproductions of Raphael's *Bella Jardiniere* and other contemporary paintings of similar subjects, see Meyer zur Capellen, *Raphael*, I, passim.

24 This work is well known in the Michelangelo literature. See, e.g., De Tolnay, *Michelangelo*, 15–16 and 192–93.

25 This large circular painting is now thought to have been painted for Pope Julius II. For a reproduction and latest discussion of this work, now in the National Gallery of Art at Washington, D.C., see Andrea Zezza, "Giovan Battista Castaldo … un tondo di Raffaello, …" in *Prospettiva*, XCIII, 1999, 29–41; and Hugo Chapman, Tom Henry, and Carol Plazzotta, eds., *Raphael: From Urbino to Rome*, London, 2004, 256–58. When this work was purchased by the National Gallery from the Hermitage, it had a different frame – a circle set into a square, probably, as Zezza suggests (in a letter to the author) not its original frame, which is deemed lost. Its present frame is modern and was separately made in Italy.

26 The role of Ovid's great hexameter poem in Michelangelo's planning of this vast painted space

is discussed at greater length in Joost-Gaugier, "Michelangelo's *Ignudi* and the Sistine Chapel as a Symbol of Law."

27 Wind's analysis is contained in his *The Religious Symbolism of Michelangelo: Sistine Ceiling*, ed. Elizabeth Sears, Oxford, 2000.

28 See Joost-Gaugier, "Michelangelo's *Ignudi* and the Sistine Chapel as a Symbol of Law."

29 Allen, *Nuptial Arithmetic*, 71–72.

30 Lomazzo, *Idea del tempio della pittura*, I, 320.

31 In 1939, Erwin Panofsky (*Studies in Iconology*, New York, 1972 ed., 180) held that Michelangelo was "the only genuine Platonic" among the many artists influenced by "Neoplatonism." Some years later, Wind proposed a number of Platonic influences in Michelangelo's sculpture ("A Bacchic Mystery by Michelangelo," in *Pagan Mysteries in the Renaissance*, 177–91).

32 Charles De Tolnay, "Le Jugement Dernier de Michel Ange," *Art Quarterly*, III, 1940 (2), 125–49.

33 Valerie Shrimplin, *Sun Symbolism and Cosmology in Michelangelo's "Last Judgment,"* Kirksville (Mo.), 2000, 106 and esp. 211–38.

34 The history of this chamber and its Pythagorean characteristics are discussed more extensively than is possible here in Joost-Gaugier, *Raphael's Stanza della Segnatura*.

35 Regarding the many major and subsidiary opposites and their balancing, see Joost-Gaugier, *Raphael's Stanza della Segnatura*.

36 This is exemplified in the Pantheon, a temple dedicated to Hadrian/Apollo (see Joost-Gaugier, *Measuring Heaven*, ch. 10).

37 See, e.g., the extensive discussions of Reuchlin on this subject in *De arte Cabalistica*. On this subject, see also Wind, *The Religious Symbolism … ,* 87–88. On the likely Kabbalistic theme of the pavement, see Joost-Gaugier, *Raphael's Stanza della Segnatura*, 147–53.

38 See, e.g., Pseudo-Iamblichus's discussion of the tetrad in *The Theology of Arithmetic,* 56.

39 Cf. Stahl, *Martianus Capella and the Seven Liberal Arts*, II, 281; Alberti, *De re aedificatura*, IX.v; and Gaffurio, *The Theory of Music*, I.iii.21–33.

40 On the fundamental importance of the cube for Renaissance Pythagoreans and Platonists, see Hersey, *Pythagorean Palaces*, 19ff. See also Vitruvius, *De architectura*, V, proem, on Pythagoras's love for the cube. Mary Garrard called my attention to Raphael's cube.

41 Stahl, *Martianus Capella and the Seven Liberal Arts*, II.

42 See discussion of these subjects in Joost-Gaugier, *Raphael's Stanza della Segnatura*, 65–81.

43 Apollo as the apex of the triangle is discussed by Plotinus (*Ennead V*) and Plutarch (*Isis and Osiris*, 374A, 375F, and 381F). As the monad, he also forms the apex of the *tetraktys*, which, according to the *Golden Verses*, was the invention of Pythagoras. Cf. Ficino, *Theologia Platonica*, XVII, where Ficino describes the apex of the triangle as "unity." See also n. 52.

44 Cf. Ficino, *Letters*, I, 52 (Plato, a Pythagorean, considered Pindar a great poet); and Lomazzo, *Libro de sogni: quarto Ragionamento*, 67. On Pindar's role in this painting, see Joost-Gaugier, "Pindar on Parnassus," *Gazette des Beaux-Arts*, CXXVII, 1996, 65–80.

45 Stahl, *Martianus Capella and the Seven Liberal Arts*, II, esp. 6–18.

46 Plutarch reports that Apollo was the inventor of both music and the lyre (*On Music*, 1135–36).

47 Plato's birth and death dates, considered to have mystical significance for Pythagoreans, are reported in several ancient sources, including Plutarch (*Table-Talk*, 717). Apollo was reputed to have been born on the seventh of an unnamed month, which is why the number came to be holy (Plutarch, *Fragment no. 103* and *Table-Talk*, IX.738). Plato's birth and death dates were discussed at length by Ficino (*Letters*, III, 19).

48 On the Pantheon as a Pythagorean structure, see Joost-Gaugier, *Measuring Heaven*, 166–81.

49 Respecting the painting of *God the Father with SS. Mary Magdalen and Catherine of Siena*, now in the Pinacoteca at Lucca, see Ronald M. Steinberg, *Fra Girolamo Savonarola, Florentine Art, and Renaissance Historiography*, Athens (Ohio), 1977, 86–90. The later picture is reproduced in Serena Padovani, ed., *Fra Bartolomeo e la Scuola di San Marco*, Venice, 1996, 95–97. See also the unfinished contemporary painting by him of the *Madonna, Child, and St. Anne* in San Marco at Florence in ibid., 101–3.

50 See Wittkower, *Architectural Principles …* , 90–94; and Antonio Foscari and Manfredo Tafuri, *L'armonia e i conflitti, la Chiesa di San Francesco della Vigna*, Turin, 1983.

51 The first Vitruvius text to be enriched with illustrations, Fra Giocondo's edition of *De architectura* was published in Venice by Ioannis de Tridino in 1511. For a photo of the Palazzo del Consiglio with surrounding structures, see Penelope Brownell and Francesco Curcio, *Verona: Guida Storico-artistica*, Verona, 1998, 97.

52 Ficino, *Theologia Platonica*, XVII.xiii. (See with commentary in edition of Marcel at III.154.) See also Ficino, *Commentary on Plato's Symposium*, II.1, in *Commentaire sur le Banquet de Platon*, 145. The idea of Apollo as the apex of a triangle was suggested by Hierocles of Alexandria in the fifth century A.D. (*Hieroclis Philosophi commentarius in aurea Pythagoreorum carmina*, ed. Joannes Curterio, London, 1654, 47), an idea that persisted in later versions of the *Golden Verses* attributed to Pythagoras. Hierocles said that Apollo was the top, or number 1, in the *tetraktys*. See also n. 43.

53 On the iconography and history of this painting, see Joost-Gaugier, "The Mute Poetry of the Fête Champêtre: Titian's Memorial to Giorgione," *Gazette des Beaux-Arts*, CXXXIII, 1999, 1–13.

54 On this picture, now in the Kunsthistorisches Museum at Vienna, see Terisio Pignatti and Filippo Pedrocco, *Giorgione*, Milan, 1999, 164–66 (photo at 165).

55 Giorgio Valla, *De expetendis, et fvgiendis rebvs opus …* , Book III (on astronomy). For the astronomical deliberations of the wise men, Nicholas of Cusa may also be of considerable importance. See esp. his Sermon for the Feast of the Epiphany, in Thomas M. Izbicki and Christopher M. Bellitto, eds., *Nicholas of Cusa and His Age: Intellect and Spirituality*, Leiden, 2002, 115.

56 Andrea Palladio, *The Four Books of Architecture* (1570), trans. Robert Tavernor and Richard Schofield, Cambridge (Mass.) and London, 1997, xvi.

57 Nicholas Cusanus, *De staticis experimentis*, 194; on the Pythagorean claims of the antiquity of this idea as their own, see Joost-Gaugier, *Measuring Heaven,* 174 and 313.

58 Primarily known as a theorist (whose *Trattato d'architettura* was also indebted to Vitruvius and Alberti), Serlio is also known for a number of buildings he designed in France. Among these the Chateau at Ancy-le-Franc and the Episcopal Palace at Auxerre stand out for establishing proportionality through the use of number and geometry.

59 On Sicilians teaching in Salamanca during the Renaissance, and on the interest in Vitruvius, Alberti, and other Italian works there, see Felipe Pereda, *La arquitectura elocuente: El edificio de la Universidad de Salamanca bajo el reinado de Carlos V*, Madrid, 2000.

60 An excellent history of the entire project can be found in Earl E. Rosenthal, *The Palace of Charles V in Granada*, Princeton, 1985.

61 See, e.g., Raphael's drawing of the Pantheon interior (Uffizi 164A) in Paul Johannides, *The Drawings of Raphael*, Berkeley and Los Angeles, 1983, fig. 196r.

62 Among these was Pico della Mirandola's most numerological work, the *Heptaplus*, a work (of unknown authorship) on the perfection of the number 10, and most of Ficino's works. Respecting Herrera's library, see Agustín Ruiz de Arcaute, *Juan de Herrera*, Madrid, 1936, 166–70 and, esp., René Taylor, "Architecture and Magic: Considerations on the Idea of the Escorial," in *Essays in the History of Architecture Presented to Rudolf Wittkower*, ed. Douglas Fraser, Howard Hibbard, and Milton J. Lewine, London, 1967, 81–109. For an example of Herrera's seeking out information on harmonic ratios, see Catherine Wilkinson, "Observations on Juan de Herrera's View of Architecture," *Studies in the History of Art*, XIII, Washington, D.C., 1984, 182; respecting Herrera's thirst for Italian editions, see Taylor, "Architecture and Magic," 84. For his works on the cube and mathematics, see Juan de Herrera, *Discurso de la figura cúbica*, ed. Julio R. Pator, Madrid, 1935; and idem, *Institvcion de la Academia Real Matemática*, ed. José Simón Diaz and Luis Cervera Vera, Madrid, 1995. See also n. 63.

63 See the large fresco of the *Gloria* by Luca Cambiaso in Lauro Magnani, *Luca Cambiaso de Genova all'Escorial*, Genoa, 1995, 260–64.

64   The plan of the Jesuit Church in Málaga is illus-
trated in René Taylor, "Hermetism and Mystical
Architecture in the Society of Jesus," in *Baroque Art:
The Jesuit Contribution*, ed. Rudolf Wittkower and
Irma B. Jaffe, New York, 1972, 71.

65   For a description of the library, see Juan Páez de
Castro in Juan de Herrera, *Discurso del Señor Juan de
Herrera aposentador Mayor de S.M., sobre figura cubica*,
ed. Edison Simons and Roberto Godoy, Madrid,
1976, 475-86. In his treatise on architecture, Tibaldi
(who was an architect as well as a painter) makes his
admiration for Pythagoras and Pythagorean values
clear. See Tibaldi, *L'Architettura*, passim.

66   See Heinrich Wölfflin, *Die klassiche Kunst*, Basel, 1899,
translated into many subsequent editions, e.g., *Classic
Art*, trans. Peter Murray and Linda Murray, London,
1952.

67   On the influence of Ficino, Pico, and, esp. Zorzi on
sixteenth-century Hermeticism, see esp. Gilly and
van Heertum, *Magia, alchima, scienza*, vols. I and II.

68   Joscelyn Godwin, *The Pagan Dream of the Renaissance*,
Grand Rapids, 2002, 99-106.

TEN: CONCLUSIONS

1   Trinitarian concepts in Antiquity are the subject of
an important study by Wind, "Pagan Vestiges of the
Trinity," 241-56.

2   Pythagorean impulses in Gothic architecture are
discussed in Joost-Gaugier, *Measuring Heaven*, ch. 12.

3   Iamblichus, *Life of Pythagoras*, 12.

APPENDIX A: PYTHAGOREAN WORKS
IN SIX RENAISSANCE LIBRARIES

1   For the history of the Visconti library see Elisabeth
Pellegrin, *La Bibliothèque des Visconti et des Sforza*,
Paris, 1955.

2   Bessarion is usually known as "Cardinal Bessarion."
Regarding the question of his baptismal name see
the bibliography in J. E. Martin, *Cardinal Bessarion*,
46, n. 66. His bequest is preserved in the Biblioteca
Marciana at Venice. It was first published by Henri
Omont, "Inventaire des manuscrits grecs et lat-
ins donnés à Saint-Marc de Venise par le Cardinal
Bessarion," *Revue des Bibliothèques*, IV, 1894, 129-87.
For his *Letter to the Doge and Senate of Venice* of 31 May

1468, see Lotte Labowsky, *Bessarion's Library and the
Biblioteca Marciana: Six Early Inventories*, Rome, 1979,
147-53.

3   Vespasiano da Bisticci, *Lives of Illustrious Men of
the XVth Century*, ed. W. G. and E. Waters, 138. Cf.
Labowsky, *Bessarion's Library and the Biblioteca Marciana*,
147-53.

4   Concerning the nucleus of Bessarion's library, brought
by him to Italy from Mistra, in Greece, where he had
studied mathematics and Neoplatonic philosophy,
see Elpidia Mioni, "Bessarione bibliofilo e filologo,"
Rivista di Studi Bizantini et Neoellenici, n.s. 5 (XV),
1968, 61-83. See also Labowsky, *Bessarion's Library and
the Biblioteca Marciana*.

5   Though this text is preserved in the corpus of works
of the famous Pythagorean Iamblichus, its author is
not known. Normally cited as Pseudo-Iamblichus,
The Theology of Arithmetic, it is a compilation of the
symbols and meanings of the first ten numbers of the
Pythagorean decad.

6   *Tor. Bib. Naz. Gr. 146.* On this text, see Mioni, "Bessarione
scriba e alcuni collaboratori," in *Miscellanea Marciana
di studi Bessarionei*, Padua, 1976, 290.

7   The development of the Vatican Library, actually
founded by Nicholas V, is admirably studied in Jeanne
Bignami Odier, *La Bibliothèque Vaticane de Sixte IV à Pie
XI: Recherches sur l'Histoire des Collections de Manuscrits*,
Vatican City, 1973. For lists as known through various
inventories of the contents of the library of Sixtus IV,
see Eugène Müntz and Paul Fabre, *La Bibliothèque du
Vatican au XVe Siècle*, Amsterdam, 1970, esp. 185-306.
For details on the organization of Sixtus's library into
four chambers and their adornment by Domenico
Ghirlandaio, see Fabre, *La Vaticane de Sixte IV*, Rome,
1896.

8   An inventory of 1,697 books and manuscripts in
Pico's library, based on a list made in 1498, four years
after his death, was published by Pearl Kibre, in *The
Library of Pico della Mirandola*, New York, 1936.

9   A list of Reuchlin's books is provided in *BAV. Palat.
Lat. 1925.* This list was published by Karl Christ in
"Die Bibliothek Reuchlins in Pforzheim," *Beiheft
zum Zentralblatt für Bibliothekswesen*, LII, 1924,
1-96.

10   Although many inventories of different parts of the
Escorial library are mentioned, only two partial ones
(previous to the first of 1671) survive, one of 1579
and the other of 1587. See Charles Graux, *Essai sur
les Origines du Fond Grec de l'Escurial*, Paris, 1880.

SELECT BIBLIOGRAPHY

This bibliography represents a selection of primary and secondary sources that form the background for this work. Because many of the well-known primary sources were used in various editions, particular editions may not always be cited for these. For works contained in printed collections, both sources will be cited when possible. However, most of those works contained in Migne will be listed only by title.

PRIMARY SOURCES

Agapitus (librarian). [Inventory of library of Federigo da Montefeltro.] Vatican (*BAV.Urb.Lat.167*).

Agrippa, Cornelius. *De incertitudine et vanitate scientiarum et artium.* Antwerp, 1526.

    De occulta philosophia libri tres. Antwerp, 1531.

    La philosophie occulte (1910). Trans. A. Levasseur. 2nd ed. Paris, 1968 (4 vols.).

    Opera. Intro. Richard H. Popkin. Hildesheim, 1970 (2 vols.).

    Of the Vanitie and Vncertaintie of Artes and Sciences. Ed. Catherine M. Dunn. Northridge (Calif.), 1974.

    De occulta philosphia libri tres. Ed. V. Perrone Compagni. Leiden, 1992.

    Three Books of Occult Philosophy. Ed. Donald Tyson. St. Paul (Minn.), 1993.

    Declamation on the Nobility and Preeminence of the Female Sex (1532). Ed. Albert Rabil, Jr. Chicago and London, 1996.

Alberti, Leon Battista. *Della pittura.*

    De scultura.

    Ludi matematici.

    Leonis Baptiste Alberti De re aedificatoria. Florence, 1485.

    Opera volgare. Ed. Cecil Grayson. Bari, 1960–73 (3 vols.).

    Intercenales. In *Dinner Pieces.* Ed. David Marsh. Binghamton (N.Y.), 1987.

    On the Art of Building in Ten Books. Trans. Joseph Rykwert, Neil Leach, and Robert Tavernor, Cambridge (Mass.), 1988.

    Descriptio urbis Romae. Ed. M. Forno and M. Carpo. Geneva, 2000.

    Momus. Ed. Virginia Brown and Sarah Knight. Cambridge (Mass.) and London, 2003.

Anatolius of Laodicea, *On the Decad*, Described in Eusebius of Caesarea, *Ecclesiastical History*, VII.xxii.5–23.

Anon. *Homeric Hymn to Pythian Apollo.*

    Prenostica Pitagorice. Oxford (*MS. Digby 46*).

    Sumari und ausszug von dem furnemesten. Washington, D.C. (*Cath.Univ.America.MS.129*).

    Turba philosophorum. Paris (*Bib.Nat.MS.Fr.1978*).

    [Untitled MS.] New York (*Morgan.M5.B.27*).

    Aureorum carminvm Pythagore versio. Ed. Prigenti Calvarini. Paris, 1539.

    Avrea dicta Pythagore. Ed. M. Georgium Prechtium Rotenpurgensem. Vienna, 1558.

    Carmina aurea. Ed. Michaelis Neandri. Leipzig, 1559.

    Speculum humanae salvationis (ed. Jean Miélot, no loc., 1448). Rep. ed. Jules Lutz and Pierre Perdrizet. Leipzig, 1907.

    Turba philosophorum. Ed. Julius Ruska (1931). Rep. Berlin, 1970.

Anonimo Fiorentino (Antonio Manetti?). *Il Codice Magliabechiano.* Ed. Karl Frey (1892). Rep. Franborough (U.K.), 1969.

Ariosto, Lodovico. *Orlando Furioso.* Ed. Giovanni Mazzocci. Ferrara, 1516.

    Orlando Furioso. Trans. W. S. Rose. Ed. Stewart Baker and Bartlett Giamatti, Indianapolis, 1968.

Aristotle, *De caelo.*

Pseudo-Averroës, *Averroeana: Being a Transcript of Several Letters from Averroes … to Metrodorus … also several letters from Pythagoras to the King of India together with his reception at the Indian Court.* London, 1695.

Baldi, Bernardino. *Memorie concernenti la città di Urbino.* Rome, 1724.

    Vita di Pitagora (1588). In *Bullettino di bibliographia e di storia delle scienze, matematiche e fisiche.* Ed. Enrico Narducci, XX, 1897, 197–308.

    "Fra'Luca dal Borgo S. Sepolcro," "Nicolò di Cusa," "Niccolò Copernico," "Paolo Fiorentino," "Pavolo di Middelburgo." In *Le vite de' matematici* (1589). Ed. Elio Nenci. Milan, 1998, 330–45, 255–71, 402–13, 291–95, and 355–97, respectively.

    Le vite de' matematici (1589). Ed. Elio Nenci. Milan, 1998.

Bandini, Aloysii. *De vita et rebus gestis Bessarionis.*

Beroaldo, Filippo, Junior. *Heptalogos septem sapientium* and *Symbola Pythagorica moraliter explicata*. In *Orationes & opuscula Philippi Beroaldi Bononiensis* ... . Basel, 1515.

Beroaldo, Filippo, Senior. *De felicitate opusculum*.

Symbola Pythagorae Philippo Beroaldo moraliter explicata. Bologna, 1503.

Declamatio an orator sit philosopho & medico anteponendus in Libellus Quo Septem Sapientium Sententiae. In *Philippi Beroaldi libe ilus quo septem saptientium sententia*. Ed. Leone Argento. Paris, 1505.

Bessarion, Joannes Cardinal. *Ad Graecos Epistola*.

De natura et arte.

De Sacramento Eucharistae..

De verbis consecrationis et transsubstantiatione.

Oratio dogmatica sive de unione quam Graece ... Latinam.

Adversus calumniatorem Platonis. Ed. Conradus Sweynheym and Arnoldus Pannartz. Rome, 1468.

In calumniatorem Platonis libri quattuor. Venice, 1516.

Orazione dogmatica sull'unione dei Greci e dei Latini. Ed. Gianfrancesco Lusini. Naples, 2001.

Biondo, Flavio. *Roma trionfante, tradotta per hora per Lucio Fauno di latino in buona lingua* (1482). Venice, 1548.

Blasius, Johannes Martinus. *Liber arithmetica practice astrologis* (1513). Rep. Cambridge, 1960 (no ed.).

Boethius Severus. *Arithmetica Boetij*. Ed. Erhardum Ratdolt. Augsburg, 1488.

Arithmetica geometria et musica Boetii (no ed.). Venice, 1492.

Epitome in libros arithmeticos and *Elementa musica*. Ed. Jacobi Fabri Stapulensis. Paris, 1510.

Diviseverini Boetii arithmetica. Ed. Simonem Colinaeum. Paris, 1521.

Opera, quae extant, omnia. Henricus Loritua Glareanus. Basel, 1546.

Iacobi Fabri Stapulensis in Arithmetica Boëthi epitome ... . Ed. Henricvm Petri. Basel, 1553.

Anitii Manlii Severini Boethi philosophorvm et theologorvm principis opera omnia. Ed. Henricvs Petrina. Basel, 1570.

De arithmetica. In Jacques-Paul Migne, *Patrologia Latina*, LVIII. Paris, 1882.

Bracciolini, Poggio. *Opera omnia*. Ed. Riccardo Fubini. Turin, 1964 (4 vols.).

Bradwardine, Thomas. *Arithmetica Thome bravardini*. Paris, 1495.

Browne, Thomas. *The Works of Sir Thomas Browne*. Ed. Geoffrey Keynes. Chicago, 1964 (4 vols.).

Bruni, Leonardo. *De studiis et literis*.

Letter to Lauro Quirini.

Commentarius rerum suo tempore gestarum. Ed. G. B. Di Pierro, *Rerum italicarum scriptores*, n.s. 193. Bologna, 1926, 341–42.

Dialogi ad Petrum Paulum Histrum. Ed. Stefano Ugo Baldassarri. Florence, 1994.

Bruno, Giordano. *Asino cillenico*.

Cabala del cavallo Pegaseo.

Il candelaio.

La cena delle ceneri.

De la causa, principio, et uno.

De l'infinito universo e mondi.

De monade, numero et figura.

Oeuvres Complèts. Ed. Giovanni Aquilecchia. Paris, 1993.

Bryennius, Manuel. [*Harmonics*.] Trans. Gian Francesco Burana. Lodi (*Bib.Comm.Cod.XXVIII.A8*), fols. 3–118.

The Harmonics of Manuel Bryennius. Ed. Goverdus H. Jonker. Groningen, 1970.

Busnoys (de Busne), Antoine. *Antoine Busnoys Collected Works*. Ed. Richard Taruskin. New York, 1990.

Calandri, Filippo. *Trattato di aritmetica* (ca. 1485). Florence (*Bib.Ricc.Cod.2669*).

Aritmetica. Ed. Lorenzo de Morgiani and Giovanni Thedesco da Maganza. Florence, 1491.

Calcagnini, Celio. *Amatoriae magiae compendium*.

Epistole a Andrea Minotto.

Epistolicarum questionum.

Pythagoras musicis modulis.

Opera aliquot. Basel, 1544.

Calvo, Fabio. *Antiqvae vrbis Romae cvm regionibvs simvlachrvm*. Eds. Frobenivm and Episcopivm. Basel, 1558.

Vitruvio e Raffaello, Il De Architectura di Vitruvio nella traduzione inedita di Fabio Calvo Ravennate. Ed. Vincenzo Fontana and Paolo Marachiello. Rome, 1975.

Caponsacchi (?), Pietro. *Vita Ficini*. Florence (*Bib.Naz. Palat.488*).

Cardano, Girolamo. *Artis Magnae sive de regulis algebraicis*. Nuremberg, 1545.

Encomivm geometriae recitatvm in De subtilitate libri XXI. Basel, 1554.

Book of My Life (1557). Trans. Jean Stoner (1930). Rep. New York, 1962.

De subtilitate (1554). Ed. Elio Nenci. Milan, 2004.

De immortalitate animorum (1545). Ed. José M. Garcia Valverde. Milan, 2006.

Castiglione, Baldassare. *Il cortegiano*. Ed. Aldus Manutius. Venice, 1528.

Il cortegiano (1528). Ed. Mario Luzi. Milan, 1941.

The Book of the Courtier. Trans. Charles S. Singleton. New York, 1959.

Chalcidius. *Platonis Timaeus interprete Chalcidio*. Ed. J. Wrobel. Leipzig, 1876.

Champier, Symphorien. *Liber de quadruplici vita. Theologia Asclepij hermetis*. Lyon, 1507.

Cicero, Tullius. *De natura deorum*.

De re publica.

In somnium Scipionis.

Tusculanae disputationes.

In M.T. Ciceronis de somnio Scipionis. Ed. Petri Olivarii. Basel, 1538.

M.Tvlli Ciceronis Timaeus. Ed. Franciscvs Pini. Milan, 1965.

Epistulae ad familiares. Ed. D. R. Shackelton Bailey. Cambridge, 1977 (2 vols.).

Clement of Alexandria, *Stromateius*.

Clichtove, Josse. *De mystica numerorum significatione opusculum*. Ptr. Henricum Stephanum. Paris, 1513.

Cocchi, Antonio. *Régime de Pythagore*. Paris, 1762.

Colet, John. *Treatise on the Sacraments of the Church, Two Treatises on the Hierarchies of Dionysius*, and *Letters to*

Radulphus on the Mosaic Account of the Creation. Ed. and trans. J. H. Lupton. Rep. w. Latin titles (no ed.). Ridgewood (N.J.), 1965–66.

Colonna, Francesco. *Hypnerotomachia Poliphili* (1499). Trans. Joscelyn Godwin. London, 1999.

Comanini, Gregorio. *The Figino or On the Purpose of Painting: Art Theory in the Late Renaissance*. Ed. and trans. Ann Doyle-Anderson and Giancarlo Maiorino. Toronto, 2001.

Copernicus, Nicholaus. *De revolutionibus orbium celestium*. Ed. Johannes Petreius. Nuremberg, 1543.

 Three Copernican Treatises. Ed. Edward Rosen (1939). 3rd ed. New York, 1971.

 Six Books on the Revolutions of the Heavenly Spheres. Ed. Jerzy Dobrzycki. Trans. Edward Rosen. Baltimore, 1978.

Corsi, Giovanni. *Life of Marsilio Ficino* (1506). In *Letters of Marsilio Ficino*. Ed. Paul Oskar Kristeller. Trans. Dept. School Economic Science. London, 1975, III, 133–48.

Cusanus, Nicholas. *De coniecturis*.

 De docta ignorantia.

 De la caccia de la sapienza.

 Idiota de mente.

 Nicolai de Cusa, Opera omnia. Ed. Felicis Meiner. Vols. I (*De docta ignorantia*), II (*Apologia doctae ignorantiae*), and III (*Idiota de sapientia …*). Leipzig, 1932–37.

 Nicholas of Cusa on Learned Ignorance. Ed. and trans. Jasper Hopkins. Minneapolis, 1981.

 De ludo globi. Ed. Pauline M. Watts. New York, 1986.

 Nicholas of Cusa on Interreligious Harmony (De pace fidei). Ed. James E. Biechler and H. L Bond. Lewiston (N.Y.), 1990.

 De concordantia catholica. In *The Catholic Concordance*. Ed. Paul E. Sigmund. Cambridge, 1991.

 Toward a New Council of Florence, On the Peace of Faith, and Other Works. Ed. William Wertz, Jr. Washington, D.C., 1993.

 De staticis experimentis. In Nicholas of Cusa on Wisdom and Knowledge. Ed. Jasper Hopkins. Minneapolis, 1996.

 The Complete Philosophical and Theological Treatises of Nicholas of Cusa. Ed. and trans. Jasper Hopkins. Minneapolis, 2001 (2 vols.).

Cyriaco d'Ancona. *Cyriac of Ancona, Later Travels*. Ed. and trans. Edward W. Bodnar with Clive Foss. Cambridge (Mass.), 2003.

De Bruxella, Arnaldus. "Library of Alchemy." Bethlehem, Pa. (*Lehigh Univ. MS. No. 1*).

De la Fontaine, Caluy. *Foelicité humaine*. Paris, 1543.

Della Porta, Giovanni Battista. *Magiae natvralis libri XX*. Naples, 1589.

 Magiae naturalis libri viginti (1589). Rouen, 1650.

Del Monte, Pietro. *De veritate unius legis et falsitaete sectarum*. Milan, 1509.

Diogenes Laertius. *Lives of Eminent Philosophers*.

Domninos de Larissa. *Le Manuel d'Introduction Arithmétique du Philosophe Domninos de Larissa*. Ed. Paul Tannery. In *Memoires Scientifiques: Sciences Exactes dans l'Antiquité*. Paris, 1915, III, 255–85.

Egidio da Viterbo. *Scechina e libellus de litteris hebraicis*. Ed. François Secret. Rome, 1959, 2 vols.

Enrique Gómez, Antonio. *El siglo pitagorico y Vida de Don Gregorio Guadaña*. Ed. Teresa de Santas. Madrid, 1991.

Erasmus, Desiderius. *Antibarbarorum liber*.

 Declamatio in laudem artis medicae.

 De contemptu mundi.

 De duplici copia verborum ac rerum commentarii.

 Dialogus Ciceronianus.

 Enchiridion militis christiani.

 Letters to Adrian VI, Christopher Urswick, François Deloynes, Guillaume de Croy, Hendrik van Bergen, Henry VIII, Jean de Nève, and Krysztof Szydowiecki; Letter from Herman Lethmaet.

 Lingua.

 Moriae encomium.

 In nucem Ovidii.

 Oratio de virtute amplectenda.

 Apotheosis capnionis/seu de incomparabili heroe iohanne Reuchlino in divorum numerum relato. In *L'apoteosi di Giovanni Reuchlin*. Ed. Giulio Vallese. 3rd ed. Naples, 1964.

 Collected Works of Erasmus. Various eds. Toronto, Buffalo, and London, 1974–93 (84 vols.).

Euclid, *Elements*.

Federigo da Montefeltro. *Lettere di stato e d'arte di Federico da Montefeltro*. Ed. Paolo Alatri. Rome, 1949.

Ficino, Marsilio. *Commentarium*.

 De laudibus philosophiae.

 Ex Porphyrio De Abstinentia Animalum.

 Florentini versiones variae quae sequntur (XV cent.). Oxford (*Bod. Lib. 163*).

 In librum de sole.

 In Timaeum Platonis.

 Pythagorae philosophi avrea verba.

 Spevsippi Platonis discipvli liber de Platonis definitionibus.

 Symbola Pythagorae.

 Libro di Marsilio Ficino Fiorentino della Christiana religione. Ed. Lorenzo Fiorentini. and Seragno Fiorentini. Pisa, 1484.

 Liber de vita. Ptr. Antonius Mischominus. Florence, 1489.

 Iamblichi de secta pythagorica in svpplementvm ficianvm. Ed. Paul Oskar Kristeller / Scuola Normale Superiore of Pisa. Florence, 1937, II, 98–103.

 Svpplementvm ficianvm: Marsilii Ficini Florentini Opvscvla inedita et dispersa. Ed. Paul Oskar Kristeller / Scuola Normale Superiore of Pisa. Florence, 1937 (2 vols.).

 Marsilio Ficino's Commentary on Plato's Symposium. Ed. Sears R. Jayne. Columbia (Mo.), 1944.

 Convivium Platonis in Commentaire sur le Banquet de Platon. Ed. Raymond Marcel. Paris, 1956.

 Opera omnia. Ed. Henrico Petrina. Basel, 1561–76. Rep. ed. Paul Oskar Kristeller. Turin, 1959 (2 vols.).

 Théologie Platonicienne de l'Immortalité des Ames. Ed. Raymond Marcel. Paris, 1964 (3 vols.).

 Letters of Marsilio Ficino. Ed. Paul Oskar Kristeller. Trans. Dept. of the School of Economic Science. London, 1975 (6 vols.).

Three Books on Life. Trans. Carol V. Kaske and John R. Clark. Binghamton (N.Y.), 1989.

Marsilio Ficino: The Philebus Commentary. Ed. Michael J. B. Allen. Tempe (Ariz.), 2000.

The Platonic Theology of Marsilio Ficino. Ed. James Hankins and William Bowen. Trans. Michael J. B. Allen and John Warden. Cambridge (Mass.), 2001–6 (6 vols.).

Filarete, Antonio Averlino. *Treatise on Architecture*. Ed. and trans. John R. Spencer. New Haven and London, 1965 (2 vols.).

Filelfo, Francesco. *Espistula de opinionibus philosophorum*.

Fine, Oronce. *De arithmetic practica libri quatuor*. Ptr. Simon de Colinaei, Paris, 1542.

Les canons & docvmens tresamples, touchant lusaige & practique des comuns almanachz … Ptr. Simon de Colines. Paris, 1543.

De quadratura circuli, tandem inventa…. Paris, 1544.

Firmani, Nicolo. *Oratio in Funere Bessarionis*. In Ludwig Mohler, *Kardinal Bessarion als Theologe, Humanist und Staatsmann* (1923–42). Rep. Aalen, 1967, III, 404–14.

Francesco di Giorgio Martini. *Trattato di architettura*.

Trattati di architettura, ingegnetia e arte militare. Ed. Corrado Maltese. Milan, 1967 (2 vols).

Gaffurio, Franchino. *Theoricum opus musice discipline*. Milan, 1492.

De harmonia musicorum instrumentorum opus. Milan, 1518.

De harmonia musicorum instrumentorum opus. Ed. Clement A. Miller. Stuttgart, 1979.

The Theory of Music. Ed. Claude V. Palisca. Ed. and trans. Walter K. Kreyszig. New Haven and London, 1993.

Theoricum opus musice discipline. Ed. Cesarino Ruini, Bologna, 1996.

Galatinus, Petrus. *Opus de arcanis catholicae veritatis*. Basel, 1550 and 1561.

Galilei, Galileo. *Le opere di Galileo Galilei* (1846). Rep. ed. Antonio Favaro. Bologna, 1890 (20 vols.).

Sidereus nuncius or the Sidereal Messenger. Ed. and trans. Albert van Helden. Chicago, 1989.

Galileo on the World Systems. Ed. and trans. Maurice A. Finocchiaro. Berkeley, 1997.

Galilei, Vincenzo. *Dialogo della musica antica e della moderna* (1581). Ed. Fabio Fano. Milan, 1947.

Gellicus, Johannes. *Ritus canendi* (ca. 1460). Ed. Albert Seay. Colorado Springs, 1981.

Giorgio (Zorzi), Francesco. *De harmonia mvndi totivs cantica tria*. Ed. Bernardini de Vitalibus. Venice, 1525.

L'Elegante poema. Ed. Jean-François Maillard. Milan, 1991.

Giovio, Paolo. *Elogia virorum illustrium*. Basel, 1577.

Guarino da Verona. *Adulescentem generosum discipulum suum, de ordine docendi et studendi*.

Hermes Trismegistus. *Liber de potestate et sapientia Dei tradvctus a Marsilio Ficino [in Poimandrem]*. Vatican City (*Bib. Apos. Vat. Lat. 1009*).

Poimandres. Paris (*Bib. Nat. Par. Graecus 1220*).

Pimander. Sapientia et potestate dei. Ed. Lefèvre d'Étaples, Paris, 1505.

Herrera, Juan de. *Discurso de la figura cúbica*. Ed. Julio R. Pator. Madrid, 1995.

Discurso del Señor Juan de Herrera aposentador Mayor de S. M., sobre figura cubica. Ed. Edison Simons and Roberto Godoy. Madrid, 1976.

Institvcion de la Academia Real Matemática. Ed. José Simón Diaz and Luis Cervera Vera. Madrid, 1995.

Hierocles of Alexandria. *Commentarius in aurea Pythagoreorum carmina*. Ed. Joannes Curterio. London, 1654.

Hippolytus (bishop of Rome). *Philosophumena*.

Homer. *Odyssey*.

Iamblichus. *De mysteriis Aegyptiorum, Chaldaeorum, Assyriorum*. Trans. Marsilio Ficino. Ptr. Aldus Manutius. Venice, 1497.

De vita Pythagorica liber. Ed. August Nauck. Amsterdam, 1965.

De vita Pythagorica liber. Ed. Ludwig Deubner (1937). Rev. ed. Ulrich Klein. Stuttgart, 1975.

On the Pythagorean Way of Life. Trans. and intro. Gillian Clark. Liverpool, 1989.

Iamblichus attrib. *Jamblique: Les Mystères d'Égypte*. Ed. Édouard des Places. Paris, 2003.

Pseudo-Iamblichus. *The Theology of Arithmetic*. Trans. Robin Waterfield. Grand Rapids, 1988.

Jordanus Nemorarius. *De elementis arithmetice artis: A Medieval Treatise on Number Theory*. Ed. H. L. L. Busard. Stuttgart, 1991.

Josephus, Flavius. *Jewish Antiquities*.

Kallendorf, Craig, ed. *Humanist Educational Treatises*, ed. Craig Kallendorf. Cambridge (Mass.) and London, 2002.

Kelly, Edward. *The Alchemical Writings of Edward Kelly* (1676). London, 1893.

Kepler, Johannes. *Cosmographicum di stella nova* (1596). In *Johannes Kepler Gesammelte Werke*. Ed. Max Caspar. Munich, 1938, I.

Letter to Galileo. In *The Portable Renaissance Reader*. Ed. James B. Ross and Mary M. McLaughlin (1953). New York, 1968, 598–600.

Mysterium cosmographicum (The Secret of the Universe). Trans. A. M. Duncan. New York, 1981.

The Harmony of the World. Trans. and ed. E. J. Aiton, A. M. Duncan, and J. V. Field. Philadelphia, 1997.

Landino, Cristoforo. *Apologia nella quale si difende Dante e Florenzia da' falsi calunniatori*.

Commento Dantesco.

Disputationum camaldulensium.

Orazione … quando cominciò a leggere le comedia di Dante.

Prolusione Dantesca Praefatio in Tusculanis.

Scritti critici e teorici. Ed. Roberto Cardini. Rome, 1974.

Disputationes camaldulenses. Ed. Peter Lohe. Florence, 1980.

Lascaris, Constantinus. *De scriptoribus Graecis patria calabaris*.

Epistola ad Joannem Gatum.

Ne aurea Pythagorae in *De octo partibus orationes*. Ptr. Aldus Manutius. Venice, 1503.

Greek Grammar (1476). Trans. C. M. Breuning-Williamson. Amsterdam, 1966.

Lefèvre d'Étaples, Jacques. *Elementa musicalia*.

Epitome in duos libros Arithmeticos divi Severum Boetij (1496). Rep. ed. Henrichvm Petri. Basel, 1553.

The Prefatory Epistles of Jacques Lefèvre d'Étaples and Related Texts. Ed. Eugene F. Rice Jr. New York, 1972.

Leonardo da Vinci. *The Literary Works of Leonardo da Vinci* (1883). Ed. Jean Paul Richter. New York, 1970 (2 vols.).

The Madrid Codices. Ed. Ladislao Reti. New York, 1974.

The Literary Works of Leonardo da Vinci Compiled & Edited by Jean Paul Richter. Carlo Pedretti, *Commentary.* Oxford, 1977.

The Notebooks of Leonardo da Vinci (1938). Ed. Edward MacCurdy. London, 1977 (2 vols.).

Leonardo on Painting: An Anthology of Writings by Leonardo da Vinci. Ed. Martin Kemp. New Haven and London, 1989.

Leonardo da Vinci's Paragone. Ed. Claire Farago. Leiden and New York, 1992.

Lomazzo, Giovanni Paolo. *Libro de sogni: Secondo Ragionamento.*

Libro de sogni: Quarto Ragionamento.

Libro de sogni: Settimo Ragionamento.

Trattato dell'arte de la pittura.

Scritti sulle arti. Ed. Roberto P. Ciardi. Florence, 1973–74 (2 vols.).

Della forma delle muse (1591). Ed. Alessandra Ruffino. Trent, 2002.

Idea del tempio della pittura (1590). Ed. Robert Klein. Florence, 1974 (2 vols.).

Lucian of Samosata. *Dialogues of the Dead.*

Fray Luis de León. *The Unknown Light: The Poems of Fray Luis de León.* Ed. and trans. Willis Barnstone. Albany (N.Y.), 1979.

Macrobius. *Commentary on the Dream of Scipio.* Trans. William Harris Stahl. New York, 1952.

Maffei, Raffaele. *Commentaria Urbana.* Rome, 1506.

Manetti, Antonio. *The Life of Brunelleschi.* Trans. Catherine Enggass. Ed. Howard Saalman. University Park (Pa.) and London, 1970.

Martianus Capella. *Martiani Capelle De nuptijs Philologie & Mercurij libri duo.* Ed. Henricvm de Sancto Vrso. Vicenza, 1499.

Martiai Capellae De nvptiis Philologiae et Mercvrii liberi dvo. Ed. Dionysiu Berthocum. Modena, 1500.

M. Capella Martiani Minei Capella Carthaginensis De nuptijs Philologiae & Septem artibus liberalibus libri novem. Ed. Haeredes Simonis Vincentij. Lvgdvni, 1539.

De nuptis Mercurii et Philologiae (The Marriage of Mercury and Philology). Ed. William Harris Stahl. New York, 1977.

Migne, Jacques-Paul. *Patrologia Latina.* Paris, 1844–64 (221 vols.).

Patrologia Graeca. Paris, 1857–66 (161 vols.).

Nanni, Giovanni. *Berosus sacerdotis caldaici.* Ed. J. Steelsius. Antwerp, 1545.

Neander, Michael. *Lapidis indago totius philosophiae et magiae naturalis.*

Nicomachus of Gerasa. *Introduction to Arithmetic.* Ed. Martin L. D'Ooge. New York, 1926. 2nd ed., 1972.

The Manual of Harmonics. Ed. Flora R. Levin. Grand Rapids, 1994.

Ovid. *Heroides.*

Metamorphoses.

Pacioli, Luca. *Summa de arithmetica geometria proportioni e proportionalita.* Ed. Paganino de Paganini. Venice, 1494.

De divina proportione. Ed. A. Paganius Paganius. Venice, 1509.

Divine proportione. Ed. Constantin Winterberg. Vienna, 1896.

Palladio, Andrea. *The Four Books of Architecture* (1570). Trans. Robert Tavernor and Richard Schofield. Cambridge (Mass.) and London, 1997.

Paracelsus. *Sieben Defensiones: Antwort auf etliche Verunglimpfungen … und Labyrithus medicorum.* Basel, 1538.

Paracelsus His Aurora, & Treasure of the Philosophers as also the Water-stone of the Wise Men. Ed. J. H. Oxon. London, 1659.

Opera omnia. Geneva, 1662 (3 vols.).

Sämtliche Werke. Ed. Bernhard Aschner. Jena, 1922–28 (4 vols.).

Patrizi, Francesco. *De regno et regis institutione.* Paris, 1519.

Compendiosa epitome commentariorum Francisci Patritii senensis episcopi. Ed. Hiérosme de Marnef. Paris, 1577.

Della nuova geometria. Ferrara, 1587.

Nova de universis philosophia. Ed. A. L. P. Bleuel. Florence, 1993.

Paulus de Middelbourg. *Prognostica, ad viginti annos duratura* (incun.). Antwerp, 1484.

Pereira, Gomez. *Antoniana margarita.* 1554.

Petrarca, Francesco. *De vita solitaria.*

Familiarum rerum.

Philo Judaeus. *De vita Mosis.*

Librum de vita Moysi. Vatican City (*Vat. Lat. 182*).

Photius. *Bibliothèque.* Ed. René Henry. Paris, 1967, VII, (9 vols.).

Piccolomini, Aeneas Sylvius. *De liberorum educatione.*

The Education of Boys.

Lettera a Maometto II (Epistola ad Mahumetem). Ed. Giuseppe Toffanin. Naples, 1953.

Pico della Mirandola, Giovanni. *Epistole.*

Heptaplus, Apologia, De hominis dignitate, and *De ente et uno.* In *Opera omnia.* Basel, 1557.

A Platonik Discourse upon Love. In *Poems.* Ed. Thomas Stanley. London, 1651, 215–43.

De hominis dignitate. Ed. Eugenio Garin. Florence, 1942.

Disputationum adversus astrologos. Ed. Eugenio Garin. Florence, 1943 (2 vols.).

On the Dignity of Man, On Being and the One, Heptaplus. Trans. Charles Glenn Wallis, Paul, J. W. Miller, and Douglas Carmichael. Indianapolis, 1965.

Conclusiones sive Theses DCCCC. Ed. Bohdan Kieszkowski. Geneva, 1973.

Conclusiones nongentae. Ed. Albano Biondi. Florence, 1995.

Syncretism in the West: Pico's 900 Theses. Ed. S. A. Farmer. Tempe (Ariz.), 1998.

Kommentar zu einem Lied der Liebe. Ed. Thorsten Bürklin. Hamburg, 2001.

Giovanni Pico della Mirandola: His Life by His Nephew … (1510?). Trans. Sir Thomas More. Ed. J. M. Rigg. London, 1890.

In examen vanitatis christianae disciplinae. In Pico della Mirandola. *Opera omnia: Ioannis Pici Mirandvlae concordi-acque comitis … * Basel, 1557, II, 729–39.

Piero della Francesca. *Libellus de quinque corporibus regularibus* (no ed.). Florence, 1995 (3 vols.).

De la perspetive en peinture. Ed. Hubert Damish. Trans. Jean-Pierre Le Goff. Paris, 1998.

De prospectiva pingendi. Ed. Giustina Nicco-Fasola. Florence. 2005.

Pins, Jean du. *Divae Catherinae Senensis simvl et clarissimi viri Philippi Beroaldi bononiensis vita per Ioannem Pinvm gallum tolosanvm.* Bologna, 1505.

Platina, Bartolomeo. *Panegyricus in laudem amplissimi patris D. Bessarionis.*

De honesta volvptate. Ptr. Ulrich Han. Rome, 1475.

Plato. *Cratylus.*

Critias.

Laws.

Timaeus.

Pletho, George Gemistus. *Commentary on the Chaldean Oracles.*

Contra Scholarii Defensionem Aristotelis.

De differentis.

Explanation of Obscure Passages.

Magica Zoroastri oracvla, Plethonis commentariis enarrata. Ed. Iacobo Marthano. Paris, 1539.

Oracula magica Zoroastris cum scholiis Plethonis. Ed. Joannes Opsopäus. Paris, 1599.

Pléthon. Traité des Lois. Ed. Charles Alexandre. Trans. A. Pellissier. Paris, 1858.

Pliny the Elder. *Historia naturalibus.*

Plotinus. *Enneads.*

Plutarch. *The E at Delphi.*

Isis and Osiris.

On Music.

Table Talk.

Fragments from *Moralia.* Ed. F. H. Sandbach. In *Plutarch,* ed. F. C. Babbitt. Cambridge (Mass.) and London, 1969, XV.

Poliziano, Angelo. *Collectanea in enarrationem fastorum.*

Oratio in expositione Homeri.

Praefatio in expositione Homeri.

Omnia opera. Ptr. Aldus Manutius. Venice, 1502.

Opera qvae qvidem extite. … Basel, 1553.

Commento inedito all'episode ovidiana di Saffo e Faone. Ed. Elisabetta Lazzeri. Florence, 1971.

Commento inedito ai Fasti di Ovidio. Ed. Francesco Lo Monaco. Florence, 1991.

Silvae. Ed. Francesco Bausi. Florence, 1996.

Silvae. Ed. Charles Fantazzi. Cambridge (Mass.), 2004.

Letters. Ed. Shane Butler. Cambridge (Mass.) and London, 2006.

Pomponazzi, Pietro. *Trattato sull'immortalità dell'anima.* Ed. Vittoria P. Compagni. Florence, 1999.

Porphyry of Tyre. *De vita Pythagorae.* In *Porphyrii philosophi Platonici opuscvla tria.* Ed. Augustus Nauck. Leipzig, 1860.

Postel, Guillaume. *Quatuor librorum de orbis terrae concordio primus.* Paris, 1543.

De la republique des Turcs et là où l'occasion s'offrira. Poitiers, 1560.

De vniuersitate liber, in qvo astrônomiae doctrinaeue coelestis. Paris, 1563.

Des Admirable Secrets des Nombres Platoniciens (1549). Ed. Jean-Pierre Brach. Paris, 2001.

Petit Traité de la Signification ultime des Cinq Corps Réguliers. Ed. Jean-Pierre Brach. In Sylvain Matton. *Documents oubliés sur l'alchimie, la Kabbale e Guillaume Postel.* Geneva, 2001, 223–44.

Ptolemy. *Tetrabiblos.* Ed. and trans. F. E. Robbins. Cambridge (Mass.) and London, 1980.

Quintilianus, Marcus Fabius. *Instituto oratoria.* Ed. Adriano Pennacini. Turin, 2001.

Regiomontanus, Joannes. *Oratio introductoria in omnes scientias mathematicas.* In *Joannis Regiomontani Opera collectanea.* Ed. Felix Schmeidler. Osnabrück, 1949, 43–53.

De triangulis omnimodis. In *Regiomontanus on Triangles.* Trans. Barnabas Hughes. Madison (Wis.), 1967.

Reuchlin, Johannes. *De arte Cabalistica libri tres,* Tübingen, 1517.

Illvstrivm virorvm epistolae hebraicae, graece et latinae. … Stuttgart, 1519.

On the Art of the Kabbalah / De arte Cabalistica (1517). Trans. M. Goodman and S. Goodman. Intro. Moshe Idel. Lincoln (Neb.) and London, 1993.

Recommendation on Whether to Confiscate, Destroy and Burn all Jewish Books (1510). Ed. and trans. Peter Wortsman. New York, 2000.

Rinuccini, Alammano. [Trans. of Philostratus's *Life of Apolonius of Tyre.*] Vatican City (*Vat. Lat. 5732,* fols. 1–158).

De libertate. In *Humanism and Liberty: Writings on Freedom from Fifteenth Century Florence.* Ed. and trans. Renée Neu Watkins. Columbia (S.C.), 1978, 186–224.

Salinas, Francisco. *De musica libri septem* (1577). Ed. Cornelius Bonardi. Salamanca, 1592.

Siete libros sobre la musica. Ed. Ismael Fernández de la Cuesta. Madrid, 1983.

Salutati, Coluccio. *Linus Colucius Salutatus to His Venerable Father in Christ, Brother John Dominici of the Order of Preachers.* Trans. Ephraim Emerton. In *Humanism and Tyranny: Studies in the Italian Trecento.* Cambridge (Mass.), 1925, 364–65.

De laboribus Hercules. Ed. Berthold L. Ullman. Zurich, 1951.

De fato et fortuna. Ed. Concetta Bianca. Florence, 1985.

Santi, Giovanni. *La vita e le gesta di Federico di Montefeltro duca d'Urbino* (ca. 1482). Ed. Luigi M. Tocci. Vatican City, 1985 (2 vols.).

Serlio, Sebastiano. *L'Architettura.* Ed. Francesco P. Fiore. Milan, 2001 (2 vols.).

Speusippus. Fragment preserved by Iamblichus. In *Greek Mathematical Works.* Ed. and trans. Ivor Thomas. Cambridge (Mass.), 1951, I, 75–81.

Stobaeus, Ioannis. *Anthologium.*

Theon of Smyrna. *Expositio rerum mathematicarum ad legendum Platonem.* Ed. Eduard Hiller. Leipzig, 1878.

Thierry of Chartres. *Heptateuchon.*

Tibaldi, Pellegrino. *L'Architettura.* Crit. ed. Giorgio Panizza. Milan, 1990.

Tory, Geofroy. *Champ Fleury ou L'art et Science de la Proportion des Lettres* (1529). Ed. G. Cohen. Paris, 1931. Rep. Geneva, 1973.

Toscanelli, Paolo dal Pozzo. Untitled MS. Florence (*Bib. Ricc. 2110*).

Della prospettiva. Ed. Alessandro Parronchi. Milan, 1991.

(ref.). *Castato della Famiglia Toscanelli*. In Florence, *Arch. di Stato, Catasto, 17*, as rep. in *Firenze e la scoperta dell'America*, exh. cat., Ed. Sebastiano Gentile. Florence, 1992, 136–38.

Trogus, Pompeius. *Justinus, epitome in trogi Pompeii historias*. Cambridge (Mass.), Harvard University (*Houghton MS. typ. 123*).

Tryon, Thomas. *Pythagoras and his Mystick Philosophy revived, or the Mystery of Dreams Unfolded*. London, 1691.

Valla, Giorgio. *Cleonidae Harmonicum interprete*. Venice, 1497.

De expetendis, et fvgiendis rebvs opvs. … Ed. Aldus Romano. Venice, 1501.

Valla, Lorenzo. *De rebus a Ferdinando gestis*.

Dialecticarum disputationum.

Opera omnia. Ed. Eugenio Garin. Turin, 1962 (2 vols.).

Laurentii Valle epistole. Ed. Ottavio Besomi and Mariangela Regoliosi. Padua, 1984.

Vasari, Giorgio. *Le vite de' più eccellenti pittori scultori ed architettori*. Ed. Gaetano Milanesi. Florence, 1906 (9 vols.).

Vergerio, Pier Paolo. *De ingenuis moribus et liberalibus adulescentae studiis liber*.

Epistolario. Ed. Leonardo Smith. Rome, 1934.

Vergil, Polydore. *On Discovery*. Ed. and trans. Brian Copenhaver. Cambridge (Mass.), 2002.

Vespasiano da Bisticci. *Vite di uomini illustri del secolo XV* (ca. 1480–85). Ed. A. Greco. Florence, 1970.

The Vespasiano Memoirs: Lives of Illustrious Men of the XVth Century. Trans. Walter George and Emily Waters. Ed. Renaissance Society of America. Toronto, 1997.

Vitruvius Pollio. *L. Victrvvii Pollionis De architectura libri decem*. Ed. Iohannis Sulpicio da Veroli. Rome, 1486.

L. Vitrvvii Pollionis ad Caesarem agvstvm De architectura. Venice, 1497.

L. Vitruuii Pollionis De architectura libri decem. Ed. Fra Giovanni Giocondo. Ptr. Ioannis de Tridino. Venice, 1511.

Dieci libri dell'architettvra. Ed. Daniele Barbaro. Venice, 1556.

Il "Vitruvio Magliabechiano" di Francesco di Giorgio Martini. Ed. Gustina Scaglia. Florence, 1985.

Ten Books on Architecture. Ed. Ingrid D. Rowland. Rome, 2003.

Vives, Ioannes Lodovicus. *De anima et vita* (1538). Rep. ed. Mario Sancipriano. Turin, 1959.

Yagel, Abraham ben Hananiah. *A Valley of Vision: The Heavenly Journey*. Ed. and trans. David B. Ruderman. Philadelphia, 1990.

Zarlino, Gioseffo. *Le istitutioni harmoniche* (1558). Ed. Paolo da Col. Bologna, 1999.

SECONDARY SOURCES

Allen, Michael J. B. *The Platonism of Marsilio Ficino*. Berkeley, Los Angeles, and London, 1984.

"Marsilio Ficino's Interpretation of Plato's *Timaeus* and Its Myth of the Demiurge." In *Svpplementvm Festivvm: Studies in Honor of Paul Oskar Kristeller*. Ed. James Hankins, John Monfasani, and Frederick Purnell, Jr. Binghamton (N.Y.), 1987, 339–441.

Nuptial Arithmetic: Marsilio Ficino's Commentary on the Fatal Number in Book VIII of Plato's Republic. Berkeley, Los Angeles, and London, 1994.

Synoptic Art. Florence, 1998.

Anstey, Tim. "Theology and Geometry in the Façade of S. Maria Novella." *Albertiana*, IV. Florence, 2003, 27–49.

Athanassiadi, Polymnia. "Psellos and Plethon on the Chaldean Oracles." In *Byzantine Philosophy and Its Ancient Sources*. Ed. Katerina Ierodoakonou. Oxford, 2002.

Bainton, Roland. *Erasmus of Christendom*. New York, 1969.

Baldassarri, Stefano Ugo, and Arielle Saiber. *Images of Quattrocento Florence*. New Haven and London, 2000.

Barbierato, Federico. "Magical Literature and the Venice Inquisition from the Sixteenth to the Eighteenth Centuries." In *Magi, alchimia, scienza dal '400 al '700*. Ed. Carlos Gilly and Cis van Heertum. Florence, 2002, I, 159–75.

Barnes, Jonathan. *Early Greek Philosophy*. London, 1987.

Barucci, Emo. *Il Tempio di San Biagio* (1979). Montepulciano, 2002.

Bedouelle, Guy, and Franco Giacone. *Lefèvre d'Étaples et ses disciples: Épistres et Évangiles pour les cinquante et deux dimanches de l'an*. Leiden, 1976.

Belluzzi, Amedeo. "Templi Albertiani a painta centrale." In *Leon Battista Alberti: Architettura e cultura*. Ed. Acc. Naz. Virgiliana. Florence, 1999, 317–29.

Benzing, Josef. *Bibliographie des Schriften Johannes Reuchlins im 15. und 16. Jahrhundert*. Vienna, 1955.

Bernstein, Eckhard. *German Humanism*. Boston, 1983.

Bertelli, Carlo. *Piero della Francesca* (1991). Trans. Edward Farrelly. New Haven and London, 1992.

Berti, Luciano. *Masaccio*. University Park (Pa.) and London, 1967.

Bianca, Concetta. "L'accademia del Bessarione tra Roma e Urbino." In *Federico di Montefeltro: La cultura*, ed. Giorgio C. Baiardi, Giorgio Chittolini, and Piero Floriani. Rome, 1986.

Billoret, Roger. "Circonscription de Lorraine." *Gallia*, XXVIII, 1970, 308ff.

Birkenmajer, Ludwik A. *Stromata Copernica*. Krakow, 1924.

Blankenburg, Walter. "Jubal." In *Die Musik in Geschichte*. Ed. Friedrich Blume. Basel, London, and New York, 1958.

Blau, Joseph L. *The Christian Interpretation of the Cabala in the Renaissance*. New York, 1944.

Bloch, Joseph. *Venetian Printers of Hebrew Books*. New York, 1932.

Boas, Marie. *The Scientific Renaissance, 1450–1630*. New York, 1962.

Bodmer, Heinrich. "Die Fresken des Annibale Carracci im Camerino des Palazzo Farnese in Rom." *Pantheon*, XIX, 1937, 146–49.

Bolgar, R. R. *The Classical Heritage and Its Beneficiaries* (1954). Cambridge, 1977.

Bouwsma, William J. *Concordia mundi: The Career and Thought of Guillaume Postel (1510–1581)*. Cambridge (Mass.), 1957.

Bowen, William R. "Ficino's Analysis of Musical *Harmonia*." In *Ficino and Renaissance Neoplatonism*. Ed. Konrad Eisenbichler and Olga Z. Pugliese. Toronto, 1986.

Brachert, Thomas. "A Musical Canon of Proportion in Leonardo da Vinci's *Last Supper*." *Art Bulletin*, LIII (4), 1971, 461–66.

Briganti, Giuliano. *Il Manierismo e Pellegrino Tibaldi*. Rome, 1945.

Brown, Beverly Louise. "The Patronage and Building History of the Tribuna of SS. Annunciata in Florence." *Mitteilungen des Kunsthistorischen Institutes in Florenz*, XXV, 1981, 59–146.

Brown, Howard Mayer. *Music in the Renaissance*. Englewood Cliffs (N.J.), 1976.

Brown, John William. *The Life of Leonardo da Vinci*. London, 1828.

Brumbaugh, Robert S. *Plato's Mathematical Imagination*. Bloomington (Ind.), 1954.

Bruschi, Arnaldo. *Bramante* (1969). Trans. Peter Murray. London, 1977.

Burlamacchi, Pacifico. *Vita di Frate Girolamo Savonarola*. Lucca, 1761.

Cammelli, Giuseppe. *I dotti Bizantini e le origini dell'umanesimo*. Florence, 1941–54 (4 vols.).

Campbell, Lily. "The First Edition of Vitruvius." *Modern Philology*, XXIX, 1931, 107–10.

Carcopino, Jerôme. "Encore la Basilique de la 'Porta Maggiore.'" *Revue Archéologique*, XVIII, 1923, 1–23.

Cardini, Roberto. *La critica del Landino*. Florence, 1973.

Casalini, Eugenio M. *Michelozzo di Bartolommeo e l'Annunziata di Firenze*. Florence, 1995.

Cassirer, Ernst, Paul Oskar Kristeller, and John H. Randall, Jr., eds. *The Renaissance Philosophy of Man*. Chicago, 1948.

Castelli, Patrizia. *I geroglifici e il mita dell'Egitto nel Rinascimento*. Florence, 1979.

  "Matematici e astrologi tedeschi alla 'corte' dei Montefeltro." *Die Kunst und das Studium der Natur von 14. zum 16. Jahrhundert*. Weinheim, 1987, 237–51.

Caye, Pierre. "Commentaire sur *De Architectura* de Vitruve." In *Le Savoir de Palladio*. Klincksieck, 1995.

Celenza, Christopher S. "Pythagoras in the Renaissance: The Case of Marsilio Ficino." *Renaissance Quarterly*, LII (3), 1999, 667–711.

  Piety and Pythagoras in Renaissance Florence. Leiden and Boston, 2001.

  The Lost Italian Renaissance: Humanists, Historians, and Latin's Legacy. Baltimore and London, 2004.

Chapman, Hugo, Tom Henry, and Carol Plazzotta, eds. *Raphael: From Urbino to Rome*. Exh. cat. London, 2004.

Chastel, André. *L'Art et Humanisme a Florence au Temps de Laurent le Magnifique*. Paris, 1959.

Cheles, Luciano. *The Studiolo of Urbino*. Wiesbaden, 1986.

Christ, Karl. "Die Bibliotek Reuchlins in Pforzheim." *Beiheft zum Zentralblatt für Bibliothekswesen*, LII, 1924, 1–96.

Clark, Kenneth. *Leonardo da Vinci*. Cambridge, 1952.

Piero della Francesca (1951). London and New York, 1969.

Clausse, Gustave. *Les San Gallo*. Paris, 1900–1902 (3 vols.).

Collins, Bradley I. *Leonardo, Psychoanalysis, and Art History*. Evanston (Ill.), 1997.

Copenhaver, Brian P. *Iamblichus, Synesius and the Chaldaean Oracles in Marsilio Ficino's De vita libri tres*. Binghamton (N.Y.), 1987.

  Natural Magic, Hermeticism, and Occultism in Early Modern Science. Cambridge, 1990.

  Hermetica: The Greek Corpus Hermeticum and the Latin Asclepius … . Cambridge, 1992.

  "L'Occulto in Pico." In *Giovanni Pico della Mirandola: Convegno internazionale … .* Ed. Gian Carlo Garfagnini. Florence, 1997.

  Magic and the Dignity of Man: De-Kanting Pico's Oration. Florence, 2002.

Cornford, F. M. "Mysticism and Science in the Pythagorean Tradition." *Classical Quarterly*, XVII, 1923 (II), 1–12.

Cranz, F. Edward. *Nicholas of Cusa and the Renaissance*. Aldershot (U.K.) and Brookfield (Vt.), 2000.

Cumont, Franz V. *Recherches sur le Symbolisme Funéraire des Romains*. Paris, 1942.

  Lux Perpetua. Paris, 1949.

D'Amico, John F. *Renaissance Humanism in Papal Rome*. Baltimore and London, 1983.

D'Ancona, Paolo. "Le rappresentazione allegoriche delle arti liberali nel Medio Evo e nel Rinascimento." *L'Arte*, V, 1902, 137–55, 211–29, 269–89, and 370–85.

D'Ascia, Luca. *Erasmo e l'umanesimo romano*. Florence, 1987.

  "Bessarione al Concilio di Firenze." In *Bessarione e l'umanesimo*, cat., ed. Gianfranco Fiaccadori. Naples, 1994, 67–79.

Davis, Margaret Daly. *Piero della Francesca's Mathematical Treatises*. Ravenna, 1977.

  "Piero's Treatises: The Mathematics of Form." *Cambridge Companion to Piero della Francesca*, ed. Jeryldene M. Wood. Cambridge, 2002, 134–51.

Debus, Allen G. *The English Paracelsians*. New York, 1965.

  "Mathematics and Nature in the Chemical Texts of the Renaissance." *AMBIX: Journal of the Society for the Study of Alchemy and Early Chemistry*, XV, 1968, 1–28.

  Man and Nature in the Renaissance. Cambridge, 1978.

Dell'Acqua, G., and L. Münster, "I rapporti di Giovanni Pico della Mirandola con alcuni filosofi ebrei." In *L'Opera e il pensiero di Giovanni Pico della Mirandola*. Ed. Ist. Naz. di studi sul Rinascimento. Florence, 1965, II, 149–69.

De Tolnay, Charles. "Le Judgement Dernier de Michel Ange." *Art Quarterly*, III, 1940 (2), 125–49.

  Michelangelo. 2nd rev. ed. Princeton, 1969–71 (5 vols.).

  Michelangelo, Sculptor, Painter, Architect. Trans. Gaynor Woodhouse. Princeton, 1975.

Di Cesare, Mario A., ed. *Reconsidering the Renaissance*. Binghamton (N.Y.), 1992.

Diller, Aubry. "The Autographs of Georgius Gemistus Pletho." *Scriptorium*, X, 1956, 27–41.

Duhem, Pierre. *Système du monde: Histoires des doctrines cosmologiques de Platon à Copernic* (1914). Paris, 1954–59 (10 vols.).

To Save the Phenomena: An Essay on the Idea of Physical Theory (1906). Trans. E. Doland and C. Maschler. Chicago and London, 1969.

*Medieval Cosmology: Theories of Infinity, Place, Time … (1914). Ed. and trans. Rogier Ariew. Chicago, 1985 (2 vols.).

Durán, Manuel. *Luis de León.* New York, 1971.

Ettlinger, Leopold. *The Sistine Chapel before Michelangelo.* Oxford, 1965.

Evans, R. J. W. *Rudolf II and His World.* Oxford, 1973.

Fabre, Paul. *La Vaticane de Sixte IV.* Rome, 1896.

Fez, Carmen de. *La estructura barroca de "El siglo pitagórico."* Madrid, 1978.

Fiaccadori, Gianfranco, ed. *Bessarione e l'umanesimo.* Catalogo della mostra. Naples, 1994.

Field, J.V. "Rediscovering the Archimedean Polyhedra: Piero della Franesca, Luca Pacioli, Leonardo da Vinci." *Archive for the History of the Exact Sciences,* L (3/4), 1997, 244–53.

"Piero della Francesca's Mathematics." In *Cambridge Companion to Piero della Francesca.* Ed. Jeryldene M. Wood. Cambridge, 2002, 152–70.

Piero della Francesca: A Mathematician's Art. New Haven and London, 2005.

Fiore, Francesco P., and Manfredo Tafuri, eds. *Francesco di Giorgio architetto.* Milan, 1993.

Fontaine, Marie Madeleine. "Les Attaques de Pietro del Monte Contre l'Alchimie dans le *De Veritate Unius Legis* de 1509." In *Documents oubliés sur l'Alchimie, la Kabbale et Guillaume Postel.* Ed. Sylvain Matton. Geneva, 2001.

Fontaine, Petrus F. M. *The Light and the Dark: A Cultural History of Dualism.* Amsterdam, 1986 (21 vols.).

Foscari, Antonio, and Manfredo Tafuri. *L'armonia e i conflitti: La Chiesa de San Francesco della Vigna.* Turin, 1983.

Freedberg, Sydney J. *Painting of the High Renaissance in Rome and Florence.* Cambridge (Mass.), 1961.

Gadol, Joan. *Leon Battista Alberti, Universal Man of the Early Renaissance.* Chicago, 1969.

Gandillac, Maurice de. *La Philosophie de Nicolas de Cues.* Paris, 1941.

"Neoplatonism and Christian Thought in the Fifteenth Century: Nicholas of Cusa and Marsilio Ficino." In *Neoplatonism and Christian Thought.* Ed. Dominic J. O'Meara. Albany, 1982, 143–69.

Gardenal, Gianna. "Giorgio Valla e le scienze esatte." *Giorgio Valla tra scienza e sapienza.* Ed.Vittore Branca. Florence, 1981.

Garin, Eugenio. "Il problema delle fonti di Leonardo." *La cultura filosofica del Rinascimento italiano.* Florence, 1961, 388–401.

"Magia e astrologia nella cultura del Rinascimento." In *Magia e civiltà.* Ed. Ernesto de Martino. Milan, 1976.

Astrology in the Renaissance (1976). Trans. Carolyn Jackson and June Allen. London, 1983.

La magia naturale nel Rinascimento. Ed. Paolo Rossi. Turin, 1989.

Gaye, Giovanni, ed. *Carteggio inedito d'artisti dei secoli XIV, XV, XVI.* Florence, 1839–40 (3 vols.).

Geanakoplos, Deno J. *Greek Scholars in Venice: Studies in the Dissemination of Greek Learning from Byzantium to Western Europe.* Cambridge (Mass.), 1962.

Geiger, Ludwig. *Johann Reuchlin sein Leben und seine Werke.* Leipzig (1871). Rep. 1964.

Gentile, Sebastiano, Sandra Niccoli, and Paolo Viti, eds. *Marsilio Ficino e il ritorno di Platone.* Exh. cat. Florence, 1984.

Gersh, Stephen. *Concord in Discourse: Harmonics and Semiotics in Late Medieval and Early Modern Platonism.* Berlin and New York, 1996.

Gies, Joseph, and Frances Gies. *Leonard of Pisa and the New Mathematics of the Middle Ages.* New York, 1969.

Gill, Joseph. *The Council of Florence.* New York, 1982.

Gillert, Karl. *Der Briefwechsel des Conradus Mutianus.* Halle, 1890 (2 vols.).

Gilly, Carlos, and Cis van Heertum, eds. *Magia, alchimia, scienza dal '400 al '700.* Florence, 2002 (2 vols.).

Gilmore, Myron. "Beroaldo, Filippo, senior." In *Dizionario biografico degli italiani.* Rome, 1967, IX, 382–84.

Ginzburg, Carlo. *Indagini su Piero.* Turin, 1981.

Girill, T. R. "Galileo and Platonistic Methodology." *Journal of the History of Ideas,* XXXI, 1970, 501–15.

Giusti, Enrico, and Carlo Maccagni, eds. *Lvca Pacioli.* Florence, 1994.

Giustiniani, Vito R. *Alamanno Rinuccini, 1426–1499.* Cologne, 1963.

Godwin, Joscelyn. ed. *Harmony of the Spheres.* Rochester (Vt.), 1993.

Harmonies of Heaven and Earth. Rochester (Vt.), 1995.

The Pagan Dream of the Renaissance. Grand Rapids, 2002.

Gordan, Phyllis W. G. *Two Renaissance Book Hunters: The Letters of Poggius Bracciolini to Nicolaus de Niccolis.* New York, 1974.

Graf, Arturo. *Roma nella memoria e nelle immaginazioni del medio evo* (1923). Bologna, 1987.

Graux, Charles. *Essai sur les Origines du Fond Grec de l'Escurial.* Paris, 1880.

Griffiths, Gordon, James Hankins, and David Thompson, eds. *The Humanism of Leonardo Bruni: Selected Texts.* Binghamton (N.Y.), 1987.

Gualdo, R. "Fabio Calvo, Marco." In *Dizionario biografico degli italiani.* Rome, 1993, XLIII, 723–27.

Guasti, Cesare. "La biblioteca di Urbino." *Giornale storico degli archivi toscani, n.s.* XV and XVI, 1862, 133–47 and 127–47, respectively.

Guthrie, W. K. C. *A History of Greek Philosophy.* I: *The Earlier Presocratics and the Pythagoreans.* Cambridge, 1962.

Hankins, James. "Plato in the Middle Ages," In *Dictionary of the Middle Ages.* New York, 1987, IX, 694–704.

The Myth of the Platonic Academy of Florence. New York, 1991.

Plato in the Italian Renaissance. Leiden, New York, Copenhagen, and Cologne, 1991 (2 vols.).

Repertorium Brunianum. Rome, 1997.

"Leonardo Bruni." In *Encyclopedia of the Renaissance.* New York, 1999, I, 301–6.

"Lo studio del greco in Occidente fra medioevo ed età moderna." In *I Greci: Storia, cultura, arte, società,* ed. Salvatore Settis. Turin, 2001, III, 1245–62.

Chrysoloras and the Greek Studies of Leonardo Bruni. Naples, 2002.

Humanism and Platonism in the Italian Renaissance. Rome, 2003–4 (2 vols.).

Hautecoeur, Louis. *Mystique et Architecture: Symbolisme du Cercle et de la Cupole.* Paris, 1954.

Heath, Thomas. *Aristarchus of Samos … A History of Greek Astronomy to Aristarchus.* Oxford, 1913.

Heiberg, Johann Ludwig. "Philologische Studien zu griechischen Mathematik." *Jahrbuch für Classische Philologie,* supp. XII, 1881, 377–99.

"Beiträge zur Geschichte Georg Valla's und seiner Bibliothek." *Beihefte zum Centralblatt für Bibliothekswesen,* XVI, 1896, 353–482.

Heninger, S. K., Jr. *Touches of Sweet Harmony: Pythagorean Cosmology and Renaissance Poetics.* San Marino (Calif.), 1974.

The Cosmological Glass: Renaissance Diagrams of the Universe. San Marino (Calif.), 1977.

Hersey, George L. *Pythagorean Palaces: Magic and Architecture in the Italian Renaissance.* Ithaca and London, 1976.

Heydenreich, Ludwig H., and Wolfgang Lotz. *Architecture in Italy, 1400–1600.* Trans. Mary Hottinger. Harmondsworth, 1974.

Higgins, Paula, ed. *Antoine Busnoys: Method, Meaning, and Context in Late Medieval Music.* Oxford, 1999.

Höfler, Janez. *Der Palazzo Ducale in Urbino unter den Montefeltro.* Regensburg, 2004.

Holzer, Hans. *The Alchemist: The Secret Magical Life of Rudolf von Habsburg.* New York, 1974.

Huntley, H. E. *The Divine Proportion.* New York, 1970.

Izbicki, Thomas M., and Christopher M. Bellitto, eds. *Nicholas of Cusa and His Age: Intellect and Spirituality.* Leiden, 2002.

Jacks, Philip. "The Renaissance *Prospettiva.*" In *Cambridge Companion to Piero della Francesca,* ed. Jeryldene M. Wood. Cambridge, 2002.

Janson, H.W. "Ground Plan and Elevation in Masaccio's *Trinity* Fresco." In *Essays in the History of Art Presented to Rudolf Wittkower.* Ed. Douglas Fraser, Howard Hibbard, and Milton J. Lewine. London, 1967, 83–89.

Jayawardene, S. A. "The 'Trattato d'Abaco' of Piero della Francesca." In *Cultural Aspects of the Italian Renaissance.* Ed. Cecil H. Clough. Manchester and New York, 1976, 229–43.

Jeauneau, Édouard. *L'Âge d'or des Écoles de Chartres.* Chartres, 1995.

Johannides, Paul. *The Drawings of Raphael.* Berkeley and Los Angeles, 1983.

Joost-Gaugier, Christiane L. "Michelangelo's *Ignudi* and the Sistine Chapel as a Symbol of Law and Justice." *Artibus et Historiae,* XXXIV, 1996, 19–43.

"Pindar on Parnassus." *Gazette des Beaux-Arts,* CXXVII, 1996, 65–80.

"The Mute Poetry of the Fête Champêtre: Titian's Memorial to Giorgione." *Gazette des Beaux-Arts,* CXXXIII, 1999, 1–13.

"Plato and Aristotle and Their Retinue: Meaning in Raphael's *School of Athens.*" *Gazette des Beaux-Arts,* CXXXVII, 2001, 149–64.

Raphael's Stanza della Segnatura: Meaning and Invention. Cambridge, 2002.

Measuring Heaven: Pythagoras and His Influence on Thought and Art in Antiquity and the Middle Ages. Ithaca and London, 2006.

Kibre, Pearl. *The Library of Pico della Mirandola.* New York, 1936.

Studies in Medieval Science: Alchemy, Astrology, Mathematics and Medicine. London, 1984.

Kieszkowski, Bohdan. *Studi sul platonismo del Rinascimento in Italia.* Florence, 1936.

King, Ross. *Brunelleschi's Dome.* New York, 2000.

Klein, Robert. *Form and Meaning* (1970). Trans. Madeline Jay and Leon Wieseltier. New York, 1979.

Knorr, Wilbur Richard. *Textual Studies in Ancient and Medieval Geometry.* Boston, Basel, and Berlin, 1989.

Kokole, Stanko. "'Cognitio formanum' and Agostino di Duccio's Reliefs for the Chapel of the Planets in the Tempio Malatestiano." In *Quattrocento Adriatico.* Ed. Charles Dempsey. Bologna, 1996, 177–206.

Koyré, Alexandre. *From the Closed World to the Infinite Universe.* Baltimore, 1957.

Krautheimer, Richard. *Lorenzo Ghiberti.* Princeton, 1970 (2 vols.).

Kristeller, Paul Oskar. *The Philosophy of Marsilio Ficino* (1938). Trans. Virginia Conant. New York, 1943.

Kubler, George. *The Building of the Escorial.* Princeton, 1982.

Labowsky, Lotte. *Bessarion's Library and the Biblioteca Marciana: Six Early Inventories.* Rome, 1979.

Lanciani, Rodolfo. *The Golden Days of the Renaissance in Rome.* London, 1906.

Lavin, Marilyn Aronberg. *Piero della Francesca: The Flagellation.* New York, 1972.

Lawlor, Robert. *Sacred Geometry.* New York, 1982.

Lazzari, A. "Un enciclopedico del secolo XVI – Celio Calcagnini." *Atti e memorie della Deputazione ferrarese di storia patria,* XXX, 1936, 159–69.

Lenormant, François. *La Grande Grèce, Paysages et Histoire.* Paris, 1881.

Lesley, Arthur M., Jr. *The Song of Solomon's Ascents by Yohanan Alemanno.* Ann Arbor, 1976.

Lotz, Wolfgang. "Notes on the Centralized Church of the Renaissance." *Studies in Renaissance Architecture.* Cambridge (Mass.), 1977, 66–74.

Luiso, Francesco Paolo. *Studi su l'epistolario di Leonardo Bruni.* Ed. Lucia Gualdo Rosa. Rome, 1980.

Lutz, Werner. *Luciano Laurana und der Herzogspalast von Urbino.* Weimar, 1995.

Mack, Charles R. *Pienza.* Ithaca and London, 1987.

Magnani, Lauro. *Luca Cambiaso de Genova all'Escorial.* Genoa, 1995.

Mancini, Girolamo. *Vita di Leon Battista Alberti* (1911). 2nd ed. Rome, 1971.

Marcel, Raymond. *Marsile Ficin.* Paris, 1958.

Marcucci, L. "Giovanni Sulpicio e la prima edizione del De architettura di Vitruvio." *Studi e Documenti di Architettura,* VIII, 1978, 193–95.

Martin, Jacquilyne E. "Cardinal Bessarion, Mystical Theology and Spiritual Union between East and West" (diss.). Winnipeg, 2000.

Martin, John Rupert. *The Farnese Gallery*. Princeton, 1965.

Marzi, Demetrio. *Le questione della riforma del calendario nel Quinto Concilio Lateranese (1512–17)*. In *Pubblicazioni del R. Istituto di studi superiori pratici e di perfezionamento in Firenze*, 1896, 39–72.

Masai, François. *Pléthon et le Platonisme de Mistra*. Paris, 1956.

Massaut, Jean-Pierre. *Josse Clichtove, L'Umanisme et la Réforme du Clergé*. Paris, 1968 (2 vols.).

Matracchi, Pietro. *La Chiesa di Santa Maria delle Grazie al Calcinaio*. Cortona, 1991.

Matton, Sylvain, ed. *Documents oubliés sur l'Alchimie, la Kabbale et Guillaume Postel* (hon. François Secret). Geneva, 2001.

McColley, Grant. "Giorgio Valla: An Unnoted Advocate of the Geo-Heliocentric Theory." *Isis,* XXXIII, 1941, 312–14.

Menninger, Karl. *Number Words and Number Symbols* (1934). Trans. Paul Broneer. Cambridge (Mass.), 1969.

Meyer zur Capellen, Jurg. *Raphael*. Ed. and trans. Stefan B. Polter. Landshut, 2001 (2 vols.).

Milne, James Lee. *Saint Peter's*. Boston, 1967.

Mioni, Elpidia. "Bessarione bibliofilo e filologo." *Rivista di studi Bizantini e Neoellenici,* n.s. 5 (XV), 1968, 61–83.

"Bessarione scriba e alcuni collaboratori." In *Miscellanea Marciana di studi Bessarionei*. Padua, 1976, 290–91.

Moesgaard, Kristian Peder. "Copernican Influence on Tycho Brahe." In *Colloquia Copernicana: The Reception of Copernicus' Heliocentric Theory*. Ed. Jerzy Dobrzycki. Dordrect and Boston, 1972, 31–57.

Mohler, Ludwig. *Kardinal Bessarion als Theologe, Humanist und Staatsmann* (1923–42). Rep. Aalen, 1967 (3 vols.).

Mommsen, Theodor E. "Petrarch and the Story of Hercules" (1953). Rep. in *Medieval and Renaissance Studies*. Ed. Eugene F. Rice, Jr. Ithaca, 1959.

Monfasani, John. "Bessarion, Valla, Agricola, and Erasmus." *Rinascimento*, ser. 2, XXIII, 1988, 319–20.

"L'insegnamento universitario e la cultura bizantina in Italia nel Quattrocento." In *Sapere e/è potere. Discipline, dispute e professioni nell'università medievale e moderna: Atti del 4 convegno*, I. Ed. Luisa Avellini. Bologna, 1990, 43–65.

"Platonic Paganism in the Fifteenth Century." In *Reconsidering the Renaissance*. Ed. Mario A. Di Cesare. Binghamton (N.Y.), 1992, 45–61.

Byzantine Scholars in Renaissance Italy: Cardinal Bessarion and Other Émigrés. Aldershot and Burlington, 1995.

Greeks and Latins in Renaissance Italy. Aldershot and Burlington, 2004.

Morison, Stanley. *Fra Luca de Pacioli*. New York, 1933.

Müntz, Eugene, and Paul Fabre. *La Bibliothèque du Vatican au XVe Siècle*. Amsterdam, 1970.

Mussini, Massimo. *Francesco di Giorgio e Vitruvio: Le traduzioni del "De architecture … ."* Florence, 2003 (2 vols., text and trans.).

Napolitani, Pier Daniele, and Pierre Souffrin, eds. *Medieval and Classical Traditions and the Renaissance of Physico-Mathematical Sciences in the 16th Century*. Turnhout, 2001.

Nardi, Bruno. "La scuola di Rialto e l'umanesimo veneziano." In *Umanesimo europeo e umanesimo veneziano*. Ed. Vittore Branca. Venice, 1960, 93–141.

Narducci, Enrico. *Vite inedite di matematici italiani scritte da Bernardino Baldi*. Rome, 1887.

Nauert, Charles, Jr. *Agrippa and the Crisis of Renaissance Thought*. Urbana, 1965.

Nofrini, Umberto. *Il Tempi del Bramante a Todi*. Intro. Arnaldo Bruschi. Todi, 1990.

Odier, Jeanne Bignami. *La Bibliothèque Vaticane de Sixte IV à Pie XI: Recherches sur l'Histoire des Collections de Manuscrits*. Vatican City, 1973.

O'Malley, John W. *Giles of Viterbo on Church and Reform*. Leiden, 1968.

Praise and Blame in Renaissance Rome. Durham (N.C.), 1979.

Omont, Henri. "Inventaire des manuscrits Grecs et Latins donnés à Saint-Marc de Venise par le Cardinal Bessarion." *Revue des Bibliothèques*, IV, 1894, 129–87.

Özdural, Alpay. "The Church of St. George of the Latins in Famagusta: A Case Study on Medieval Metrology and Design Techniques." In *Ad Quadratum*. Ed. Nancy Y. Wu. Aldershot and Burlington, 2002, 217–42.

Padovani, Serena, ed. *Fra Bartolomeo e la Scuola di San Marco*. Venice, 1996.

Pagliara, P. N. "La Roma antica di Fabio Calvo." *Psicon,* III, 1976 (8/9), 65–70.

Palisca, Claude. *Humanism in Italian Renaissance Musical Thought*. New Haven and London, 1985.

Panofsky, Erwin. *Studies in Iconology*. New York, 1939.

Patai, Raphael. *The Jewish Alchemists*. Princeton, 1994.

Pellati, Francesco. "Giovanni Sulpicio da Veroli primo editore di Vitruvio." In *Atti, secondo congresso nazionale di studi romani*, III. Rome, 1931, 382–86.

Pellegrin, Elisabeth. *La Bibliothèque des Visconti e des Sforza*. Paris, 1955.

Bibliothèques Retrouvées: Manuscrits, Bibliothèques et Bibliophiles du Moyen Âge et de la Renaissance. Paris, 1988.

Pereda, Felipe. *Le arquitectura elocuente: El edificio de la Universidad de Salamance bajo al reinado de Carlos V*. Madrid, 2000.

Pernis, Maria Grazia. *Le Platonisme de Marsile Ficin et la Cour d'Urbin*. Ed. and trans. François Roudaut. Paris, 1997.

Piccaluga, Gabriella Ferri. "Leonardo, Pico e L'ambiente Ebraico." In *Leonardo e Pico* (Atti del Convegno di Mirandola, 2003). Ed. Fabio Frosini. Florence. 2005, 37–53.

Pieper, Jan. *Pienza: Il progetto di una visione umanistica del mondo*. Stuttgart, 2000.

Pignatti, Teresio, and Filippo Pedrocco. *Giorgione*. Milan, 1999.

Planiscig, Leo. *Luca della Robbia*. Florence, 1948.

Pope-Hennessy, John. *Luca della Robbia*. Oxford, 1980.

Portoghesi, Paolo. *Il Tempio Malatestiano*. Florence, 1965.

Preyer, Brenda. "The Rucellai Palace." In *Giovanni Rucellai ed il suo Zibaldone*. Ed. Alessandro Perosa. London, 1981, II, 156–225.

Puliafito, Anna Laura. "Searching for a New Physics: Metaphysics … in Franesco Patrizi." In *Magia, alchimia, scienza dal '400 al '700*. Ed. Carlos Gilly, and Cis van Heertum. Florence, 2002, 255–66.

Radetti, Giorgio. "Un'aggiunta alla biblioteca di Pierleone Leoni da Spoleto." *Rinascimento*, ser. II 2,V, 1965, 87–101.

Ragghianti, Carlo. *Filippo Brunelleschi*. Florence, 1977.

Reese, Gustave. *Music in the Renaissance (1954)*. New York, 1959.

Reeves, Eileen. *Painting the Heavens: Art and Science in the Age of Galileo*. Princeton, 1997.

Reti, Ladislao. "The Two Unpublished Manuscripts of Leonardo da Vinci in the Biblioteca Nacional of Madrid" (I and II). *Burlington Magazine*, CX, 1968, 10–22 and 81–89.

Ricci, Corrado. *Il Tempio Malatestiano (1925)*. Rimini, 1974.

Ricci, Saverio. *Giordano Bruno nell'Europa del Cinquecento*. Rome, 2000.

Rice, Eugene F., Jr. *The Prefatory Epistles of Jacques Lefèvre d'Étaples and Related Texts*. New York, 1972.

Rigo, Antonio. "Gli interessi astronomici del cardinal Bessarione." In *Bessarione e l'umanesimo*. Ed. Gianfranco Fiaccadori. Naples, 1994, 105–19.

Ritman, Joost R., ed. *Bibliotheka Philosophica Hermetica Hermes Trismegistus Pater Philosophorum*. Amsterdam, 1990.

"Bessarion and the Influence of Hermes Trismegistus." *Magia, alchimia, scienza dal '400 al '700*. Ed. Carlos Gilly and Cis van Heertum. Florence, 2002, I, 11–23.

Robin, Diana. *Filelfo in Milan*. Princeton, 1991.

Rose, Paul Lawrence. "Universal Harmony in Regiomontanus and Copernicus." In *Copernic (1473–1973)*. Palais de la Découverte, exh. cat. Paris, 1973, 35–43.

"Copernicus and Urbino." *Isis*, LXV, 1974, 387–89.

The Italian Renaissance of Mathematics. Geneva, 1975.

"Bartolomeo Zamberti's Funeral Oration for the Humanist Encyclopaedist Giorgio Valla." In *Cultural Aspects of the Italian Renaissance*. Ed. Cecil H. Clough. Manchester and New York, 1976, 299–310.

Rosenthal, Earl. *The Palace of Charles V in Granada*. Princeton, 1985.

Rotondi, Pasquale. *Il Palazzo Ducale di Urbino*. Urbino, 1950–51 (2 vols.).

Ruffo, Patrizia L. "Lorenzo Bonicontri e alcuni suoi scritti ignorati." *Rinascimento*, 2nd ser.,V, 1965, 184–88.

Ruiz de Arcaute, Agustin. *Juan de Herrera*. Madrid, 1936.

Saalman, Howard. *Filippo Brunelleschi – The Buildings*. London, 1993.

Sabbadini, Remigio. *Le scoperti dei codici latini e greci ne'secoli XIV e XV (1905)*. Ed. Eugenio Garin. Florence, 1967 (2 vols.).

Saiber, Arielle. *Giordano Bruno and the Geometry of Language*. Aldershot (U.K.) and Burlington (Vt.), 2005.

Sandys, John E. *History of Classical Scholarship (1906)*. Rep. New York, 1958, I.

Sarton, George. *A History of Science*. Cambridge (Mass.), 1952 (2 vols.).

Sarton, George, and Alexander Pogo, eds. *Catalogue of Alchemical MSS. Osiris*,VI, Bruges, 1939.

Savelli, Divo. *La rotonda del Brunelleschi: Storia e documenti*. Florence, 1992.

Scalzo, Marcello. "La facciata Albertiana di Santa Maria Novella a Firenze." In *Leon Battista Alberti architettura e cultura*. Ed. Acc. Naz.Virgiliana. Florence, 1999, 265–83.

Schapiro, Meyer. "Leonardo and Freud: An Art Historical Study." *Journal of the History of Ideas*, XVII, 1956, 147–79.

Schlosser, Julius von. "Giusto's Fresken in Padua und die Vorläufer der Stanza della Segnatura." *Jahrbuch der Kunsthistorischen Sammlungen des Allerhöchsten Kaiserhauses*, XVII, 1896, 13–100.

Scholem, Gershom. *On the Kabbalah and Its Symbolism (1965)*. Trans. R. Manheim. New York, 1988.

Secret, François. "Pico della Mirandola e gli'inizi della cabala cristiana." *Convivium*, n.s. I, 1957, 31–47.

"Le Symbolisme de la Kabbale Chretienne dans la 'Scechina' de Egidio da Viterbo." *Archivio di Filosofia*, II-III, 1958, 152–55.

Les Kabbalistes chrétiens de le Renaissance. Paris, 1964.

"Nouvelles Precisions sur Flavius Mithraidates Maitre de Pic de la Mirandole et Traducteur de Commentaires de Kabbale." In *L'Opera e il pensiero di Giovanni Pico della Mirandola*. Ed. Ist. Naz. di studi sul Rinascimento. Florence, 1965, II, 169–89.

Bibliographie des Manuscrits de Guillaume Postel. Geneva, 1970.

Shorey, Paul. *Platonism Ancient and Modern*. Berkeley, 1938.

Shrimplin, Valerie. *Sun Symbolism and Cosmology in Michelangelo's "Last Judgment."* Kirksville (Mo.), 2000.

Shumaker, Wayne. *The Occult Sciences in the Renaissance*. Berkeley, Los Angeles, and London, 1972.

Fray José de Sigüenza. *La fundación del Monasterio de El Escorial*. Ed. Antonio Fernandez Alba. Madrid, 1986.

Singer, Dorothea W. *Giordano Bruno: His Life and Thought*. New York, 1968.

Siraisi, Nancy. *Arts and Sciences at Padua: The Studium of Padua before 1350*. Toronto, 1973.

Smith, David E. *Rara arithmetica*. Boston and London, 1908.

Smith, Fenella, K.C. "Pacioli, Luca." In *Encyclopedia of the Renaissance*. New York, 1999, IV, 357–58.

Solmi, Edmondo. *Le fonti dei manoscritti di Leonardo da Vinci (Giornale storico della letteratura italiana*, supp/s. 10–11), 1908, 1–344.

Stahl, William Harris. *Martianus Capella and the Seven Liberal Arts*. New York, 1971.

Steinberg, Leo. "Leonardo's *Last Supper*." *Art Quarterly*, XXXVI, 1973, 297–410.

Steinberg, Ronald M. *Fra Girolamo Savonarola, Florentine Art, and Renaissance Historiography*. Athens (Ohio), 1977.

Steinmann, Ernst. *Die Sixtinische Kapelle*. Munich, 1901–5 (2 vols.).

Struik, D. J. "Paulus van Middelbourg." *Mededeelingen van het Nederlandsch Historisch Institut te Rome*,V, 1925, 79–118.

Taylor, René. "Architecture and Magic: Considerations on the Idea of the Escorial." In *Essays in the History of Architecture Presented to Rudolf Wittkower*. Ed. Douglas Fraser, Howard Hibbard, and Milton J. Lewine. London, 1967, 81–109.

"Hermetism and Mystical Architecture in the Society of Jesus." In *Baroque Art: The Jesuit Contribution*, ed. Rudolf Wittkower and Irma B. Jaffe. New York, 1972, 63–99.

Thoenes, Christof. "Renaissance St. Peter's." In *St. Peter's in the Vatican*. Ed. William Tronzo. Cambridge, 2005.

Thomas, Ivor, ed. *Greek Mathematical Works*. Cambridge (Mass.) and London, 1951 (2 vols.).

Thorndike, Lynn. *A History of Magic and Experimental Science*. New York, 1929–58 (6 vols.).

   The Place of Magic in the Intellectual History of Europe. New York, 1967.

Tiberi, Claudio. "Misure e contemporaneità di disegno del chiostro di S. Maria della Pace e del Tempietto." Com. Naz. per le celebrazioni Bramantesche. *Studi Bramanteschi*. Rome, 1974, 437–82.

Tomlinson, Gary. *Music in Renaissance Magic*. Chicago, 1993.

Toni, Giovanni Battista de. "Leonardo da Vinci e Luca Paciolo." *Atti del Reale Istituto Veneto di Scienze, Lettere ed Arti*, LXV, 1905, 1145–49.

Torre, Arnaldo Della. *Storia dell'Accademia Platonica di Firenze*. Florence, 1902.

Toussaint, Stéphane. "Leonardo filosofo dei contrari." In *Leonardo e Pico* (Atti del Convegno di Mirandola, 2003). Ed. Fabio Frosini. Florence, 2005, 13–37.

Uzielli, Gustavo. *La vita e i tempi di Paolo dal Pozzo Toscanelli*. In *Raccolta di documenti e studi*, Part V. I Rome, 1848.

Valori, Niccolò. *La Vie de Laurent de Médicis* (1492). Paris, 1761.

Vasoli, Cesare. "Hermetism in Venice. From Francesco Giorgio to Agostino Steuco." In *Magia, alchimia, scienza dal '400 and '700*. Ed. Carlos Gilly, and Cis van Heertum. Florence, 2002, I, 31–69.

Vast, Henri. *Le Cardinal Bessarion*. Paris, 1878.

Verner, Juan. "Copernicus in Spain." In *Colloquia Copernicana: The Reception of Copernicus' Heliocentric Theory*. Ed. Jerzy Dobrzycki. Dordrecht and Boston, 1972, 171–93.

Vogel, Cornelia de. *Pythagoras and Early Pythagoreanism*. Assen, 1966.

   Rethinking Plato and Platonism. Leiden, 1986.

Waerden, Bartel van der. *Science Awakening: The Birth of Astronomy*. Trans. Arnold Dresden. Leiden, 1975.

Weiss, Roberto. *The Renaissance Discovery of Classical Antiquity*. Oxford, 1969.

"Gli inizi dello studio del greco a Firenze." In *Medieval and Humanist Greek: Collected Essays*. Padua, 1977, 227–54.

Wilkinson, Catherine, "Observations on Juan de Herrera's View of Architecture." In *Studies in the History of Art*. Ed. National Gallery. Washington, D.C., XIII, 1984, 181–88.

Wind, Edgar. "A Bacchic Mystery by Michelangelo." In *Pagan Mysteries in the Renaissance* (1958). Rev. ed. New York, 1968, 177–91.

   "Bessarion's Letter on Palingenesis." In *Pagan Mysteries in the Renaissance* (1958). Rev. ed. New York, 1968, 256–58.

   "Gaffurius on the Harmony of the Spheres." In *Pagan Mysteries in the Renaissance (1958)*. Rev. ed. New York, 1968, 265–70.

   "The Medal of Pico della Mirandola." In *Pagan Mysteries in the Renaissance* (1958). Rev. ed. New York, 1968, 36–53.

   "Pagan Vestiges of the Trinity." In *Pagan Mysteries in the Renaissance* (1958). Rev. ed. New York, 1968, 241–55.

   The Religious Symbolism of Michelangelo: Sistine Ceiling. Ed. Elizabeth Sears. Oxford, 2000.

Wirszubski, Chaim. *Pico della Mirandola's Encounter with Jewish Mysticism*. Cambridge (Mass.), 1989.

Wittkower, Rudolf. *Architectural Principles in the Age of Humanism* (1940). 2nd ed. London, 1952.

   "Brunelleschi and 'Proportion in Perspective.'" *Journal of the Warburg and Courtauld Institutes*, XVI, 1953, 275–91.

Wittkower, Rudolf, and B. A. R. Carter. "The Perspective of Piero della Francesca's 'Flagellation.'" *Journal of the Warburg and Courtauld Institutes*, XVI, 1953, 292–302.

Wölfflin, Heinrich. *Die klassische Kunst*. Basel, 1899.

Woodhouse, Christopher M. *George Gemistos Plethon: The Last of the Hellenes*. Oxford, 1986.

Woodward, Harrison. *Vittorini da Feltre and Other Humanist Educators*. Cambridge, 1963.

Yates, Frances A. *Giordano Bruno and the Hermetic Tradition*. Chicago, 1964.

Yriarte, Charles. *Un Condottiere au XVe Siècle: Rimini*. Paris, 1882.

Zezza, Andrea. "Giovan Battista Castaldo … un tondo di Raffaello." *Prospettiva*, XCIII, 1999, 29–41.

Zorzi, Marino. "Ermete Trismegisto nelle biblioteche veneziane." In *Magia, alchimia, scienza dal '400 al '700*. Ed. Carlos Gilly and Cis van Heertum. Florence, 2002, I, 113–35.

INDEX

Abaris, 47

Abel, 224

Abraham, 131

Abraham ben Yagel, 139

Adam, 48, 52–53, 59, 131

Adrian VI, Pope, 50

Aelian, 145

Aeneas Sylvius Piccolomini (Pius II), 23, 66, 70, 181, 183, 243

Aëtius, 6

Agrippa, Cornelius, of Nettesheim, 45–46, 130–32, 141, 239, 241

Alamanno Rinuccini, 92, 94

Alberti, Leon Battista, 25–26, 33, 68–69, 75–77, 79, 93–96, 98, 109, 114–15, 140, 175–82, 184–85, 189–90, 192, 194–95, 200–01, 204, 207, 215, 227–28, 233–35, 238, 243

Alexander VI, Pope, 120

Allen, Michael J. B., 4, 185

Amalfi, Archbishop of, 82

Ambrose, Saint, 37

Anatolius, 6, 76, 99

Anaximander, 98, 227

Andrea Pisano, 171

Annibale Carracci, 159–60

Anonimo Magliabecchiano, 200

Antiquario, Jacopo, 99, 105

Antonio da Sangallo the Elder, 216

Apollo, 7, 17, 22, 26, 28–29, 47, 53–54, 66–67, 74, 81–82, 84–88, 93, 103, 105, 108–09, 113, 130, 165–66, 173, 187–88, 191, 199, 201, 225, 228–29, 231, 232–33

Apollonius of Tyana, 29, 40, 46, 50, 92, 94

Apuleius, 112

Archytas of Tarentum, 20, 32, 47, 111, 127, 139

Aretino, Pietro, 52–53

Ariosto, Ludovico, 47

Aristobulus, 8, 29, 44, 108

Aristotle, 7, 9, 24, 37, 51, 57, 67, 70–71, 91, 126, 133, 146, 227–28

Aristoxenus of Tarentum, 32, 36, 100, 139

Arithmetic, Lady, 17, 154

Athena, Palla, 188

Atlas, 160

Augustine, Saint, 2, 27, 30, 37–38, 48, 71, 86, 88, 105, 125–26

Ausonius, 65

Baldi, Bernardino, 55–57, 59, 94, 139, 188, 225, 240, 242

Barbaro, Daniele, 52

Bembo, Bernardo, 82

Benozzo Gozzoli, 173

Bentivoglio, family, 40

Bernardo Rossellino, 181–84

Beroaldo, Filippo Senior, 39, 40, 120

Bessarion, Cardinal, 25–27, 47, 68–72, 75, 79–80, 93–94, 134, 181, 183, 200, 214, 238, 242

Biondo, Flavio, 23

Blasius, Johannes, 119

Boethius Severus, 8, 41, 65, 73–76, 88, 99–101, 103, 110–16, 119, 120, 123, 128, 130, 139, 141, 154–56, 185, 235

Bonincontri, Lorenzo, 101

Botticelli, 203, 238

Bracciolini, Poggio, 21, 173

Brache, Tycho, 136

Brachert, Thomas, 207

Bradwardine, Thomas, 101

Bramante, Donato, 95, 102, 105, 185–87, 194–97, 201–02, 208, 211–16, 234–35, 238

Browne, Thomas, 132

Brunelleschi, Filippo, 68, 162–70, 173, 176, 190, 200, 243

Bruni, Leonardo, 20–21, 35, 63, 66, 147–48, 161–62, 171, 200

Bruno, Giordano, 55, 136, 138, 239

Bryennius, Manuel, 102

Busnoys, Antoine, 33

Cademosto, Giovanni, 100

Cain, 53

Calandri, Filippo, 101, 151–53

Calcagnini, Celio, 51, 135, 141

Calvo, Marco Fabio, 121–22, 135, 140, 213–14, 230, 242

Cambiaso, Luca, 237

Capella, Martianus, 8, 17, 41, 65, 93, 100, 146, 177, 227, 228–29

Caponsacchi, Piero, 83

Caradosso, Cristoforo, 215

Cardano, Girolamo, 51–52, 136

Carter, B. A. R., 189

Cassiodorus, 2, 53

Castiglione, Baldassare, 47, 120, 140, 184

Celenza, Christopher, 4

Chalcidius, 15, 54

Charles V, Emperor, 234

Chastel, André, 4

Christ, Jesus, 1, 29, 41, 50, 82, 84, 89, 91, 105, 125, 129, 158, 162, 171–72, 179, 190–91, 196, 207, 220, 225, 236

Chrysoloras, Manuel, 16

Church Fathers, 9, 16, 37–38

Cicero, 6, 8, 21–22, 41, 47–48, 93, 101, 106, 121, 123, 137, 140, 188

Clark, Kenneth, 189

Clement of Alexandria, 2, 44

Clement VII, Pope, 125

Cleonides, 100

Clichtove, Josse, 41, 58, 128

Colet, John, 126

Colleoni, Bartolomeo, 35

Comanini, Gregorio, 54, 59

Constantine, Emperor, 198

Copenhaver, Brian, 4

Copernicus, Nicholaus, 51–52, 58, 74, 99, 133–36, 141, 225, 230

Cornazzano, Antonio, 35

Corsi, Giovanni, 80, 83

Cosimo de' Medici, 69, 164, 243

Cumont, Franz, 3, 60

Cusanus, Nicholas, Cardinal, 25–27, 58, 68–70, 72–75, 79, 112, 134–36, 138, 141, 181–83, 190, 195, 200, 202–03, 205–06, 215, 217–18, 233, 238, 242

Cyriaco of Ancona, 22–23

D'Abano, Pietro, 53

D'Amico, John, 37

Damo, 25, 45

Dante, 9, 70

De Tolnay, Charles, 225

Debus, Allen, 4

Dee, John, 132

Della Porta, Giambattista, 58, 132–33, 141, 239, 242

Democritus of Abdera, 5, 52, 88

Diogenes Laertius, 22, 28, 41, 44, 72, 98, 104, 227

Dionysius of Halicarnassus, 41

Dionysius the Areopagite, 27, 41, 72, 88, 126

Domenico Veneziano, 173

Domninos of Larissa, 17

Egidio da Viterbo, Cardinal, 48, 125, 140, 242

Empedocles of Agrigento, 5, 29, 32, 54, 87–88, 102, 133

Enriquez Gómez, Antonio, 60

Erasmus, Desiderius, 45, 48–53, 58, 124–27, 135, 140, 242

Euclid, 97, 146–47, 160, 228

Euphorbus, 21, 53

Eusebius of Caesarea, 44

Faon, 53, 93

Federigo da Montefeltro, Duke, 93–97, 105, 184–86, 188, 190–91, 243

Fibonacci (Leonardo da Pisa), 97, 156

Ficino, Marsilio, 25, 27–30, 37, 41–43, 47, 53, 58, 68–69, 80–87, 91–95, 104–06, 108–09, 113, 119, 126, 128–32, 134, 136, 140–41, 165, 186, 188, 190, 200–02, 205, 207, 212, 215, 224–26, 229, 238–39, 242

Field, J.V., 4

Filarete (Antonio Averlino), 23

Filelfo, Francesco, 22

Filippino Lippi, 238

Fine, Oronce, 128, 130

Fludd, Robert, 126, 138

Fra Angelico, 173

Fra Bartolomeo della Porta, 230–31, 238
Fra Filippo Lippi, 173, 203
Francesco di Giorgio Martini, 95–97, 100, 105, 114–15, 185, 192–94
Francesco I de'Medici, Grand Duke of Tuscany, 239
Freedberg, Sydney J., 204

Gaffurio, Franchino, 33, 58, 102–03, 105, 113, 115–16, 123, 153–54, 157, 194, 200–02, 207, 215, 227, 238
Galatino, Pietro, 124
Galen, 121
Galilei, Vincenzo, 123
Galileo Galilei, 58, 135, 138, 141, 160–61
Garzoni, Giovanni, 34
Gemistus, George (see Pletho)
Gherardini, Niccolo, 138
Ghirlandaio, Domenico, 203
Giacopo da Spira (Jacob of Speyer), 94
Giocondo, Fra Giovanni, 96, 112, 230
Giorgio, Francesco (see Zorzi, Francesco)
Giorgione, 231–32, 238
Giovanni Francesco Pico della Mirandola, 46–47, 92, 126
Giuliano da Sangallo, 193–94, 216
Glaucus, 32
God, 21, 23, 27–28, 30, 32, 35, 40, 43–44, 48, 57, 66, 70, 73–74, 79–80, 82, 84–89, 91–92, 105, 108, 134–35, 137–38, 164, 181, 188, 198, 200–01, 205–06, 212, 215, 217–18, 223, 226, 230, 236, 241–42
Godwin, Joscelyn, 239
Gregory, Saint, 37
Guarino da Verona, 66
Guidobaldo da Montefeltro, Duke, 38, 93, 95, 98, 105, 109–10

Hankins, James, 4
Helen of Troy, 53
Heninger, S. K. Jr., 4
Henry VIII, King, 50
Heraclitus of Ephesus, 5, 34, 227
Hercules, 19–20, 47, 52, 65, 124, 159–60, 209
Hermes Trismegistus, 17, 27, 31, 35, 58, 81, 88, 90, 102
Hermippus, 7, 44, 46, 108
Hermodamante, 56
Herrera, Juan de, 235–39, 243
Hersey, George, 4, 96, 174, 176, 184

Hesiod, 9
Hipparchus, 25, 47
Hippasus of Metapontum, 32
Hippocrates, 121
Homer, 53, 56

Iamblichus of Chalcis, 7, 17, 28, 39, 41, 46–47, 49, 72, 76, 81, 84, 88, 90, 101, 123, 150, 153, 157
Ignudi, 224
Inghirami, Tommaso, 120–21, 140, 229, 243
Isidore of Seville, Bishop, 2, 8, 65

Jacopo de'Barbari, 152
Jerome, Saint, 2, 21, 37–38, 48, 65
Johanan ben Isaac Alemanno, 29
Jörg Syrlin the Elder, 150–51
Joseph, Saint, 210
Jubal, 153, 157–58
Julius II, Pope, 95, 120, 135, 140, 224–25, 243

Kelly, Edward, 132
Kepler, Johannes, 58–59, 136–38, 141, 160–61, 242
Kircher, Athanasius, 136

Landino, Cristoforo, 26
Lascaris, Constantinus, 32, 100
Laurana, Luciano, 95, 184–85, 191–92
Lavin, Marilyn Aronberg, 190–91
Lefèvre d'Étaples, Jacques (Faber Stapulensis), 41, 128
Lenormant, François, 3, 60
Leo X, Pope, 42–43, 120
Leonardo da Vinci, 38, 74, 95, 98–99, 102, 104–05, 109, 111–19, 139–40, 194–95, 201–07, 218–20, 224, 230, 238, 242–43
Leoni, Ambrogio, 50
Livy (Titus Livius), 23, 41
Lomazzo, Giovanni Paolo, 52–54, 59, 229, 242
Lorenzo de'Medici, 29, 37, 80–81, 84, 87, 207
Lorenzo Ghiberti, 171–72, 175
Luca della Robbia, 145–46, 148, 152, 157, 171
Lucian of Samosata, 7, 49–50
Lysides, 32
Lysis of Tarentum, 25, 47

Machuca, Pedro, 234–35
Macrobius, 6, 8, 20–21, 28, 54, 65, 76, 84, 93, 123, 133

Maffei, Raffaele, 40–41
Magi, the, 32, 43, 46, 82, 84, 132, 204, 233
Manetti, Antonio, 168, 170
Manutius, Aldus, 112
Marsyas, 231
Masaccio, 171–73, 200, 204, 243
Mathias Corvinus, King, 17
Maximilian I, Emperor, 42, 119
Melanchthon, Philip, 124
Michelangelo Buonarotti, 158–60, 196, 202,
    207–09, 214, 220–25, 230, 238, 243
Michelozzo di Bartolomeo, 173–75, 184, 200
Mithridates, Flavius (Raimundo Moncada), 94
Mohammed, 87
Monfasani, James, 4
More, Sir Thomas, 126
Moses, 27, 29, 31, 35, 43–44, 46, 48, 51–52, 56,
    58–59, 78, 82, 85, 88, 90–91, 108, 124, 126,
    129, 131, 139–40, 171, 196, 198, 226, 235
Muses, the, 7, 20, 54, 57, 66–67, 84, 186–88, 229
Mutianus, Conrad, 125

Nanni, Giovanni (Annius da Viterbo), 38, 39
Napolitani, Pier Daniele, 4
Neander, Michael, 131
Neanthes Satyrus, 7
Nemorarius, Jordanus, 101
Nicomachus of Gerasa, 6–7, 17, 31, 34, 41, 51,
    66, 75–77, 90, 93, 97, 99–100, 110, 116, 120,
    123, 153, 157, 174, 176, 200
Nigidus Figulus, 121
Noah, 224
Numa Pompilius, 23
Numenius, 29, 44, 108

Ockeghem, Johannes, 33
Orpheus, 27, 89
Ortiz de Zúñiga, Diego, 135
Ottaviano Ubaldini, 189, 191
Ovid, 16–17, 93, 116, 223–24

Pacioli, Luca, 38, 57–59, 95, 98, 105, 109, 110–16,
    119, 152, 189–90, 194, 201–02, 206, 208, 215,
    242
Palladio, Andrea, 233–34
Paracelsus, Theophrastus, 46, 130–32, 141, 239,
    241
Parmenides of Eleata, 32, 86
Patrizi da Cherso, 123
Patrizi, Francesco, Bishop, 34

Paul, Saint, 45, 91
Paulus de Middelbourg, 94–95, 97, 100, 105,
    109, 135, 188, 190
Pereira, Gómez (Gometius), 131
Persius, 41
Peter, Saint, 162
Petrarch, 9, 15, 19, 21, 65, 71, 79, 170, 173, 209
Pfefferkorn, Johannes, 42, 44
Pherecydes, 29, 32, 52
Philip II, King, 157, 235, 237, 243
Philo of Alexandria (Philo Judaeus), 6, 8, 17, 29,
    44, 78, 88, 90, 104, 108, 196, 198, 200, 224,
    237
Philolaus of Croton, 5, 20, 32, 65, 74, 81, 133–34,
    153, 157
Philostratus, 41
Pico della Mirandola, 30–31, 34, 41–43, 46–48,
    63, 68, 87–91, 94, 104–05, 108–09, 119–20,
    124–26, 128, 130, 132, 140–41, 200–01, 226,
    228, 238–39, 242
Piccolomini (see Aeneas Sylvius Piccolomini)
Piero della Francesca, 95, 97–98, 100, 105,
    185–86, 189–92, 201, 207, 243
Pietro d'Abano, 53
Pietro del Monte, 40
Pindar, 229
Pinturricchio (Bernardino di Betto), 238
Pius II (see Aeneas Sylvius Piccolomini)
Planudes, Maximus, 99
Platina (Bartolomeo dei Sacchi), 78, 103–04,
    106
Plato, 5, 6, 8–9, 15–18, 20–22, 24–30, 35, 37–39,
    41–42, 46–48, 51–52, 54, 57–58, 64, 66–72,
    76, 79, 81–82, 84–88, 91, 95, 97, 99–100,
    102–06, 110–13, 115, 121, 123–24, 129–30, 132,
    134, 137, 139, 146–48, 162, 164, 173, 181, 185,
    190, 200–01, 204–05, 207, 224–25, 227–29,
    238, 240, 242
Pletho (George Gemistus), 24–25, 37, 66–70, 72,
    77, 79, 164, 171, 173–75, 178, 200, 238
Pliny the Elder, 23, 32, 34, 45
Plotinus, 46, 83, 85, 88, 104, 242
Plutarch, 47, 75
Poliziano, Angelo, 31–32, 80–81, 92–93
Polydore Vergil, 32, 98, 105, 215, 227
Pope-Hennessy, John, 147
Porphyry of Tyre, 7, 28, 39, 41–42, 46, 49, 81, 83,
    88, 123, 150, 242
Postel, Guillaume, 51–52, 54, 59, 128–29, 141,
    239, 241

Proclus, 8, 67, 89
Psellus, Michael, 67
Ptolemy, 101, 133, 147

Quintilian, 21, 23, 151

Raphael, 94–95, 98, 105, 121–22, 135, 156–57,
    161, 207–11, 213, 219–22, 225–30, 238, 243
Reeves, Eileen, 4
Regiomontanus (Joannes Müller) or Giovanni
    di Monteregio, 75
Reisch, Gregorius, 119, 154–56
Reticus, George Joachim, 134
Reuchlin, Johannes, 42–45, 48, 50, 55, 58, 85,
    123–25, 127, 130–32, 135, 140, 151, 208, 226,
    240–41
Rose, Paul Lawrence, 4
Rudolf II, Emperor, 132, 243

Saiber, Arielle, 136
Salinas, Francisco de, 123
Salmoxis, 27, 46, 88
Salutati, Coluccio, 19–20, 65–66, 75, 79, 147–48,
    161–62, 164, 171–73, 200, 209
Salvator Rosa, 161
Santi, Giovanni, 94
Sappho, 53, 93, 229
Schlosser, Julius von, 146–47
Serapis, 103
Serlio, Sebastiano, 233
Servius (Maurus Servius Honoratus), 65
Seth, 130
Seven Liberal Arts, 23, 66, 119, 147, 154, 157,
    159, 179
Sforza, Francesco, Duke, 35
Sforza, Lodovico, Duke, 113
Shrimplin, Valerie, 225
Shumaker, Wayne, 4
Sigismundo Pandolfo Malatesta, 114–15, 178
Sigüenza, Fray José de, 158
Sixtus IV, Pope, 78, 104, 106, 196–98, 200, 243
Socrates, 16
Solomon, King, 8, 55, 175, 191, 237
Souffrin, Pierre, 4
Speusippus, 31, 81
Syracuse, King of, 23

Taylor, René, 236

Theano, 45, 56
Theon of Smyrna, 6, 8, 31, 76, 81, 130
Thierry of Chartres, 90
Three Graces, 103, 209–10
Tibaldi, Pellegrino, 158–59, 238
Tifernate, Lilio, 78, 94
Timaeus of Locri, 16, 22, 32
Titian, 231–32
Titus, Emperor, 198
Tory, Geofroy, 127
Toscanelli, Paolo, 41, 68, 72, 75, 115, 170, 200
Trogus, Pompeius, 41
Tubalcain, 147

Valla, Giorgio, 98–100, 105–06, 112, 115–16, 122,
    134–35, 165, 230–33, 242
Valla, Lorenzo, 21, 71
Varro, Marcus, 8, 90
Vasari, Giorgio, 68, 146–47, 239
Vergerio, Pier Paolo, 21, 66
Veroli, Giovanni Sulpizio da, 96–97, 120, 233
Verrocchio, Andrea, 203
Vespasiano da Bisticci, 94
Villalpando, Juan Battista, 237, 239, 243
Virgil, 20
Virgin Mary (Madonna), 45, 150, 179, 204,
    207–09, 211, 220–21
Vitruvius, 6–7, 21, 26, 35, 52, 57, 76, 79, 93,
    96–98, 100, 109, 111–12, 114–15, 120, 122–23,
    127, 139–40, 170, 174, 176, 180, 185, 212–13,
    216, 228, 231, 233–35, 238
Vives, Juan Luis, 50
Vogel, Cornelia de, 4
Von Iniching, Matheiss Passinger, 131
Von Sickingen, Franz, 125

William of Bavaria, Duke, 125
William of Conches, 85
Wind, Edgar, 224
Wittkower, Rudolf, 4, 189, 230

Zamberti, Bartolomeo, 100
Zarlino, Gioseffo, 123
Zelada, Cardinal, 17
Zeus, 188
Zoroaster, 22, 24, 27, 68, 132
Zorzi, Francesco (Francesco Giorgio), 47–48,
    52, 58, 122–23, 129, 140, 230, 238–39